The Enterprise Big Data Framework

The Enterprise Big Data Framework

Building critical capabilities
to win in the data economy

Jan-Willem Middelburg

KoganPage

First published in Great Britain and the United States in 2024

2nd Floor, 45 Gee Street
London
EC1V 3RS
United Kingdom

8 W 38th Street, Suite 902
New York, NY 10018
USA

4737/23 Ansari Road
Daryaganj
New Delhi 110002
India

www.koganpage.com

Kogan Page books are printed on paper from sustainable forests.

ISBNs

Hardback   978 1 3986 0174 1
Paperback   978 1 3986 0171 0
Ebook   978 1 3986 0172 7

British Library Cataloguing-in-Publication Data

A CIP record for this book is available from the British Library.

Library of Congress Control Number
2023946440

Typeset by Integra Software Services, Pondicherry
Print production managed by Jellyfish
Printed and bound by CPI Group (UK) Ltd, Croydon, CR0 4YY

For Marthe, Julie and Maurits

CONTENTS

PART FIVE Big Data Algorithms

PART EIGHT AI and Big Data

ACKNOWLEDGEMENTS

This book is the culmination of more than two years of relentless research, writing and rewriting, aimed at providing a comprehensive guide to establishing a data-driven organization. Throughout this journey, I have strived to delve beyond the realm of technology and focus on the critical capabilities necessary for success in the ever-evolving data landscape.

The rapid advancements in Big Data have revolutionized the way organizations operate, presenting new challenges and opportunities. In recognition of this reality, I have endeavoured to capture the latest developments in the field, ensuring that this book reflects the most up-to-date understanding of Big Data. By doing so, I aspire to equip readers with the knowledge and insights required to navigate the complexities of the data economy effectively.

This book is not merely an academic exploration of Big Data; it is a practical guide designed to empower professionals and organizations alike. As you delve into its pages, you will find a wealth of practical strategies, methodologies and frameworks that can be readily applied to real-world scenarios. I hope that this work will serve as a valuable resource enabling you to unleash the power of data and drive meaningful transformation within your own organization.

I would be remiss if I did not express my deepest gratitude to APMG-International for wholeheartedly embracing the Enterprise Big Data Framework. In particular, I extend my appreciation to Richard Pharro for facilitating the connection to Kogan Page. The dedication and support of the Kogan Page team have been invaluable throughout the process and I am profoundly grateful for their commitment to bringing this book to market.

Finally, I must extend a special thank you to my wife, Marthe Bosma, whose unwavering belief in me has been a constant source of inspiration. Amidst the arduous journey of creating this book, we welcomed the arrival of our second child, Maurits Middelburg. Balancing the demands of writing and family life was no easy feat, and I am forever grateful for Marthe's understanding, patience and unwavering support.

In closing, I invite you to embark on this journey through the Enterprise Big Data Framework. May this book serve as your trusted guide, and I hope it will help you to win in the data economy. Enjoy reading it, and I hope it will convince you that building a data-driven organization is all about establishing the right capabilities.

PART ONE
Introduction to Big Data

Introduction to Big Data   01

1.1 Big Data in a world of big decisions

It needs very little explanation that data sets have been exploding in recent years. Our worlds are happening increasingly more online, and the Covid-19 pandemic has accelerated digital adoption at an unprecedented rate. Where we used to go to offices, went to stores in person and paid with cash, we have switched our behaviour to online Zoom or Teams meetings, online shopping, and digital currencies and transactions. However, what very few people still realize is that every click, swipe or digital interaction creates data. The combination of all these swipes, clicks and online meeting results in insurmountable amounts of data that are created at record speed – and it results in Big Data.

A significant amount of that data contains little to no value for people or business. Who cares that someone posted on Twitter that he just went out to get ice cream? And is it really interesting to know what your neighbour just ordered groceries? The fact that most data provide little decision-making value is a commonly heard argument from technology agnostics and analytics sceptics. And to a large extent, this view is valid and true. To recognize the value in data sets, it is necessary to look at them from a higher level of abstraction. When we combine the data of all the people who just posted on Twitter that they went out for ice cream or combine the data of all grocery orders in a particular neighbourhood, we obtain datasets that contain predictive power. The value of data is not so much in an individual action or singular behaviour, but in the combined patterns that start to emerge when multiple data entries or data sets are combined. At a higher level of abstraction, we can start to see patterns. These patterns provide a representation of human behaviours, and which contains significant value for organizations.

An organization that is better able to predict which customers might be interested in their products can set up more effective marketing campaigns. Organizations that understand customer preferences better than their competitors can reduce churn. Even in government organizations, insight in the behaviours of populations can help with infrastructure planning and decision-making. The predictive value of large data sets only leads to one conclusion: data and value are strongly correlated. This conclusion explains the rapid growth and interest in Big Data and data science of the last few years, and the significant investments that have been made to professionalize organizations. Most commercial companies are now racing to make better and more informed decisions than their competitors to stay ahead in an increasingly competitive market. Additionally, most governments have started to adopt analytics to start developing their economies and create better living conditions for their citizens.

Extracting value from data is, however, easier said than done. Although there are many great resources and publications available that explain the core techniques and approaches to Big Data and data science, the reality is that many companies are still struggling to achieve a positive return on investment on their data and analytics programmes. Many CIOs realize the need for a data analysis or analytics department, but very few can claim that this department is bringing in more revenue than their associated costs. If you recognize this in your own organization, rest assured that you are by no means alone. And this is exactly why the Enterprise Big Data Framework was created.

The Enterprise Big Data Framework – which we will discuss in great depth in this book – provides organizations with a structured approach to retrieve value from Big Data sets. And with value, we mean something that can be justified in board meetings, can be written down in business cases and can be measured and tracked by finance departments and auditors that seek to justify expenditures and optimize profit margins. To obtain value from massive data sets, a more structured approach is required, especially in large organizations. Enterprise organizations will need to consider processes, capabilities, enterprise IT architecture, skills development and legal and regulatory requirements, amongst a great many other things. Hiring several data scientists and some Big Data analysis tools is easy. But building a Big Data or analytics department that brings traceable long-term business value to the decision-making process in the organization is a completely different ballgame.

In this book, we will present the Enterprise Big Data Framework, which will focus on the capabilities that organizations require to extract quantifiable value from massive quantities of data. Although many of the principles that are discussed in this book can also easily be applied to the public and non-profit sectors, one of the primary premises of this book is that most organizations work under competitive pressure, and therefore require a return on their investments. Because data sets are created and stored in such incomprehensible volumes these days, organizations could spend months (or even years) creating all kinds of fascinating insights and graphs. And in many organizations, many interesting graphs and picture are created by the analytics teams and data scientists. Yet, a fundamental question about many of these 'interesting' insights remains the explanation of business value. In what way does the analysis, model or algorithm contribute to the bottom line of the organization?

The primary scope of *The Enterprise Big Data Framework* will therefore be organizations that function in a competitive environment. In the following chapters, we will consider which capabilities are required to incorporate data-driven decision-making, and how to quantify value from Big Data and analytics. Of course, we will also discuss technical requirements and IT considerations, because Big Data would simply not be possible without its underlying infrastructure. However, in this book, we will continue to review Big Data from a business point of view.

If the organization you work for can realize the capabilities of Big Data and incorporate the practices you will see in this book, many new and exciting possibilities will start to occur. Not only will it change the culture of the organization towards data-driven approaches and decision-making, but it will also empower new ideas and growth. If applied well, the appropriate use of Big Data can help solve the world's most pressing problems and can power executives' big decisions.

Before we introduce the structure and set-up of the Enterprise Big Data in Part 2, we need to determine its scope. In this first chapter, we will therefore begin with introducing the most important definitions of Big Data, common taxonomies and provide the context of the knowledge domain that is now known as Big Data.

1.2 Defining Big Data

The first important aspect to grasp about the term 'Big Data' is that it is an arbitrary definition. It is not a concept or technology that was introduced at a specific moment in time, but rather the convergence of several technologies over a period of time. Through the rapid rise and adoption of data-generation devices, the technological advancement in cloud computing and the application of smart algorithms, it became possible for enterprises to store and analyse large quantities of data in a secure and cost-effective way. Big Data can therefore be characterized as the convergence of several different technologies that gained traction in the last decades.

Although it is not exactly known who used the term 'Big Data' for the first time, most people credit John R Mashey (who worked at Silicon Graphics at the time) for making the term popular.[1] In the general sense of the term, Big Data deals with all the aspects that organizations face in storing, processing and analysing large data sets to support their decision-making. Many people and organizations have tried to define Big Data over the years. For this publication, we will use the following definition:

> Big Data is the knowledge domain that explores the techniques, skills and technology to deduce valuable insights out of massive quantities of data.

There are three important reasons this definition best resonates with the purpose of this book:

1 We consider Big Data primarily as a **knowledge domain**. Whether organizations are successful with Big Data primarily depends on the way they apply existing knowledge. In this book, our main objective is to contribute to this knowledge.

2 The knowledge domain of Big Data can be broken down into the sub-categories of **techniques, skills and technology.** To be successful with Big Data in any organization, there is more than just technology required. Throughout this book, we will therefore provide additional emphasis on the techniques and skills required to establish a successful Big Data organization.

3 The primary objective of Big Data for enterprise organizations is to obtain **valuable insights.** In the end, just like any other business decision, there need to be justifications and business cases for investing in Big Data. It is therefore important to keep constantly considering the value that Big Data solutions will bring to the enterprise.

The primary objective of this definition is to provide a practical and operational context for Big Data. The three components listed above provide an overview of the core focus areas of Big Data, and they will resonate throughout the rest of this publication.

1.3 Big Data complexities and focus areas

This definition of Big Data provides a high-level overview of the core capabilities that organizations will need to master to achieve value from large data sets. To realize this objective, organizations will need to combine data from a variety of different sources (for example data from your CRM systems and external data) in a smart and efficient way. As a result, several complexities will need to be addressed that make this by no means an easy task. These complexities can be summarized into several different categories which Big Data solutions will need to address, as depicted in Figure 1.1.[2]

Figure 1.1   Categories of complexities in Big Data

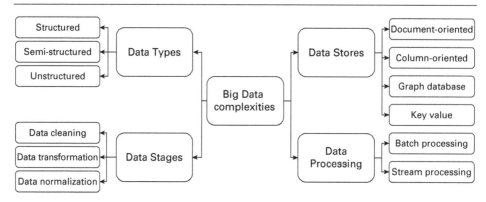

Data types

Value in Big Data is frequently created by combining data from various sources together. Unfortunately, in most cases the structure of these **data sources** is not the same. For example, it is easy to see that combining CCTV footage with data captured in an Excel sheet will not be an easy task. Because Big Data will need to incorporate all kinds of data, the first complexity that would need to be addressed for valuable results is the way in which **data structures** can be combined. Data can be **structured** (e.g. financial, electronic, medical records, government statistics), **semi-structured** (e.g. text, tweets, emails) or **unstructured** (e.g. audio and video)). All these applications share the potential for providing invaluable insights, if organized and analysed appropriately.[3]

- **Structured data:** Structured data is data that adheres to a pre-defined data model and is therefore straightforward to analyse. Structured data conforms to a tabular format with relationships between the different rows and columns. Common examples of structured data are Excel files or SQL databases. Each of these have structured rows and columns that can be sorted.

- **Semi-structured data:** Semi-structured data is a form of structured data that does not conform with the formal structure of data models associated with relational databases or other forms of data tables, but nonetheless contains tags or other markers to separate semantic elements and enforce hierarchies of records and fields within the data. Therefore, it is also known as self-describing structure.[4] Examples of semi-structured data include JSON and XML.

- **Unstructured data:** Unstructured data is information that either does not have a pre-defined data model or is not organized in a pre-defined manner. Unstructured information is typically text-heavy, but may contain data such as dates, numbers and facts also. This results in irregularities and ambiguities that make it difficult to understand using traditional programmes compared with data stored in structured databases. Common examples of unstructured data include audio, video files or NoSQL databases.

Since the processing of unstructured data (and to a lesser extent semi-structured data) is complex, many solutions make use of metadata. In essence, metadata can be considered structured data about an unstructured data set. A common example of metadata is the timestamp and location details about a photograph. Without considering the pixels in the photograph itself, the metadata provides information about the image. The additional benefit is that metadata allows the easy sorting and re-ordering of structured data.

- **Metadata:** Metadata is data that provides information about other data. In other words, it is 'data about data'. Many distinct types of metadata exist, including descriptive metadata, structural metadata, administrative metadata, reference metadata, statistical metadata and legal metadata.[5]

Although this is technically not a separate data type, many Big Data solutions use metadata to speed up the process of analysing unstructured or semi-structured data.

Data stores

A second key complexity is brought by the fact that structured, semi-structured and unstructured data are typically stored in different data stores. A data store is a repository for storing, managing and distributing data sets on an enterprise level. It is a broad term that incorporates all types of data that is generated, stored and used in the enterprise.[6]

The term 'data store' references data that is at rest and used by one or more data-driven applications, services, or individuals. Big Data solutions would need to integrate with a data store, which is why it is important to understand different types of data stores. Table 1.1 provides an overview of the most important data stores.

Table 1.1   Overview of the most common data stores

Type	Description
Document-oriented	Document-oriented data stores are mainly designed to store and retrieve collections of documents or information and support complex data forms in several standard formats, such as JSON, XML and binary forms (e.g. PDF and MS Word). A document-oriented data store is similar to a record or row in a relational database but is more flexible and can retrieve documents based on their contents (e.g. MongoDB, SimpleDB, and CouchDB).
Column-oriented	A column-oriented database stores its content in columns aside from rows with attribute values belonging to the same column stored contiguously. Column-oriented is different from classical database systems that store entire rows one after the other (e.g. BigTable).
Graph database	A graph database is designed to store and represent data that utilizes a graph model with nodes, edges and properties related to one another through relations (e.g. Neo4). In Big Data environments, graph databases are, for example, used by social media companies.

(continued)

Table 1.1   (Continued)

Type	Description
Key-value	Key-value is an alternative to relational database systems that stores and accesses data designed to scale to a very large size. Dynamo [20] is a good example of a highly available key-value storage system; it is used by Amazon.com in some of its services. Other examples of key-value stores are Apache HBase, Apache Cassandra and Voldemort. HBase uses HDFS, an open-source version of Google's BigTable built on Cassandra. HBase stores data into tables, rows and cells. Rows are sorted by row key, and each cell in a table is specified by a row key, a column key and a version, with the content contained as an un-interpreted array of bytes.

Data stages

The next level of complexity is introduced by the process-oriented nature of data processing. Processing data typically happens in a sequential nature, moving from left to right in the Big Data Value Chain (discussed in further detail in section 1.4). This means that the steps to process or analyse data need to be coordinated.

Within in the data analysis and Big Data domains, there are several terms that are frequently used to indicate 'the stage' in which the data currently is. Most Big Data solutions will follow a similar terminology in the design of their solutions. Additionally, the data stages are frequently referenced by practitioners in discussing design options or to assist in problem solving.

Common stages that need to be addressed by Big Data solutions include:

- **Data cleansing** or **data cleaning** is the process of detecting and correcting (or removing) corrupt or inaccurate records from a record set, table or database and refers to identifying incomplete, incorrect, inaccurate or irrelevant parts of the data and then replacing, modifying or deleting the dirty or coarse data.[7] Data cleansing may be performed interactively with data-wrangling tools or as batch processing through scripting.

- **Data transformation** is the process of transforming data into a form that is suitable to be used by system or tool. The technical challenges of data transformation come from an unbounded variety of inputs and outputs to the problem, which in many cases requires manual work.[8] Many Big Data professionals cite the complexities of data transformation as one of the major bottlenecks of Big Data processes.

- **Data normalization** is the method of structuring a database schema to minimize redundancy and ensure that different variables in data can be used for modelling.

Most data that enterprises will collect will be in completely different dimensions (e.g. pricing in US dollars or length in metres) and in different data ranges. For many algorithms and processing techniques (which we will discuss in further detail in Chapter 5) this might potentially create problems, requiring normalized versions of the data. Normalization can therefore be seen as a pre-processing stage, but we would like to avoid the situation where copies of the normalized data would need be stored in Big Data sets.

Each of these stages will bring additional levels of complexity in the design of valuable Big Data solutions. The list above is by no means a complete overview and will be further detailed and outlined in section 1.4.

Data processing

The last level of complexity that we will review in this section has to do with the timeliness and velocity of data. In some Big Data solutions, time is of the essence. Solutions that aim to analyse stock market information, for example, will need the ability to process incoming data instantly. In other solutions, time is less urgent. A financial report that needs to be generated with sales data, for example, does not need to rely on data that was generated minutes or seconds ago.

The timeliness with which data needs to be processed introduces a next level of complexity, and something that Big Data solutions will need to consider. There are generally two ways in which data can be processed:

1 **Batch processing** is a method of running high-volume, repetitive data jobs. In batch processing, data (or a batch of information) is collected over time and then processed when computing resources are assigned or have become available.

2 **Stream processing** is a method to query continuous data streams and detect conditions (or variations) within a short period from the time the data is received. In stream processing, data is analysed within seconds after the data was created or made available, which is the reason it is also frequently referred to as **real-time processing.**

Technically speaking, a combination of these two solutions is also possible (a concept known as **hybrid processing**). We will discuss further the technical implications of batch processing and stream processing in detail in section 2.3.

1.4 The Big Data Value Chain

As noted in the first paragraphs, Big Data and value are inherently correlated. The larger a data set, the more potential power it has to provide predictions for the future. But the big paradox in Big Data, however, is that data itself, objectively viewed, has no value at all. In its very essence, data is a binary collection of zeros and ones that is stored in a physical location in some data centre or storage device.

To extract value from Big Data, organizations require techniques, skills and technology, as defined in the definition of Big Data in section 1.2. These techniques need to be applied in a systematic and sequential order. With every step, the underlying data will become more valuable to an organization. Because every step creates more value, the application of Big Data techniques, skills and technology can be considered a value-chain approach; every step in the process will give an organization more complete insights, empowering better decision-making.

The Big Data Value Chain, depicted in Figure 1.2, showcases how every step adds value in the process. Using a value-chain approach helps us to break down the various business activities that are required to make better and more data-driven decisions.[9] The purpose of the decomposition of the Big Data Value Chain is to provide an overview of the main and supporting activities required to translate data into value.

The Big Data Value Chain is a useful conceptualization for a variety of reasons. First, the Value Chain clearly depicts that, as you move from left to right in the Value Chain, data becomes more valuable for an organization. In most enterprise organizations, the primary interest will be in the outcome (i.e. the **presentation stage**) of the Big Data Value Chain. Managers and business leaders will make decisions based on reports, visualizations and dashboards. But to arrive at the presentation stage, the **ingestion, preparation and analysis stages** are required.

The second main part that the Big Data Value Chain clearly depicts is that the various stages are typically not independent or easy to separate. Data frequently

Figure 1.2   The Big Data Value Chain

OBJECTIVES	INGESTION	PREPARATION	ANALYSIS	PRESENTATION
DESCRIPTIVE EXPLORATORY INFERENTIAL PREDICTIVE CAUSAL MECHANISTIC	DATA PIPELINE / LOCAL ONLINE DATABASES / DISTRIBUTED STORAGE & PROCESSING	CLEANSING WRANGLING	INFERENCE REGRESSION CLASSIFICATION CLUSTERING OUTLIER DETECTION	REPORTS VISUALIZATION DASHBOARDS

Security, Governance, Ethics

VALUE

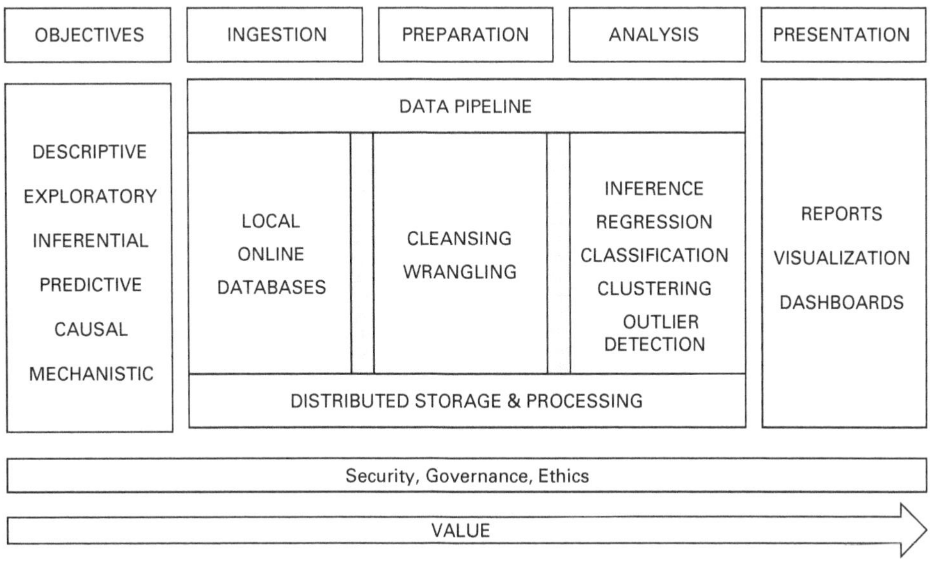

'flows' through organizations and is not stopped in different queues. To accommodate this 'flow', organizations typically establish data pipelines, which guide information from import to result. A data pipeline can be defined as a set of connected data processes where the output of one element is the input of the next one. The elements of a pipeline are often executed in batch or real-time (as discussed in section 1.3). To support the flow of these data pipelines, Big Data organization typically work with **distributed storage and processing technologies**. Distributed processing and storage technologies help to deal with the volume, velocity, variety and veracity characteristics (further discussed in Chapter 2 section 2.2).

Lastly, it is clear that the Big Data Value Chain consists of several stages, which can be subdivided into several sub-activities. To retrieve value from data, these stages in almost every business objective will be quite similar. To solve a business problem, data will need to be ingested, prepared and analysed. But which sub-activities are required will vary based on the structure of the incoming data, the complexity of the problem and the constraints from different algorithms. To illustrate this with an example, it is clear that creating a daily report with the number of mentions of a company on social media is a way easier and more straightforward problem compared with building a solution that can automatically recognize faces in movies.

The five different stages of the Big Data Value Chain are briefly outlined below.

Business objectives

The first step in any value chain must happen before valuable time and resources are spent on exploring or investigating data sets. The goals and business objectives of a Big Data project need to be determined. This step, which is frequently overlooked in many organizations, enables an organization to consider what the key outcomes or results of Big Data projects need to be. Because of the massive number of data sets and algorithms that exist in the world, it is important to establish scope and purpose right from the start. Including this stage at the beginning of the Value Chain enables an organization to reflect on the purpose of the problem: What value does a Big Data project bring to the organization? Is it possible to obtain this value with the known and available data sets that exist? And what kind of complexities are likely to be expected?

Within the Big Data and data analytics domain, there are six main business problems for which Big Data typically can provide valuable insights and answers.[10] These common business problems can be translated into objectives that bring real and tangible value to an enterprise. In many cases the type of business objective already determines, to a significant extent, the complexity and scope of any Big Data project:

1 **Descriptive business objective:** A descriptive business objective aims to summarize the key characteristics of one or multiple data sets, based on the inherent properties of the data set.

2 **Exploratory business objective:** An exploratory business objective aims to find (unknown) patterns, trends or relationships in one or multiple data sets. The exploratory business objective is also referred to as the **data mining** business objective.

3 **Inferential business objective:** An inferential business objective aims to find generalizations about populations by examining smaller subsets (i.e. samples) with available data about the population. Inferential business objectives are used to make inferences about the expected properties or a target group.

4 **Predictive business objective:** A predictive business objective aims to make the best possible prediction for an unknown, uncertain situation in the future. This objective aims to 'predict' what will happen in the (near) future so that businesses can anticipate their actions accordingly.

5 **Causal business objective:** A causal business objective (sometimes referred to as causal discovery) aims to understand why a certain phenomenon happened. This objective tries to find the underlying cause to business questions. For example, why did we sell more of a particular product last month?

6 **Mechanistic business objective:** Mechanistic business objectives provide answers to business questions which explain phenomena in purely physical or deterministic terms. In simple terms, a mechanistic business objective is used to understand exact changes in variables that lead to other changes in other variables.

Understanding the business objective in any Big Data problem is of significance. In most cases, it will define the complexity of the solution. Additionally, the business objective marks the official 'beginning' of the Big Data Value Chain. The final solution or presentation should provide an answer to the business objectives.

Data ingestion

The second phase in the Big Data Value Chain is data ingestion. Before any kind of analysis can take place, an organization needs to have access to data. In Big Data environments, data will be generated and created at high velocity and in high volume. As a result, dealing with data ingestion will already bring significant challenges for storage and processing.

Enterprises that generate data on a constant basis, in particular, will need significant infrastructures to import and store data sets. For example, think about financial institutions that need to track and store stock-price information on an ongoing basis. Or social media companies that generate new photos and videos every second. To perform any form of data analysis, an organization first needs to control the way that it ingests data.

Data ingestions can happen in many different forms and with many different technologies. To narrow the discussion a bit further, we will discuss three major components in the Enterprise Big Data Framework. The first is the difference between batch (local) processing and stream (online) processing. The difference between these two approaches will be further considered in Part 2. In addition, a critical component in data ingestion is storage. All the enormous amounts of data need to be stored somewhere on the planet, and this storage requires many different forms of databases. In Part 4 (Designing a Big Data Architecture), we will focus in more depth on different database and storage solutions. Data ingestion forms the start of the **data pipeline** (depicted horizontally in Figure 1.2), which will accommodate the 'flow' of data throughout the enterprise.

Data preparation

The third stage in the Big Data Value Chain is data preparation. Data ingestion (i.e. the start of the data pipeline) is valuable, but is missing one important element: data ingestion does not provide you with any relevant understanding of the **quality of the data**. Most data sets contain data that is duplicate, erroneous or even just plain missing. Frequently, data sets have been built up over years and years, during which time fields in databases have changed, were renamed or simply ignored. As a result, most organizations have databases and data sets that are far from perfect in terms of their accuracy or preciseness.

A large part of managing an Enterprise Big Data environment is therefore to evaluate and clean up the data sets before they can be processed. Research figures vary, but according to some interviews, data analysts spend 50 per cent to 80 per cent of their time on data cleaning and data wrangling activities, something the *New York Times* has labelled as the janitor's job of data science.[11]

Data preparation is an essential part of the Big Data Value Chain and involves all activities of cleaning and wrangling data before it is analysed. The difference between data cleaning and data wrangling can be expressed as follows:

1 **Data cleaning** is the process of detecting and correcting (or removing) corrupt or inaccurate records from a record set, table or database. It refers to identifying incomplete, incorrect, inaccurate or irrelevant parts of the data and then replacing, modifying or deleting the dirty or coarse data.

2 **Data wrangling**, sometimes referred to as data munging, is the process of transforming and mapping data from one 'raw' data format into another format with the intent of making it more appropriate and valuable for a variety of downstream purposes such as analytics.

In summary, data cleaning is the act of altering existing records, whereas data wrangling concerns itself with creating new records. Obviously, there is a grey area between these two domains and many tools are available that combine elements of both approaches. In the end, both data cleaning and data wrangling have the same objective – to ensure that correct and accurate data is being processed.

Data analysis

The fourth step in the Big Data Value Chain is data analysis. In this stage, the actual processing of Big Data sets takes place to (hopefully) extract value from data. In almost all cases, data analysis is done through the creation, development and testing of algorithms and models. These models will need be created, tested and refined on an ongoing basis. It is therefore fair to say that data analysis is more of a process, rather than a single step in the data pipeline.

Conducting Big Data analysis is difficult and requires significant knowledge about the way different algorithms work. In the Enterprise Big Data Framework (which will be introduced in Part 2), we will look further at the capabilities required to make data analysis successful. Part 5 (Big Data Algorithms) will cover the individual capabilities (**inference, regression, clustering, classification** and **outlier detection**) in more detail.

Data presentation

The fifth and final step of the Big Data Value Chain is data presentation. Although this stage is technically less complex than data analysis, it is of paramount importance for the success of Big Data initiatives, especially in enterprise organizations. Many Big Data initiatives fail because the information that is analysed is not properly presented or communicated. As a result, valuable analysis results can be questioned or plainly ignored.

At the end of the Big Data Value Chain, organizations need to consider how to present the finding of their analysis and explain how these results were obtained. In most organizations, senior management does not have expert knowledge in data analysis, statistical techniques or algorithms, nor do they need to have this knowledge to effectively lead the company or make decisions. It is therefore a crucial job of data analysts and data scientists to present their work in a structured way that not only demonstrates the key results of the data analysis, but also how these results were generated and what the underlying assumptions were.

Notes

1 S Y Piskorskaya and Y N Malanina. Big data technologies in environmental monitoring, *Journal of Physics: Conference Series*, April 2020 1515 (3), 032058. IOP Publishing

2 I A T Hashem, I Yaqoob, N B Anuar, S Mokhtar, A Gani and S U Khan. The rise of 'big data' on cloud computing: Review and open research issues, *Information systems*, 2015 47, 98–115

3 K Kambatla, G Kollias, V Kumar and A Grama. Trends in big data analytics. *Journal of Parallel and Distributed Computing*, 2014 74 (7), 2561–73

4 P Buneman (1997) Semi-structured data. In proceedings of the sixteenth ACM-SIGACT-SIGMOD-SIGART. In *Symposium on Principles of Database Systems*, Tucson, Arizona

5 J Greenberg. Understanding metadata and metadata schemes. *Cataloging & Classification Quarterly*, 2005 40 (3–4), 17–36

6 D Slamanig and C Hanser (2012) On cloud storage and the cloud of clouds approach, *2012 International Conference for Internet Technology and Secured Transactions*, December, 649–55. IEEE

7 E Rahm and H H Do. Data cleaning: Problems and current approaches, *IEEE Data Engineering Bulletin*, 2000 23 (4), 3–13

8 J Heer, J M Hellerstein and S Kandel (2015) Predictive Interaction for Data Transformation. In *CIDR*, January

9 A Z Faroukhi, I El Alaoui, Y Gahi and A Amine. Big data monetization throughout Big Data Value Chain: a comprehensive review, *Journal of Big Data*, 2020 7 (1), 1–22

10 J T Leek and R D Peng. What is the question?, *Science*, 2015 347 (6228), 1314–15

11 M Kim, T Zimmermann, R DeLine and A Begel (2016) The emerging role of data scientists on software development teams. In 2016 IEEE/ACM 38th International Conference on Software Engineering (ICSE), May, 96–107, IEEE

The State of Big Data in Today's Organizations   02

2.1 The four dimensions of Big Data

The quick rise of Big Data, data science and analytics techniques is not something completely new. In fact, many organizations have consistently identified Big Data analysis and data analytics as one of their core strategic objectives since the early 2010s. Famous research companies, such as Gartner and Forrester, have consistently indicated that data analysis and Big Data should be the priorities of enterprise IT executives.[1]

As a result, many organizations have already taken (some) steps to build capabilities within the Big Data domain. Before we introduce the capabilities of the Enterprise Big Data Framework, it is necessary to first provide an overview of where we are today. Which business and technological developments have emerged over the last decade that have led to current Big Data best practices?

In this section, we will therefore explore the most fundamental techniques and technologies that are currently in use in most enterprise organizations. By understanding the techniques that have driven Big Data, analytics and data science in the last decade, you will start to understand the key challenges that most organizations face. The Enterprise Big Data Framework subsequently aims to address these challenges by introducing a comprehensive and measurable capability framework.

We will discuss the current 'state of Big Data' by reviewing four different dimensions, which is a common approach in the IT industry: technology, processes, people and partners. Each of these four dimensions has made considerable progress over the last decade and will help form a comprehensive picture of the current adoption of Big Data practices. After we have addressed the current state within each dimension, we will discuss the corresponding challenges of each domain to provide a better understanding of key drivers behind the Enterprise Big Data Framework.

The rapid growth of the Big Data domain over the last decade is primarily driven by advancements in technology. To process the massive quantities of data that are created by social media posts, sensory devices and smart phones, organizations first

Figure 2.1   The four dimensions of Big Data

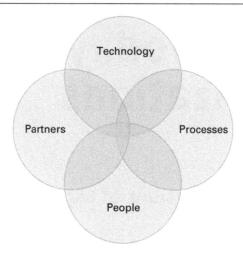

need to set up IT systems and architectures that can deal with these large quantities of data sets, and which are frequently generated in different file formats (for example text, images or audio files). If you consider the data that your organization creates every single day, it is not hard to imagine that specialized technology capabilities are required to store, analyse and process these data sets. To build effective and efficient Big Data organizations, it is therefore important to first understand the technological challenges of Big Data, and the different solutions that have been developed to address these problems.

2.2 Key characteristics of Big Data

The primary reason there are technological considerations in Big Data in the first place is that 'traditional' computers are not able to process Big Data sets with enough speed on which to build business decisions. For example, an analysis of stock market fluctuations would be worthless if a data set took a day to process. By that time, the financial markets would have already adjusted, and an organization would quite literally be analysing yesterday's news. Similarly, analysis patterns of financial transactions (or, for example, medical data), frequently warrant immediate action.

A common way to review the technological requirements of Big Data sets is to first review the characteristics of the data that needs to be processed.[2] The nature of the data sets that need to be processed are inherently different from 'regular' data sets, for which most organizations have business intelligence (BI) solutions in place. The reason Big Data is considered different is because the volume, velocity, variety

Figure 2.2   Big Data characteristics

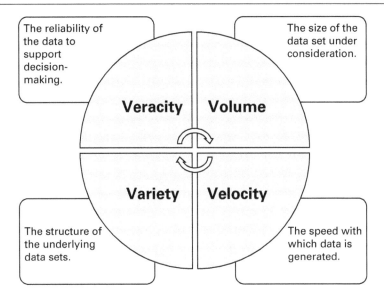

The reliability of the data to support decision-making.

The size of the data set under consideration.

Veracity   **Volume**

Variety   **Velocity**

The structure of the underlying data sets.

The speed with which data is generated.

and veracity of Big Data sets is different from other data, and therefore requires distinct storage and processing technologies.

The four key characteristics of Big Data require distinct technologies because of the following reasons:

- The volume of Big Data sets is typically so large that ordinary (personal) computing systems and storage solutions would be unable to cope with these type of data sets. When organizations are considering the analysis of Big Data, this frequently means the storage and processing of a multitude of terabytes or even petabytes. This volume immediately introduces storage and networking constraints, which need to be addressed by Big Data solutions.

- The velocity of Big Data refers to the speed with which data is generated, and therefore the speed with which data needs to be stored and analysed. The data that is generated through social media applications is a primary example of 'high-velocity' data. High velocity applications create significant data volumes per unit of time (for example terabytes per second). As a result, storage solutions need to have the capability to store this information and the corresponding networks need to be able to deal with high volumes of traffic. Additionally, if there is a requirement to analyse these data sets in real-time (consider for example stock market information), processing of high-velocity data needs be done instantly.

- Big Data is created in a variety of different data formats, depending on the creator or the source data. If data is created by sensors, it will commonly have a structured format that is organized in relational tables (neatly organized in rows and columns). But if the sensor is a traffic camera, the data format will be an image (for example in .jpg or .png format). CCTV cameras, which are now present in almost every large city, create thousands of video files (for example in .mp4 formats). All these different data formats bring different requirements to Big Data technology. Some solutions have been optimized for the storage and processing of images, whereas other solutions are optimized for storing and analysing videos. Because different data formats bring different requirements, technology solutions need to be optimized for file formats accordingly.

- The veracity of Big Data measures the extent to which a data source can be trusted, given the reliability of the source. Although many organizations collect massive quantities of data, a fundamental question is how reliable this data is. Can it be used as input for strategic decisions and is the data trustworthy enough to make reliable predictions? The veracity characteristic of Big Data introduces technological challenges, because solutions need to provide safeguards to ensure the integrity, provenance and quality of the data in the enterprise.

This broad classification of Big Data, based on its functional use, can be further extended to include other characteristics. However, the purpose of this overview is to demonstrate that the key characteristics of data in any modern organization require Big Data technology. For example, Facebook processes 10 billion messages, 4.5 billion 'Like' activities and 350 million photo uploads per day.[3] Although most enterprise organizations will process only a fraction of that volume and variety of data formats per day, it illustrates how massive data sets have become in recent years.

2.3 Batch processing vs. stream processing

The four characteristics of Big Data (volume, velocity, variety and veracity) require specific technologies and tools, so that data can be processed within a timely fashion. From a technology point of view, each of these Big Data solutions can be categorized based on the way it processes data as a function of time. As we saw in Chapter 1, there are three ways in which organizations process Big Data:

- **Batch processing** is a method of running high volume, repetitive data jobs. In batch processing, data (or a batch of information) is collected over time and then processed when computing resources are assigned or have become available.

- **Stream processing** is a method to query continuous data streams and detect conditions (or variations) within a short period from the time the data is received. In stream processing, data is analysed within seconds after the data was created or made available, which is the reason it is also frequently referred to as 'real-time' processing.

- **Hybrid processing** is a combination of batch processing and stream processing. Hybrid processing tools and solutions aim to combine the benefits of both batch processing and stream processing in one architecture.

The difference between batch processing and stream processing is crucial to understand the state of Big Data technology today. Over the last 20 years, most innovations in the Big Data domain have been aimed at resolving constraints within one of these three categories. To provide a comprehensive overview of the technologies that are available today, an overview of the development in each of the three categories is discussed next. This overview will provide you with the historical perspective on the way Big Data technologies have evolved and will provide you with an understanding of the technological constrains of Big Data that enterprise organizations are still facing today.

Batch processing – MapReduce and Hadoop

The first major development in Big Data (and probably the reason we are considering Big Data as a separate knowledge domain today) started with the introduction of the MapReduce framework, which was created by Google in 2003.[4] The MapReduce framework offers three major components within an integrated framework: an easy and simple programming model, automatic and linear scalability, and built-in fault tolerance. Within the Google set of products, the components were introduced as the MapReduce execution engine, a distributed file system called *Google File System (GFS)* and a distributed NoSQL database labelled *Google BigTable.*[5] To this day, Google still uses (a modified version of) the MapReduce framework to deal with large-scale batch processing.

After the introduction of the MapReduce framework by Google, the Apache software foundation started on the development of an open-source version, which resulted in the launch of the Hadoop framework in 2006. The creation of this open-source version of batch processing technology is accredited to Doug Cutting (who at the time worked at Yahoo!) and Mike Carafella. In the Hadoop framework, Hadoop MapReduce and Hadoop YARN were introduced as execution engines, together with the Hadoop Distributed File System (HDFS) for file distribution, and HBase as the corresponding NoSQL database. The introduction of Hadoop propelled the adoption of Big Data batch processing towards the mainstream domain, and it is used by major corporations like Facebook, Twitter and Yahoo!

In essence, Hadoop is the most well-known and popular implementation of the MapReduce framework. It provides a software library that allows for the distributed processing of large data sets across clusters of computers using simple programming models. Hadoop is designed to scale up from single servers to thousands of machines, each offering local computation and storage. Rather than rely on hardware to deliver high availability, the library itself is designed to detect and handle failures at the application layer, so delivering a highly available service on top of a cluster of computers, each of which may be prone to failures.[6]

Distributed processing and storage form the fundamental design principle of batch processing. Figure 2.3 illustrates how distributed processing is executed based on Hadoop MapReduce.

Distributed processing (using the MapReduce framework) works in two basic steps. First, the master node evaluates the input file and splits the input data across different worker nodes. A worker node may do this process again, leading to a multi-level tree structure, depending on the size of the input file. This step is known as the *Map* phase because the master node executes a map function to assign the workload over the different worker nodes.

After the map operation has been executed successfully, the second reduce function is invoked by the master node. The reduce function instructs the worker nodes to read the intermediary files (which were processed and stored locally as the result of the map function) and combine these files together into the final output files. This final operation will return the requested output files that contain the answer to the analysis. With this two-step approach, data is distributed across different machines so that it can be processed locally before it is combined into a result.

Figure 2.3 Execution of Apache Hadoop MapReduce

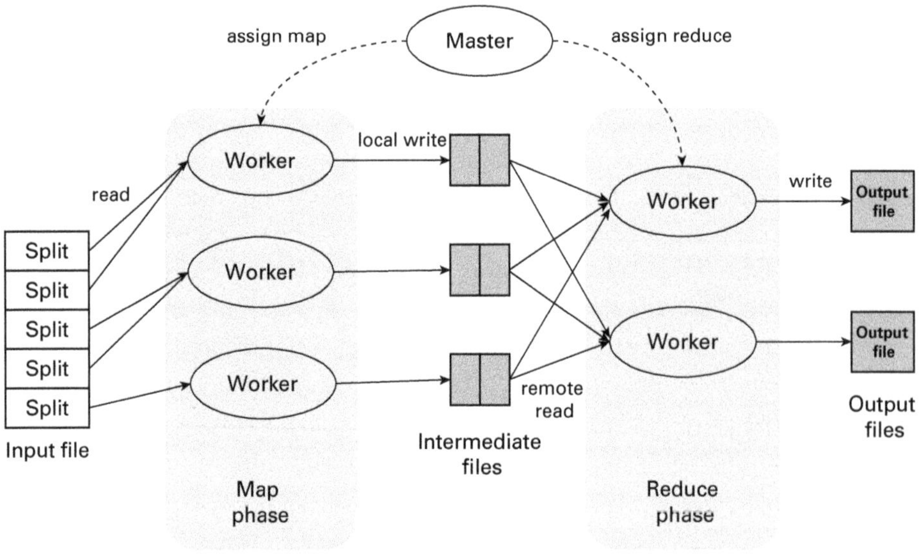

SOURCE hadoop.apache.org

Batch processing, using the Hadoop implementation of MapReduce, has several important benefits. First, Hadoop can work with different database designs. Although the standard implementation utilizes HDFS to store input and output files, available extensions provide the opportunity to store data in the other NoSQL databases (such as HBase or Cassandra) or even to store data in traditional SQL databases. Secondly, Hadoop has near linear scalability and built-in fault tolerance, providing a robust solution for most enterprise organizations.

Although there are many advantages to using MapReduce and Hadoop, there is one significant constraint. By design, the MapReduce function requires that all input data is available before the batch is executed. And it is exactly this property that prohibits the execution of interactive jobs and real-time processing. As a result, a completely different technical design is required for the execution of real-time Big Data analysis: stream processing.

Stream processing – micro-batching and native streams

Nowadays, most enterprise organizations are creating Big Data every single second, generating a continuous stream of data. Examples include log streams, click streams, message streams and photo or video streams. CCTV cameras, which are now present in almost every major city, are a suitable example to illustrate the way in which data is generated 24/7, in a continual pace and with tremendous volume. To deal with these distinct requirements, stream processing technology is required.

In the previous paragraph, we saw that one of the major constraints of the MapReduce and Hadoop technologies is that all input data needs to be available before the processing job is executed. The MapReduce framework processes a complete set of input data, and the result (for example an analysis report) will only be available when all the computations are done.

To overcome the constraints of the Hadoop framework, micro-batching is a solution that is adequate for many enterprise organizations. Although this solution is technically not a pure streaming technology, it resembles streaming behaviour by breaking up the input data into smaller (micro) batches, which can subsequently be analysed using the scalable Hadoop framework that many organizations already have in place.

The fundamental idea in micro-batching is that data streams are broken down in small batches, as depicted in Figure 2.4. The most popular and common micro-batching technology that supports micro-batching is Apache Spark.[7] With Spark Streaming, a continuous data stream can be broken down into several micro input-batches. The Spark Engine will subsequently process these micro input-batches into several micro-output-batches.

Figure 2.4   Micro-batch processing with Apache Spark

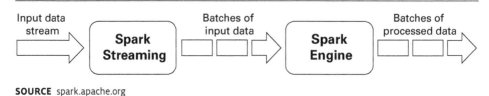

SOURCE spark.apache.org

Whilst micro-batching will provide a suitable technology for many enterprise organizations, it is not a pure form of batch processing. Micro-batching still utilizes the basic architecture and design of batch processing and is therefore by definition not suitable for high-velocity stream processing requirements (for example at social media companies).

In stream processing, data is processed continuously and in an ongoing manner. Since the stream is continuous, there is a non-stop influx of new data that needs to be analysed. And it is exactly in the ability to process real-time data that organizations can create value. A common use case, for example, is the ability to detect fraudulent credit card transactions. New credit card transactions are generated every single second. Within this continuous stream of ever-ongoing transactions, credit card companies would like to detect fraudulent transactions as quickly as possible. In this example, time is of the essence, and therefore requires stream processing. In general, time-sensitive information (stock values, credit card transaction or traffic data) depreciates in value if it is not processed immediately.[8]

Stream processing requires high-volume, high-velocity data to be processed instantly. It processes the raw data immediately as it arrives, meeting the constraints of variability, scalability and fault tolerance. Although there are a variety of technical solutions to support this, the most popular stream processing frameworks are Storm (developed at Twitter), S4 (developed at Yahoo!), Splunk and Apache Kafka.[9] These solutions can be considered as the second-generation Big Data technology tools for real-time processing, and most of these solutions aim to combine batch and stream processing into single or parallel data processing pipeline.[10] The reason that most of these solutions combine the batch and stream processing is that one of the primary use cases of Big Data tools is the application of machine learning. In machine learning new data (the streaming data) is instantly compared with historic data (the batch data) to make instant real-time decisions.

To understand the state of Big Data technology today, having a sound understanding of how stream processing works is of fundamental importance. Figure 2.5 provides a high-level overview of the architecture of stream processing systems. Most modern Big Data systems (that support real-time analysis) are based on this underlying design. A streaming solution can be deployed on a single machine that

consists of multiple components, where each component calls on the next component to be executed in the processing pipeline. Alternatively, for larger scale implementations, multiple distributed machines can be set up, where each of the
components is orchestrated (i.e. managed) by another software tool.

As shown in Figure 2.5, every stream processing solution will have a stream op
input data, which can arrive in different sizes (volumes), different formats (variety)
and with a different pace (velocity). This sequence of potentially never-ending data
(for example new Facebook comments) will enter the data pipeline as a continuous
stream.

To process this continuous data stream, stream processing solutions consist of a
few key components (from top to bottom):

- A **resource management layer,** which manages and coordinates the distributed
  computing and storage systems. The resource management layer coordinates and
  manages the interaction between the different computing resources (both
  computing and storage nodes) and deals with the scheduling and allocation of
  resources. The resource management layer is the central coordinator that ensures
  that data streams can analysed at the required speed.

- A **data stream ingestion layer,** at the beginning of the data pipeline, which is
  responsible for accepting data into the pipeline. Data ingestion is the process of
  getting data streams from its source to its processing or storage system as efficiently
  and correctly as possible. The data stream ingestion layer deploys a variety of
  tools to accept different types of input data streams from one or more sources.

Figure 2.5   Architecture of a stream processing solution

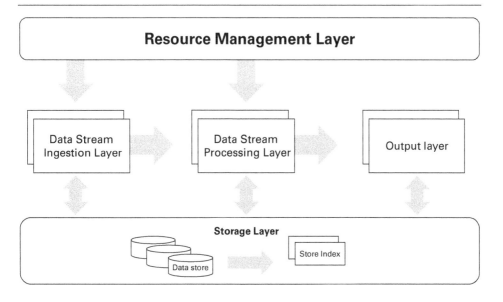

- A **data stream processing layer**, which processes or analyses data in one or multiple steps. The data stream processing layer is where the streaming data processing applications or jobs are executed. A central component of the streaming solution, the data stream processing layer consists of one or more data stream processing engines (DSPE) to process data in real-time and for any given time interval, as well as to peek into the data within a sliding window of time.[11]

- An **output layer**, which directs the output of the data stream to other databases, systems or visualization tools. The results from data stream processing pipelines will in most cases be directed to an application, visualization tool or dashboarding application. At the same time, data and extracted knowledge can be passed to other storage solutions or databases for subsequent analysis and query.

- A **storage layer**, which stores and manages the data and the generated knowledge. The data stream processing layer (and their DSPEs) typically need to store data that has been analysed and which is the result of different processing queries. Typical database solutions (both SQL and NoSQL) can be used in the storage layer to integrate with the stream processing solution.

In summary, every stream processing solution includes a fixed number of components that can be utilized in the design of the underlying architecture. A further and more detailed overview of Big Data architecture will be discussed in Chapter 4. However, the design of modern enterprise Big Data organization builds upon the technological developments that were made in the last decade, and which are continually improved. From a technology point of view, the difference between batch processing and stream processing is of crucial importance in subsequent design decisions.

Hybrid processing

Hybrid processing is a combination of batch processing and stream processing and aims to combine the benefits of both technologies. With the hybrid processing approach, it becomes possible to utilize a single architecture to process Big Data. This approach provides several significant benefits for organizations because they can use (more cost-efficient) batch processing for bulk workloads, whilst leveraging stream processing for critical business operations.

Hybrid processing is realized with the *lambda architecture*, which is depicted in Figure 2.6.[12] The lambda architecture provides access to batch processing and stream processing methods with a hybrid approach. Lambda architecture is used to solve the problem of computing arbitrary functions and consists of three components:

1 The batch layer, which typically uses the Hadoop framework to execute computations based on incoming batches of data. The batch layer is typically designed and organized using the same structure as traditional batch processing systems.

Figure 2.6   Hybrid processing with the lambda architecture

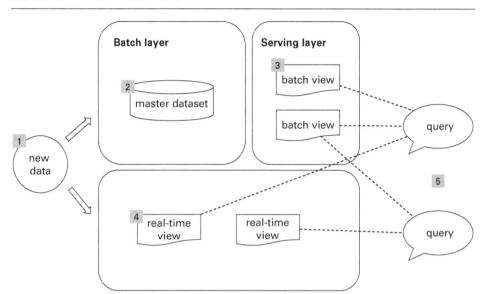

2 The speed layer, which deals with the most recent (or real-time) data and which processes the incoming data instantly to produce near real-time results. For the speed layer, common implementations are based on the stream processing architecture, as shown in Figure 2.5. A popular approach is to utilize *Storm* to implement this layer.[13]

3 The serving layer indexes the batch views so that they can be queried in low-latency on an ad hoc basis. With the serving layer, it becomes possible to run queries on data that has either been processed as a batch, or data that has been processed with the streaming solution (see number 5 in Figure 2.6).

Hybrid processing solutions provide organizations with additional flexibility in the design of their Big Data architecture, and the option to utilize different technologies for different data streams. For this reason, hybrid processing technologies provide a promising solution towards the future design of Big Data architectures. We will further explore hybrid processing solutions and architectures in Chapter 4.

2.4 Big Data types and data structures

In Big Data (and computer science in general) a data structure is a particular way of organizing and storing data in a computer such that it can be accessed and modified efficiently. More precisely, a data structure is a collection of data values, the relationships between them and the functions or operations that can be applied to the data.

As we briefly introduced in Chapter 1, for the analysis of data, it is important to understand that there are three common types of data structures:

1 **Structured data:** Structured data is data that adheres to a pre-defined data model and is therefore straightforward to analyse. Structured data conforms to a tabular format with relationships between the different rows and columns. Common examples of structured data are Excel files or SQL databases. Each of these have structured rows and columns that can be sorted.

2 **Unstructured data:** Unstructured data is information that either does not have a pre-defined data model or is not organized in a pre-defined manner. Unstructured information is typically text-heavy, but may contain data such as dates, numbers and facts also. This results in irregularities and ambiguities that make it difficult to understand using traditional programmes compared with data stored in structured databases. Common examples of unstructured data include audio, video files or NoSQL databases.

3 **Semi-structured data:** Semi-structured data is a form of structured data that does not conform with the formal structure of data models associated with relational databases or other forms of data tables, but nonetheless contain tags or other markers to separate semantic elements and enforce hierarchies of records and fields within the data. Therefore, it is also known as self-describing structure. Examples of semi-structured data include JSON, XML, SWIFT and EDI.

Most 'traditional' data analysis and analytics techniques (including most BI solutions) have the ability to process structured data. Processing unstructured or semi-structured data is, however, much more complex and requires distinct solutions for analysis.

A last category of data type is metadata. From a technical point of view, this is not a separate data structure, but it is one of the most important elements for Big Data analysis and Big Data solutions. Metadata is data about data. It provides additional information about a specific set of data. In a set of photographs, for example, metadata could describe when and where the photos were taken. The metadata then

Figure 2.7   Data types and data structures

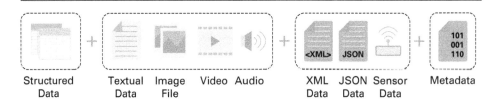

| Structured Data | Textual Data | Image File | Video | Audio | XML Data | JSON Data | Sensor Data | Metadata |

provides fields for dates and locations which, by themselves, can be considered structured data. Because of this reason, metadata is frequently used by Big Data solutions for initial analysis.

2.5 Storing unstructured data

In the previous sections, we have seen that data volume, velocity and variety have a significant impact on the way Big Data environments need to be managed, set up and maintained. An essential part of any Big Data environment is the ability to capture and store unstructured contents which (as discussed in section 2.4) frequently consists of videos, audio files, documents, etc.

To deal with this wide variety of data, Big Data platforms need be able to store unstructured data. The traditional SQL relational databases don't have the capability (or speed) to deal with high-volume data that comes in a variety of different formats. To allow storage of Big Data, non-relational databases have been designed, which are collectively called NoSQL (Not only SQL) databases.[14] NoSQL databases are designed to import, store and export data that is non-tabular in nature. Because no relational scheme is required, the data can be inserted in a NoSQL database without defining any table structures.

Since the 'traditional' relational structure of an SQL database (i.e. tables, rows and columns) is no longer required in NoSQL solutions, they can be optimized for specific purposes. Whereas SQL databases are all similar in structure, NoSQL databases are optimized to store a specific type of data. For example, some NoSQL databases will be optimized for storing documents (document database), whereas others might be optimized to store network relationships (graph database). An overview of the most popular NoSQL databases is outlined in Table 2.1.

Table 2.1 Common NoSQL databases

Category	Descriptions
Columnar Database	A columnar database is a database management system that stores data primarily in columns instead of the 'traditional' storage in rows. The purpose of a columnar database is to efficiently write and read data to and from hard disk storage to speed up the time it takes to return a query. Columnar databases store data in a way that greatly improves disk I/O performance. They are particularly helpful for data analytics and data warehousing.

(continued)

Table 2.1   (Continued)

Category	Descriptions
Document Database	A document database (also known as a document-oriented database or a document store) is a database that stores information in documents. Document databases rely on the internal structure of documents to extract metadata that the database engine uses for further optimization.
Graph Database	A graph database is defined as a specialized, single-purpose platform for creating and manipulating graphs. Graphs contain nodes, edges and properties, all of which are used to represent and store data in a way that relational databases are not equipped to do.
Key-Value Pair Database	A key-value database is a type of nonrelational database that uses a simple key-value method to store data. A key-value database stores data as a collection of key-value pairs in which a key serves as a unique identifier. Both keys and values can be anything, ranging from simple objects to complex compound objects. Key-value databases are highly partitionable and allow horizontal scaling at scales that other types of databases cannot achieve.
Spatial Database	A spatial database (or geodatabase) is optimized to store and query data that represents objects defined in a geometric space. It allows representing geometric objects such as lines, points and polygons.

2.6 Current challenges in Big Data organizations

Despite the many advancements and technological innovations with Big Data in the last decade, there remain many challenges for organizations to fully harness the power of Big Data. Many, if not most, of these challenges are non-technical in nature. Today's technology solutions are able to process unimaginable amounts of data within record time. However, the most common challenges that obstruct organizations from benefiting from Big Data are caused by a lack of adequate processes, lack of trust in data quality and a lack of data analysis skills in general.

Many studies have been conducted to try to find and answer to the question of why adoption of Big Data solutions is so difficult.[15] What almost all studies conclude is that the challenges in adoption do not originate from underestimation of its importance, management commitment or a lack of budget; rather, most challenges arise from the complexity that is inherent to large and complicated (technical) analysis. The list below outlines some of the most common challenges.

Lack of strategic direction

In most enterprise organizations, there are hundreds of business problems to solve. And to solve these business problems, there are thousands of data sets that can potentially be analysed. Whereas most senior leaders and data teams recognize the importance of Big Data (and the analytics function in general), they find it difficult to articulate how Big Data should bring monetary value to the organization. In more simple words: when is it worth the investment to get Big Data teams involved?

Most enterprise organizations create tremendous amounts of data, internally, through customer transactions or the supply chain. Whilst handling all that data is already a challenge on its own, it is even harder to determine what 'tangible' value can be generated from these data sets. Most organizations have not clearly identified how a Big Data function should provide a return on investment.

Lack of trust in data quality

A second major obstacle in the successful adoption of Big Data in enterprise organizations is the lack of trust in data quality. Most organization don't have adequate processes in place to govern or steward enterprise data, making it easy to challenge results and recommendations. In some cases, the lack of trust is warranted, especially if there are no proper procedures in place to safeguard data quality. A commonly heard question is: can I trust the data in this report? This question inherently implies doubt with regards to the data source. Since data can be easily changed, altered and manipulated, it is always good to question the validity and veracity of data sets.

In other cases, data quality is challenged because of a personal agenda or individual motive. If data or the outcome of data analysis does not correspond with the personal agenda of an executive or decision-making, the easiest thing that executive can do is question the validity of the data set. Especially since early 2020, there is much more doubt around the concept of 'truth', and it has become more accepted to challenge (scientifically) data-driven conclusions. The challenge is way more difficult to address, since none of the underlying technologies or processes are at fault. In the end, whether to adopt data-driven advice remains a decision that is strongly rooted in the organizational culture.

Legal and governance complexities

As the power of data becomes more visible, so too has the interest from government and regulators. In the last decade, most governments have significantly tightened their data privacy and data security regulations. The most famous example is the General Data Protection Regulation (GDPR), which was introduced by the European

Union in 2018.[16] These new or additional regulations provide additional protections for individuals and are – in most cases – an extension of personal freedoms. From an enterprise compliance point of view, however, they make Big Data significantly more complex.

Organizations need to set up governance processes to showcase how they process data, how it is stored and create additional safeguards when personal data from individuals is processed, especially if this data crosses certain borders (which is almost always the case for enterprises). These legal and governance complexities don't prohibit an organization from obtaining value from Big Data, but they do make it more of a significant effort.

The war for Big Data talent

Lastly, and maybe most famously, it is no surprise that the world of Big Data is, by its very essence, complex. Very few people fully understand how Big Data environments work, and even fewer have the capacity to write or develop algorithms that can provide value to organizations. As a result, between most enterprises there is a war for data and analytics talent.

Although there is a strong effort from government and academia to speed up the capacity building programmes, and fund Big Data educational programmes, there is still a significant skills gap, which is not expected to be resolved anytime soon.[17] Demand for people with Big Data skills (whether technical or analytical) keeps on growing, and Big Data skills are consistently rank as the 'most in-demand' on job vacancy websites.

Addressing Big Data challenges

The four listed above are by no means a complete list of all the challenges that exist in the successful adoption of Big Data technologies and solutions. However, they all have one thing in common: each of these challenges touches upon an organizational competency. In essence, these challenges represent a lack of organizational competency.

The challenges (and lack of competencies) that enterprise organizations struggle with to adopt and adapt Big Data are by no means unique. Most organizations have similar problems and are lacking similar processes and skills. All organizations need Big Data talent, all organizations need proper data quality management and all organizations need to have governance and management processes to comply with increasing data rules and regulations. And this raises the question of how an organization can structurally build capabilities to address these challenges. Is there a way to structurally build capabilities to win in the data economy?

The reason for writing this book is to propose an answer to this question. To win in the data economy (further explained in the next chapter), organizations need a structural way to build capabilities consistently. They need a framework. They need an Enterprise Big Data Framework.

Notes

1 B Hostmann, N Rayner and G Herschel. Gartner's business intelligence, analytics and performance management framework, *Gartner Research Note*, 2009

2 A Mohamed, M K Najafabadi, Y B Wah, E A K Zaman and R Maskat. The state of the art and taxonomy of big data analytics: view from new big data framework, *Artificial Intelligence Review*, 2020 53 (2), 989–1037

3 R Kitchin and G McArdle. What makes Big Data, Big Data? Exploring the ontological characteristics of 26 datasets, *Big Data & Society*, 2016 3 (1), 2053951716631130

4 J Dean and S Ghemawat. MapReduce: a flexible data processing tool, *Communications of the ACM*, 2010 53 (1), 72–77

5 F Chang, J Dean, S Ghemawat, W C Hsieh, D A Wallach, M Burrows, T Chandra, A Fikes and R E Gruber. Bigtable: A distributed storage system for structured data, *ACM Transactions on Computer Systems (TOCS)*, 2008 26 (2), 1–26

6 T White (2012) *Hadoop: The definitive guide*. O'Reilly Media, Inc.

7 A Spark (2018) Apache spark, p.2018. https://spark.apache.org/ (archived at https://perma.cc/2KNR-QSKY)

8 M D de Assuncao, A da Silva Veith and R Buyya, R. Distributed data stream processing and edge computing: A survey on resource elasticity and future directions, *Journal of Network and Computer Applications*, 2018 103, 1–17

9 L Neumeyer, B Robbins, A Nair and A Kesari (2010) S4: Distributed stream computing platform. In *2010 IEEE International Conference on Data Mining Workshops*, December, 170–77. IEEE

10 A Ferranti, F Marcelloni, A Segatori, M Antonelli and P Ducange. A distributed approach to multi-objective evolutionary generation of fuzzy rule-based classifiers from big data, *Information Sciences*, 2017 415, 319–40

11 R Thottuvaikkatumana (2016) *Apache Spark 2 for Beginners*. Packt Publishing Ltd

12 M Kiran, P Murphy, I Monga, J Dugan and S S Baveja (2015). Lambda architecture for cost-effective batch and speed big data processing. In *2015 IEEE International Conference on Big Data (Big Data)*, October, 2785–92. IEEE

13 Z Hasani, M Kon-Popovska and G Velinov. Lambda architecture for real time big data analytic, *ICT Innovations*, 2014, 133–43

14 R Burtica, E M Mocanu, M I Andreica and N Ţăpuş, N. (2012) Practical application and evaluation of no-SQL databases in Cloud Computing. In 2012 IEEE International Systems Conference SysCon, March, 1–6. IEEE

15 R H Hariri, E M Fredericks and K M Bowers. Uncertainty in big data analytics: survey, opportunities, and challenges, *Journal of Big Data*, 2019 6(1), 1–16

16 J P Albrecht. How the GDPR will change the world, *European Data Protection Law Review*, 2016 2, 287.

17 K Nair (2019) Overcoming today's digital talent gap in organizations worldwide, *Development and Learning in Organizations: An International Journal* 33, 16–18

Win in the Data Economy 03

3.1. The data economy – integrating Big Data, cloud, IoT and AI

As discussed in the first chapter, Big Data is not a standalone concept. Rather, it consists of skills, technologies and procedures to extract value from massive quantities of data. First, this means that the data needs to be generated somewhere, either by people or machines. Since sensors provide the means to generate consistent and massive data, there is a strong correlation between the increasing number of Internet of Things (IoT) devices and the ever-increasing size of data. It is estimated that in 2018, there were 22 billion IoT devices connected to the internet. And this number is expected to increase further towards around 50 billion by 2030.[1]

The ever-increasing affordability of IoT sensors means that it will become even easier to generate more data about individual behaviours. Wearable devices, such as the Fitbit or Apple Watch, measure the heart rate, sleep cycles and physical activity of their owners. They collect data on the number of steps, movement, intensity and general health of the people who wear them, and generally report these findings back with comprehensive reports and summaries. And to produce these results it means that this data needs to be stored in a database, somewhere in the world.

Besides the obvious ethical and privacy questions that IoT devices will bring (and which will be further discussed in Part 6), it is easy to see that the IoT will be a significant driver of further research and the development of enterprise solutions, simply because the data generated by IoT devices will have significant enterprise value. In line with the examples mentioned above, the analysis of sleep cycles will have value for pharmaceutical companies. Sports and apparel companies will find data about exercise behaviour valuable. And health insurance companies will probably be able to make better and more predictive estimations based on all the data points that wearable devices generate.

The increasing quantities of data, like the data generated by IoT devices, all need to be stored somewhere in databases across the world, requiring a significant number of data centres. From a technical perspective, the only solution that can accommodate the massive influx and storage of data is provided by cloud solutions. It is fair to say that the concept that we know as Big Data today would not have been possible without the technological infrastructure that is provided by cloud computing concepts. Cloud computing provides an affordable, secure and instant opportunity to store and retrieve data in an efficient and consumer-friendly way.

To accommodate the ever-increasing quantities of Big Data, it means that additional data centre capacity will become an imperative, a fact that is well known to the major cloud providers in the world (Microsoft, AWS, Google and Alibaba). Demand for data centre services doubled from 2018 to 2020, and data centre providers keep increasing their infrastructure by building new data centres at strategic locations across the world.[2] As long as the velocity with which we as a society keep generating data increases, the demand for storage solutions in the form of cloud solutions will continue to grow.

The last major technology domain that continues to integrate with Big Data is the knowledge domain of artificial intelligence. Artificial intelligence (popularly abbreviated as AI) is the domain that aims to mimic human-grade decision-making, by combining several scientific techniques. And although the exact working of the human brain is still not fully discovered, one thing is certain: the brain is able to store massive quantities of information – enough to last a lifetime.

Therefore, to deploy AI algorithms, or solutions that are coming close, massive Big Data sets are required. Just like a human would search through years of experiences in their physical memory to make a judgement or decision, a computer would need to have the ability to search through massive quantities of Big Data to make the optimal decision. In other words, AI solutions depend heavily on Big Data. And, conversely, AI algorithms provide the opportunity to extract meaningful business value from data sets, creating a symbiotic relationship between the two domains. Because of this strong relationship, AI is an integral part of the Enterprise Big Data Framework (discussed in Part 2).

Figure 3.1 The data economy: convergence of knowledge domains

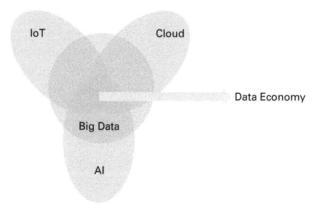

In summary, Big Data is not a standalone function or knowledge domain. For Big Data to bring enterprise value, it would need to be integrated with the technology domains of IoT, cloud computing and AI. However, the common denominator between these four domains is data. Companies and organizations that can smartly and efficiently integrate data from these domains are able to win in the data economy. The next generation of successful enterprises will generate and collect data from customer or business processes utilizing IoT technologies, they will then store those massive quantities of data in an efficient and secure way utilizing the infrastructure of the cloud, and they will subsequently make better, faster and more accurate decisions by employing AI algorithms.

However, winning in the data economy is by no means an easy task. It requires knowledge, capabilities and skills. The knowledge domains of IoT, cloud, AI and Big Data are vast, and rooted in strong theoretical foundations. How can this be translated to something that is workable, comprehensive and practical for organizations? The Enterprise Big Data Framework, which we will introduce in Part 2 in detail, integrates the practical aspects of Big Data and related technologies into a capability model. With the capability model, organizations can structurally start to build capabilities in different domains – with the ultimate goal to win in the data economy.

3.2 The Internet of Things and Big Data

The IoT is one of the primary drivers behind the existence of Big Data. IoT devices, and their embedded sensors, can create data around the clock. As such, IoT devices are to a large extent responsible for the volume and velocity characteristics of Big Data that we discussed in Chapter 2.

Because the creation of data (or data generation processes) by IoT devices plays a significant role in the creation, storage and analysis of Big Data, this section will explore the most common structure, applications and taxonomies in further detail. Because to obtain value from Big Data, we would first need to know where the data comes from.

The IoT is – like Big Data – a container term that addresses a number of underlying technologies. Although many definitions of IoT exists, one that is commonly used to explain the term comes from the Institute of Institute of Electrical and Electronics Engineers (IEEE) which defines it as follows:[3]

A network of items – each embedded with sensors – which are connected to the Internet.

The primary focus in IoT is therefore primarily the creation of a network of sensors, connected through the internet. From a data perspective – which will be the leading point of view in this publication – this is significant for two main reasons:

1 Sensors can generate data continuously and without limits. The more sensors become operational, the more data (per unit of time) is produced.

2 Because the sensors are networked through the internet, they create continuous data streams (i.e. velocity) that need be stored in databases, and which provide real-time information.

Through these two main characteristics – the continuous creation of data and its direct accessibility – data sets inherently become massive (i.e. Big Data), but, more importantly, data sets become valuable. For example, if a sensor detects an abnormal heart rate through a wearable device, this might be a reason to visit a doctor instantly. Similarly, the ability to detect that someone is in store, or looking at a particular product, provides a variety of marketing opportunities for companies. The main advantage IoT brings is that data becomes actionable immediately.

The data that is generated by IoT devices is frequently contrasted with data that is generated by people, also known as the Internet of Computers. The main difference between these **data generators**, as illustrated in Figure 3.2, comes from the source.[4] Are humans actively creating the data (for example through social media) or

Figure 3.2 Human-generated vs. machine-generated data

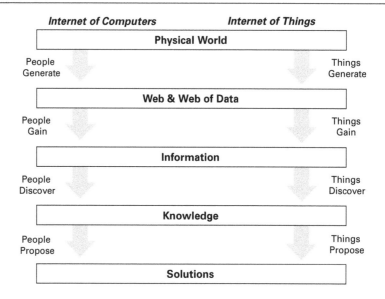

is the data generated by things? A common classification of data generators is to distinguish between human-generated and machine-generated data:[5]

- **Human-generated data:** this refers to the vast number of social media, such as photos, tweets or videos. The data generated in this category are normally very unstructured.

- **Machine-generated data:** this refers to data generated from real-time sensors in industry machinery or vehicles. Data comes from various sensors, cameras, satellites, log files, bio informatics, activity trackers, personal health care trackers and many other sense data resources.

A visual representation of the difference between Internet of Computers (human-generated) and IoT (machine-generated) data is depicted in Figure 3.2.

A valid question is to ask why the primary focus of this publication will be on IoT or machine-generated data. Is human-generated data not equally important in making predictions and obtaining value from data sets? The answer to this question is obviously yes, and data generated by people will also be addressed. However, the main purpose and scope of this book is to address the capabilities that will help enterprises win in the data economy. In other words, we will primarily look at defining Big Data strategies and building Big Data capabilities that an organization can control. Machine-generated data is typically something an organization can control proactively, whereas human generated data is not. Additionally, and maybe more importantly, the contribution of machine-generated data far outpaces the Big Data that is created every day. If we think about the analysis of website traffic or behaviour, for example, although a person clicks on pages, it is a sensor that logs the

Figure 3.3   IoT markets and key stakeholders

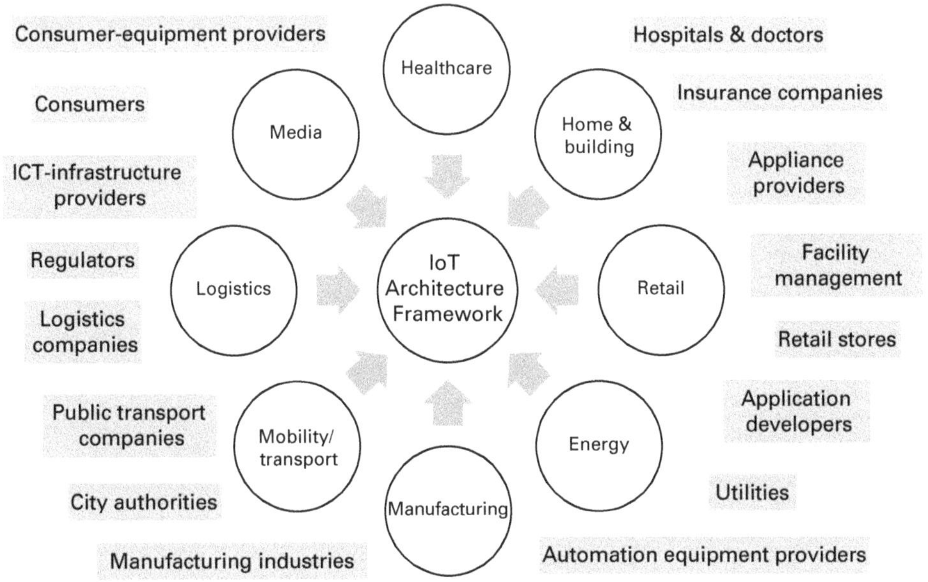

behaviours and traffic. In most business and enterprise contexts, it will therefore be the machine-generated data that we are interested in for our analysis.

A comprehensive overview of the wide application and use cases of IoT traffic is depicted in Figure 3.3, outlining common markets and stakeholders that can benefit from Big Data created through IoT devices. Not surprisingly, these are the same markets that were discussed in the first chapter.

The relation between IoT and Big Data is apparent in all markets, across all stake-holders. IoT devices and sensors can generate and produce significant quantities of data. IoT devices function as **data generators** or the beginning of the **data pipeline**. The data that is generated by these devices is subsequently stored in databases which reside in the cloud (which will be discussed in detail in in the next section). Because data can be collected by sensors every minute, for example with every step you take, the data stream will in most cases be continuous, causing databases to expand and expand over time.

The data that is generated by IoT devices is frequently structured or semi-structured in nature (as discussed in Chapter 2), but more modern IoT devices also have the capacity to capture unstructured data. Common examples include CCTV cameras, which capture ongoing data streams of videos every single second. If you consider that the City of London alone houses 691,000 CCTV cameras, it becomes easy to understand the tremendous storage required.

The data that is generated by IoT devices can be structured into a taxonomy of key characteristics. Understanding these key characteristics will provide insights into

Table 3.1 Taxonomy of the IoT domain and its impact on Big Data

Category	Characteristics	Description
Data Generation	Velocity	Data generated by IoT devices is generated with different speeds and creates data at different rates. Wearable devices, for example, might generate new data points every millisecond, second or maybe every minute. The frequency with which data is generated is dependent on the needs for accuracy (more is better) versus the cost of processing the data.
	Scalability	As the number of IoT devices, and hence the number of sensors, continues to grow, the scalability of solutions becomes a significant question. Every new sensor will add to the stack of data-generating devices, and solutions will need to be designed to deal with scaling requirements.

(continued)

Table 3.1   (Continued)

Category	Characteristics	Description
	Dynamics	IoT sensors are frequently part of moving components and wearable devices. Examples include mobile phones, smart watches and/or cameras. Sensors will therefore move around, could be damaged or break altogether. Big Data solutions that rely on IoT data therefore need to consider these dynamics and the fragility of the technical components.
	Heterogeneity	The number of devices that are connected to the internet keeps increasing – we now connect mobile devices, smart TVs and smart home equipment. But new solutions are developed rapidly in lighting, home appliances and medical care. New sensors might generate different data formats, which will need to be connected in Big Data environments.
Data Quality	Uncertainty	Sensory data that is created at massive scale can come with many levels of uncertainty. Sensors might malfunction and produce corrupt or erroneous values. In addition, the precision (the degree of reproducibility) or accuracy (the difference between measured and actual value) might provide levels of uncertainty.
	Redundancy	Sensors can create multiple versions of the same observation or data point. For example, when an RFID scanner detects the same object multiple times as it is detected by the sensor. Big Data solutions need the ability to deal with redundant versions of the same data points.
	Ambiguity	Data can have a different meanings to different data consumers, and Big Data solutions therefore must deal with ambiguity in data sets. Medical data, for example, can be interpreted in different ways by a medical professional or by an insurance provider.
	Inconsistency	Data that is created by sensors is not always consistent. For example, a sensor might miss a particular reading or experience an error in the generation of data. Inconsistencies therefore need to be detected by Big Data solutions.

(continued)

Table 3.1   (Continued)

Category	Characteristics	Description
Data Interoperability	Incompleteness	To make accurate predictions for Big Data sets, data frequently needs to be combined from a variety of sources, especially if the data needs to be analysed in real-time. In particular, if there are many different data sources, it is important to determine which data point will provide a complete representation of the real world.
	Semantics	The semantics of data sets becomes more complex as data sizes increase. Understanding the meaning of the data generated will lead to improved decision-making and enhanced solutions. Therefore, semantics within machine-generated data will play an important role in the process of enabling sensors to understand and process data by themselves.

some of the key storage requirements and design choices that will need to be made to set up a Big Data environment in the enterprise. Table 3.1 provides an overview of this taxonomy, which separates the key characteristics of IoT into three main categories: data generation, data quality and data interoperability.

Data generation, data quality and data interoperability will have a profound impact on the way Big Data solutions need to be architected, and how data streams need to be processed to make quality predictions. For example, filtering or data-cleaning steps will need to be included if the data quality is poor or inconsistent. In later parts of this book, we will consider the technical requirements for Big Data environments in further detail and explore the relationship the way we can incorporate the key characteristics of data generation, data quality and data interoperability in technical Big Data architectures and solutions.

3.3 Cloud computing and Big Data

After data is generated, it needs to be stored in a secure and easily accessible way. Cloud computing or cloud infrastructure provides the technology with which this goal can be accomplished. Like IoT, we can therefore state that cloud computing is a foundational technology for Big Data. Without the cloud, Big Data would probably not exist, or at least not at the scale that we know it today.

With cloud computing, we are referring to virtualized storage and processing resources, which can be requested by any organization or enterprise on demand. Like IoT, there are many definitions available, but one that is commonly used is from the National Institute of Standards and Technology (NIST)[6]:

> Cloud computing is a model for enabling ubiquitous, convenient, on-demand network access to a shared pool of configurable computing resources (e.g., networks, servers, storage, applications, and services) that can be rapidly provisioned and released with minimal management effort or service provider interaction. This cloud model is composed of five essential characteristics, three service models, and four deployment models.

The key characteristic of cloud computing, as provided by the NIST definition above, is that it provides enterprises with almost unlimited computing resources. And from a data perspective, this means that organizations will have access to **data storage** and **data processing** solutions to accommodate the massive quantities of data that were generated by the **data generators** (most notably IoT devices, as discussed in the previous section). With cloud data storage and cloud data processing, organizations can collect, access and process Big Data sets at affordable pricing over the internet. And because resources can be pooled and shared across multiple customers, cloud solution providers are able to process massive quantities of data in seconds for the customers.

A visual representation of the definition of cloud computing as provided by NIST is shown in Figure 3.4, and includes the essential characteristics, service models and deployment model referenced in the definition.

The key characteristics, delivery and deployment models offer a number of significant benefits for storing Big Data sets. The rapid elasticity offers enterprises the

Figure 3.4   Visual representation of cloud computing

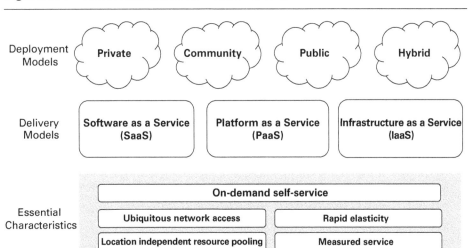

SOURCE NIST

ability to quickly scale their storage capacity endlessly. No matter how much data an enterprise generates, leading cloud providers can dynamically scale up their storage capacity. Combined with the measured usage resource pooling characteristics, this offers enterprises the ability to store massive data sets at optimized cost levels, generally significantly cheaper than purchasing and managing IT infrastructure independently.

The following key cloud characteristics (as depicted in Figure 3.4) make cloud computing a suitable – if not the preferred – option to store and process Big Data:

- **On-demand self-service:** Organizations can decide unilaterally how much data they want to store or process and what IT resources need to be provisioned to accomplish their objectives. As a result, companies are in complete control with regards to the quantities and formats of data they store, and how frequently they want to process their data sets.

- **Ubiquitous network access:** Cloud resources can be accessed via networks (usually the internet) by heterogeneous thin or thick client platforms (e.g. mobile phones, tablets, laptops and workstations). Big Data solutions can therefore collect and process data from different types of devices and through different platforms. Through the ubiquitous network access characteristics, data that is generated by IoT devices (discussed in the previous section) can be collected and stored.

- **Resource pooling:** In cloud environments, a customer's computing resources are pooled to serve multiple consumers using a multi-tenant model, with different physical and virtual resources dynamically assigned and reassigned according to consumer demand. In other words, IT infrastructure is shared between different organizations. With resource pooling, storing and processing Big Data sets becomes cost-efficient. Since most companies only need to process Big Data sets at certain intervals, the resource pooling option enables organizations to keep costs under control.

- **Rapid elasticity:** In cloud environments IT resources can be elastically provisioned and released, in some cases automatically, to scale rapidly proportional to demand. This means that if suddenly massive quantities of data need to be stored or processed, the IT infrastructure can accommodate this. There is (virtually) no limit to the size of data sets that can be stored in cloud environments.

- **Measured service:** Automated listeners that are embedded in cloud computing environments can measure the amount of IT resources that are consumed per client. The measure service characteristic is expressed in most cloud environments in a utility-based pay-per-use system. The more data you store or process, the higher the corresponding costs. Through measure service usage, organizations can predict the costs of their Big Data solution, which provides primary input to the business case of Big Data solutions (discussed further in Part 3).

A second key benefit includes the various deployment models, as depicted in Figure 3.4. Organizations that have strict IT security protocols or regulatory requirements (think about the medical sector, financial institutions or government-linked agencies) can still utilize the benefits of cloud computing to store and process Big Data sets by utilizing a deployment model rather than the public cloud. With private cloud environments, for example, resources are not shared between multiple tenants and are tailored for a particular client.

Table 3.2 outlines deployment models that are frequently used to address different organizational perspectives and visions with regards to security concerns and data ownership.

The essential characteristics of cloud computing (Table 3.1) combined with the various deployment models have made it possible to store and process massive

Table 3.2 Deployment models of cloud and their implications for Big Data

Deployment model	
Public Cloud	In public cloud environments IT infrastructure is provisioned for open use by the public. The data sets stored in public cloud environments may be owned, managed and operated by organizations, but exist on the premises of the cloud provider. In public clouds, IT resources are shared between different organizations, making it the most cost-efficient form of Big Data storage and processing.
Private Cloud	In private cloud environments infrastructure is provisioned for exclusive use by a single organization comprising multiple consumers (e.g. business units). The private cloud is typically the preferred option for organizations that store and process sensitive data or for which regulatory requirements apply. Because IT resources are dedicated to one customer, private clouds are the most expensive deployment option.
Community Cloud	In community cloud environments resources are shared between an exclusive group of consumers, for example government departments. Community clouds are primarily set up to address some of the security concerns of public clouds. In essence, a community cloud is a private cloud shared by a limited number of known tenants, and therefore will have a similar cost structure to private clouds.
Hybrid Cloud	A hybrid cloud is a combination between a public and private cloud and is of special interest to the design of Big Data solutions. By choosing a hybrid cloud, organizations can achieve the cost benefits of public clouds, combined with the additional security that is provided by private clouds. In practice, this means that organizations store Big Data sets of (unprocessed) data in private clouds (leveraging the cost benefits) and store the results of Big Data analysis (i.e. the value obtained from the data sets) in private clouds.

quantities of data securely and efficiently. Cloud infrastructure environments enable organizations to store (almost) unlimited sets of data without building their own data centres, or without building the knowledge to set up and maintain complex IT environments. Additionally, the services that most professional cloud providers typically offer make it possible to integrate data from different sources (i.e. building a **data lake**) and run common machine learning algorithms across the data sets, providing quick and effective mechanisms to leverage the value of Big Data.

With the proliferation and rapid request for Big Data storage and processing solutions, the number of cloud services has expanded linearly in the last decade. The number of hyperscale data centres (defined as data centres to offer a complete mix of hardware and facilities that can scale a distributed computing environment up to thousands of servers) has been growing steadily in the last few years, with no end in sight.[7] An overview of the growth of cloud provider data centres is depicted in Figure 3.5.

Commensurate with the growth (and demand) for cloud providers that can store and process all the Big Data that is generated across the world is the energy consumed. Global data centres will become the world's largest users of energy consumption, with the ratio rising from 3 per cent in 2017 to 4.5 per cent in 2025.[8] The ever-increasing demand for Big Data will therefore also bring pressing questions with regards to the way energy will need to be sourced. In Part 3, we will further discuss the implication of energy on enterprise Big Data strategies.

Because most Big Data environments are hosted in these hyperscale data centres, it is beneficial to have a further understanding of the key players involved. Although we will keep a vendor-neutral perspective throughout this publication, it is important to understand that Big Data technology (most notably the storage and processing capabilities) is dominated by a select number of private companies. In 2020, the top five cloud providers accounted for 80 per cent of the market, and nearly 90 per cent of cloud service providers exhibited growth.[9]

Figure 3.5   Growth of hyperscale data centres

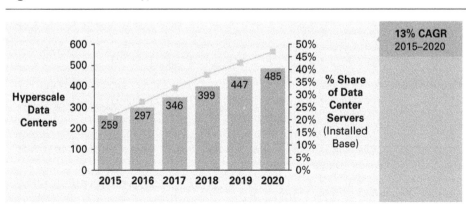

SOURCE Cisco

Understanding the competitive landscape of cloud providers is important for several reasons. First, because of the limited number of cloud providers that have the capacity to support Big Data environments, the design choices (in terms of architecture) that are made by these companies will have an impact on the Big Data solutions that are used in the enterprise. We will further discuss the technical implications of these design choices in Part 4.

Second, choosing a cloud provider is a strategic decision. The choice of your cloud provider to store and analyse your data is frequently a long-lasting one. Migration between major cloud providers is by no means an easy or cost-efficient operation. The choice of a cloud provider in essence means choosing a long-term partnership, which will last many years. Choosing a cloud provider for your Big Data environments should therefore be a strategic consideration, involving top management approval. We will further discuss the strategic aspects of Big Data in Part 3.

Third and lastly, there are regulatory requirements and considerations to consider. Note that all the cloud providers listed in Table 3.3 are commercial companies, incorporated under the laws of their respective countries. The countries where these companies are incorporated have different views, laws and regulations with regards to data privacy, data security and accessibility of data hosted at different locations. These regulations are incredibly complex, and are typically also under political influence. The regulatory, privacy and security consideration that are relevant for Big Data, and which will be influenced significantly by the choice of cloud provider, will be further discussed in Part 6.

3.4 Artificial intelligence and Big Data

Once data is generated and stored securely in a cloud environment, the value in the data sets needs to be extracted. Although cloud computing environments provide the

Table 3.3 Top cloud providers (measured by IaaS)

Company	2020 Revenue	2020 Market Share (%)	2019–2020 Growth (%)
Amazon	26,201	40.8	28.7
Microsoft	12,658	19.7	59.2
Alibaba	6,117	9.5	52.8
Google	3,932	6.1	66.1
Huawei	2,672	4.2	202.8
Others	12,706	19.8	25.6
Total	64,286	100.0	40.7

SOURCE Gartner

computing resources to process massive quantities of data, there is still a requirement to instruct the compute engines which script or algorithm to run. The last major knowledge domain that enterprise organizations need to win in the data economy is therefore artificial intelligence – more popularly known as AI.

Artificial intelligence is a scientific domain that encompasses major areas of research which aim to mimic human decision-making into decision-making by machines. And when we draw a comparative model with 'intelligence' in humans, and 'intelligence' in machines, we can easily see why the domains of AI and Big Data are intertwined.[10]

As humans, we make decisions and predications every day based on information that we have obtained over a lifetime. You know the answer to a maths problem because you learned it in high school. You decide to invest in specific stock on the stock market because you have read about them in the news and learned the principles and theory of investments. In all these decisions, you instruct your brain to think (i.e. 'process') information based on the knowledge and memories (i.e. 'storage') that is archived at some specific location in your brain. With Big Data in an enterprise context, our objective is similar: we have the storage and processing capacity, yet we still must instruct the machine how to **search, learn or reason**. To accomplish this objective, we can apply knowledge from the domain of artificial intelligence.

Although AI has risen to tremendous new levels of popularity in the last decade, the study of trying to mimic human decision-making by computers is not. Alan Turing (1912–1954) is credited with laying the groundwork of machine learning and AI. In his famous 'Computing Machinery and Intelligence' paper, published in 1950, he asked the now famous phrase:

> I propose to consider the question, 'Can machines think?' This should begin with definitions of the meaning of the terms 'machine' and 'think'.

Alan Turing's paper laid the groundwork for the domain of artificial intelligence as we now know it today. Creating computers and machines that have the ability to reason or 'think' can have a significant amount of value, both for society as a whole, but in particular for corporate organizations. The ability to make better predications better, faster or cheaper than a competitor can have significant monetary results. It is therefore no wonder that AI has been a main focus point of some of the biggest companies in the world, and the investments in AI have been significantly growing.[11] This trend is also reflected in the growing spend on AI software, as depicted in Figure 3.6.[12]

In AI solutions, the primary purpose is to mimic the process of human decision-making. Like the other knowledge domains that we discussed in earlier sections, there are many definitions of AI available. Throughout the rest of this book, we will adhere to the one utilized by the International Standards Organization (ISO) and published in ISO/IEC 2382:2015[13]:

> Artificial Intelligence is the capability of a functional unit to perform functions that are generally associated with human intelligence such as reasoning and learning.

Retrieving 'value' from data is generally the most challenging part of Big Data. With enough resources, every organization can generate large data sets, store them somewhere and pay for enough processing power to analyse them. But the most important thing is to identify 'how' value can be obtained. If you have access to large quantities of data (which most enterprises have), what can you do with it? How can you use customer data to optimize your marketing campaigns? How can you use data from wearables to increase sales? Or how can you use data from network monitoring tools to predict failure of different components?

To answer these questions, you will need to have a 'beyond basic' understanding of how data can be translated into value. And this begins with a fundamental understanding of AI. To accomplish this objective and provide organizations with the capabilities to retrieve enduring value from Big Data, we will cover AI extensively. In Part 4, we will provide a practical overview of most common **AI techniques** and **AI engines** that organizations can use to obtain value from Big Data sets. Additionally, in Part 8 we will provide an in-depth overview of AI use cases and applications.

Since the applications of AI are vast, we will focus primarily on the practical applications of AI that can be used for Big Data. In other words, this means we will

Figure 3.6   Artificial intelligence (AI) software market revenue worldwide from 2018 to 2025

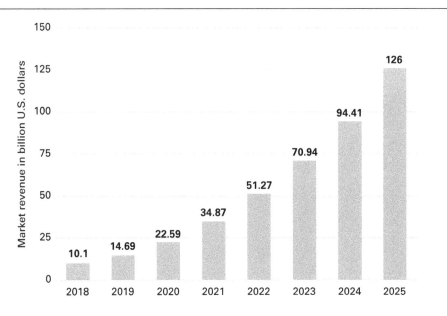

limit our focus to AI techniques and AI engines. These are practical, proven and available applications or algorithms that can be applied to Big Data sets in organizations. The goal of this book is to help identify strategies with which organizations can win in the data economy, based on proven best practices and techniques.

Notes

1 Statista (2023) Number of Internet of Things (IoT) connected devices worldwide from 2019 to 2021, with forecasts from 2022 to 2030, www.statista.com/statistics/802690/worldwide-connected-devices-by-access-technology/#statisticContainer (archived at https://perma.cc/S2GW-CY8D)

2 E Masanet, A Shehabi, N Lei, S Smith and J Koomey, Recalibrating global data center energy-use estimates, *Science* 2020, 367 (6481), 984–86

3 R Minerva, A Biru and D Rotondi. Towards a definition of the Internet of Things (IoT), *IEEE Internet Initiative*, 2015 1 (1), 1–86

4 Y Qin, Q Z Sheng, N J Falkner, S Dustdar, H Wang and A V Vasilakos. When things matter: A survey on data-centric internet of things, *Journal of Network and Computer Applications*, 2016 64, 137–53

5 M Ghotkar and P Rokde. Big data: How it is generated and its importance, *IOSR Journal of Computer Engineering*, 2016, 5

6 P Mell and T Grance (2011) The NIST definition of cloud computing, https://nvlpubs.nist.gov/nistpubs/legacy/sp/nistspecialpublication800-145.pdf (archived at https://perma.cc/E8VZ-SKE3)

7 Cisco (2015) Forecast and methodology, www.cisco.com/c/dam/m/en_us/service-provider/ciscoknowledgenetwork/files/622_11_15-16-Cisco_GCI_CKN_2015-2020_AMER_EMEAR_NOV2016.pdf (archived at https://perma.cc/Y2QA-RNH8)

8 Y Liu, X Wei, J Xiao, Z Liu, Y Xu and Y Tian. Energy consumption and emission mitigation prediction based on data center traffic and PUE for global data centers, Global Energy Interconnection, 2020 3 (3), 272–82, www.researchgate.net/publication/343907273_Energy_consumption_and_emission_mitigation_prediction_based_on_data_center_traffic_and_PUE_for_global_data_centers (archived at https://perma.cc/7VQX-8RPS)

9 M Rimol (2021) Gartner says worldwide IaaS public cloud services market grew 40.7% in 2020, Gartner, www.gartner.com/en/newsroom/press-releases/2021-06-28-gartner-says-worldwide-iaas-public-cloud-services-market-grew-40-7-percent-in-2020 (archived at https://perma.cc/Q33M-AADF)

10 A M Turing (2009) Computing machinery and intelligence. In *Parsing the Turing Test*, Springer, Dordrecht, 23–65

11 A Ghimire, S Thapa, A K Jha, S Adhikari and A Kumar (2020) Accelerating business growth with big data and artificial intelligence. In 2020 Fourth International Conference on I-SMAC (IoT in Social, Mobile, Analytics and Cloud)(I-SMAC), October, 441–448. IEEE

12 L Blake (2020) The success factors influencing AI ecosystems and AI startups: a
multi-level analysis, doctoral dissertation, HEC Montreal

13 S Samoili, M L Cobo, E Gomez, G De Prato, F Martinez-Plumed and B Delipetrev
(2020) *AI Watch. Defining Artificial Intelligence. Towards an operational definition and
taxonomy of artificial intelligence.* Publications Office of the European Union

PART TWO
The Enterprise Big Data Framework

The Enterprise Big 04
Data Framework

4.1 Introduction to the Big Data Framework

In the previous segment, we provided a comprehensive overview of the key drivers behind Big Data, the most important underlying technologies, and emphasized the need for capability building in the enterprise. It is now time to introduce the Enterprise Big Data Framework, the main model behind this book.

The **Enterprise Big Data Framework** was developed to assist enterprise organizations to structurally develop their capabilities in Big Data, providing them with an approach and strategy to win in the data economy – an explanation of this book's title. Since enterprise organizations are characterized by the fact that they are inherently complex, a structural approach and programmatic approach is required. Hence, the need for a framework.

Frameworks bring structure and are applied in a variety of different domains. There are frameworks for project management, IT architecture, IT governance and automation best practices.[1] Yet, for the domain of 'Big Data', no such framework exists. Although there are technical programming frameworks (like the Hadoop software library that we introduced in Chapter 2) in the Big Data domain, none of these focus on building **capability**.

The Enterprise Big Data Framework is different because it is a capability model. As such, it will not only focus on the technical capabilities required (although these will also be covered) but aims to provide a holistic approach. With this holistic approach, we aim to cover all the knowledge, skills and technologies that are required to be successful with Big Data in an enterprise. We therefore position the Enterprise Big Data Framework as an end-to-end capability model. High level enough to facilitate a discussion in the boardroom, yet also detailed enough to start planning improvement projects in any of its six capabilities.

To be successful in Big Data best practices, more is required than just technology. Investing in tools or hiring skilled data scientists is the easy part. The difficult part is to facilitate a culture of data-driven decision-making and building a structured Big Data practice. Building this practice takes time and requires organization to take a variety of different aspects into considerations. Organizations that process massive quantities of data will have to ensure that the data they are processing is valid, they need to consider data privacy regulations or security policies. They will need to monitor changes to data, and ensure reproducibility and auditability of processing results. They will need to build skills and talent development programmes to keep upskilling their analytics, architecture and data governance teams. And this list could go on for a considerable number of pages.

In the Enterprise Big Data Framework, we have tried to capture all the required capabilities that are necessary to win in the data economy, and we will cover all the before-mentioned topics in the upcoming chapters. But before we can do this, a co-herent approach is necessary that will bind all these different topics together – hence the choice for the development of this Enterprise Big Data Framework, which is de-picted in Figure 4.1.

Although the Framework looks simple at first glance, every capability domain covers a variety of in-depth topics as well as key guidance on how to develop capa-bilities in that area. In this section, we will start with providing the background of the Framework, its core capabilities and some practical advice on how to work with the Framework and where to get started. In the subsequent chapters, we will cover each of the six capability domains in detail, together with an outline that explains how organizations can grow their capability in every domain.

Figure 4.1   The Enterprise Big Data Framework

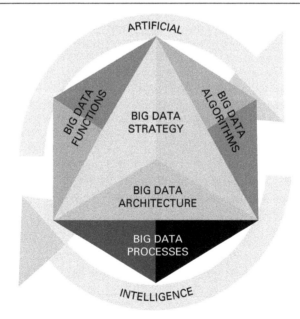

4.2 The six capabilities of the Enterprise Big Data Framework

A schematic overview of the Enterprise Big Data Framework is depicted in Figure 4.1. The Framework consists of six capability domains, providing an overview of the areas that any organization should address to leverage long-term business results from Big Data. Each of the six capability domains is complementary to the other domains, with strong interfaces and connections between every domain. In this section, we will first provide a high-level overview of each of the six essential capabilities. In the subsequent sections, each of the capabilities will be discussed in greater detail.

Big Data strategy

The Big Data strategy is positioned at the centre of the Enterprise Big Data Framework. It is at the centre of the Framework for a variety of reasons. For many enterprise organizations, a strategy is at the core of their operations, and the knowledge domain of Big Data is no different. A first and fundamental question that every organization should ask is what strategic advantage they aim to achieve by analysing massive data sets.

The quantities of data that are generated across the world are so massive that you can spend a vast amount of time and resources on data analysis. There are many 'interesting' facts hidden in data sets, and correlations or insights that can be discovered. And many organizations start their Big Data projects taking that approach: they hire a team of data analysts, source several Big Data analysis tools and the team comes back with interesting dashboards and reports. Although these insights might prove to be useful, they frequently don't warrant the investment and provide limited returns on the capital spent. Analysis just for the sake of analysis provides little value.

To overcome this problem, organizations (and especially those of scale) should start with the creation of a Big Data strategy. A Big Data strategy will provide focus to the objectives of a Big Data programme and outline the competitive advantage the company is aiming to achieve by the analysis for Big Data sets. The strategy will need to outline the business case, the return on investment and the way data-driven decision-making will ultimately lead to a competitive advantage.

Although it sounds straightforward that the creation of a Big Data strategy should be the starting point for any organization, the reality is different. Many companies fail to define their strategic objectives beforehand, and some studies even suggest that most Big Data programmes do not reach their completion stages because of a lack of strategic direction.[2] Many managers that are leading data analysis teams are unsure how to quantify their contributions towards the organization's bottom line.

How can an organization objectively say that they are making better decisions because of Big Data?

The formulation of a Big Data strategy is therefore the starting point of the Enterprise Big Data Framework. In Part 3, we will define the steps that organizations can take to formulate a practical Big Data strategy. Only if a Big Data strategy has been adequately defined can it be communicated, explained and shared with other stakeholders in the organization. It is therefore a crucial exercise that needs to be performed regularly to assess whether the organization is still on track to meet its strategic goals, or whether any revisions would need to be made.

Building a Big Data strategy is a capability. Organizations that have more experience, and who have done this more frequently, perform better in this area. It is a capability that can grow and develop, allowing organizations to continually refine their strategy. For example, it is very clear that an organization that has defined strategic metrics to determine the success of their Big Data programme operates at a higher capability level than an organization that does not have this in place.

Big Data architecture

The Big Data architecture capability represents the technical capabilities that an organization requires to process massive quantities of data. As we have discussed in the previous section, the analysis of high-volume, high-velocity data requires different (distributed) storage and processing approaches and a corresponding IT architecture.

In this second domain, we therefore need to consider what an organization needs in terms of technology, tools and IT infrastructure. Organizations will need to make strategic choices which vendors will provide technologies and tools (the Big Data tool stack) to process their Big Data. In many cases, this represents a strategic choice with strong long-term implications in terms of partnerships, contractual arrangements and costs. It is therefore not difficult to see that there will be a strong integration between the Big Data strategy (discussed in the previous section) and the Big Data architecture capability.

There are many key considerations that come into play in designing an enterprise Big Data architecture. How will data pipelines be constructed? How do we build an enterprise data lake? How robust and secure does the environment need to be? Are there technical constraints from a regulatory point of view? The choices that are made in answering these questions will, to a large extent, determine the cost levels of the technical Big Data environment and therefore the return on investment of Big Data solutions. Organizations that have designed their Big Data architecture in a sound and robust way will experience significant benefits from compliancy and cost perspectives.

Given the fact that Big Data is in essence data, is it not possible to set up a Big Data architecture without taking the wider context of enterprise IT into consideration. The IT environment that an organization currently has will to a large extent determine what will be necessary to facilitate the processing and storage of Big Data. Vice versa, design choices that are made to set up a Big Data architecture will inherently impact the enterprise IT architecture. As such, it would be a fair statement to claim that Big Data architecture is a critical subset of any organization's IT architecture.

Since IT architecture as a knowledge domain is inherently complex, Big Data architecture is a critical capability. Organizations can make smart or poor design choices; they can set up their systems and infrastructure in different ways and can incorporate different toolsets to build their Big Data products and solutions. It is therefore important to start building from a few structured design principles, which we will discuss in further detail in Part 4.

Big Data algorithms

To extract value from massive data sets, computers will need to run algorithms. To find the proverbial needle in the haystack (i.e. the value in the data), you need to know what you are looking for. Big Data algorithms is the capability that concerns itself with the techniques and algorithms that can sift through data sets to obtain the desired results. It is very clearly a knowledge capability because it requires a firm understanding of what algorithm to apply in what situation. Given an existing set of enterprise data, there are many ways in which data can be analysed. Some of these methods might be good, some might even be better. Having the capability to predict half a percentage point better than a competitor can lead to additional millions in profits.

The Big Data algorithms capability is frequently denoted as data science. A common definition of data science is the one from the National Institute of Standards and Technology[3]:

> Data science is the extraction of actionable knowledge directly from data through a process of discovery, or hypothesis formulation and hypothesis testing.

Although this definition covers the objectives that we are aiming for with Big Data algorithms to a significant extent, it does not provide any guidance as to the volume, velocity and variety characteristics that are determining for Big Data. For that reason, we have chosen to adhere to the term **Big Data algorithms** to indicate the capability that is necessary to extract actionable knowledge from Big Data sets. In simpler terms, we could state that this capability covers data science in the context of Big Data.

Regardless of the characteristics of the data set under consideration, it is important to have a sound understanding of how algorithms work. For example, if there are multiple ways to predict which customers will purchase a product, it is important to understand what the best choice will be, and especially why. Organizations may have the resources to store all the information in the world, but without the knowledge to extract value, a Big Data set will just remain a data set.

Since this is a crucial and necessary capability to retrieve value, the last years have seen a significant proliferation of educational programmes, university degrees and job vacancies related to the ability to understand Big Data algorithms. Most of these roles in enterprises are denoted by the popular terms **data analysts** or **data scientists**. Although the fundamental skills for these roles are still to this day strongly rooted in maths and statistics, the significant demand for people with these skills have greatly popularized this capability. *Harvard Business Review* even labelled the role of the data scientist the 'sexiest job of the 21st century'.[4]

The increased interest in Big Data algorithms, and the techniques to extract value from data sets, is beneficial for organizations for multiple reasons. The collective knowledge about algorithms is growing, and it is becoming easier for organizations to hire and retain employees that possess these skills. In addition, because the community of **data professionals** is growing, more knowledge is exchanged and shared, leading to increased innovation. Over the last years, the number of open-source data science and machine learning packages that are available in the two most famous **Big Data programming languages** (Python and R) has increased dramatically.[5] The significant advantage of this development is that the community becomes more open, less proprietary and therefore more cost-effective. In fact, many complex algorithms are today available for free without the need to write complex mathematical equations.

Building capability in Big Data algorithms goes further than just hiring the right team of data analysts or data scientists; they can always decide to move to other organizations. To build enduring value, organizations will need to start building standardized analysis practices, create libraries of commonly used algorithms or even build proprietary algorithms that can provide a competitive advantage. The best example that shows that building capabilities in Big Data algorithms has significant (or maybe even exorbitant) monetary value is Google, whose famous and proprietary web searching algorithm is in fact a Big Data algorithm.

Big Data processes

The next and maybe most overlooked capability in the Framework is Big Data processes. By Big Data processes, we specifically mean the processes that organizations need to set to ensure consistency in their operations. Countries that are operating in multiple countries, for example, would need different processes in place to ensure that they are compliant with **data privacy** and **data security** regulations. Another common example is the processes that organizations need for data governance, or for data management.

Which processes an organization requires will be highly dependent on the nature of their business, geographical location and the amount of sensitive information they are processing. Heavily regulated industries, like banking and healthcare, typically have a more process-oriented approach because they are required to showcase compliance. These organizations will require more stringent processes than for example companies in the hospitality industry.

There are, however, several processes that apply to any organization that deals with Big Data. These processes include the steps that organizations need to take to ensure that data that is processed is accurate. Every enterprise organization will therefore need to set up several data management processes to safeguard the quality of their analysis. Data management is the practice of collecting and keeping enterprise data safe, secure and accessible.[6] And to accomplish this goal, it is necessary to set up measurable processes. Ensuring that the data in an enterprise remains accurate (so that it has predictive value) is by no means an easy task, especially given the volume, velocity, variety and veracity characteristics of Big Data.

A second major area of processes that are required for any enterprise organization are data governance processes. Whereas data management primarily concerns itself with the quality of data in the enterprise, data governance focuses on the regulatory and compliancy issues. Data governance refers to the exercise of authority and control over the management of data.[7] It determines who should be able to access data, and how this access can be provided in a controlled manner. For this reason, data governance is typically very heavily structured around processes and process management. And together with data management, they form the core of the processes that we will consider in the Enterprise Big Data Framework.

The focus on Big Data processes has increased significantly in the last few years, especially since Big Data brings up challenging ethical dilemmas with regards to the way organizations keep and use their data. Many governments around the world have started to sharpen their regulatory requirements and have imposed stricter regulations on the way companies can collect, store and utilize their data. A good example in this regard is the European Data Protection Regulation (better known as GDPR) which came into effect in 2018, and which imposed strict regulations about data protection and data privacy.[8] Through these regulations, companies are mandated to set up processes that safeguard data privacy, data security and to strictly control the transfer of personal data. Since GDPR is an enforced regulation (and non-compliance penalty fees can be in the millions of dollars), having suitable Big Data processes is no longer an optional exercise – it is mandatory.

Setting up the right Big Data processes is therefore a key imperative, and every organization aiming to professionalize their Big Data operation should start building capability in this area. For that reason, we will cover the area of Big Data processes to a very significant extent and provide in-depth guidance on maturing capabilities in this area.

Big Data functions

All the capabilities that we have discussed so far evolve around technology, processes and the required infrastructure to process Big Data. In the Big Data functions capability, we will consider the maybe most important asset to retrieve value from massive data sets – people. To set up a successful Big Data practice, organizations need a function that focuses on the continual improvement of Big Data best practices. The Big Data functions capability will therefore focus on the ways organizations can build knowledge, skills and organizational structures to support a culture of data-driven decision-making.

We noted earlier in the book that Big Data is about more than just technology. Moving towards a data-driven enterprise journey requires commitment and dedication, and will not happen without a few setbacks. For example, organizations can have the best predictive models in the world, but if senior management does not act upon the data they have been provided with, the whole analysis process is pointless. Moving towards a data-driven organization is therefore an exercise that is the equivalent of organizational change management. It is quite literally a digital transformation, which has become the popular term to denote the steps that organizations are taking in this journey. Big Data is in that sense no different. For any Big Data organization to be successful, it requires the hearts and minds of the people. This includes the people who are directly involved in a function that processes Big Data, but also decision-makers, the vendor ecosystem and other key stakeholders that can either accelerate or hinder the adoption of Big Data best practices.

The Big Data functions capability combines the organizational and human aspects that are required for success in Big Data. We will look at organizational aspects, such as the best way teams can be structured and the way the Big Data function can interact with other parts of the organization. How can, for example, a finance or marketing department leverage the power of Big Data without setting up individual teams in each department? How can knowledge effectively be shared across organizational silos, and how can knowledge and lessons learned be captured, so that the enterprise can improve its capability over time?

Additionally, we will also review Big Data functions from one lower level of abstraction, which is the individual perspective. What makes a good data engineer, data analyst or data scientist? What are the key skills required, and how do personal characteristics help in building Big Data analysis teams? These are key questions to answer and key capabilities to build in any Big Data organization. In the end, people are still at the heart of Big Data, and they are the reason a Big Data organization exists in the first place.

The Big Data functions capability – the people aspect of Big Data – requires more attention in most professional organizations. It is a capability that many organizations have not properly structured, and one that requires a dedicated place in the organization. In this book, we will therefore emphasize the importance of setting up and structuring the Big Data Centre of Excellence. A Big Data Centre of Excellence (BDCoE) will provide organizations with a centralized place to build human capabilities in a world of data. By setting up a Big Data Centre of Excellence, organizations can start developing use cases, embed processes and, maybe most importantly, provide an opportunity to learn from each other. As such, it can embed the human capability of Big Data as an enterprise function.

Artificial intelligence

The last critical capability of the Enterprise Big Data Framework is artificial intelligence (AI). As depicted in Figure 4.1, the AI capability surrounds the other five capabilities of the Framework. The reason for this design choice is that the knowledge domain of AI utilizes the same underlying strategy, architecture and processes that are necessary in Big Data. AI solutions in almost all cases need to have the ability to process massive quantities of data in real-time.

If you consider popular examples of AI, such as self-driving cars or AI chatbots, you can easily verify this property. Self-driving cars need to have the ability to make instant decisions based on a variety of input sensors, such as traffic lights, road signs, the weather and other external conditions. Based on these input conditions, a computer needs to combine this information with data from external sources, for example a database with traffic rules or the car's previous driving history. This computation will need to happen within spilt seconds, so that the self-driving car can make the optimal decision given the input data: increase or decrease speed, turn or hit the emergency brakes. If the AI solution does not have the ability to process large data sets within split seconds, it could have life-altering implications.

Self-driving cars are a great example to illustrate the significant overlap of the knowledge domains of Big Data and AI. Although the purpose of each domain is different (Big Data is focused on the storage and processing of massive data sets, whereas AI is focused on mimicking human decision-making), it is apparent that there is a significant overlap. AI solutions are using the same data, the same storage mechanism and (in most cases) the same algorithms that we utilize in the Big Data domain.

More importantly, from an enterprise perspective, the functional capabilities that are required to build AI solutions are building upon the capabilities required for Big Data. Fundamental processes, such as data privacy and data security, will not be different for AI solutions, since the underlying object (i.e. the data) will remain the same. As a result, we will therefore consider AI as an extension of the Big Data domain. Although this consideration is functional in nature (instead of scientific), the core purpose of the Enterprise Big Data Framework is to present an approach that is, first and foremost, practical to implement. It would therefore not be functional to set up a separate framework solely for the purpose of AI.

Building capability in the AI domain can therefore be considered the last step of the Framework. Whereas the first five domains of Big Data have grown to relative maturity in the last years, the AI capability is still under constant and rapid development. Investment in AI is ever increasing, and both professional corporations and governments are racing to fund and develop further use cases of these technologies.[9]

To bring the AI capability in line with the other capabilities in the Enterprise Big Data Framework (and to provide a practical and measurable way to increase this capability), we will therefore consider practical AI use cases as a measurement of capability. For most corporations that have only just begun their explorations in the domain of AI, this approach will be more than sufficient. Organizations that are involved in research and development of AI solutions, or who are leading the AI revolution, might need to expand these capabilities to a more scientific level.

One of the key reasons for including the AI capability in the Enterprise Big Data Framework is to highlight the strong overlap between the different domains. In addition, it is practical to realize that AI builds upon Big Data capabilities. An organization cannot just 'start' with AI, because any AI project (no matter how small) will require control of the underlying data. It will build upon the other capabilities of the Enterprise Big Data Framework.

4.3 Working with capability models

In the previous section, we introduced the Enterprise Big Data Framework as a capability model. The word capability quite literally means the 'extent of someone's or something's ability'.[10] In order to understand how to work with a capability model, we will therefore first explain the basic structure of a capability model, its core principles and the underlying philosophy that underpins the Enterprise Big Data Framework. A sound understanding of how capabilities work will provide any reader with a better understanding on how to use the capabilities in the remaining chapters for further improvement.

Organizational capabilities

Every organization is based on several capabilities. These capabilities combined provide the organization with a differentiating, often unique, place in the market. Based on their capabilities, organizations can charge for their products or services. Other organizations that are lacking these capabilities are willing to pay a fee to utilize the capabilities of other organizations.

The capabilities that organizations acquire over their existence are a combination of people, processes, intellectual property and technology. Collectively, they work together to coordinate the actions and behaviours of individuals and groups. An IT company that specializes in database systems, for example, will have specialist capabilities in the database domain, which will drive the innovations and decisions the company makes. Over time and with experience, a company will become better in utilizing their capabilities, and these capabilities become more efficient and effective. The capabilities that an organization builds up over time is therefore labelled an organizational capability, which can be defined as the following:

> An organizational capability refers to an organization's ability to perform a set of coordinated tasks, utilizing organizational resources, for the purposes of achieving a particular result.

The result, or ultimate goal, that we are aiming for with the Enterprise Big Data Framework is for organizations to enable data-driven decision-making or, as the subtitle of this book indicates, to win in the data economy. To win in the data economy, organizations will need to build and expand on the six critical capabilities of the Enterprise Big Data Framework, which were introduced in the previous section.

Organizational capabilities will bring focus and consistency to any organization. Organizations that have developed capabilities are able to perform activities in repeated and effective ways. For this reason, the Big Data domain is well suitable to a capability model. Building up knowledge, skills and efficiency in analysing data sets requires experience and time, and no organization will have an efficient Big Data organization right from the onset. Instead, by building Big Data capabilities progressively in a process of trial, feedback and learning, the organization will become better (i.e. more capable) over time. Because this process requires time, it also means that capabilities become embedded in the organization's operating procedures and culture. A focus on developing capabilities will therefore change the organization over time, enabling it to perform activities more effectively.

To grow capabilities, organizations require resources. These resources can be tangible, such as human capital, IT infrastructure or financial resources. But to build lasting capabilities, intangible resources are equally important. An organization's intangible resources include intellectual property, knowledge and, most importantly, culture. In the Framework, we will therefore discuss both tangible and intangible resources.

The Enterprise Big Data Framework has been structured in such a way that organizations can start building the capabilities they need to retrieve value from data to enhance their decision-making process. The six organizational capabilities that we will cover in the upcoming parts each cover a different aspect of Big Data. At the same time, they are functioning collectively to increase the knowledge, skills and systems required to find value in massive data sets. Organizations that have built these capabilities will be better positioned to utilize their data to drive future decisions, especially compared to organizations who will not have developed these capabilities. As a result, companies can differentiate themselves based on their capabilities.

Capability maturity

One of the primary benefits of using capability models is that they are measurable. With capability models, organizations can measure how well they are progressing towards a goal, and where further improvement efforts are required. In other words, they can set goals for the future, and subsequently start to measure how well they are progressing towards these goals.

In the previous section, we discussed 'the state of Big Data' in enterprises and noted that most organizations recognize the value of data-driven decision-making. Where most organizations are struggling is to define the path toward this goal. Because capabilities are measurable, they can provide the requested guidance on the path towards data-driven decision-making. The fact that capabilities are measurable makes the Framework easy to adopt and adapt in any organization.

A second key benefit of using a capability approach is that it recognizes the fact that every organization will be at a different point in their journey. Some organization might already be highly data-driven, whilst others might still be in the infancy stages. Each organization will have a unique starting point and unique context in which data will be used. Since different organization will be operating at different levels (i.e. maturity levels), they can each apply the Enterprise Big Data Framework in their own way. Similarly, to 'grow' capabilities, each organization will have their own approach. An approach that might work for one organization might not necessarily be successful in another organization. To recognize these differences, the Enterprise Big Data Framework should be adapted to different situations. The Framework is deliberately not structured as a one-size-fits-all, but aims to take into account the individual differences between organizations. Although the goal of the Enterprise Big Data Framework is to enable every organization to win in the data economy, the journey towards these destinations will be different. Using a capability model with corresponding maturity levels supports this differentiated approach.

Capability models and corresponding maturity levels have grown to great popularity in recent years, primarily because they provide a practical approach that companies can use in a repetitive manner.[11] In essence, the purpose of capability models is to assist an organization with several iterative steps from infancy stage to a more sophisticated stage, whereby an entity will have to go through some transitional stages.[12] For the capabilities that we are using in the Enterprise Big Data Framework, the purpose is similar in nature. Through the different maturity levels, we aim to showcase how any organization can move from limited application of data in day-to-day decision-making towards a data-driven enterprise.

For each of the capabilities that have been introduced at the beginning of this chapter, the Enterprise Big Data Framework defines five maturity levels. These five maturity levels support a systematic and incremental approach to capability improvement, without becoming overly complex or too detailed. A breakdown into five maturity levels is widely used in the IT domain and for this reason is therefore equally suitable for the Enterprise Big Data Framework.[13] The five maturity levels that we will be using throughout this book are depicted in Table 4.1.

The definition of the maturity levels will be used consistently over the six capabilities of the Enterprise Big Data Framework. By keeping a uniform and consistent approach to maturity, organizations can address gaps and opportunities for improvement in every capability. For example, in in the first capability (Big Data Strategy) a lack of documented Big Data strategy will clearly indicate that an organization is more probably operating at the "initial" level of maturity than the

Table 4.1   Maturity levels used in the Enterprise Big Data Framework

Level	Approaches Quality of practices or activities	Scope Breadth of coverage and focus	Outcomes Predictability of outcomes
1 – Initial	Approaches are inadequate and unstable	Scope is fragmented and incoherent	Repeatable outcomes are rare
2 – Managed	Approaches are managed, but inconsistent	Scope is limited to partial areas of business	Repeatable outcomes are achieved occasionally
3 – Defined	Approaches are standardized, inconsistencies addressed	Scope includes business function or department	Repeatable outcomes are often achieved
4 – Controlled	Approaches are systematically improved	Scope covers the organization end-to-end	Repeatable outcomes are often achieved
5 – Optimized	Approaches are considered leading	Scope extends the borders of the organization	Repeatable are almost always achieved

"defined" level. Addressing all the capabilities in a consistent way through maturity levels will therefore help to defined structured roadmaps and improvement plans.

4.4 Macro- and micro-capabilities

Now that we have introduced the concepts of organizational capabilities and maturity levels, it is time to present a secondary level of abstraction. The six capabilities of the Enterprise Big Data Framework are, on their own, too large to summarize, and we could easily fill six entire books on every domain. From this moment forward, we will therefore refer to the primary six capabilities of the Enterprise Big Data framework as **macro-capabilities**. The six capabilities of the Framework (strategy, architecture, algorithms, processes, functions and AI) will therefore be labelled the six macro-capabilities.

Each of these macro-capabilities will subsequently be subdivided into a few more specific (and therefore more measurable) capabilities, which we will label **micro-capabilities**, correspondingly. The actual measurement of capabilities will therefore happen at the level of micro-capabilities. The micro-capabilities will make the Framework more tangible, more practical and provide every organization with a consistent way to use the Framework. A breakdown of the macro- and micro-capabilities is depicted in Table 4.2.

Table 4.2   The 30 micro-capabilities of the Enterprise Big Data Framework

Macro Capability	Micro Capability	Description
Big Data Strategy	Strategy Formulation	Defines the vision, goals and objectives of the Big Data programme, and ensures that all relevant stakeholders are aligned on priorities and the Big Data programme's implementation and management.
	Innovation Management	Defines how Big Data can exploit new and pioneering ways in which organizations bring new products and services to market.
	Leadership and Governance	Defines the required leadership and governance structure through which an organization can successfully execute a Big Data strategy.

(continued)

Table 4.2   (Continued)

Macro Capability	Micro Capability	Description
	Communication	Defines the ability to communicate the motives and purpose of Big Data strategies, policies and processes, so that they are understood by internal and external stakeholders in the organization.
	Sustainability	Defines the ability of an organization to achieve their Big Data strategy in a sustainable way with minimal environmental impact, and positive social contributions.
	Programme Funding	Defines the ability to secure the availability of adequate and sustainable financing to support Big Data initiatives and their corresponding budgets.
Big Data Architecture	Big Data Architecture Management	Defines the ability to plan, design, manage and control the conceptualization of Big Data systems and processes and the relationships between them.
	Infrastructure Management	Defines the ability to manage all physical and virtual components of the IT infrastructure to support the introduction, maintenance and retirement of Big Data services.
	Data Platform Management	Defines the ability to control enterprise data in line with the enterprise data strategy so that data is safeguarded as a corporate asset.
	Master and Metadata Management	Defines the ability to establish infrastructure and processes for specifying and extending clear and organized information about the enterprise data assets under management.
	Information Security Management	Defines the ability to protect enterprise data and information from damage, theft or inappropriate use.
Big Data Algorithms	Software Engineering	Defines the ability to maintain a structured and reliable code base of algorithms, which can be easily maintained.
	Data Cleaning and Wrangling	Defines the ability to structurally deal with missing, incomplete, inconsistent, inaccurate, duplicate and dated enterprise data, in order to establish quality data that stakeholders trust.

(continued)

Table 4.2 (Continued)

Macro Capability	Micro Capability	Description
	Descriptive Data Analysis	Defines the ability to summarize internal and external enterprise data to support decision-making.
	Supervised Machine Learning	Defines the ability to use classification algorithms for predictive decision-making.
	Unsupervised Machine Learning	Defines the ability to use clustering algorithms and techniques to support predictive decision-making.
Big Data Processes	Data Governance Process	Defines the ability to establish a process to govern the availability, usability, integrity and security of enterprise data, based on internal data standards and policies.
	Data Management Process	Defines the ability to establish a process to collect, process, validate and store enterprise data in line with corporate quality criteria.
	Data Analysis Process	Defines the ability to set up a structural process for the day-to-day execution data analysis activities in the enterprise.
	Data Lifecycle Management Process	Defines the ability to set up a process to understand, map and control its enterprise data flows throughout the data lifecycle, from creation or acquisition to retirement.
	Data Vendor Management	Defines the ability to manage interactions between the Big Data function and suppliers of critical Big Data technology or data.
Big Data Functions	Knowledge Management	Defines the ability to create, share, use and manage internal knowledge about big data best practices in the organization.
	Service Catalogue	Defines the ability to define which Big Data and data science services they provide to internal and external customers, including offered service levels and costs.
	Workface and Talent Planning	Defines the ability to manage the Big Data workforce to ensure adequate availability of competent employees.

(continued)

Table 4.2 (Continued)

Macro Capability	Micro Capability	Description
	Education and Skills Development	Defines the ability to set up educational programmes to increase knowledge about Big Data.
	Data Literacy	Defines the ability to establish a culture of data-driven decision-making by data-literate employees.
Artificial Intelligence	Deep Learning	Defines the ability to use deep learning algorithms for cognitive decision-making.
	Reasoning	Defines the ability to develop systems and solutions that can mimic human decision-making.
	Knowledge Representation	Defines the ability to effectively store knowledge in the enterprise, so it can be used by information systems.
	Ethics	Defines the ability to develop, create and deploy AI solutions in a responsible and socially acceptable manner.

The 30 micro-capabilities listed in Table 4.2 provide a summary of the required capabilities that enterprise organizations can build to win in the data economy. Each of these capabilities is discussed in further detail in the following chapters.

4.5 The Enterprise Big Data Framework Capability Maturity Model

As organizations feel pressure to gain competitive advantage, retaining their market position, identifying ways to cut costs, improving quality, reducing time to market and recognizing the need to invent or reinvent new products and services becomes increasingly important. The capability maturity model, introduced in section 4.3, has been developed to assist organizations in this endeavour. In short, the Enterprise Big Data Framework Capability Maturity Model (EBDFCMM) allows an organization to have its methods and processes assessed according to Big Data best practice, and provides an opportunity to benchmark with other organizations.

In management theory, the term 'maturity' is defined as the state of being complete, perfect or ready.[14] As such, it provides organizations with a long-term objective to strive for, regardless of personnel changes, technology updates or management hierarchies. Maturity provides a long-term goal, which can be achieved in several steps or iterations.

Because of its iterative nature, organizations progress towards maturity in steps. Each step can be broken down into projects or activities, which makes progress towards maturity comprehensible. Most organizations start with an 'initial' state of maturity, which means they have little capability in a specific domain. Over time, they progress towards 'total' maturity, which means they are fully capable in the specific domain.

The EBDFCMM assists organization to progress from an initial state of maturity, with little or no capability in Big Data and analytics, towards total maturity. In this last stage, the organization uses information from data sources (both internal and external) for everyday decision-making. Consequently, the EBDFCMM guides organizations towards data-driven decision-making.

Conducting a maturity assessment

Big Data maturity can be defined as the evolution of an organization to integrate, manage and leverage all relevant internal and external data sources. As a result, the EBDFCMM helps to build an ecosystem that includes technologies, data management, analytics, governance and organizational components. Organizations might conduct a capability assessment for one of the following two reasons:

1 **To track overall progress toward data-driven decision-making.** The EBDFCMM functions as a measurement scale to track progress.

2 **To identify relevant initiatives to advance capability.** The EBDFCMM provides information to identify and prioritize projects and activities.

Both objectives help organizations to further their capabilities in Big Data. Whereas the first objective provides an independent snapshot of the current state of the organization (Where are we now?), the second objective provides input to advance the maturity towards a higher level (How do get there?). Both objectives reinforce each other.

The EBDFCMM helps to create structure around a Big Data programme and determines where to start. It is a simple yet effective tool for organizations to determine goals around the programme and communicate their visions for data-driven decision-making across the organization.

Additionally, the EBDFCMM provides a methodology to measure, monitor and direct the state of the Big Data programme and the efforts needed to move towards the next maturity level. The model measures and manages the speed of adoption, reporting both the progress and obstacles that organizations face in their journey towards data-driven decision-making.

The goal of the EBDFCMM is to provide a capability assessment approach that focuses on specific Big Data key areas in organizations, helping to guide development milestones and to avoid known pitfalls. Because of its strong focus on capabilities (i.e. the ability to succeed), in this book we want to provide a practical way of working with the Framework. For this reason, every section of the book will end with a questionnaire through which capability for a particular macro-capability can be identified.

The EBDF assessment questions

To objectively measure capability across organizations (to be used as the benchmark) a total of 180 questions have been developed. These consist of the 30 capabilities (outlined in Table 4.2), for which six questions have been developed.

An example of the questions for the 'data governance process' (part of Big Data processes) is illustrated in Figure 4.2.

Figure 4.2   Example of Big Data capability maturity questions

Big Data Processes - Data Management

* In our organization, we have specified metrics and performance indicators for the quality of our data.

Strongly Disagree   Strongly Agree
(1)   (2)   (3)   (4)   (5)

* We have a function (department or people) in place that actively monitors and manages our enterprise data.

Strongly Disagree   Strongly Agree
(1)   (2)   (3)   (4)   (5)

* We have practices (tools or processes) in place to validate the quality of our data and make data quality improvements.

Strongly Disagree   Strongly Agree
(1)   (2)   (3)   (4)   (5)

* We communicate and educate our staff on data management practices and procedures to ensure data quality in the organization.

Strongly Disagree   Strongly Agree
(1)   (2)   (3)   (4)   (5)

Submit

The Enterprise Big Data Framework Capability Maturity Assessment can be conducted in organizations through either external audit or individual self-assessment using the questions in this book. It is recommended that the latter should be approached as a team exercise involving people from different functional groups, to ultimately eliminate single-respondent bias.

Results and benchmarking

During the Enterprise Big Data Framework Capability Maturity Assessment, every area of the Enterprise Big Data Framework is assessed to determine the level of capability. The outcome of the Enterprise Big Data Framework Capability Assessment is depicted in Figure 4.2 and provides valuable information on the potential improvement areas for the enterprise.

Because of the objective nature of the Enterprise Big Data Framework Capability Maturity Assessment and the corresponding questionnaires, the results provide input information for a global benchmark report. Because a comparative model was selected (see earlier in this section), the maturity results can be used by organizations to determine how they compare with industry or regional peers. Benchmarking can

Figure 4.3   Results of the Enterprise Big Data Capability Maturity Assessment

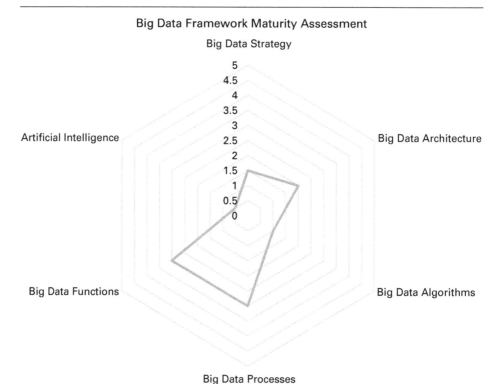

compare an actual situation with industry-specific best practice to support management decisions for continual improvement.

With the Enterprise Big Data Framework and the Maturity Assessment, this book provides both the theory (the capabilities) and the practical steps (assessment questions) to win in the data economy.

Notes

1   J W Middelburg (2016) *Service Automation Framework*. Van Haren Publishing
2   M J Mazzei and D Noble. Big data dreams: A framework for corporate strategy, *Business Horizons*, 2017. 60 (3), 405–14
3   D.N.B.D.I. Framework (2015) DRAFT NIST Big Data Interoperability Framework, vol 1, Definitions. *NIST Special Publication*, 1500, 1
4   T H Davenport and D J Patil. Data scientist. *Harvard Business Review*, 2012 90 (5), 70–76
5   J Hao and T K Ho. Machine learning made easy: a review of scikit-learn package in python programming language, *Journal of Educational and Behavioral Statistics*, 2019 44 (3), 348–61
6   T P Raptis, A Passarella and M Conti. Data management in industry 4.0: State of the art and open challenges. *IEEE Access*, 2019 7, 97052–93
7   R Abraham, J Schneider and J Vom Brocke. Data governance: A conceptual framework, structured review, and research agenda, *International Journal of Information Management*, 2019 49, 424–38
8   P Voigt and A Von dem Bussche. The EU general data protection regulation (GDPR). *A Practical Guide*, 1st edn, 2017 10, 3152676. Cham: Springer International Publishing
9   D Gunning and D Aha. DARPA's explainable artificial intelligence (XAI) program, *AI Magazine*, 2019 40 (2), 44–58
10   M C Paulk, B Curtis, M B Chrissis and C V Weber. Capability maturity model, version 1.1, *IEEE software*, 1993 10 (4), 18–27
11   H T Braun (2015) *Evaluation of Big Data maturity models–a benchmarking study to support Big Data maturity assessment in organizations*, master's thesis
12   S M Drus and N H Hassan. Big data maturity model–a preliminary evaluation, *ICOCI Kuala Lumpur. University Utara Malaysia*, 2017 117, 613–20
13   C P Team (2006) CMMI for Development, version 1.2
14   M Comuzzi and A Patel. How organisations leverage big data: A maturity model, *Industrial Management & Data Systems*, 2016 116 (8), 1468–92

PART THREE
Defining a Big Data Strategy

Big Data Strategy   05

5.1 Introduction to Big Data strategy

At the centre of the Enterprise Big Data Framework, the capability of a Big Data strategy is depicted. The reason it is situated in the middle is because it is – or should be – the starting point for any organization. As we discussed in the previous chapters, the amount of data in the world is overwhelming, and organizations and individuals could potentially spend the rest of their lifetimes analysing interesting and complex data sets.

The pivotal question that every organization needs to answer, before investing any money into Big Data technology and solutions, is their definition of value. What constitutes value in an organization, and how can that value be expressed in return on investment? For example, if a company is able to have a 2 per cent better marketing conversion than a competitor, what is that worth? Or what is the financial value of a 5 per cent more accurate inventory prediction? Although these financial estimations seem trivial, they form the crux to success in Big Data. Organizations that can determine the financial value of enhanced decision-making are able to select the right optimization projects and can prioritize different analysis projects over others. Organizations that don't have this capability will come to recognize that their investments in Big Data teams and Big Data solutions are frequently not paying off.

In this section, we will therefore start at the very beginning and consider the essence of strategy: the ability to determine an organization's direction by setting the right priorities. A very famous quote from Lewis Carroll's famous children's book *Alice in Wonderland* exemplifies the essence of strategy[1]:

> If you don't know where you are going, any road will take you there.

Although the book was written in 1865, this quote is as true today as ever before. Because the data sets in the world have become so incomprehensibly large, it is necessary to focus – on the data that matters and, more importantly, on the way that data brings value to an organization. Since this book is primarily intended for corporate organizations, we will choose to define value in a utilitarian way, by considering the return on investment in financial terms. Although most examples in this section will be in financial terms, it is equally possible to quantity 'non-financial' returns, such as increased life expectancy, a healthier environment or increased knowledge.

By the end of this section, you should have a clear understanding about the critical components that make up a Big Data strategy. Additionally, you will understand how to define a Big Data strategy for your organization, and which steps you should take to formulate a Big Data roadmap with actionable projects.

5.2 Purpose and structure of a Big Data strategy

Participants of the famous World Economic Forum in Davos, Switzerland already declared during the annual meetup of 2012 that Big Data has become a strategic economic resource, similar in significance and liquidity to currency and gold.[2] Most organizations have long-term plans and strategies in place to deal with their economic plans. Enterprises and companies go through yearly budgeting cycles, in which the planning for the subsequent year, and their strategic choices, are defined and explained. If we consider Big Data as an economic resource, similar in nature to other assets, defining a Big Data strategy is a logical step. A Big Data strategy can help any organization to define their strategic choices with regards to their data.

The Big Data strategy macro-capability, introduced in Chapter 4, is a logical starting point for any organization to ensure that the different initiatives in an organization are aligned. It can be considered the glue that holds the other capabilities together. Choices regarding technology and tool selection, or the way that analytics or Big Data departments should be structured, or the way professional training programmes should be set up, should all cascade down from the organization's Big Data strategy.

The Big Data strategy capability

The Big Data strategy capability is defined as an organization's ability to clarify how it uses internal and external data to obtain a competitive advantage and realize a positive return on investment.

The Big Data strategy capability provides focus and guidance for everyone in the organization. It helps to determine where organizations should focus their efforts and investments, and what the medium and long-term objectives are through which an organization can outperform competitors.

Despite the great growth and popularity of analytics and Big Data solutions over the last decade, and the realization that data contains value that can provide a way to obtain a competitive advantage, multiple research reports show most fail dramatically, with reported failure rates as high as 85 per cent.[3] In addition, other studies

Figure 5.1   Micro-capabilities of Big Data strategy

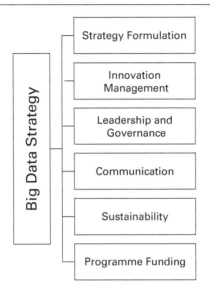

show that the vast majority of organizations have not defined measurable success criteria or key performance indicators (KPIs) to measure whether their Big Data programmes are successful.[4] They have, in other words, not defined how success in Big Data should be measured and lack a Big Data strategy.

To interpret these high failure rates in the correct way, and to provide guidance to others on how to avoid this in future (i.e. building a capability), it is important to note that an effective Big Data strategy is more than just a written document. Although a formulated Big Data strategy document is a great first (and necessary) step towards effectiveness, it is also important that the formulated Big Data strategy is meaningful, executable and innovative.

Because an effective Big Data strategy is more than just a document, the Big Data strategy capability has been subdivided into several **micro-capabilities**, as depicted in Figure 5.1. Not surprisingly, strategy formulation is an important micro-capability. However, for a robust and competitive strategy, organizations also need to consider innovation management, leadership and governance, sustainability and communication. Only if these micro-capabilities are effectively combined can an organization claim that it has a future-proof Big Data strategy.

5.3 Barriers to an effective Big Data strategy

In the previous segment, we saw that many organizations are struggling with the implementation and execution of a Big Data strategy. As a result, many Big Data

Figure 5.2   Barriers to a successful Big Data strategy

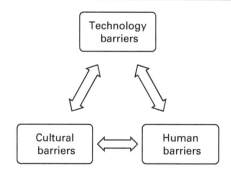

initiatives fail, or do not provide the value that was anticipated beforehand. So, before it is possible to introduce capabilities that help to overcome this problem, it is advisable to take a step back and consider the main reasons why Big Data strategies have failed. What is the reason that large and successful companies have difficulties with making Big Data (and hence data-driven decision-making) a successful enterprise function? And what are the common denominators that can be used in the micro-capabilities?

Over the years, many organizations have tried to understand common inhibitors and barriers to Big Data success. A common classification is to subdivide these barriers into technological barriers, human barriers and cultural barriers, as depicted in Figure 5.2.[5] Whether this classification is fully complete or whether there are some additional inhibitors is, from a strategy perspective, not a very interesting discussion. The main point is to learn from these barriers to determine which capabilities can help organizations overcome failure in their Big Data strategy. By considering barriers to success closely, we can identify critical capabilities that are necessary to overcome any inhibitions.

The difficulty with each of these barriers is that they cannot be placed in isolation. For example, hosting training programmes to address a lack of skills (a human barrier) will elevate skill levels for a certain group, but is by no means a guarantee that a Big Data programme will subsequently be successful. In a similar way, a successful Big Data strategy cannot be seen in isolation. It is the result of several different components (which we labelled micro-capabilities) which will need to work together in a coherent way.

Technological barriers

The technical capacity to analyse hundreds of thousands or even millions of records or data points within an acceptable time frame is by no means an easy task. Organizations will require distinct and specialized IT infrastructure for the analysis of massive data sets. Building an IT infrastructure that can support this will require significant investments in software and hardware solutions that are necessary to support this. Despite all the technological advancements that have been made, and the easy accessibility to cloud computing (discussed in Chapter 2 section 2.2), setting up a Big Data environment is still a challenging technological task.[6]

Additional technological complexities, and therefore barriers to a successful Big Data strategy, are the result of the ever-increasing velocity and variety of characteristics of Big Data. Since data sets are growing so rapidly, keeping an infrastructure in place that can support this is a challenge. A Big Data environment that might have been suitable a few years ago might pose technical challenges or security risks today. Keeping up with the rapid developments, innovations and product updates requires full-time attention.

Although most of these technological barriers can be addressed by setting up an appropriate IT architecture (the capability that we will discuss in Part 4 of this book), it all starts with strategy. A Big Data strategy should outline technological design choices and priorities, which will be addressed in the micro-capability of **strategy formulation**. Additionally, a Big Data strategy should be future proof, considering development in the industry such as ethnological advancements and expected data growth. These aspects are bundled together in the **innovation management** micro-capability.

Human barriers

A second and commonly understood barrier to any Big Data strategy are human factors. Even if you have defined the most innovative and exciting Big Data strategy in the world, it will be worthless if people deviate from its objectives. There are many examples across the world where human behaviour is contrary to the facts that are shown by data. The classic example is smoking, where even though data sets make a compelling case to abstain from smoking, many people don't act based on that data.

It can even be stated that mistrust in scientific facts and data is growing, and more people are taking deliberate choices to act contrary to the facts that data provide.[7] A great example comes from the classic 1956 book *When Prophecy Fails*, where psychologist Leon Festinger and his co-authors described what happened to a UFO cult when the mother ship failed to arrive at the appointed time[8]:

> Instead of admitting error, members of the group sought frantically to convince the world of their beliefs and they made a series of desperate attempts to erase their rankling dissonance by making prediction after prediction in the hope that one would come true.

Festinger called this **cognitive dissonance**, which is arguably one of the larger problems that the world is facing today. Cognitive dissonance is important in the context of analytics and Big Data. If a Big Data strategy is aimed at data-driven decision-making, but people don't make decisions in line with this strategy, it will not have any effect. To address cognitive dissonance, it is important that senior leaders in the organization promote data-driven decision-making, and that they lead by example. Additionally, it is important that there are processes and systems in place to safeguard the data analysis process, so that the outcome of data analysis can be trusted. To address this barrier the **leadership and governance** micro-capability will look at best practices that can be executed by the leadership of an organization.

A second important barrier to the successful execution of a Big Data strategy is a lack of skills. A lack of technical and analytical skills in organizations is consistently identified as one of the major reasons why progress with Big Data solutions has been delayed, or why strategies have failed.[9] To take it further, some CIOs have even stated that Big Data skills shortages have hindered their organization's ability to keep pace with innovation and change.[10]

Addressing the skills gap is therefore not something that should only be addressed once a Big Data organization is up and running. Rather, it should be addressed as an integral part of the Big Data strategy itself. Without adequate knowledge and skills, it becomes impossible to execute the strategy. Although it sounds straightforward that skills are required, in practice this is one of the major barriers to successful implementation. In the Enterprise Big Data Framework, we have therefore included the **continuous learning** micro-capability as a critical part of a Big Data strategy – one that should be an integral part of any organization's approach to Big Data.

Cultural barriers

The last major barrier for implementing a Big Data strategy has to do with organizational culture. By organizational culture we mean the set of assumptions and beliefs that are prevalent in a particular organization. In many organizations, barriers are not just formed by technology or individuals (as discussed in the previous paragraphs) but can also be the result of the way organizations are fundamentally structured. For example, some organizations lack the overall understanding of how Big Data can improve their business operations and consequently see little value in pursuing Big Data initiatives.[11] Cultural barriers are ultimately formed by the group of individuals that make up the organization, which is why there is a strong relationship with the human barriers.

Out of all the barriers discussed, cultural barriers might be the most difficult to overcome. An organizational culture establishes over time, and it takes time and significant effort to change culture. For Big Data strategies to be executed, it is important that there is enough support in the organization. Why is data-driven decision-making necessary, and what are the advantages for the organization and its employees? The answers to these questions need to be continuously reinforced. The **communication** micro-capability is therefore an essential component for Big Data success. Enterprises need to think how they will continuously explain and communicate the necessity of Big Data initiatives.

Besides the need to communicate what the Big Data strategy is, it is equally important to explain why this strategy has been chosen. In modern organizations, people want to relate to the purpose of what a company is doing, and in which way it will bring benefits to the organization or society at large. The most successful Big Data strategies (examples of which are discussed in the next section) have one thing in common: they have a clear purpose and clearly explain why this the strategy is important. Successful Big Data strategies are, in other words, sustainable and have a long-term orientation. The opposite is also true – a Big Data strategy that is not sustainable will attract very few people and will not create the energy and motivation necessary to execute the strategy successfully. The **sustainability** micro-capability will therefore consider the larger purpose of Big Data, and the way in which organizations can leverage this strategy for long-term success. In modern enterprises, strategy is only successful if the organization can capture employees' interest and get the organization involved.[12] The sustainability micro-capability defines the bigger picture, or purpose, that an organization needs to successfully execute this strategy.

By looking at the barriers to success in a Big Data strategy, we can learn the key components that are required to overcome them. These barriers, which are based on the collective experience from companies all over the world, provide us key insights into where organizations are, or have been, lacking capability. Understanding these barriers gives us the opportunity to structurally address the issues, and not make the same mistake. By subdividing the larger concept of 'Big Data strategy' into six micro-capabilities, organizations can focus on defining the right priorities. In chapters 6 to 12, we will consider these micro-capabilities in further detail, and provide guidance and best practices on how these capabilities can be built or enhanced.

5.4 Examples of effective Big Data strategies

Now that we have considered some of the barriers that inhibit the successful implementation of Big Data strategies, it is time to take the opposite approach. Over the last decade, there have been many organizations that were successful in the definition, execution and implementation of their Big Data strategies. This success has been made visible through rapid growth, exploding stock market value and generally a positive reputation. In many cases, it is a combination of all three.

In this section, we will consider some examples of companies and organizations that were able to successfully execute their Big Data strategies. By looking at these case studies, we can identify common characteristics that support the Big Data strategy micro-capabilities.

DBS Bank: intelligent banking

DBS is one of the premier and largest banks in Singapore, and has a strong Big Data strategy in place, focused on leveraging Big Data capabilities to increase customer service, and intelligent banking capabilities. DBS Bank was the first to add predictive technology to its mobile applications, which proactively offers suggestions to customers on how to manage their money more effectively or cut losses on investments.

As part of their strategy, DBS Bank has a company-wide training and upskilling programme in place, to ensure that its implementations are effective and long-lasting. To accomplish this goal, DBS Bank trained more than 16,000 of its employees with Big Data and data analytics skills within a period of 18 months.[13]

The case study from DBS Bank showcases several important capabilities that the organization concentrated on. Their strategy is focused on intelligent banking (innovation management) to provide better service and intelligent banking capabilities (sustainability). More importantly, the strategy was executed as part of a larger plan where top management (leadership) set up an enterprise-wide training programme (continuous learning) for more than 16,000 employees.

5.5 Big Data strategy: a leadership responsibility

The implementation of a business strategy is a complicated process, and a Big Data strategy is no exception to this rule. It can even be stated that the execution of a Big Data strategy is more complicated, given the technical complexities inherent in Big Data. The formulation (i.e. the documentation) of a Big Data strategy alone is not enough for successful implementation. The additional capabilities that have been outlined in the previous segment are required.

When it comes to the implementation of Big Data strategies, leadership and decision-making play a critical role. Because of the technological, human and cultural barriers (as discussed in section 5.3), the leadership of an organization is ultimately responsible for the success or failure of the Big Data strategy. Individual leaders are required to create and sustain the vision of the organization, and to subsequently build the required capabilities.

Whereas the six micro-capabilities introduced in this chapter will provide organizations with best practice guidance and key areas of focus, in the end it comes down to the individuals that define, promote and execute a Big Data strategy. Leaders in this domain will need to have an adequate understanding of the basic concept of Big Data, stay committed to their Big Data initiatives and promote and communicate the goals of Big Data initiatives.[14] With the tools that are outlined in this book, we hope that this responsibility becomes (slightly) easier.

Notes

1   L Carroll (1889) *The Nursery 'Alice': Containing Twenty Coloured Enlargements from Tenniel's Illustrations to "Alice's Adventures in Wonderland" with Text Adapted to Nursery Readers*. Bodley Head

2   J E Johnson. Big data + big analytics = big opportunity: big data is dominating the strategy discussion for many financial executives. As these market dynamics continue to evolve, expectations will continue to shift about what should be disclosed, when and to whom, *Financial Executive*, 2012 28 (6), 50–54

3   M Asay. 85% of big data projects fail, but your developers can help yours succeed, TechRepublic, 2017 11, 1, www.techrepublic.com/article/85-of-big-data-projects-fail-but-your-developers-can-help-yours-succeed/ (archived at https://perma.cc/PNM9-C43B)

4   H Baldwin (2015) When big data projects go wrong. *Forbes*

5   A Alharthi, V Krotov and M Bowman, M. Addressing barriers to big data, *Business Horizons*, 2017 60 (3), 285–92

6   O Trelles, P Prins, M Snir and R C Jansen. Big data, but are we ready?, *Nature Reviews Genetics*, 2011 12 (3), 224–24

7   M Shermer. How to convince someone when facts fail, *Scientific American*, 2017 1

8   L Festinger, H W Riecken and S Schachter. When prophecy fails, *Social Psychology in Life*, 1973, 257–68

9   S Bonesso, E Bruni and F Gerli (2020) How big data creates new job opportunities: Skill profiles of emerging professional roles. In *Behavioral Competencies of Digital Professionals*, Cham: Palgrave Pivot, 21–39

10 C Pompa and T Burke (2017) Data science and analytics skills shortage: equipping the APEC workforce with the competencies demanded by employers. APEC Human Resource Development Working Group

11 S LaValle, E Lesser, R Shockley, M S Hopkins and N Kruschwitz. Big data, analytics and the path from insights to value, *MIT Sloan Management Review*, 2011 52 (2), 21–32

12 C A Bartlett and S Ghoshal. Changing the role of top management: Beyond strategy to purpose, *Harvard Business Review*, 1994 72 (6), 79–88

13 Dbs.com (2021) DBS equips employees with skills to become everyday 'Data Heroes', www.dbs.com/newsroom/DBS_equips_employees_with_skills_to_become_everyday_Data_Heroes (archived at https://perma.cc/R43D-CS8X)

14 P Tabesh, E Mousavidin and S Hasani. Implementing big data strategies: A managerial perspective, *Business Horizons*, 2019 62 (3), 347–58

Strategy Formulation

06

6.1 Introduction to strategy formulation

The first micro-capability that we will discuss in detail is the strategy formulation capability. In very simple words, the strategy formulation capability represents an organization's ability to define a comprehensive Big Data strategy, and to put this on paper (or other shareable format) in a structured and explainable way.

Libraries of books have been written on the way corporate strategies need to be defined, since it justifies – in essence – the decision-making process of companies. In this book, we will not try to reinvent the wheel when it comes to strategy formulation. Rather, we aim to provide a comprehensive and practical approach to the steps with which organizations can build the strategy formulation capability. To accomplish this goal, we will draw upon existing management theories and research, but will apply it specifically to the Big Data domain.

Strategy formulation is an interesting and fascinating topic, which has been the focus of management consulting companies for decades. Large strategy consulting companies have, almost without exception, set up departments, divisions or entire daughter companies that now focus on the development or formulation of Big Data strategies. In fact, the top strategy consulting firms, McKinsey, BCG and Bain, all have active services for the formulation of Big Data strategies.[1] All consulting firms use different techniques and approaches, which is why it is difficult to pinpoint one approach as the 'best practice' when it comes to strategy formulation. When it comes to Big Data strategy formulation, there are multiple roads that lead to Rome.

In this chapter, we will focus mostly on the process of strategy formulation. What are the steps that organizations need to go through when defining a Big Data strategy? What are the key inputs that need to be taken into consideration? And what are the main deliverables that come out of this process? As you will soon see, finding an answer to these questions requires significant time and effort.

To start with the end in mind, note that in the last chapter of this part (Chapter 12) you will find a practical Big Data Strategy Maturity Assessment, with which you can measure your own organization's capability in strategy formulation. This maturity assessment can provide guidance on where your organization is today and will help you to formulate a roadmap to further improvement.

6.2 Purpose and maturity levels of strategy formulation

Purpose

Strategy formulation is a crucial capability for a successful Big Data strategy and programme. This micro-capability clarifies the purpose and goals of using Big Data technologies to optimize value generation for individuals and organizations.

The strategy formulation capability defines the ability of an organization to define and formulate a long-term vision and to translate this into an actionable Big Data strategy for the rest of the organization. Typical activities in strategy formulation include:

- Developing a long-term vision of how Big Data can provide value to the enterprise
- Alignment of Big Data strategy with the overall corporate vision and objectives
- Identification of risk and opportunities that Big Data technology can bring
- Involving crucial stakeholders in the Big Data strategic planning
- Evaluation and adjustment of the strategy and targets depending on changing circumstances
- Development of long-term Big Data roadmaps and use cases

The strategy formulation capability is frequently the way in which an organization is able to translate vision and ideas into products that can be shared and executed by others in the organization.

Strategy formulation maturity levels

In section 4.3, we explained the reason why the Enterprise Big Data Framework has been structured as a capability model. One of the primary benefits of using a capability model is that it is measurable, provides organizations with the opportunity to identify how well they master this capability, and identifies what other steps could be

Table 6.1   Purpose of strategy formulation

Capability	Purpose
Strategy formulation	Defines the vision, goals and objectives for the Big Data programme, and ensures that all relevant stakeholders are aligned on priorities and the Big Data programme's implementation and management.

Table 6.2 Maturity levels for strategy formulation

Maturity Level	Description
Level 1 – Initial	Any Big Data strategic planning that exists or resources allocated to it are informal, and opportunities and challenges are identified only in an ad hoc or informal way.
Level 2 – Managed	Big Data objectives, priorities and scope are defined and approved and are aligned with business objectives.
Level 3 – Defined	Big Data strategy representing an organization-wide scope is established, approved, promulgated and maintained.
Level 4 – Controlled	Statistical and other quantitative techniques are used to evaluate the effectiveness of strategic Big Data objectives in achieving business objectives, and modifications are made based on metrics.
Level 5 – Optimized	The organization researches and adopts selected industry best practices for Big Data strategy and helps with contributions to the Big Data industry.

taken to improve the capability. Table 6.2 indicates the five different levels that can be used to determine maturity in strategy formulation.

The five levels outlined above provide guidance on how strategy formulation capabilities can be addressed. In the next few sections, we will review in more practical details how these capabilities can be developed and improved.

6.3 Building strategy formulation capabilities

Strategy formulation is a broad domain of research that far extends the boundaries of IT and Big Data. The purpose of defining a strategy is to obtain a competitive advantage, and for the formulation of a Big Data strategy, the objective is no different. With a properly formulated Big Data strategy, organizations can outperform their competitors by analysing data in a faster, better or more insightful way. The essence of strategy formulation is well defined by the famous economist Michael Porter, who defined strategy in the following way[2]:

For companies, strategy can be defined as the search for a favorable and sustainable competitive position against the forces that determine competition in industry.

Defining a Big Data strategy is no different. Having a Big Data strategy provides organizations with a way to obtain a more favourable and sustainable position against competitors, by utilizing the data that an organization has access to. As we have seen in Chapter 1, this data can be internal in the organization or it can be externally available.

Formulating a strategy provides direction for an organization, and typically helps in defining future steps that an organization can take. These future steps are expressed in a roadmap that will help leaders with decision-making in a competitive landscape. A properly defined strategy will lead to actions, which will ultimately lead to a competitive advantage.[3]

To build capability in strategy formulation in Big Data, we will follow the same practical approach that ultimately leads to tangible action. Having words on paper does not guarantee any success. The process of formulating a Big Data strategy is therefore a clear capability: some organizations can be considered mature in strategy formulation, where other are still in their early stages. To systematically formulate a Big Data strategy, and hence build capability in this domain, organizations can follow the five-step approach as outlined in Figure 6.1.

The approach depicted in Figure 6.1 is cyclical on purpose and helps organizations to move towards data-driven decision-making in a structured and repetitive manner. It aligns the overall corporate objectives (i.e. the business objectives) of the organization with the practical and real-world projects (which we will refer to as 'use case') undertaken in analytics and Big Data departments.

Figure 6.1 Building strategy formulation capabilities

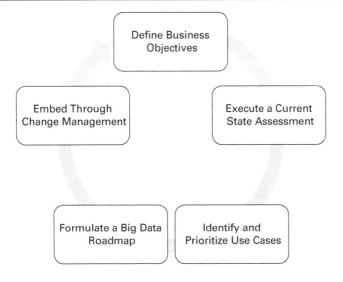

Define business objectives

The first, and maybe most important, step in defining a Big Data strategy is the realization that a Big Data strategy cannot be seen as independent of the overall corporate strategy and objectives of the enterprise. To put it even more strongly, many organizations will see that their Big Data strategy will, ultimately, become their corporate strategy.

The first step is therefore to review the overall business objectives of the organization. What makes an organization successful? Which products or services are unique? And why are customers purchasing these products and services, instead of buying from a competitor? Only if these questions can be answered will it become possible to determine where Big Data projects and use cases can improve the overall performance. Using insights and data-driven decision-making will be especially useful if it can augment the strength of an organization.

A great example of how a Big Data strategy can enhance the business objectives of an organization is observable at McDonald's. The enterprise, which is already famous for its speed and efficiency, has a Big Data strategy that analyses customer behaviour through its self-service kiosks (where you can place your food order). By analysing the data from millions of orders ever single week, McDonald's can predict (with a scary amount of certainty) what your final order will look like. With this information, they can already start preparing the meal in the kitchen, while you have not even paid yet. As a result, they are increasing their capabilities to deliver a meal speedily and efficiently, further cementing their position as leader in the fast-food market.

A critical success factor in defining business objectives is the involvement of key stakeholders, and senior leadership. Since a Big Data strategy will have a significant impact on the overall direction of the organization, it is of paramount importance to have leadership involved right from the start.

Particularly as the Big Data strategy should align to the corporate objectives of the enterprise, senior leaders should help to identify what those overall corporate objectives are. A Big Data strategy that needs to support growth in specific target markets (which you currently see in e-commerce) will differ greatly from a Big Data strategy that needs to increase efficiency and decrease operating costs (for example in the aviation and transport sectors). A fundamental understanding of the enterprise corporate objectives is therefore a crucial input.

Execute a current state assessment

Once an organization has a clear understanding of their business objectives, the question of current capability comes to mind. Strategic plans need to be placed into the context of what is possible. Overly ambitious goals, or too aggressive timelines, can be demotivating. Many organizations start out with ambitious plans and visions of how Big Data, machine learning and artificial intelligence will change their complete service offering. Yet, at the same time, these organizations don't have any skills or capabilities in-house to realize this vision. The funny paradox of Big Data is that you need to start small in order to be successful.

A current state assessment will review the existing knowledge, skills and technology capabilities in the organization, and serves as a benchmark for further improvement planning. The current state assessment will give insights into where the company is today, so that future plans can be set up and adjusted accordingly. To a large extent, it will provide a measure of the realistic goals an organization can achieve, and how feasible the Big Data strategy is in practice.

Many companies struggle most with this part of strategy formulation. Whereas it is relatively simple to formulate ambitions and outline a vision for the future, it is much more difficult to honestly review your own organization's knowledge and capability. Yet, it is a critical aspect of formulating a Big Data strategy. If the gap between current state and desired vision is too large, any Big Data strategy (no matter how professionally formulated) is doomed to fail.

A current state assessment is typically conducted through a series of interviews and structured assessments and questionnaires. The involvement of the data and analytics teams is crucial to obtain an adequate overview of the current state. In Chapter 12 of this book you can find assessment questions that can help to define the current state.

Identify and prioritize use cases

An organization that has its business objectives defined (step 1) and that is aware of its current capabilities (step 2) can move forward with identifying and prioritizing **Big Data use cases**. In essence, a Big Data use case is a feasible Big Data project that identifies how Big Data can help to expedite or realize a business objective, given the current constraints of the organization. Use cases make the strategy practical and tangible, because these can be converted into real-world projects that can be executed by the organization.[4] Some popular Big Data use cases are outlined in Table 6.3.

The main purpose of identifying use cases is that they provide an executable part of a Big Data Strategy. A use case can be analysed, planned and budgeted for. More importantly, there are many successful use cases already in existence, many of which provide a positive return on investment. These proven examples generally provide a motivation for companies to include them in their Big Data strategy as well.

Defining suitable Big Data use cases is by no means an easy task. It should, however, be an integral part of strategy formulation. Without the use cases in place, it is simply not possible to make a Big Data strategy actionable. Rather, it will remain a vision document.

Table 6.3 Big Data use cases

Industry: Financial Services

Fraud Detection	When it comes to security, it's not just a few rogue hackers. The financial services industry is up against entire expert teams, while security landscapes and compliance requirements are constantly evolving. Using Big Data, companies can identify patterns that indicate fraud and aggregate large volumes of information to streamline regulatory reporting.
Service Innovation	Big Data offers valuable insights that help organizations innovate. Big Data analytics makes the interdependencies between humans, institutions, entities and processes more apparent. With better understanding of market trends and customer needs, organizations can improve decision-making about new products and services.
Anti-Money Laundering	Financial services firms are under more pressure than ever before from governments passing anti-money laundering laws. These laws require that banks show proof of proper due diligence and submit suspicious activity reports. In this extraordinarily complicated arena, Big Data analytics can help companies identify potential fraud patterns.
Regulatory Compliance	Financial services companies must be in compliance with a wide variety of requirements concerning risk, conduct and transparency. At the same time, banks must comply with the Dodd-Frank Act, Basel III and other regulations that require detailed reporting.

Industry: Manufacturing

Predictive Maintenance	Big Data can help predict equipment failure. Potential issues can be discovered by analysing both structured data (equipment year, make and model) and multi-structured data (log entries, sensor data, error messages, engine temperature and other factors). With this data, manufacturers can maximize parts and equipment uptime and deploy maintenance more cost effectively.
Operational Efficiency	Operational efficiency is one of the areas in which Big Data can have the most impact on profitability. With Big Data, you can analyse and assess production processes, proactively respond to customer feedback and anticipate future demands.
Production Optimization	Optimizing production lines can decrease costs and increase revenue. Big Data can help manufacturers understand the flow of items through their production lines and see which areas can benefit. Data analysis will reveal which steps lead to increased production time and which areas are causing delays.

Industry: Telecommunication

Network Optimization	Optimal network performance is essential for a telecom's success. Network usage analytics can help companies identify areas with excess capacity and reroute bandwidth as needed. Big Data analytics can help them plan for infrastructure investments and design new services that meet customer demands. With new insights, telecoms are able to maintain customer loyalty and avoid losing revenue to competitors.
Customer Churn	By analysing the data telecoms already have about service quality, convenience and other factors, they can predict overall customer satisfaction. And they can set up alerts when customers are at risk of churning – and take action with retention campaigns and proactive offers.
Product Innovation	Big Data provides valuable insights to help companies design new products and features. An improved understanding of customer behaviour enables companies to tailor services to different customer segments for future offerings.

Industry: Retail

Product Development	Big Data can help you anticipate customer demand. By classifying key attributes of past and current products and then modelling the relationship between those attributes and the commercial success of the offerings, you can build predictive models for new products and services. Dig deeper by using the data and analytics from focus groups, social media, test markets and early store rollouts to plan, produce and launch new products.
Customer Experience	Big Data provides retailers with a clearer view of the customer experience that they can use to fine-tune their operations. By gathering data from social media, web visits, call logs and other company interactions, and other data sources, companies can improve customer interactions and maximize the value delivered. Big Data analytics can be used to deliver personalized offers, reduce customer churn and proactively handle issues.
Customer Lifetime Value	Big Data provides you with insights on customer behaviour and spending patterns, so you can identify your best customers. Once you know who they are, marketing can target them with special offers. Sales teams can devote more time to them. Customer service can work more proactively if it appears they may leave.
Shopping Experience	Big Data can be used to improve the in-store experience. Many retailers are starting to analyse data from mobile apps, in-store purchases and geolocations to optimize merchandizing and encourage customers to complete purchases.

(continued)

Table 6.3 (Continued)

Dynamic Pricing	Retailers need to know the true profitability of their customers, how markets can be segmented and the potential of any future opportunities. End-to-end profit and margin analysis can help with identifying pricing improvement opportunities and areas where profits may be leaking.

Industry: Healthcare

Genetics/DNA Research	Big Data can play a significant role in genetic and DNA research. Using Big Data, researchers can identify disease genes and biomarkers to help patients pinpoint health issues they may face in the future. The results can even allow healthcare organizations to design personalized treatments.
Patient Experience	Healthcare organizations seek to provide better treatment and improved quality of care – without increasing costs. Big Data helps them improve the patient experience in the most cost-efficient manner. With Big Data, healthcare organizations can create a 360-degree view of patient care as the patient moves through various treatments and departments.
Healthcare Insurance Fraud	For every healthcare claim, there can be hundreds of associated reports in a variety of different formats. This makes it extremely difficult to verify the accuracy of insurance incentive programmes and find the patterns that indicate fraudulent activity. Big Data helps healthcare organizations detect potential fraud by flagging certain behaviours for further examination.
Healthcare Billing	By analysing billing and claims data, organizations can discover lost revenue opportunities and places where payment cash flows can be improved. This use case requires integrating billing data from various payers, analysing a large volume of that data and then identifying activity patterns in the billing data.

Industry: Oil and Gas

Predictive Maintenance	Oil and gas companies often lack visibility on the condition of their equipment, especially in remote offshore and deep-water locations. Big Data can help by providing insight so companies can predict the remaining optimal life of their systems and components, ensuring that their assets operate at optimum production efficiency.
Oil Exploration and Discovery	Exploring for oil and gas can be expensive. But companies can make use of the vast amount of data generated in the drilling and production process to make informed decisions about new drilling sites. Data generated from seismic monitors can be used to find new oil and gas sources by identifying traces that were previously overlooked.
Production Optimization	Unstructured sensor and historical data can be used to optimize oil well production. By creating predictive models, companies can measure well production to understand usage rates. With deeper data analysis, engineers can determine why actual well outputs aren't tallying with their predictions.

Besides the identification of use cases, a priority should be assigned to individual use cases. Some use cases will be more beneficial to an organization compared to others. The prioritization of Big Data use cases will need to be done based on the purposes and values of the organization. For most enterprises, Return on Investment (ROI) will be the determining factor in deciding the priority of projects. However, in the last few years we have also seen increased project prioritization based on sustainability incentives (further discussed in Chapter 10) and other non-commercial motives.[5]

Prioritization of Big Data use cases will lead to an ordered list of Big Data projects that, given the business objectives and the current state, will be able to define how an organization can achieve a competitive advantage through Big Data. The next question is how these use case can and should be executed in a structured manner, and in line with begetting cycles, required timelines and approvals. The ordered list of project will need to be translated into a Big Data roadmap.

Formulate a Big Data roadmap

A Big Data roadmap is a strategic plan that outlines how an organization will be able to execute its Big Data strategy. It differs from the prioritized list of use cases (step 3) in terms of details. A Big Data roadmap includes timelines, required budgets and measurable success factors. It will, in other words, state exactly which Big Data projects will be executed, when they will be completed and when they are considered successful.

Whereas the prioritized use cases give direction on *which* projects would be strategically most beneficial for an organization, the Big Data roadmap provides guidance on *how* these projects should be executed. Critical components that should therefore be included in the Big Data roadmap are:

- A selected number of Big Data use cases, and how these initiatives cascade back towards the overall business objectives.
- Estimated timelines and interdependencies between different use cases in the roadmap. The roadmap should clearly reflect in which order the projects will be executed, with an advisable maximum horizon of three years.
- Identification of key decision-makers and owners or the roadmap. The Big Data roadmaps should identify who will be responsible for the execution of critical elements of the Big Data programme. In larger Big Data programmes, it is important to identify levels of authority and the total scope of decision-making.
- An estimation of the costs and benefits of executing the projects identified on the roadmap. For budgeting purposes, the Big Data roadmap provides insights into the overall cost of the Big Data programme.

- Identification of critical resources and skills. The Big Data roadmap will need to identify which resources (and therefore capabilities) would be necessary to successfully complete the Big Data programme.

Commonly, Big Data roadmaps are visualized in flowchart-like graphs and graphs similar to the famous Gantt chart. Visualizing a Big Data roadmap is typically a good idea, since most Big Data roadmaps will be subject to boardroom discussions. Providing a clear and understandable overview of the way in which the strategy will be executed will generally speed up the decision-making process. Additionally, it will generally help identify potential dependencies or issues, and highlight how these could be addressed.

Anchor data-driven results

The last step in the strategy formulation life cycle is to ensure that previous successful Big Data initiatives are anchored in the organization. The strategy, roadmap and corresponding projects will not have enduring value if they do not change the way in which the organization operates. In the case of Big Data projects, this means taking the step towards data-driven decision-making.

One of the famous management theories about changing the way organizations work originates from Kurt Lewin, who is widely regarded as the founding father of change management.[6] In his most famous model, he describes changing an organization in three steps, the 'unfreeze-change-refreeze' model, which is depicted in Figure 6.2.

Although Lewin's model stems from 1947, it still applies to modern-day enterprises, and especially to the opportunities that are brought by Big Data. In essence, the execution of a Big Data strategy is nothing more than a major organization change project. Maybe more than in other types of change project, people will need to start basing their decisions on the analysis that is brought by Big Data.

The last step, anchoring data-driven results, is therefore just as important as the other four steps. Only if the analysis, the algorithms and recommendations (i.e. the

Figure 6.2   Kurt Lewin's model applied to Big Data

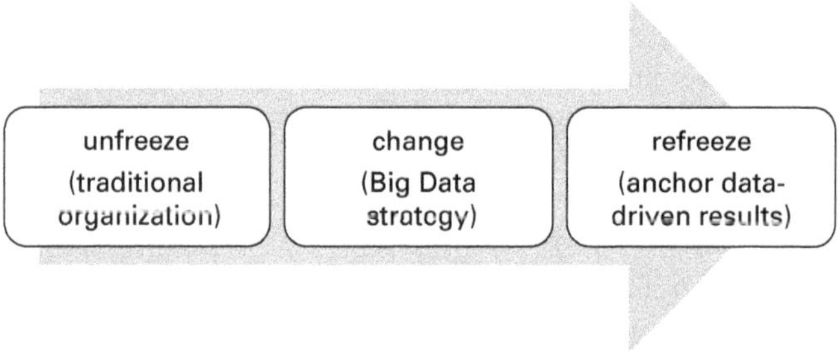

results of the Big Data projects) change decision-making process in the enterprise can we say that the strategy has been successfully executed. The opposite is also true; if data analysis and analytics don't change behaviour in an organization, the company could just as well not have taken the steps to make significant investment in setting up a Big Data organization.

Anchoring data-driven results should therefore be considered an integral part of strategy formulation. As part of the Big Data strategy, you should already be thinking about how successful projects will be embedded. How will predictive algorithms be embedded in reports? Will new solutions be integrated in company applications? And how is new information going to guide the decision-making process? To consider these questions and elements a part of your strategy will help to ensure that the organization captures the most value from their investments, and that organizations do not go backwards when talent leaves the organization.

6.4 Strategy formulation summary

The first micro-capability that we discussed in this section is a crucial step towards Big Data success. Without a properly formulated Big Data strategy, an organization will not know where it is going, and could potentially burn millions analysing 'interesting' data without ever seeing a return on investment.

The strategy formulation capability is a measure that organizations can use to identify how well they are able to express their Big Data initiatives in line with the business objectives. By following the cyclical five-step model discussed in the previous section, organizations have a step-by-step approach through which they can define their Big Data strategy. Through starting at the very beginning (the business objectives), and subsequently identifying tangible and practical Big Data projects (the use cases and roadmap), organizations can build a comprehensive Big Data programme based on a coherent strategy. As a final step in this process, organizations need to think about ways in which they can anchor success and change into the organization. If we apply the lesson from this chapter to the famous quote from *Alice in Wonderland* (see Chapter 5), we might be able to change it to:

> If you do know where you are going, many data sets will take you there.

Notes

1 J Bughin, J Livingston and S Marwaha. Seizing the potential of 'big data'. *McKinsey Quarterly*, 2011 4, 103–09

2 G Stonehouse and B Snowdon. Competitive advantage revisited: Michael Porter on strategy and competitiveness, *Journal of Management Inquiry*, 2007 16 (3), 256–73

3 W C Satyro, J B Sacomano, J C Contador, C M Almeida and B F Giannetti. Process of strategy formulation for sustainable environmental development: Basic model, *Journal of Cleaner Production*, 2017 166, 1295–304

4 I Chih-Lin, Q Sun, Z Liu, S Zhang and S Han. The big-data-driven intelligent wireless network: architecture, use cases, solutions, and future trends, *IEEE Vehicular Technology Magazine*, 2017 12 (4), 20–29

5 R D Raut, S K Mangla, V S Narwane, B B Gardas, P Priyadarshinee and B E Narkhede. Linking big data analytics and operational sustainability practices for sustainable business management, *Journal of Cleaner Production*, 2019 224, 10–24

6 S Cummings, T Bridgman and K G Brown. Unfreezing change as three steps: Rethinking Kurt Lewin's legacy for change management, *Human Relations*, 2016 69 (1), 33–60

Innovation Management

07

7.1 Introduction to innovation management

Innovation has long been recognized as one of the primary drivers for obtaining a competitive advantage.[1] Innovative products and services are more competitive and provide organizations with an opportunity to increase their market share, or to solidify their current market position. Big Data and corresponding Big Data solutions offer a unique way to embed innovation in an organization's strategy.

Innovative products and services bring something new to the market and set a company apart from its competitors. Innovation provides inspiring services and examples that can increase service and/or performance or reduce overall costs. Data analysis and Big Data can provide the required insights into new products and services. The Big Data case study at Netflix is very famous in this area, because it provides a good overview of how Big Data can be used to come up with new and different formats that did not exist before.[2] Netflix, the media streaming platform, uses their data from customer behaviours to determine which new services (i.e. shows and movies) they will produce next. They determine which story lines people prefer, which actors will be liked together and which categories of audiences are likely to enjoy their products. But the company goes even one step further, utilizing Big Data solutions to introduce innovation in the production planning cycle. Using predictive models, they forecast optimal shooting times, shoot locations and resource planning. The *New York Times* famously phrased the impact of Big Data on the company's success as knowing what consumers want before they know what they want.[3]

The Netflix case study is a good example that showcases how Big Data can be used for innovation, and how data can be leveraged to bring new products and services to market. Big Data, of all the different parts of an enterprise, is maybe best suited to address innovation, and can be the engine to bring new competitive products or services to market. With the strategic technological advancements that Big Data brings, organizations can position themselves for the future. We will therefore consider innovation management an integral part of Big Data strategy and will discuss how organizations can build innovation management capabilities to realize their strategic objectives. In the same way that an organization needs a formulated strategy (discussed in Chapter 6), it needs capabilities in innovation management to identify how Big Data can help to bring new innovative products and services to market.

Developing innovation management capabilities through the use of analytics and Big Data will help bring innovative products and services to market faster, in a more structured way. Organizations that have a high level of capability in this domain are typically considered the innovators in their market, with all the positive corresponding benefits. In this chapter, we will therefore first consider how Big Data can boost innovation, and we will subsequently outline how organizations can build a mature innovation management practice as a core part of their Big Data strategy.

7.2 Purpose and maturity levels of innovation management

Purpose

Innovation management is an organization's capability to bring new products and services to market, so that they can obtain a unique position in relation to their competitors. Innovative products or services have an advantage over other products and services because they are faster, more cost-efficient or have a higher level of quality. Innovation is a key driver for sales and growth of companies. A secondary side benefit of innovation is that is generally reflects favourably on the image of a company. Innovative companies have a more favourable reputation than others and are frequently able to attract better talent.

In this book, we will limit the scope of innovation management to Big Data, exploring the ways in which Big Data can help to drive innovation. The scope and purpose of innovation management in this context is outlined in Table 7.1.

The extent to which Big Data can be used for innovation is dependent on the type of business of an organization. For example, the use of predictive analytics and machine learning algorithms (discussed in Part 5) can be more simply used in financial services (by including it in software applications) than for instance in product manufacturing. However, there are quite a number of components that are generic to any

Table 7.1　Purpose of innovation management

Capability	Purpose
Innovation management	Defines how Big Data can exploit new and pioneering ways in which organizations bring new products and services to market.

type of business. Leveraging data to understand customer behaviour, product or service consumption, churn and customer life cycle value will be applicable and useful for any organization. The purpose of using Big Data for innovation management is therefore first and foremost to understand how market opportunities can be created, before new products and services are developed to serve that market.

Innovation management maturity levels

Building an innovation management capability will take time. Innovative companies are not 'naturally' created; they have a strong focus on research and development and are continuously exploring ways in which they can improve their products and services. In line with the capability maturity levels (outlined in Part 2), there are five maturity levels through which organizations can use Big Data to increase innovation.

The five maturity levels outlined in Table 7.2 provide an overview of the journey organizations take to use Big Data as an integral part of innovation management. At the lowest levels, data-driven innovation is typically the result of individual effort. At

Table 7.2 Maturity levels for innovation management

Maturity Level	Description
Level 1 – Initial	Individual 'innovators' help to create new products and services based on their best efforts without any formal organizational support. There is little understanding of the impact and value of data-driven innovation.
Level 2 – Managed	Data-driven innovation is limited to the technology departments. Data analysis and reports are requested to identify new market opportunities, but only on a case-by-case basis.
Level 3 – Defined	There is visible leadership within different departments that support data-driven innovation, with formal and informal networks in the organization to facilitate ideation of new products for different departments.
Level 4 – Controlled	There is an organization-wide effort to promote data-driven innovation. Leadership promotes cross-functional collaboration between different departments and ensures that the Big Data teams provide information and analysis results to the departments on a continual ongoing basis.
Level 5 – Optimized	There is an entrepreneurial culture where product innovation crosses organizational boundaries. The organization has planned innovation cycles and practices and is at the forefront in incorporating algorithms and predictive analysis in products and services.

the higher levels of maturity, data powers the decision-making process, and helps to determine which products and services are brought to market.

7.3 Structuring data-driven innovation management

Whereas using some form of data-driven decision-making is common for most organizations, most find reaching higher levels of maturity quite the challenge. And though the efforts to reach mature levels of innovation management are extensive, it is worth it. New products and services are the way in which organizations can differentiate from their competitors and which define the future path of any company.

Big Data and innovation management are a powerful combination. Whereas previously organizations only had the opportunity to analyse the market (and its products and services) from a historic perspective, Big Data makes it possible to detect needs and opportunities more quickly, or drive demand in a particular area (for example through advertising). The data itself remains data, but the transformative power of Big Data becomes apparent when it is applied to innovation.[4] What will market demand look like? For which products and services will there be a need? And what does current behaviour tell us about future product launches? The aim of data-driven innovation management is to answer these questions.

In this section, we will cover some practical considerations for more mature levels of innovation management and offer some guidance on the way organizations can structure this. To understand how to structurally drive innovation management in enterprise organizations, four different types of organizations can be classified, as depicted in Figure 7.1.

Figure 7.1   The four different archetypes of data-driven innovation management

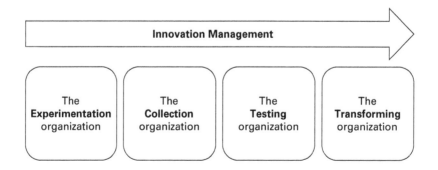

Figure 7.1 defines four different archetypes of organizations, and the ways in which they apply data-driven innovation management to devise or create new products or services. Although there is obviously no right or wrong with each individual archetype, it can be stated that organizations that have a "transformation" archetype generally have a higher level of maturity in innovation management than organizations that have a "experimentation" archetype.

The experimentation organization

The **experimentation organization** is an organization where data and analytics are used to develop new products or introduce service innovations, but where the data analysis process is separated from the product or service itself. The experimentation organization collects data about their products and services (for example through third parties) to identify new product options or enhancements. Through subsequent experiment amongst the different options and – based on trial-and-error approaches – they find the best solution for a particular market demand.

The experimentation archetype is the most dominant innovation management archetype on the market today. These organizations are characterized by the fact that they have analytics or business intelligence solutions in place, but usually as a separate department within the IT domain. This department will support R&D departments on request, but these organizational functions are clearly demarcated.

The collection organization

The **collection organization** is an organization that collects data about consumers and users as part of their product offering or service. Data (and therefore the analysis of data) is embedded in their solutions, and therefore these organizations can analyse how products and services are being consumed. By analysing this behaviour, subsequent innovation decisions can be made. If customers never use a feature, for example, then this can be eliminated in the next release of the product launch. With collection archetype organizations, a focus on data-driven decision-making is already embedded in their products and services.

It is easy to identify successful examples of the collection archetype organization. Organizations that produce products that are intended to be worn (i.e. wearables) are popular because they allow you to measure and analyse all your health data. With these products, you get the ability to download mobile applications, through which you can track your progress, or lack thereof. The data that is collected through wearables is not just valuable from a consumer perspective, it also generates data that showcases how people are using their products, and where further improvements and innovations can be made.

It is a common mistake to think that the collection archetype is only applicable for digital products, like wearables, or IT services, like applications. Through the quick rise of sensors and the Internet of Things (as discussed in Chapter 3, section 3.2), it has become much easier to make data collection an integral part of any product or service offering. Inditex, the parent company of the clothing retailer Zara, for example, is famous for collecting cashier data to optimize their supply chain.[5] Supermarkets, like Amazon Go, collect data about customer behaviour by including radio-frequency identification (RFID) tags on their products to optimize their product offering.[6] For the collection archetype organization, collecting customer or product data to make further improvements is fundamental to their innovation process.

The testing organization

The **testing organization** tests new products or service features continuously as an integrated approach to their research and development. These organizations constantly test different solutions and use the outcome data to justify further enhancements or features. The testing archetype is not to be confused with the experimentation organization. In an experimentation organization, the Big Data function is separate from the product or service itself, whereas in a testing organization innovation through data is fully integrated.

A common example of testing practices for the testing archetype is the use of A/B testing to optimize products and services. With A/B testing, hypotheses are generated, and data is used to verify or falsify optimization solutions. The statistical nature and techniques of A/B testing will be further explained in Part 5, but this technique is exemplary for data-driven innovation through testing. A testing organization is continuously trying to improve its products and services and leads its innovation strategy based on data-driven decisions.

To make adequate predications, and set up the right types of tests, massive data sets are required. As we will see in Chapter 24 (Machine learning), Big Data sets are required to make statistically significant claims. For this reason, the testing archetype is a gradual improvement on the collection archetype. Organizations first need to have the data about consumers (preferably integrated within their solutions) before optimization decisions can be made. As a result, data-driven innovation management is a capability that matures over time.

The transforming organization

The **transforming organization** continually improves their products or services based on customer feedback and preferences. For the transforming archetype, the concept of a product or service is not static but adjusted towards individual behaviours and preferences. Transforming organizations use Big Data and personalization algorithms to predict and deliver customized solutions to their customers, even if this is based on a limited number of products.

Tailoring solutions, products and services through innovation is mostly done by finding the most optimal recommendation amongst a series of alternatives. On a social media platform for example, the number of options that can be shown (though large) is finite. Yet every person that opens their LinkedIn or Instagram profile has a personalized timeline. Similarly, the number of songs or movies on Spotify or Netflix is finite, but they are nonetheless tailored to individual preferences. From a technical point of view, these organizations use recommendation engines, which are based on classification algorithms, which will be further explained in Part 5.

In transforming organizations, Big Data is used on a day-to-day basis to make instant decisions to customize or tailor products to individual needs or preferences. The only way to achieve this level of innovation is to have a strong focus on data, knowledge about algorithms and the technical infrastructure to support this. Consequently, innovation in transforming organizations is not so much in the products or services themselves, but rather in the algorithms with which they are created. The focus on innovation shifts towards optimizing algorithms to enhance predictions, forecasting more accurately or increasing conversion. It is therefore no surprise that transforming organizations have the highest level of maturity in innovation management.

7.4 Innovation management summary

The innovation management micro-capability is an indicator of the extent to which organizations drive their product or service innovations with Big Data. Organizations that are in their early stages of maturity will use traditional business intelligence solutions to provide input to product innovation decisions, the more traditional R&D model of most organizations. This type of structure is known as the experimentation archetype.

Organizations that are moving to higher levels of Big Data maturity are embedding data-driven decision-making to steer choices with regards to innovations, new product updates or the launch of new services. In their product offering, they include data collection possibilities to steer future decision-making (the collection archetype) or they continually increase the quality of their products by introducing new features or enhancements (the testing archetype). Organizations that tailor their product or service offering on an immediate or nearly real-time basis are operating at the highest levels of capability in innovation management (the transforming archetype). For these transforming organizations, the focus of innovation is the data itself.

Notes

1 L Keeley, H Walters, R Pikkel and B Quinn (2013) *Ten Types of Innovation: The discipline of building breakthroughs*, London, John Wiley & Sons

2 X Amatriain (2013) Big & personal: data and models behind Netflix recommendations. In Proceedings of the 2nd international workshop on big data, streams and heterogeneous source. Mining: Algorithms, systems, programming models and applications, August, 1–6

3 D Carr. Giving viewers what they want, *The New York Times*, 2013 24 (02), 2013

4 G George and Y Lin. Analytics, innovation, and organizational adaptation, *Innovation*, 2017 19 (1), 16–22

5 N R Sanders. How to use big data to drive your supply chain, *California Management Review*, 2016 58 (3), 26–48

6 S Junsawang, W Chaiyasoonthorn and S Chaveesuk (2020) Willingness to use self-service technologies similar to Amazon Go at supermarkets in Thailand. In Proceedings of the 2020 2nd International Conference on Management Science and Industrial Engineering, April, 135–39

Leadership and Governance 08

8.1 Introduction to leadership and governance

A Big Data strategy will not be drafted or executed out of nowhere. Nor will any kind of Big Data technology investments be done without proper business cases or support from the upper management levels of any company. For a Big Data strategy to be successful, strong leadership and adequate governance are required. The leadership and governance micro-capability will therefore consider the extent to which an organization has set up leadership and governance capabilities to execute a Big Data strategy.

That strong leadership and governance capabilities and successful Big Data strategies are strongly correlated is nothing new. Many studies have shown that Big Data and a culture of data-driven decision-making can only be successful if there is strong management support and executive buy-in. Companies succeed in the Big Data era not simply because they have more or better data, but because they have leadership teams that set clear goals, define what success looks like and ask the right questions.[1] It is therefore imperative to consider leadership and governance capabilities, and to see how these can be fostered and grown in any company. Leadership and governance capabilities determine the extent to which an organization can successfully define a Big Data strategy, but, maybe more importantly, the extent to which an enterprise can successfully execute it.

One of the frequent misconceptions about Big Data and leadership is that Big Data will make the need for, or involvement of, senior leadership obsolete, because the algorithms are able to make better decisions than people. Although it is certainly true that algorithms have the capability to make better (i.e. more accurate) decisions than people, there is a profound need for executives that can spot opportunities and bring people together who can create innovative data-driven solutions (as discussed in Chapter 7). Many organizations that have flourished over the past years in the execution of their Big Data strategies have one thing in common: strong leadership and strong executive teams. Big Data does not pose a threat to executives, but rather provides them with an opportunity to implement their strategy more quickly.

As you might have noted, the micro-capability discussed in this chapter is the combination of leadership and governance. The reason that these two elements are combined is because leadership, without a proper governance structure, still inhibits the successful execution of a Big Data strategy. Since governance is especially relevant in an enterprise organization, this topic has been made an integral part of the leadership and governance capability.

As we have already noted in Chapter 5 section 5.5, the implementation of Big Data strategies is ultimately a leadership responsibility. When it comes to the implementation of Big Data strategies, leadership and decision-making play a critical role. Because of the technological, human and cultural barriers (discussed in Chapter 5 section 5.3), the leadership of an organization is ultimately responsible for the success or failure of the Big Data strategy. Individual leaders are required to create and sustain the vision of the organization, and to subsequently build the required capabilities. In this chapter, we will take a closer look at how this can be done from a practical point of view.

8.2 Purpose and maturity levels of leadership and governance

Purpose

Leadership and governance is an organization's capability to successfully establish leadership and a governance structure that enables a Big Data strategy to be executed successfully. Successful Big Data leaders can articulate a Big Data strategy and gather enough support to successfully execute their plans. Through the leadership and governance capability, organizations ensure that plans don't just remain plans, but that they transform the organization towards data-driven decision-making.

Just as all organizations need leadership to head up separate functions, the leadership of the Big Data function is ultimately the responsibility of a person. For the sake of simplicity, the individual accountable for the formulation and execution of the Big Data strategy will be denoted as the **Chief Data Officer (CDO)** in the rest of this book. Although many different job titles exist, such as Data Director, Analytics Lead,

Table 8.1   Purpose of leadership and governance

Capability	Purpose
Leadership and governance	Defines the required leadership and governance structure through which an organization can successfully execute a Big Data strategy.

Head of Data, to name just a few, we will use a uniform name to indicate the person (or group) who ultimately bears end-to-end accountability for the Big Data function: the Chief Data Officer (CDO).

Moving any organization towards a data-driven approach requires a transformation in terms of thinking, as well as some significant organization change. Effective leadership is necessary to encourage commitment towards the formulated Big Data strategy (discussed in Chapter 6), and to set accountability for the Big Data programme's results. At the same time, appropriate governance structures (including decision-making authority and oversight mechanisms) are required to ensure the organization's leadership, and particularly the CDO, can be successful.

The leadership and governance capability enables an organization to set the conditions for success. As with all the capabilities discussed in this book, leadership and governance can be improved and developed, leading to higher levels of success. Although it is a fact that there will always be some personal characteristics in leadership that cannot be captured in any process or approach, it does not relieve organizations of the obligation to create an environment in which leaders can translate their Big Data strategy into tangible results. By establishing the right focus on leadership competences, a clear and straightforward decision authority and the appropriate oversight structure, an organization can ensure it attracts the right talent and leadership in an ever more competitive market.

Leadership and governance maturity levels

Even though the individual aspects of leadership and governance are difficult to measure, there are clear organizational maturity levels for this micro-capability. The five levels outlined in Table 8.2 provide direction for organizations who aim to grow

Table 8.2 Leadership and governance maturity levels

Maturity Level	Description
Level 1 – Initial	IT leadership and governance are carried out in an ad hoc manner, relying on the strengths of individual leaders. No documented governance processes about decision rights or accountability exists.
Level 2 – Managed	Leadership with a uniform direction towards the company's goals is visible and expressed. Some decision rules and governance bodies are in place that help steer the direction for the company.
Level 3 – Defined	Leadership can generate commitment from teams to the execution of the Big Data strategy, and there is visible proof that the teams work towards their goals. There are documented responsibilities and levels of authorization for decision-making.

(continued)

Table 8.2 (Continued)

Maturity Level	Description
Level 4 – Controlled	Leadership creates an environment that enables other teams to reach their goals by determining clear boundaries, and results are measured, reported and tracked on a continuous basis. There is a high trust in leadership decisions, and the governance system enables teams to execute their goals.
Level 5 – Optimized	Leadership inspires teams to be successful, and only manages by exception. Leadership has created a culture in which teams are self-steering and take accountability for their own work. The governance system facilitates teams to make their own decisions but sets the proper controls to track long-term success.

their leadership and governance capabilities. The Leadership element outlines the conditions through which leaders can motivate and inspire others, whereas the Governance perspective addresses crucial design aspects, such as decision rights, mechanisms for accountability and oversight.

The leadership and governance micro-capability covers the human aspect of Big Data strategies. No matter how well a strategy is defined, the human aspect and influence in the execution of this strategy should not be overlooked.

8.3 Structuring leadership and governance

Many books have been written about what constitutes effective leadership, and what conditions must be in place for potential leaders to flourish. Like the previous chapters, we will therefore focus on the practical aspects of leadership. Instead of looking at the procedural aspects, role descriptions and characteristics, we will take a practical approach. What are the key characteristics of good leadership in a Big Data environment? And what are the key activities a Big Data leaders should do? By focusing on activities instead of characteristics, we hope to inspire organizations to think about these best practices.

The same can be stated about suitable governance practices. Many best practice frameworks exist that outline suitable processes and controls for governance.[2] In this chapter, we will focus on critical governance areas that are required for successful leadership, and we will introduce several controls to measure these successfully. When we are discussing governance in this chapter, please note that we are considering the topic of leadership governance, instead of data governance (which is also an important micro-capability covered in Chapter 28). Governance in the context of leadership is about the establishment of transparent decision-making processes, and the ability to steer decision-making toward the future.

As we noted in the previous section, organizations would need to assign roles and responsibilities for Big Data leadership and governance. In this chapter, we will therefore introduce the role of the CDO. The CDO is a role that anchors and is ultimately accountable for leadership and governance in an organization. Additionally, this role makes it possible to anchor leadership and governance in a consistent and practical way.

Leadership

The ability to lead and inspire others is a crucial characteristic of leaders. Leaders focus on achieving goals, by ensuring tasks are adequately assigned amongst team members, who will then execute these tasks. A successful leader will have controls in place to ensure that these goals are met and can adjust course or direction early, whenever this is deemed to be necessary. Leadership itself is therefore predominantly a skill.[3]

> Leadership is defined as the skill of influencing people to work devotedly towards an identified common good. The key words here are skill and influence. Skill is a learned or acquired ability and influence is how you get people to voluntarily do what you task them to do.

Just like other skills, leadership is something people can learn. Some people are naturally better at this skill than others, but the same is true for skills in sports or other disciplines. Some people are naturally gifted, but through training, repetition and experience, it is possible to master the basic ideas and to master this skill. For this reason, the skill of leadership is a capability. It can be grown and cultivated, which will result in organizations that bring forward better or more effective leaders.

Because leadership is a general skill (also necessary for marketing, finance or any other domain), we will take a closer look at leadership skills that are predominantly useful for leaders in the Big Data domain. What are the key characteristics of a good leader in the Big Data domain? And what would qualify someone as a potential CDO?

The skills and capabilities of Big Data leaders are summarized in Figure 8.1 and Table 8.3 which outline the core focus activities and focus areas of Big Data leadership. As indicated in these figures there is a common 'red thread' for effective leadership in the Big Data domain: the leader should adhere to data-driven decision-making and should also encourage others to follow this way of thinking and working. When it comes to leading a Big Data organization, leadership should follow their own message, and walk the walk (or follow the data).

Even if all these skills are in place, it remains the Big Data leaders' role to continuously assess whether adjustments are necessary. As Table 8.3 indicates, leadership is not just about articulating a compelling vision or Big Data strategy. Leadership

Figure 8.1   Skills and capabilities of Big Data leaders

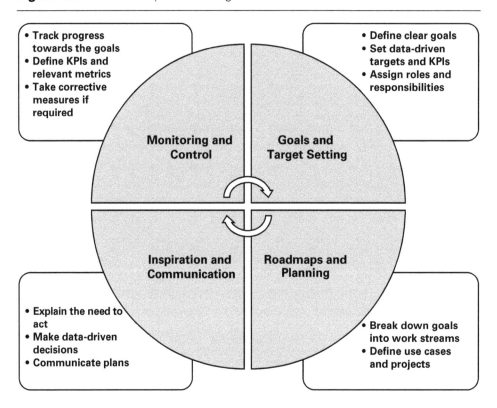

- Track progress towards the goals
- Define KPIs and relevant metrics
- Take corrective measures if required

Monitoring and Control

- Define clear goals
- Set data-driven targets and KPIs
- Assign roles and responsibilities

Goals and Target Setting

Inspiration and Communication

- Explain the need to act
- Make data-driven decisions
- Communicate plans

Roadmaps and Planning

- Break down goals into work streams
- Define use cases and projects

Table 8.3   Big Data leadership skills and focus areas

Skills	Description
Goals and Target Setting	After some initial experimentation and conceptualization, set both short- and long-term goals, in line with the organization's Big Data strategy. These goals should then be cascaded down to measurable objectives and targets which can be measured by data. Each of these targets and KPIs should then be assigned to roles that are accountable for achieving these targets.
Roadmaps and Planning	Based on the Big Data strategy, several use cases and projects can be identified, as discussed in Chapter 6. Big Data leadership is involved in the selection, prioritization and assignment of these use cases. Many of these high-level use cases will need to be broken down into actionable projects that require budget, resources and leadership support. Part of the roadmap should include the existing data products and data services.

(continued)

Table 8.3   (Continued)

Skills	Description
Inspiration and Communication	A crucial element for success, Big Data leadership should continuously communicate the value of data-driven decision-making. Expressing the benefits of data collection, data analysis and using the results are critical activities that are expected from Big Data leadership, so that all team members are moving in the same direction.
Monitoring and Control	Leadership should set up data dashboards to track and measure KPIs based on the goals and objectives that were defined in the first activity. Through data, it becomes visible what the progress of the use cases and projects is, and which activities are on track. Based on this data-driven information, leadership can make decisions and corrective actions if required.

is equally about inspiring and persuading people to embrace the strategy, managing a variety of stakeholders in the process. The most successful Big Data companies today are the ones whose leaders can do all that, whilst changing the way their organizations make decisions.

Governance

Governance is the ability of an organization to set up a structure to evaluate, direct and monitor organizational performance to meet stakeholder needs.[4] This structure, which is a requirement in every organization, requires the setup of a governance system. Governance is a complex and interwoven approach that applies to the whole organization: it is the collection of processes, people, technology and practices that define an organization. As systems are inherently complex, it is difficult to find one uniform or workable approach that applies to all different types and sizes of organization.

To establish a practical and vendor-independent approach, this book will utilize a model that follows the 'capability thinking' approach, in combination with established governance best practices.[5] The **Enterprise Big Data Framework Governance System** provides guidance for any organization that wishes to use the Enterprise Big Data Framework as a blueprint for their organizational design.

The Enterprise Big Data Framework Governance System combines three capabilities that have a direct impact on governance decisions that are necessary to evaluate, direct and monitor any Big Data organization. Each of these three is a separate micro-capability which are outlined in detail in other chapters:

- **The Leadership & Governance micro-capability** (part of the Big Data Strategy capability). Discussed in detail in this chapter, the leadership and governance capability defines the required leadership and governance structure through which an organization can successfully execute a Big Data strategy. The leadership and governance capability is at the top of the model because it is the most strategic element, and the responsibility of the leadership.

- **The Data Governance micro-capability** (part of the Big Data Processes capability). The Data Governance capability develops the ownership and operational structure needed to ensure that enterprise data is managed as a strategic asset and implemented in an effective and sustainable manner. Data governance will be further discussed in Chapter 28.

- **The Data Management micro-capability** (part of the Big Data Processes capability). The Data Management capability is a set of disciplines and techniques used to process, store and organize data in line with enterprise requirements. Data management will be further discussed in in Chapter 29.

Each of the three capabilities have their own maturity levels. Similarly, the different capabilities can be managed by separate teams with separate responsibilities. Yet it is

Figure 8.2   The Enterprise Big Data Framework Governance System

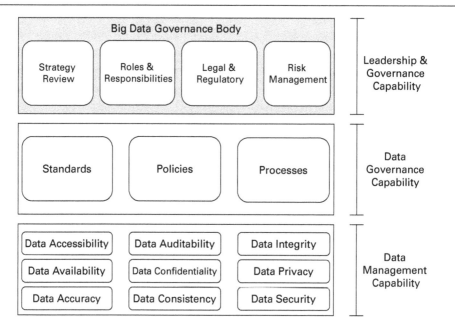

crucial to consider the governance system holistically, where all the components in-fluence each other. In practice, this will mean that maturity levels for each of these three capabilities need to be in sync. A situation where Leadership and Governance is at maturity level 4 and Data Governance is at maturity level 2 is, for that reason, highly unlikely.

Leadership and governance capability components

In any organization, roles and accountabilities need to be assigned. At the highest level, the four components of the leadership and governance capability are assigned to the Big Data Governance Body. The **Big Data Governance Body** operates at the strategic level and includes key decision-makers and senior executives that determine the direction of the organization. In most organization, the CDO (or equivalent) will chair the Big Data Governance Body.

> The Big Data Governance Body is the strategic leadership of an organization which decides on the future direction of the organization and its Big Data strategy.

The composition of the Big Data Governance Body will be different from organiza-tion to organization, depending on the way the upper management has been struc-tured. It is recommended that the governance body consists of three to seven members, and that it convenes at least on a quarterly basis. The Big Data Governance Body is tasked with the decision-making of the four strategic components of the Enterprise Big Data Framework Governance System:

1 **Big Data Strategic Review.** The Governance Body should review the formulated Big Data strategy (as discussed in Chapter 6) and determine whether this strategy is in line with the overall organizational objectives. Since Big Data strategies are not static, instead frequently including crucial innovations (as discussed in Chapter 7), the Governance Body needs to set up a formal review process to manage any changes in the strategic direction. Because the Governance Body consists of the most senior leadership of an organization, it gives the final approval on the documented Big Data strategy.

2 **Roles and responsibilities.** A fundamental requirement for any type of governance programme is the definition of clear roles and responsibilities. The Governance Body needs to be rigorous about defining roles and assigning specific responsibilities to the individuals involved in leadership and governance, data governance, and data management. Establishing clear roles and responsibilities enforce accountability, and makes it clear who oversees specific decisions.

3 **Legal and regulatory.** A core aspect of governance in any Big Data environment is to have a clear understanding of legal and regulatory requirements, and the way they influence the strategic objectives of the organization. As most enterprises conduct business across international borders, international laws and regulations with regards to data processing, data privacy and data security can become quite complex quite quickly. Legal requirements might inhibit an organization's strategic Big Data objectives, or they can function as an accelerator. In either case, it is the core responsibility of the organization to understand the legal landscape, any upcoming new laws and any industry-specific regulations. Most legal and regulatory requirements will be incorporated into specific policies and processes (further discussed in Chapter 28).

4 **Risk management.** Risk management is at the core of any organization's decision-making process. A Big Data strategy is – in essence – finding the right balance between risk and reward. Organizations that are more risk averse will have more conservative views on the way Big Data can be used to power decision-making. On the other hand, organizations with a higher risk appetite might take on more risky approaches in the hope of generating higher returns or values. Since balancing risk and reward (i.e. risk management) quickly becomes an ethical discussion, for which there is no definitive guidance or answers), risk management should be placed at the level of the Big Data Governance Body. They will be best placed and best informed to make a balanced trade-off in these decisions, and to decide which decisions are best for their stakeholders.

The four strategic components of the Enterprise Big Data Framework Governance System have significant impact on the direction of an organization. The formalized power that the Big Data governance body holds should therefore not be underestimated. For that reason, it is imperative that organizations should really consider who they nominate for positions in the Big Data Governance Body.

The role of the Chief Data Officer

In the previous section, we saw the impact that the Big Data Governance Body has on the direction and decision-making of organizations. To personify one of the crucial leadership roles in more detail, Big Data organizations should consider the creation of a CDO role, a critical role to define who should manage Big Data in the enterprise. In many organizations, Data Scientist roles have emerged to capitalize on the analytical opportunities of Big Data, but placing these specialists in operational business units without leadership at the corporate level might not be sufficient to harness the full value of Big Data.[6] To address this vacuum, many leading organizations have started to appoint a CDO.

> ## Chief Data Officers
>
> A CDO defines strategic priorities for the company in the area of data systems, identifying new business opportunities pertaining to data, optimizing revenue generation through data and generally representing data as a strategic business asset at the executive table.

The Chief Data Officer can lead the effort to enhance or mature the leadership and governance capability as outlined in this chapter. As the CDO operates at the strategic level, he or she can build bridges between business and IT, execute the plans from the Big Data strategy (discussed in Chapter 6) and chair the Big Data Governance Body. Adding this role to the organization's leadership team (or equivalent) emphasizes the strategic importance of Big Data, and signals to employees and partners the significance of data-driven decision-making.

Many large firms have started to embrace the role of the Chief Data Officer. The first recognized CDO was already established in 2003 at Capital One.[7] Other early adopters included Yahoo! and Microsoft. Nowadays, CDOs are established at investment banks, consumer banks, data companies, healthcare companies and several government organizations.[8] More and more organizations recognize that they need to start considering data as a strategic asset, and just like other strategic assets, it is beneficial to appoint an executive that oversees the strategic direction of these assets. A CDO can lead enterprise-wide initiatives on data strategy, data governance, data management and data architecture. The formalization of the role (from a governance perspective) and the appointment of an individual are therefore critical steps to develop and grow the leadership and governance micro-capability.

8.4 Leadership and governance summary

In this chapter, we explored the leadership and governance micro-capability in more detail and discussed the importance of this capability for the successful execution of a Big Data strategy. The leadership and governance capability can be brought to higher levels of maturity by focusing on three critical components:

1 **Defining a leadership structure.** Organizations need to consider how to structure a leadership domain that supports the Big Data structure. Several critical leadership skills of Big Data leaders were outlined in Table 8.3.

2 **Establishing a governance system.** Governance is a critical component for success in Big Data. In this chapter, we introduced the Enterprise Big Data Framework

Governance System (Figure 8.2) and showcased how strategic review, roles and responsibilities, legal and regulatory aspects, and risk management need to be established.

3 The appointment of a Chief Data Officer (or equivalent). The CDO can lead the effort to enhance or mature the leadership and governance capability. By appointing an individual at the strategic level, Big Data strategies are anchored in the enterprise in a consistent and sustainable way.

The leadership and governance micro-capability is essential to ensure a Big Data strategy can be executed successfully. This capability ensures that strategy-setting is not just a paper exercise, but that the support system to create success is established, and that the individuals responsible for that strategy can fulfill their jobs in a consistent way.

Notes

1 A McAfee, E Brynjolfsson, T H Davenport, D J Patil and D Barton. Big data: the management revolution, *Harvard Business Review*, 2012 90 (10), 60–68

2 G Mangalaraj, A Singh and A Taneja (2014) IT governance frameworks and COBIT – a literature review, www.researchgate.net/publication/287852898_IT_governance_ frameworks_and_COBIT_-_A_literature_review (archived at https://perma.cc/U4D4-686T)

3 J C Hunter 2008. *The Servant: A simple story about the true essence of leadership.* Currency

4 S De Haes, W Van Grembergen, A Joshi and T Huygh (2020) COBIT as a Framework for Enterprise Governance of IT. In *Enterprise Governance of Information Technology*, Springer, Cham, 125–62

5 Z Panian. Some practical experiences in data governance, *World Academy of Science, Engineering and Technology*, 2010 62 (1), 939–46

6 Y Lee, S E Madnick, R Y Wang, F Wang and H Zhang (2014) A cubic framework for the chief data officer: Succeeding in a world of big data, www.researchgate.net/ publication/282287864_A_Cubic_Framework_for_the_Chief_Data_Officer_CDO_ Succeeding_in_a_World_of_Big_Data (archived at https://perma.cc/42U7-VKTY)

7 J Peppard. Unlocking the performance of the chief information officer (CIO), *California Management Review*, 2010 52 (4), 73–99

8 P Aiken and M M Gorman (2013) *The Case for the Chief Data Officer: Recasting the C-suite to leverage your most valuable asset.* Elsevier Science

Communication 09

9.1 Introduction to communication

Communication is an important capability for every business function. The domain of Big Data is no different. For a Big Data strategy to be effective, it needs to be properly communicated to all stakeholders involved. Communication is therefore a micro-capability that contributes significantly to the success (or failure) of Big Data organizations. An impressive way to express the importance of communication in Big Data was written by the novelist William Gibson, who said:

> The future is already here. It's just not evenly distributed yet.[1]

This quote exemplifies one of the main challenges that Big Data, and Big Data technologies, face in the modern world. From a technology perspective, a lot is already possible. Yet very few people, including internal staff working at Big Data organizations, are properly informed about the impact, workings and implications of using Big Data.

This chapter will therefore introduce communication as a micro-capability that should be actively managed in any Big Data organization. Communication, which is frequently the responsibility of the corporate communications department, forms a critical success factor for successful execution of a Big Data strategy. The positive news is that communication is one of the micro-capabilities that is easily plannable. Because communication theory has been around a long time and has been a domain of study long before the term Big Data was invented, there are many best practices that will help organizations grow in their communication capability. In this chapter, we will review a number of these communication best practices and provide guidance how they can be utilized in the domain of Big Data.

9.2 Purpose and maturity levels of communication

Purpose

Communication is an organization's capability to successfully explain the needs, benefits and implications of their Big Data strategy. As is common in communication theory, the difficulty in communication is that it needs to address different stakeholders, all of whom have different preferences and interests, and who also prefer different modes of communication. As a result, communication strategies can quickly become quite complex.

Before we start to dive into some of the most applicable communication best practices, it is important to pause for a second and reflect on the purpose of communication in Big Data. Why is this necessary? And what is the benefit of good communication in Big Data? A good illustration of the need for solid Big Data communication can be learned from the Facebook Files case study, which dominated the news cycles in 2021 for many months.[2] Facebook, essentially a Big Data company, with a widely publicized and studied Big Data strategy, received a significant amount of criticism for several policy choices and governance decisions that had adverse effects on society.[3]

Leaving the ethical discussion aside (which we gladly leave to the press), there is one important and general conclusion that can be learned from this case study: communication is essential to the successful execution of a Big Data strategy. Communication strategies should be set up to address the needs and concerns of different stakeholders and, maybe even more importantly, need to explain how data is used to drive decision-making. The purpose of communication – in the context of Big Data – is therefore two-fold:

1 Organizations need to communicate to internal and external stakeholders *why* Big Data is used, and in what way it contributes to an organization's competitive position. We will refer to this purpose as **motive communication**.

2 Organizations need to communicate to internal and external stakeholders *how* Big Data is used, and in what way the organization is safeguarding ethical norms. We will refer to this objective as **purpose communication**.

It is clear to see that most objections, negative press and scandals are the direct result of a lack in purpose communication. Enterprises who are unable (or unwilling) to explain how data is processed, and who are balancing on the edge of ethical or legal norms, run the risk of severe reputational damage. As the Facebook Files clearly show, a lot of damage might have been avoided if the company had better communicated how it was using profile information, and which measures it took to ensure data could not be misused.

In the rest of this chapter, we will take a closer look at how organizations can structure their environment to ensure motive communication and purpose communication. The purpose of the communication micro-capability is therefore structured as per the definition in Table 9.1.

The communication capability should be set up as an ongoing practice and include more than just the communication of the Big Data strategies. More tactical and operation processes, such as Big Data policies and processes, are also

Table 9.1 The purpose of the communication capability

Capability	Purpose
Communication	Ensure that the motives and purpose of Big Data strategies, policies and processes are published, enacted and understood by internal and external stakeholders in the organization.

governed by the communication capability and will therefore also be considered in this chapter.

Communication maturity levels

Key stakeholders in organizations differ in how they understand and acknowledge the value of communication and implement strategic communication practices to accomplish the objectives that are defined in the Big Data strategy (as discussed in

Table 9.2 Communication maturity levels

Maturity Level	Description
Level 1 – Initial	The communication of motives and purposes happen in a reactive manner, when requested by stakeholders. There is no formalized communication plan.
Level 2 – Managed	A Big Data communications plan exists that addresses how information to critical stakeholders about Big Data strategies, policies and processes should be disseminated. The organization acts upon this communications plan.
Level 3 – Defined	The Big Data communications plan is periodically reviewed, and the organization ensures that a periodic review of stakeholder communication needs is executed. The organization has defined metrics that define the success of communication, and these metrics are actively monitored.
Level 4 – Controlled	The Big Data communications plan is improved with both internal and external stakeholders. Stakeholders can provide feedback on the communication plan, and this feedback is incorporated in revised versions. The organizations apply statistical metrics and techniques to increase the effectiveness of the communication.
Level 5 – Optimized	The communication strategy has a positive impact on internal and external stakeholders, and the communication plan is under active management. The impact of communication (internally and externally) is monitored, and there is evidence that the communication strategy positively influences the reputation of the organization.

Chapter 6).[4] Yet in general, it is possible to define a number of maturity levels that define how capable, or mature, an organization is that needs to communicate the motives and purpose of a Big Data strategy.

The communication micro-capability considers the variety of stakeholders of the enterprise. Internal stakeholders are those that can be considered as part of the organization (employees, management, shareholders, etc.). External stakeholders are those who are further removed from the organization, or those who don't have direct involvement (customers, suppliers, government regulators, media outlets, etc.). Reputational damage and consequences typically have a direct impact on external stakeholders.

9.3 Structuring communication

As discussed in section 9.1, the communication capability can have a significant impact on the reputation of a company. This impact can be positive, providing an opportunity to accelerate the Big Data strategy of an organization. The opposite is also true – (the lack of) communication can have an adverse effect on the reputation of a company.

Communication challenges

An important aspect, and one that makes communication more complex in a Big Data context, is to consider that most of the general public will be sceptical (if not to say hostile) towards the use of Big Data to improve organizational effectiveness. From a historical perspective, there are many reasons that led to this attitude to Big Data functions, but the most common ones are the following three:

1 **Complexity** – People fear what they don't know. Big Data, and the corresponding domains of machine learning and AI (as discussed in Chapter 3 section 3.1) are inherently complex.[5] Big Data systems apply statistical or machine learning algorithms that most people find complex, or don't have any background in. In many cases, people find it difficult to support or promote technologies they don't fully comprehend.

2 **Privacy and ethical considerations** – Big Data technologies, and the algorithms that use them, can bring significant privacy and ethical concerns.[6] And these concerns are for the most part valid. Big Data solutions make it possible to track and trace people, recognize preferences and make predictions about behaviours. Many people, especially in highly democratic countries, have concerns that Big Data can be used by enterprise organizations or governments, and these concerns should be addressed. This topic will be further explored in Chapter 28.

3 Scandals – The last decade has seen its fair share of misuse of Big Data technologies, and in most cases these situations were covered widely in the press. The Cambridge Analytica scandal, which used Big Data to manipulate election outcomes, is still fresh in most people's minds.[7] Other recent scandals, such as the Pegasus spyware scandal, which used Big Data techniques to listen to calls from government officials, or the Nightingale data controversy, in which patient data was used without consent, are also still well remembered.[8]

When addressing communication in Big Data, it is important to be aware that these challenges exist. Whether you agree with this bias or not, it certainly is something to recognize. In the proverbial sense of the word, any communication approach or plan is two steps behind. Not only does Big Data communication need to explain its benefits from a neutral ground, it will also need to deal with pre-existing scepticism and likely mistrust.

For this reason, growing capability in communication requires two focus points. First, organizations need to address the strategic, policy and process objectives (motive communication) in a similar way to the way other business functions communicate about their direction. Secondly, the organization needs to communicate how it is safeguarding ethical norms (purpose communication) in data storage and data processing. The second objective in this communication plan is relatively unique to the domain of Big Data, and specifically aimed to address the challenges outlined above.

Defining a communication plan

As clearly indicated in the communication maturity levels (see Chapter 9 section 9.2), one of the crucial components to grow capability in communication is the establishment of a Big Data communication plan. The **Big Data communication plan** outlines which stakeholders should receive which message, how frequently and through which communication channels.

Communication about the objectives and goals of an internal organization should be separated from external communication. For example, a company that is using Big Data to optimize its marketing budget does not want any competitors to know how it allocates its budget or resources. However, the company's data privacy policies need to be communicated clearly to all stakeholders involved.

The common components of a communication plan are:

- **Target audience:** The intended recipients of the communication. This can be an individual, another department or even a completely different company. Defining the different target audiences is one of the most crucial parts of a communication plan. An advisable way to create different target audiences is to work with personas.

- **Message:** The key content of communication. If, for example, the purpose is to let customers know how your organization processes their personal data, the message is the communication of the data privacy and data processing policy.

- **Objectives:** A description of the desired outcome that the communication is aiming to achieve. Why are we taking the effort to communicate this message in the first place? In the example of the communication of the data privacy policy to customers, the main objective is to create trust and build reputation as a reputable company. By communicating the measures that a company takes to safeguard data, customers gain trust that their data is in safe hands.

- **Medium:** A common communication principle is that the message is in the medium.[9] Different forms of communication are perceived differently according to the chosen medium. A message that is communicated through a company chat system (Slack or MS Teams, for example) will be considered more informal than a non-disclosure contract that employees are requested to sign. In many cases, the chosen mode of communication determines the gravity of importance of the message.

- **Timing and frequency:** One of the most important elements to think about in a communication plan is when and how often communication will be sent to different stakeholders. Organizations need to find a balance that will ensure stakeholders are informed properly, without resorting to over-communication. When many messages are sent, it becomes difficult to differentiate important messages from the rest.

- **Feedback mechanism:** A frequently overlooked element of a sound Big Data communication plan, the feedback mechanism allows stakeholders to respond to messages. When communication to different stakeholders is prepared, it is important to think about the way in which the company deals with return messages. In order for communication to be effective, a two-way communication channel needs to be established, even if it is something as simple as setting up a (monitored) mailbox.

A common best practice for defining and managing stakeholders in Big Data communication is to work with **personas**. Personas are fictional individuals that represent the typical – or archetypal – individual for whom communication is intended.[10] It is a simple yet effective way in which a company can structure its communication plan. A persona is a fictional character that represents a stakeholder group, and whose communication needs are required to be addressed in the communication plan. Table 9.3 provides some common personas that are typical in Big Data communication plans.

The steps to set up a Big Data communication plan are straightforward. It is more difficult to keep a communication plan up to date and in line with the changing

Table 9.3 Common personas in a Big Data communication plan

Persona	Description
Charlie the Consumer	Charlie the consumer is a paid subscriber to the services of company X. He loves the features of the app that are provided and is using the app daily. Although Charlie does not take the time to read the company's data privacy and security policies in detail, he does expect the service provider to ensure adequate measure are in place and expects proof in communication to verify that company X is taking this seriously.
Ronnie the Regulator	Ronnie the Regulator is working for the government and is tasked with overseeing compliance to local rules and regulations. Ronnie is primarily concerned with verifying a recently introduced regulation to provides customers the 'right to be forgotten,' and needs to verify compliance by the companies in his jurisdiction. It would help his job tremendously if companies proactively communicate the measures they have taken to address this new requirement.
Sandra the Supplier	Sandra provides services and resources to company X and has a long-term relationship with the company. Sandra wants to ensure that she keeps a good standing with the company (and to keep receiving purchase orders). To accomplish this objective, she would need to be aware of the latest vendor policy and any data-processing requirements her organization is required to enhance or set up.

requirements of different stakeholders. Organizations that are operating at a higher level of maturity for the communication capability therefore typically employ communication professionals to revise and update this plan on an ongoing basis.

Defining a communication approach

Besides structuring a communication plan that outlines which message will be delivered to which stakeholders, it is recommended that any organization thinks about their communication approach. A Big Data communication approach takes a bigger picture look at the topic of communication and interweaves both motive communication and purpose communication. Besides the informative nature of communication (i.e. the objective is to inform), marketing and public relations are also part of the messaging. In many cases, this approach is to specifically address the purpose of the communication objective.

An example of an organization communication approach is depicted in Figure 9.1 and is adjusted specifically for common Big Data messaging.

Figure 9.1   Big Data communication approach

Internal Communication	Marketing Communication	External Communication
Staff Communication	Product Features	Shareholder Communication
Management Communication	Data Security Certification	Customer Data Protection
	Data Privacy Certification	Vendor Data Requirements
	Corporate Identify	Policies and Processes
	Audit Compliance	

As outlined in Figure 9.1, a common communication approach is to structure messaging into three major domains. The first domain is **internal communication**. Internal communication is aimed at keeping every stakeholder within the organization informed about the company's strategy and approach with regards to data. This includes communication about the objectives, goals and KPIs the organization aims to achieve. But it also needs to address ethical internal data questions, such as the way in which employee data is being used, what data-driven practices are when it comes to HR and the hiring and promotion practices. Transparency in this domain is crucial and determines to a significant extent employee satisfaction and churn.

The second domain of the marketing communication approach is **marketing communication**. Marketing communication defines how data practices can be used to start or expand customer relationships. Many customers – both in the business-to-consumer and the business-to-business domain – nowadays care about the way in which their data is processed and protected.[11] Customers expect organizations to take adequate measures to safeguard their data, and failure to do so may constitute a major breach of trust, or even termination of the relationship. It is therefore not only important that organizations set up practices and processes to safely store and process data, but also that they actively communicate about it. This communication can be in the form of product features (especially how a particular service is secured) or can be in a more general format for the entire organization. More and more companies are choosing to independently certify their operational processes for data privacy and data security, and to subsequently use these certifications in marketing communication.[12]

The last domain of the marketing communication approach is **external communication**. External communication is targeted to specific stakeholder groups and is typically more focused than the more general marketing communication. Examples of external communication include the way in which organizations communicate their policies and processes towards, for example, shareholders, existing clients or vendors. External communication is important to keep the stakeholders that are close to the organization updated and involved in the strategic decisions that the company makes with regards to Big Data.

9.4 Communication summary

A Big Data strategy that is properly formulated but not effectively communicated will still fail to reach its goal. The communication capability is crucial to ensure Big Data strategies can be executed properly. In this chapter, we reviewed some of the most common challenges to structuring the Big Data communication capability and reviewed several practices to overcome these challenges.

In general, it can be stated that communication about an organization's Big Data strategy is difficult. Because of the complexity of Big Data, privacy and security considerations and number of highly publicized scandals about the misuse of Big Data, many individuals and organizations have concerns about the way in which their data is being used. Organizations need to address these concerns, which is why the Big Data communication capability can be subdivided into motive communication and purpose communication. Motive communication addresses *why* an organization uses Big Data, whereas purpose communication explains to interested stakeholders *how* the organization is storing and processing data.

To grow maturity in the communication capability, organizations need to create, maintain and execute a Big Data communication plan. The communication plan outlines which stakeholders or personas need to be informed about the way in which the company stores and processes data, and how frequently and through which media these goals need to be communicated. Next to the communication plan, mature organizations start to develop Big Data communication approaches, which include marketing and public relations (i.e. external communication) in the messaging and communication plan. The communication capability, although simple to establish, is a crucial enabler for achieving the goals that any organization aims to accomplish with their Big Data strategy.

Notes

1 MR Parks. Big data in communication research: its contents and discontents, *Journal of Communication*, 2014 64 (2), 355–60
2 K Thorson, K Cotter, M Medeiros and C Pak. Algorithmic inference, political interest, and exposure to news and politics on Facebook, *Information, Communication & Society*, 2021 24 (2), 183–200

3 Oxford Analytica, 'Facebook Files' intensify the firm's image problem. Emerald Expert Briefings (oxan-es), www.emerald.com/insight/content/doi/10.1108/OXAN-ES264360/full/html (archived at https://perma.cc/CBK9-N9AM)

4 C Johansson, C Grandien and K Strandh. Roadmap for a communication maturity index for organizations—Theorizing, analyzing and developing communication value, *Public Relations Review*, 2019 45 (4), 101791

5 R N Carleton. Fear of the unknown: One fear to rule them all?, *Journal of Anxiety Disorders*, 2016 41, 5–21

6 K E Martin. Ethical issues in the big data industry, *MIS Quarterly Executive*, 2015 14, 2

7 H Berghel. Malice domestic: The Cambridge Analytica dystopia, *Computer*, 2018 51 (5), 84–89

8 S Singhal (2021) Pegasus scandal shows we cannot take privacy for granted, *The Indian Express*, 23 July, https://indianexpress.com/article/opinion/columns/pegasus-scandal-shows-we-cannot-take-privacy-for-granted-7417678/ (archived at https://perma.cc/XUY2-U4W8)

9 M McLuhan and Q Fiore. The medium is the message, *New York*, 1967 123, 126–28

10 G Getto and K S Amant. Designing globally, working locally: using personas to develop online communication products for international users, *Communication Design Quarterly Review*, 2015 3 (1), 24–46

11 A Goldfarb and C Tucker. Shifts in privacy concerns, *American Economic Review*, 2012 102 (3), 349–53

12 C Hsu, T Wang and A Lu (2016) The impact of ISO 27001 certification on firm performance. In 2016 49th Hawaii International Conference on System Sciences (HICSS), January, 4842–48. IEEE

Sustainability 10

10.1 Introduction to sustainability

As the world is becoming more socially and environmentally conscious and aware, the impact of Big Data on its immediate environment is (or should be) an integral part of a Big Data strategy. In most modern organizations, social sustainability and environmental sustainability are key indicators in an organization's success.[1] As more and more organizations expand their corporate objectives towards the triple bottom line (People, Planet and Profit), a fundamental question arises: What is the impact of Big Data on an organization's sustainability?

The answer to this question is fundamentally complex. On one side, proponents of this discussion will point towards the potential for the efficiency, optimization and reduction of waste by using data to solve business problems. On the other side of the spectrum, opponents will point towards the increased use of energy consumption, the sustainability concerns of hyper data centres and the impact that Big Data and algorithms have on social issues, polarization and manipulation of facts. For both sides of the argument, there are valid arguments; however, this book will not provide any definitive answer to the question as to whether Big Data has a positive influence on sustainability. We will follow the data, which currently affirms that empirical research on the impact of Big Data on social and environmental sustainability is still in its infancy.[2]

This chapter will focus on the way sustainability needs to be incorporated into a Big Data strategy. Regardless of what the social implication or environmental impact of Big Data will be, organizations will need to take the effects into consideration. Sustainability, and the way organizations set up the processes to support its impact, is a critical capability for current and future success. Although the concept of sustainability in general is broad, we will limit sustainability to two different perspectives:

- **Social implication:** the effect that the use of Big Data technologies and applications will have on people in society, families and individuals. From a data perspective, organizations will need to consider the effect their Big Data solutions have on shaping behaviour and decision-making.
- **Environmental impact:** the effect that the use of Big Data technologies and applications have on the environment and the wellbeing of the planet. From a data perspective, organizations need to consider how their products and services will impact carbon emissions, pollution, transportation and waste.

An important thing to note about the sustainability capability is that both these per-spectives can either be negative or positive. When structuring and maturing the sustainability capability, organizations need to take both these perspectives into con-sideration.

10.2 Purpose and maturity levels of sustainability

Purpose

As discussed in Chapters 6 and 7, the formulation of a Big Data strategy helps or-ganizations to achieve a competitive advantage. With Big Data, companies can make quicker or better decisions, which ultimately leads to a monetary advantage in the form of increased profits. The sustainability capability considers the level at which companies are able to support a Big Data strategy that is not only profitable but also socially responsible and environmentally friendly. Since the importance of sustaina-bility is ever growing, this capability balances the monetary objectives of the Strategy Formulation capability (Chapter 6) and the Innovation capability (Chapter 7).

The purpose of the sustainability capability is to utilize Big Data to obtain social and environmental advantages, whilst minimizing the impact that Big Data storage and Big Data processing have on the environment. As such, sustainability is a clear opportunity for any enterprise. An organization that has a properly structured sus-tainability capability will not only see accelerated speed in the execution of the strat-egy, but also generally more positive press, industry recognition and the opportunity to attract talent. Terms like 'Green Big Data' or 'Social Big Data' are therefore fre-quently used by companies who aim to promote a more mature sustainability capa-bility in their organization.[3]

An important note about sustainability is that is a capability that must be embed-ded in the DNA of an organization and driven by the founders or senior leadership of the organization – from a sense of purpose. Setting high maturity ambitions that are unfeasible or not in line with the organization's core business can be seen as insincere

Table 10.1   The purpose of the sustainability capability

Capability	Purpose
Sustainability	Defines the ability of an organization to achieve their Big Data strategy in a sustainable way with minimal environmental impact, and positive social contributions.

or 'greenwashing', and will typically reflect negatively on the organization. It is therefore advisable to set achievable and properly motivated ambition levels for this capability.

Sustainability maturity levels

In general, sustainability and the sustainability maturity of organizations across the world is growing. Environmental and social awareness is becoming increasingly more important for any organization, and Big Data can have a significant impact on the way in which organizations achieve their sustainability targets and goals.

The sustainability maturity levels, as outlined in Table 10.2, can therefore be considered a first set of targets to make sustainability an integral part of a Big Data strategy. By defining a level of maturity for sustainability, organizations become aware of the impact that Big Data has on the organization's footprint. It will help start a discussion as to what extent Big Data contributes to the overall sustainability goals of the organization.

Table 10.2 Sustainability maturity levels

Maturity Level	Description
Level 1 – Initial	There is little or no awareness of social or environmental sustainability issues, or the way that data has an impact on sustainability. All data-related activities to increase sustainability goals are ad hoc.
Level 2 – Managed	There is an emerging level of awareness about sustainability. The organization has defined social and environmental sustainability goals that can be achieved through Big Data.
Level 3 – Defined	The organization incorporates defined sustainability goals. There is an active effort to use data analysis and Big Data to meet sustainability goals or reduce any negative social and environmental impact.
Level 4 – Controlled	The organization actively monitors how Big Data contributes towards the achievement of sustainability goals. There is an operational process that measures how Big Data is contributing to these goals, and based on these measurements and feedback, corrective actions are taken.
Level 5 – Optimized	Sustainability is an integral part of the way the organization operates. Social and environmental impact is assessed in every decision, and sustainability is considered a critical success factor in the execution of the Big Data strategy.

The sustainability maturity levels provide organizations with information that can help shape ambition levels. Although the concept of sustainability will be different depending on region, or type of industry, it is important that organizations consider this aspect of Big Data. As the world processes more and more data every day, the social and environmental impacts of data keep increasing. Making sustainability an integral part of a company's Big Data strategy is a first step towards the claim that Big Data has a positive contribution towards a more sustainable planet.

10.3 Structuring sustainability

The purpose of the sustainability capability is to ensure that organizations consider social implications and environmental impact in the execution of their Big Data strategy. Although many organizations have set high-level sustainability goals, considering the way data can contribute to the achievement of these goals is a relatively new domain. Big Data sustainability therefore offers a tremendous opportunity. Through data analysis, companies can obtain insights into their impact on the environment. Additionally, they can take measures (based on data) that can be used to actively contribute to the achievement of sustainability goals.

To benefit from the opportunities that Big Data brings in sustainability, it is first important that organizations understand how data can contribute towards the achievement or sustainability goals. Secondly, it is also important to understand what the adverse effects are from the use of Big Data, and how these adverse effects should be dealt with. Only when both these sides are properly understood can enterprises start to formulate sustainability goals for Big Data. Structuring the sustainability micro-capability is therefore a process that starts with understanding and ends with active approaches to increase the sustainability of the enterprise.

Big Data's contributions to sustainability

Big Data can be used for many purposes and many objectives. The wide variety of algorithms and models that exists (which will be further discussed in Part 5) can be used for an almost limitless number of possibilities.

As we have seen in the Strategy Formulation micro-capability (Chapter 6), many of these possibilities can be used to make the company operate in a more efficient manner, or to obtain a competitive advantage. The good news is that that many of these predictive techniques can also help to optimize social implications, or environmental impact.

Big Data's contributions can best be illustrated by an example that will showcase that Big Data is able to support an organization's financial and sustainability goals. Let's take a large grocery chain with multiple stores across a country. With Big Data technologies and algorithms, they can optimize the accuracy of the sales forecasts to 2 per cent, resulting in a better forecast of which products will be bought in which quantities by their consumers. Besides the obvious financial benefits (caused by more accurate purchasing of goods), there are numerous improvements towards sustainability objectives. Better forecasts will lead to less food waste, and fewer trucks that need to travel to supply these goods, which are clear environmental contributions. Additionally, it also means that the company is probably better able to restock supplies and can provide more stable work schedules for employees (a social contribution). Just a simple Big Data solution, like increasing forecast accuracy, can therefore have significant sustainability contributions.

The very simple example above is just a (non-numerical) illustration of the way in which Big Data can have a positive effect on a company's supply chain. We have chosen this high-level example because, at the moment of this book's publication, only very few case studies exist that showcase how enterprises use Big Data to achieve sustainability goals. Even fewer companies have actual processes and practices in

Table 10.3 Big Data sustainability categories

Category	Description
Supply Chain & Logistics	The most direct and visible optimizations are in operations and logistics. Sensors and data from supply chains can be used to optimize shipping, logistics and transportation. Big Data might provide more realistic and timely sales forecasts and, consequently, this might lead to reduction of unnecessary transport and waste.
Energy Usage	Big Data analytics can provide significant savings in the form of a reduction of energy consumption. Though sensors and predictive models, organizations can better forecast at which times energy is required, and either spread demand or reduce the need altogether.
Product Customization	Through Big Data, companies are in a better position to understand customer requirements. This will result in a better understanding of what is necessary from a customer point of view, so that companies can adjust or tailor products to individual needs. This subsequently leads to more durable products that will last for a longer period, hence reducing waste.
Work Predictability	A social optimization comes in the form of work predictability. Any company that is better able to predict workloads can plan resources and staff accordingly. This provides stability for employees and schedules, reducing the need for overtime and other disruptive work.
Performance Transparency	Big Data can make a fairer business ecosystem, where people are rewarded and promoted on personal, measurable merits. Through data, it is possible to achieve a fair and unbiased understanding of performance and results. These techniques can be utilized in HR and hiring processes, making the organization more transparent.

place that measure the contribution of data analysis and Big Data on their sustainability goals. It is fair to say that domain still provides a great opportunity for further development and enhancement. To address this void, a first step would be to outline major **Big Data sustainability categories**, as outlined in Table 10.3. These sustainability categories provide guidance on where organizations can find contributions of Big Data to their sustainability objectives.

The sustainability categories are a good place to get started for companies who would like to assess the way Big Data has a social or environmental impact. The difficult second step is to try to quantify savings and goals and express a way in which Big Data (and analytics decisions) contribute to achieving sustainability goals. There are many different ways to make these calculations, but it is common to use a standardized approach, such as the Global Reporting Initiative (GRI), and report on the organization's impacts on the economy, environment and people in a comparable and credible way.[4]

Big Data's adverse impact on sustainability

Besides the benefits that Big Data brings to organizations, it is important to also consider the adverse impacts on sustainability. The processing of data, almost by definition, consumes energy. The larger the dataset that needs to be analysed, the larger the energy consumption will be. And since everyone in the world is creating more and more data, and enterprises at the same time are processing more and more data, it means Big Data has a significant environmental impact. Globally, data centres that store and process data will become the world's largest users of energy consumption, with the ratio rising from 3 per cent in 2017 to 4.5 per cent in 2025.[5] And as this growth continues, criticism about the impact that Big Data has from an environmental point of view is growing. In many countries, laws are passed that regulate the allocation of data centre space and energy, and scrutiny of these operations is becoming more intense. These effects certainly need to be taken into consideration when determining the sustainability of Big Data.

Secondly, the social impact of Big Data needs to be considered. The fact that analytics and algorithms shape our lives and decisions, and the question of whether or not this is desirable, is a topic currently under heavy debate. The much-discussed Netflix documentary *The Social Dilemma* showcased that Big Data does not always lead to better decisions or better lives. And like with many other contested topics, organizations should consider the impact that their Big Data strategy has on people's lives, and the social impact it makes. Admittedly, it is a very fine line to walk, and many of the issues that Big Data brings highlight difficulties in our society. Is personalized information through algorithms beneficial, so that you can see news that interests you? Or is personalized information confirming people's currently belief systems (the confirmation bias), making society more polarized? There is not just one uniform answer to this question, and it is up to companies to balance enterprise needs with social impact.

Like the contributions towards sustainability, it is important that organizations find a suitable, consistent and effective way to measure how Big Data impacts sustainability, and also if it means these impacts are negative. Earlier, we discussed an example of a company that used Big Data and predictive analytics to optimize its supply chain. But suppose that – in this example – the energy cost of running the analysis in terabytes of data is higher than the potential savings in reduced shipping. Would that still contribute to the organization's sustainability goals? The main point here is that there are pros and cons to using Big Data to reach sustainability goals.

Table 10.4 Categories of adverse effects of Big Data

Category	Description
Energy consumption	Data storage and data analysis require the consumption of energy. For complicated and more advanced algorithms, this energy consumption can be significant. As part of its Big Data strategy, organizations need to take into consideration how much (additional) energy they will consume.
Targeting vulnerabilities	Algorithms (and especially classification algorithms) can be optimized to identify subgroups. This also means these algorithms can be used to identify vulnerable target groups that might be receptive to promotional advertisement, making donations or unhealthy products. Targeting vulnerable groups is known as algorithmic profiling, and a clear adverse effect of the use of Big Data.[1]
Discrimination	The use of Big Data can intentionally or unintendedly lead to discrimination. Discrimination happens when algorithmically driven solutions and services are offered differently to different people, based on religion, race, sexual orientation or disability.[2] Predictive algorithms (like multivariate regression and classifiers) can use feature selection and optimization methods to optimize based on discriminatory factors. Even though this form of discrimination is not always intentional, it has strong negative implications.
Political manipulation and social harm	Fake news, confirmation bias and political manipulation have been in the news frequently and have significant negative social implications. Even after the Cambridge Analytica scandal, different studies have shown that political manipulation and social harm are still practiced.[3]

1 M Büchi, E Fosch-Villaronga, C Lutz, A Tamò-Larrieux, S Velidi and S Viljoen. The chilling effects of algorithmic profiling: Mapping the issues, *Computer Law & Security Review*, 2020 36, 105367
2 T B Gillis and J L Spiess. Big data and discrimination, *The University of Chicago Law Review*, 2019 86 (2), 459–88
3 S C Woolley and P N Howard (2017) Computational Propaganda Worldwide: Executive Summary, Working Paper, 11. Oxford, UK: Project on Computational Propaganda, https://demtech.oii.ox.ac.uk/wp-content/uploads/sites/12/2017/06/Casestudies-ExecutiveSummary.pdf

Common categories that organizations need to take into consideration when it comes to sustainability in Big Data are listed in Table 10.4.

Are these adverse effects so significant that they outweigh the potential benefits? Only time will tell. The reality is that the vast majority of enterprise organizations are not significantly involved in any practices that might willingly or unwillingly lead to significant adverse effects. Being aware, and measuring any adverse effects, will already make most organizations far ahead of other competitors. In addition, maturity in the communication capability (discussed in Chapter 9) will help organizations to communicate about any issues transparently.

Defining a Big Data sustainability process

In the two previous sections, we considered Big Data's positive contributions towards sustainability, as well as a few adverse effects. Understanding sustainability is truly the first step towards incorporating the Big Data strategy. The next step is to grow maturity in this micro-capability. To grow maturity in this capability, the most crucial step is recognition. Recognition that Big Data and sustainability are strongly correlated (further explained in Part 5), and recognition that activities would need to be undertaken to measure and mitigate social implications and environmental impact.

One of the first steps that every organization can take is to set up a **Big Data sustainability process**. A Big Data sustainability process consists of several repetitive steps and activities that ensure sustainability is firmly embedded in the Big Data strategy. A high-level design of such a process is depicted in Figure 10.1. The process starts with defining yearly sustainability goals, and end with a yearly report on the progress, results and lessons learned. With this simple process, which can be adapted and adopted as the enterprise sees fit, a major step is established: sustainability becomes part of the Big Data strategy.

The Big Data sustainability process, although depicted linearly, is in fact cyclical and this cycle should be completed on an annual basis. For consistency with annual reporting and planning, it is recommended that this cycle follows the yearly accounting period of the organization.

The establishment of a Big Data sustainability process, even in its most rudimentary form, says something about the visions and drivers for sustainability in an organization. Organizations who have established (mature) sustainability processes typically drive on sustainable progress and view Big Data as a means to reach this goal. Organizations that lack any form of sustainability, on the other hand, frequently see Big Data as a commercial opportunity, and have quite a few steps to take to realize the potential of Big Data in a sustainable way.

Figure 10.1 Big Data sustainability process

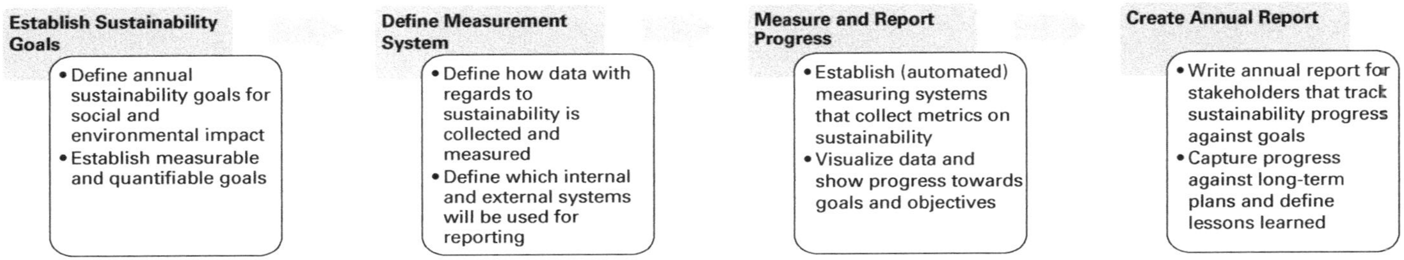

Establish Sustainability Goals

- Define annual sustainability goals for social and environmental impact
- Establish measurable and quantifiable goals

Define Measurement System

- Define how data with regards to sustainability is collected and measured
- Define which internal and external systems will be used for reporting

Measure and Report Progress

- Establish (automated) measuring systems that collect metrics on sustainability
- Visualize data and show progress towards goals and objectives

Create Annual Report

- Write annual report for stakeholders that track sustainability progress against goals
- Capture progress against long-term plans and define lessons learned

Sustainability profiles

The Big Data sustainability process covers quite a bit of ground for organizations who have just started building their sustainability micro-capability. More mature organizations, who typically already have these processes in place, are confronted with a second challenge. As we discussed in section 10.1, the major domains of sustainability in Big Data are **social implications** and **environmental impact**. And since both domains are different, some organizations can focus more on their social impact, whereas others prefer to focus more on their environmental impact.

It is important to consider that in sustainability it is not the case that one domain is better than the other. Although the environmental aspects (Green Big Data) are recently featured more, it does not mean that they are more important than social considerations. Organizations can choose to focus or excel in one domain or can chose to focus on both.

A model that showcases different approaches is depicted in Figure 10.2, which views social implications and environmental impact as two different axes that describe sustainability.

Social implications and environmental impact are the two axes of sustainability. Organizations that choose to focus more on social achievements (for example oil

Figure 10.2   The Enterprise Big Data Framework sustainability model

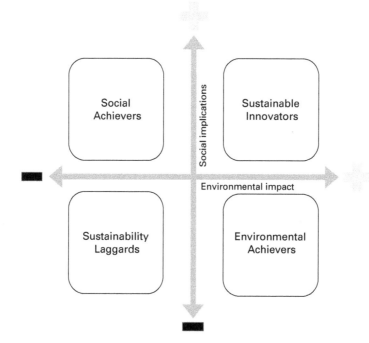

and gas companies) leverage Big Data to enhance social benefits through data analysis and can therefore be considered **Social Achievers**. Companies that are clearly taking environmental aspects into consideration (for example Electric Vehicle manufacturers) focus on using Big Data to reduce carbon emissions and can be labelled as **Environmental Achievers**. Both types of organizations are achievers from a sustainability point of view but choose to use Big Data for different purposes.

Organizations that don't focus on either of the two domains (**sustainability laggards**) are characterized by low levels of maturity in the sustainability micro-capability. Organizations that are in the top right corner are those who use Big Data for a greater purpose, and typically gather positive press (and sometimes fame) with their approach. These **sustainable innovators** include companies like the toy manufacturer Lego, who are using Big Data to drive sustainable innovation.[6] For a company that started out producing and selling plastics as its main product, it provides a good case study on how Big Data and sustainability can reinforce each other.

10.4 Sustainability summary

In this chapter, we covered the sustainability micro-capability in quite some detail. It is nothing new to state that sustainability is becoming increasingly more important. What is new, however, is the impact that Big Data has on achieving sustainability targets. The topics of Big Data and sustainability are strongly correlated, and organizations who aim to become Sustainable Innovators will need to make sustainability an integral part of their strategy.

There are many aspects to consider when it comes to Big Data and sustainability. Some of these aspects have very positive effects, whereas others might bring adverse impact to sustainability. Even though much of the research regarding these effects is still in the early stages, organizations can already start defining goals, processes and measurement systems to build their own sustainability agenda. They can determine how Big Data can be used to create positive social implications and reduce their carbon footprint (environmental implications).

There are many ways in which organizations can make sustainability an integral part of their Big Data strategies. The most important first step in building capability is that organizations start understanding how Big Data can be used to achieve sustainability targets, where potential opportunities lie and also which risks need to be considered. The sustainability micro-capability is an integral part of a Big Data strategy. Because to win in the data economy, data should be used in a sustainable manner.

Notes

1 P Shrivastava and N Guimarães-Costa. Achieving environmental sustainability: The case for multi-layered collaboration across disciplines and players, *Technological Forecasting and Social Change*, 2017 116, 340–46

2 M Song, L Cen, Z Zheng, R Fisher, X Liang, Y Wang and D Huisingh. How would big data support societal development and environmental sustainability? Insights and practices. *Journal of Cleaner Production*, 2017 142, 489–500

3 J Wu, S Guo, J Li and D Zeng. Big data meet green challenges: Greening big data, *IEEE Systems Journal*, 2016 10 (3), 873–87

4 Global Reporting Initiative (2021) www.globalreporting.org/Pages/default.aspx (archived at https://perma.cc/4F8H-6C35)

5 Y Liu, X Wei, J Xiao, Z Liu, Y Xu and Y Tian. Energy consumption and emission mitigation prediction based on data center traffic and PUE for global data centers, *Global Energy Interconnection*, 2020 3 (3), 272–82

6 R N Lussier (2016) *Lego Learns to Make Sustainable Environmental Decisions*. SAGE Publications, Inc.

Programme Funding

11

11.1 Introduction to programme funding

Big Data is a business decision. The analysis of large data sets is only useful if it provides value, and when it provides a sound return on investment (ROI). The programme funding micro-capability considers the financial aspects of structuring and running a Big Data programme. Programme funding should be an integral part of a Big Data strategy, bringing focus to the question of whether the investments in Big Data tools and technology are worth it, and whether the Big Data programme is generating enough funds to sustain itself.

Many if not most organizations have limited experience and practice in managing this capability as part of their Big Data strategy. Funding for Big Data programmes usually comes from the enterprise IT budget, and is allocated to specific cost centres (instead of profit centres). There are, however, two strong reasons why it is beneficial for any organization to consider Big Data programme funding as a separate capability:

- The discussion about how a Big Data programme needs to be funded implicitly starts the discussion about the value of the programme. It is apparent that any Big Data initiative or programme requires investment and running cost. But the question of funding is not as straightforward. Where does the money come from to sustain the programme? Does the Big Data programme provide additional revenues? Or does it cut costs in other business lines that can be allocated to the Big Data programme? Answering these questions will inherently bring back the discussion about the ROI, as discussed in Chapter 6 (Strategy Formulation).

- How the Big Data programme will be funded will determine the internal positioning of the Big Data organization, and in particular the Big Data Centre of Excellence (introduced in Part 7). A Big Data function that will be operating as a cost centre will have a different position than a Big Data function operating as a profit centre. In the former, there is frequently increased focus on cost containment, whereas in the latter there is primary focus on innovation.

It is therefore safe to say that a strong programme funding capability enhances the strength of an organization's overall Big Data Strategy. By establishing this capability, organizations can determine and set the appropriate funding levels to drive their Big Data programmes not just as individual projects, but on a long-term strategic basis.

11.2 Purpose and maturity levels of programme funding

Purpose

With a strong and mature programme funding capability, the Big Data programme will be considered a strategic initiative in the enterprise. By establishing this capability, organizations will move into a continuous cycle of planning, budgeting and control of the Big Data activities that the organization is conducting.

Besides the obvious financial benefits of establishing this capability (more structured oversight and cost control), there are several non-financial benefits. These benefits include internal and external perception, the importance of Big Data in the organization and the commitment towards a long-term data-driven organization.

The purpose of the programme funding micro-capability is outlined in Table 11.1.

The programme funding capability will link the Big Data function (typically part of the IT organization) to the finance department of the organization. A strong finance function can therefore significantly help with establishing (or expediting) the development of this capability.

Maturity levels

To develop and grow the maturity of the programme funding capability, organizations need to develop a structured approach to **budgeting, benchmarking, and funding models.** This structured approach can help move an organization from a case-by-case decision-making process towards a planned, organized and proactive programme funding capability. These individual topics will be further explained in section 11.3.

Table 11.1 The purpose of the programme funding capability

Capability	Purpose
Programme funding	Defines the ability to secure the availability of adequate and sustainable financing to support Big Data initiatives and their corresponding budgets.

Whether an organization currently has a separate programme funding capability for Big Data solutions (or a Big Data Centre of Excellence) says a lot about the strategic importance of Big Data. Organizations where Big Data programme funding is considered typically use data more strategically. Organizations that are still in the early stages of developing this capability, on the other hand, generally still have work to become a data-driven enterprise. Table 11.2 outlines the five maturity levels of the programme funding capability.

At the highest level of maturity, the programme funding capability would be akin to corporate business planning. The Big Data function, at this level, operates as if it was an individual company or organization. This means that the Big Data services and solutions create such a level of visible or monetary value that the Big Data function is self-sustainable. If there is no demand from internal business units, there would be demand for these services from external companies.

It is important to note this highest level of programme funding maturity, because it means that at the level 5 (optimized) level of maturity, the Big Data function is a company within a company. Even without the mandated internal usage, the organization

Table 11.2 Programme funding levels

Maturity Level	Description
Level 1 – Initial	Funding levels and budget allocations for Big Data initiatives and solutions are determined in an ad hoc manner. Funding for Big Data projects is a sub-component of the enterprise IT budget.
Level 2 – Managed	Big Data programme funding levels are based on historic overviews, with minimal deviations and a limited number of funding allocations based on the requirements of specific Big Data projects. Big Data programme funding is considered a cost centre within the enterprise IT budget.
Level 3 – Defined	The funding of Big Data projects is determined on business cases and individual merits. The organization realizes that Big Data solutions and services can have a positive ROI, and therefore programme funding is adjusted accordingly. Programme funding is available from the centralized IT budget, but also from individual business units.
Level 4 – Controlled	Programme funding of the Big Data functions is adjusted in line with the business strategy and can be dynamically adjusted. The Big Data function operates as a profit centre, where Big Data solutions and services are funded by the value they generate.
Level 5 – Optimized	Programme funding levels and allocations for Big Data projects can be dynamically adjusted based on continual review cycles. The Big Data function operates as a separate organization which is self-sustainable.

would prosper. It is not hard to see that at this level, Big Data programmes are considered an essential part of the strategy of any organization.

11.3 Structuring programme funding

Structuring the programme funding capability starts with sound control of financial processes. In every enterprise organization, financial planning processes are undertaken on an annual basis, and are led by the senior executives of the organization.[1] In this section, we will consider approaches and techniques that can help to shape and grow this capability.

By establishing a mature programme funding capability, organizations can safeguard adequate investments that deliver on the strategic initiatives of the organization. By determining adequate funding levels, selecting the appropriate funding sources and assigning the proper funds for Big Data programmes, it become possible to effectively govern the value of the Big Data function.

In this section, we will focus on three structuring approaches: budgeting, benchmarking and funding models. Each of these structuring techniques is relatively easy to apply, and each of them provide significant contributions to develop the programme funding capability.

Programme budgeting

The first question that comes with any corporate investment is: Where does the budget come from? In Big Data programmes and initiatives this is no different. For any Big Data function to operate, a significant amount of money is required. Salaries need to be paid, storage and processing costs need to be paid to vendors and significant investments are required to manage large volumes of enterprise data daily.

A Big Data programme budget plan is a financial statement that outlines proposed expenditures for the Big Data function over a predetermined period, usually a year. An example of common line items of a Big Data programme budget plan includes hardware, software, processing and storage (cloud) expenses, personal and training expenses.

A Big Data budget plan should be complete in itself and provide enough visibility to indicate which expenses would be required to operate a Big Data function independently, and without reliability on other enterprise functions. It should reflect the 'true cost' of operating a Big Data function, and pro-rata shared resources. For example, if cloud computing power is shared between the Big Data analytics team and the finance team, the Big Data budget plan should allocate the percentage of resources they use.

It is important to separate the Big Data budget plan from the overall enterprise IT budget. The Big Data budget plan is obviously a subset of the enterprise IT budget, but it is important to know the exact costing of the Big Data function. To establish sound programme funding, it is first imperative to have an exact overview of the incurred costs. Allocating a fixed percentage of the overall IT budget to the Big Data function does not meet this requirement.

The purpose of preparing an annual Big Data budget plan is twofold:

1 It provides a precise overview of the cost for operating the Big Data function (or Big Data Centre of Excellence) as if it were a separate entity. Understanding the cost model is important to determine how the programme will be funded.

2 It establishes a sense of the value a Big Data function needs to deliver in providing the organization with a suitable return on investment. This values perception is important, because it can subsequently be used to define and calculate the business case for the Big Data function.

The Big Data budget plan should be reviewed and accepted by senior management and be 'owned' by the person in charge of the Big Data function. In most organizations, Big Data Centres of Excellence have different names (Analytics Team, Data Discovery Team, Big Data Team, etc.), but regardless of the name, it should be the budget that covers the functional unit concerned with extracting value from massive quantities of data.

Benchmarking

Benchmarking will help grow the capability of programme funding. With benchmarking, we mean comparing the organization's Big Data budget plan with other (similar or competitive) organizations. The purpose of benchmarking is to gain a better understanding as to whether the cost component of an organization's Big Data budget plans are above or below industry averages.

If a Big Data budget plan is above industry average (in terms of cost), it might be the case that the Big Data function can increase efficiency or become leaner. In a competitive environment, this would indicate that the Big Data function is underperforming (compared to its peers) and would not be self-sustaining. It is important to know this information to structure where funding needs to come from.

Finding sound Big Data benchmarking information is difficult, and there is not one single, absolute authority in this field. Reliable sources generally include IT research firms (Gartner, Forrester, etc.) that periodically benchmark Big Data spend across leading organizations.

The purpose of the benchmarking exercise is simple: is the organization spending (comparatively) more or less than industry peers? Knowing this information provides insights to how a Big Data function can be funded to become self-sustaining (i.e. maturity level 5).

Funding models

As soon as the (benchmarked) expense model of the Big Data function is established, an organization can devise its funding model. With the funding model, an organization can establish where the funds (or revenues) are coming from to sustain itself. The main choice that any organization needs to make is whether the Big Data function will be considered a **cost centre** or **profit centre**. An overview of different funding options is shown in Table 11.3.

The main difference between a cost centre and a profit centre is that a cost centre is only responsible for its costs whereas a profit centre is responsible for both its revenues and costs. Another difference is that cost centres tend to be organizationally simple, while profit centres are more likely to have a complex structure.

From an experience and perception perspective this difference is of paramount importance. Organizations that operate their Big Data function as a cost centre will

Table 11.3   Big Data funding models

Cost Centre (internal funding models)

Corporate IT budget: a fixed percentage of the IT budget is allocated to the Big Data budget plan.

Fixed contribution: different business units contribute a fee per employee to account for the Big Data function.

Pay-per-use: different business units contribute fees based on usage of Big Data solutions (e.g. data processes or data stored).

Profit Centre (external funding models)

Internal sales: The Big Data function sells its services to other business units, without mandatory purchase by the business units.

External sales: The Big Data functions sells its services to external clients and is paid through charging fees (revenue-generating model).

Vendor payment: The Big Data function is (partially) funded by vendors.

Government contributions: The Big Data function is funded by (partial) government (innovation) grants to support its cost structure.

---

face more challenges in the execution of their strategy. Internal units pay fixed fees, so there is typically a low perception of the value that the Big Data organization brings. In contrast, organizations that operate their Big Data function as a profit centre see a stronger focus on innovation, customer services and meeting the demands of the business.

Moving towards a profit centre is challenging, but ultimately worth the effort. A Big Data function that is self-sustaining, in control of its own cost and needs to 'sell' its services to others (even if it is internally) will have more incentives to adapt to customer demand, and provide Big Data products and services that are relevant in the market.

11.4 Programme funding summary

The programme funding capability considers the financial aspect of the Big Data strategy macro-capability. It helps every organization to determine not only what their strategy is (or should be), but how this strategy can be financially sustainable. How will the cost of the Big Data function be structured and, ultimately, who is going to pay for this?

In this chapter, we looked in more depth at the establishment of the programme funding capability, and how it can be developed. The goal of the programme funding capability is to ensure that Big Data programmes have sufficient resources and money to operate, whilst staying competitive to industry peers. Different techniques, such as budgeting, benchmarking and funding models, contribute to the establishment and growth of this capability.

Note

1 L Cao, K Mohan, B Ramesh and S Sarkar. Adapting funding processes for agile IT projects: an empirical investigation, *European Journal of Information Systems*, 2013 22 (2), 191–205

Big Data Strategy Maturity Assessment

## 12

Please respond to the following questions by indicating the relevant level of maturity for each activity in question and its importance to your organization.

The Capability Maturity Model levels are shown in Table 12.1.

Please note that responses to this survey should reflect how the organization performs the task today, not how you would like to see the organization perform the task in the future. Your choices should be based on your opinion of the organization, not just the way the task is performed in your own workgroup.

Table 12.1 Capability Maturity Model levels

Score	Description
0 – Non-existent	Describes a total lack of activity or lack of recognition that the activity exists.
1 – Initial	Describes evidence that the organization recognizes issues exist and need to be addressed.
2 – Managed	Describes activities designed so that similar procedures are followed by individuals. There is a high reliance on individual knowledge and skill level.
3 – Defined	Describes a standardized and documented level of activities, which is being communicated through training, processes and tools.
4 – Controlled	Describes activities which are good practice and under constant improvement. Automation and tools are used to support the activities.
5 – Optimized	Describes activities that are considered leading and 'best practice' and can be considered an example to other organizations.

Table 12.2 Big Data Strategy Maturity Assessment

Strategy Formulation	Score

1.1 A long-term vision has been documented that outlines how Big Data can provide value to our organization.

1.2 Our organization periodically identifies the risk and opportunities that Big Data technology can bring.

1.3 There is a uniform approach to capturing and evaluating potential Big Data Use Cases that bring value to the organization.

1.4 Senior leadership formulates the Big Data strategy and communicates this to other parts of the organization.

1.5 Our organization has a clearly identified Big Data roadmap with documented use cases that contribute to business value.

1.6 The organization periodically assesses its Big Data capabilities and makes plans to improve these capabilities.

Innovation Management	Score

2.1 Big Data tools and solutions are used to drive innovation and develop new products and services.

2.2 Our organization encourages innovation and provides resources to foster a culture of innovations.

2.3 Big Data is used to collect and analyse customer feedback so that this feedback can be used in future products and services.

2.4 Internal training programmes are organized to teach staff how data can be used to drive innovation.

2.5 Senior leadership leads innovation efforts and is driving awareness on data-driven innovation.

2.6 Our organization uses Big Data tools and solutions to measure the performance of products to determine how they can be improved.

Leadership and Governance	Score

3.1 Our organization has established a Big Data Governance Body that formulates data governance policies.

3.2 Clear goals and targets have been defined that measure the success of our Big Data programmes and initiatives.

3.3 Large-scale Big Data programmes are broken down into manageable roadmaps and corresponding planning.

3.4 Leadership provides inspiring communication to showcase how Big Data can transform the organization.

(*continued*)

Table 12.2   (Continued)

3.5	Monitoring and control processes and frameworks have been established that measure whether the organization meets its strategic objectives.
3.6	A clear leadership structure has been established that defines roles and responsibilities within the Big Data function.

Communication	**Score**
4.1	The goals and objectives of the enterprise Big Data strategy are documented in a communication plan and are communicated across the enterprise.
4.2	Employees in the organization are familiar with and knowledgeable on how Big Data is impacting work and roles over the next few years.
4.3	There is periodic communication about Big Data roadmaps, plans, use cases and expected timelines.
4.4	There is periodic communication about Big Data policies, including data privacy and data security policies.
4.5	Our organization uses a mix of communication media to cater to different target audiences and matches the message to the medium.
4.6	There are guidelines and procedures about data that can be shared internally and data that can be shared externally.

Sustainability	**Score**
5.1	A sustainability policy has been documented that outlines how the organization aims to use Big Data (products and service) in a sustainable way.
5.2	Our organization has documented sustainability goals for social and environmental impact.
5.3	A measurement system exists through which our organization measures and collects data about the social and environmental impact of using Big Data.
5.4	Our organization has processes in place that report measurements on social and environmental impact, and measures are taken to mitigate impact.
5.5	Our organization creates an annual public report that showcases how the organization deals with social and environmental impact.
5.6	Awareness campaigns and communication exist that explain the impact of using Big Data solutions and services in the organization.

(continued)

Table 12.2   (Continued)

Programme Funding	Score
6.1 Our organization is aware of the cost structure of the Big Data organization and has a detailed breakdown of these costs.	
6.2 An annual Big Data budget plan is created and approved by senior management, outlining the costs of the Big Data function.	
6.3 Our organization performs benchmarking exercises to determine whether the costs of the Big Data function is in line with industry peers.	
6.4 Our Big Data function operates as a profit centre and can charge, or cross-charge, other business units based on services provided.	
6.5 It is clear to everyone in the organization how Big Data programmes are funded, and how budgets are obtained for proceeding with Big Data projects.	
6.6 Our enterprise Big Data function is considered competitive and could operate as a self-sustaining organization.	

PART FOUR
Designing a Big Data Architecture

Big Data Architecture

13

13.1 Introduction to Big Data architecture

Processing terabytes of data within seconds to make real-time decisions sounds like something that is simple to realize nowadays. We all experience the speed with which it is possible to search through large collections of data sets when we are using search engines, or search for directions on our phones. However, from a technical perspective, this is not nearly as easy as it seems. Storing massive quantities of data, and analysing these massive amounts of data, brings some significant technical constraints. In order to overcome these constraints, organizations that aim to leverage the benefits of Big Data (as discussed in Part 3) need to design and structure a technology stack that can process data in high volumes, and with high velocity. In other words, these organizations need to design a Big Data architecture.

In this next section of the Enterprise Big Data Framework, we will cover the technological capabilities that are required to make Big Data successful in an enterprise. We will look at the technical limits of storing and processing data, and how organizations can design solutions to address these limits. To design a sound Big Data architecture, it is important to have an in-depth understanding of how exactly data is stored and processed. In this section we will therefore introduce some technical concepts and technologies, which will explain common design choices in Big Data architecture. For readers who don't have a computer science background, we will also explain some fundamental technical concepts about data storage and data processing.

As we noted in Part 2, one of the primary characteristics of the Enterprise Big Data Framework is that it is **vendor independent**. The capabilities that are presented in this book can be applied to any organization, regardless of its technology stack and choice of software vendors. From a Big Data capability point of view, it does not matter which vendors provide the data stores or the analytics applications to obtain value from data.

Yet the reality is that most enterprises will purchase commercial solutions to design their Big Data architecture and to set up their technology stack. It would be an mistake to think that every company builds their Big Data solutions from scratch. To address this paradox, we will be using the structure of **reference architectures**.

A **reference architecture** is a high-level design that explains the structure and purpose of individual components of a system, without going into the specifics of vendors that deliver this technology. To make a simple analogy, a reference architecture explains the components that are necessary to build a car, without advising whether the engine is coming from Honda, Volkswagen or Ferrari. The main benefit of this approach is that every enterprise can decide by themselves which solutions are best utilized to realize their Big Data strategy. A reference architecture enables us to present a uniform approach, which can subsequently be tailored by every organization.

Just like the sound architecture of a building determines the quality, durability and ultimately cost of a structure, a sound Big Data architecture determines the quality, speed and costs of processing massive quantities of data. Some architectural designs are robust and able to weather unexpected situations or accommodate growth, whereas other architectures might collapse (or crash in IT terms) if unexpected situations occur. It can, without a doubt, be stated that some architectures are just better than others, which makes the topic of Big Data architecture a distinct capability. By the end of this section, we hope you will have mastered some of the capabilities that contribute to a sound design for your own Big Data architecture, and that you understand the fundamental components that contribute to this architecture. To quote one of the most famous architects of all time:

> The noblest pleasure is the joy of understanding – Leonardo Da Vinci

13.2 Fundamental structure of Big Data architecture

Before we dive into the technical details of Big Data architecture, and the many smart variations that have been invented over the last decades, it is important to compartmentalize some of the main operations that make up any Big Data environment. When we think about contemporary Big Data solutions, we always start from the point of collection of data (for example through human-generated or machine-generated data, as discussed in Chapter 3 section 3.2). This first function is known as **data ingestion**, and from an architectural point of view, this means that tools and processes are required to facilitate these operations.

The data that is collected needs to be stored in a particular location. In most enterprise scenarios, this storage will be provided by cloud solutions (as discussed in Chapter 3 section 3.3). The function of **data storage** is essential to any Big Data solution and will therefore be a central component of any Big Data architecture. As we will discuss later, there are dozens of different Big Data storage solutions, but they all have one thing in common: ultimately, they store bits and bytes on physical storage devices.

Figure 13.1 Three basic components of Big Data architecture

Once data has been ingested, and it is properly stored, we can perform activities where hidden knowledge is uncovered through algorithms, which represents the **data processing** function of Big Data architecture. Although there are hundreds, if not thousands, of algorithms that can be applied (we will discuss the most important statistical, machine learning and AI algorithms in Part 5), they all require processing power to be executed. Figure 13.1 illustrates how these three building blocks work together to provide the basic structure of Big Data architecture:

- **Data ingestion** refers to the architectural function to collect (from multiple disparate sources), categorize and clean data before it is imported into the enterprise data lake. Data ingestion remains one of the main Big Data challenges from an infrastructure requirement. The infrastructure required to support the acquisition of Big Data must deliver low, predictable latency in both capturing data and in executing queries. Additionally, it must be able to handle very high transaction volumes, often in a distributed environment and support flexible and dynamic data structures.[1]

- **Data storage** refers to the architectural function that needs to store high-volume, disparate formats in a scalable and efficient way. In most enterprise environments, the data storage that is used for Big Data solutions and applications is referred to as an enterprise data lake. A data lake is a distributed storage repository that holds a vast amount of raw data in its native format until it needs to be processed by Big Data applications or solutions. A data lake uses a flat architecture to store data, so that the data requirements are not defined until the data is processed.[2]

- **Data processing** refers to the architectural function that is able to translate the raw data (frequently from a data lake) into a meaningful result for the organization. In almost all cases, this means specific algorithms need to run that can query or process the data. The required capacity that is necessary to 'crunch the numbers' is provided by the processing infrastructure. Because speed is of the essence for data processing, most architectures use distributed data processing designs, where resources (i.e. data processing units) run parallel to facilitate large workloads.

Throughout the rest of this section, where we introduce common architectural models and designs, we will adhere to this division into three fundamental components.

13.3 Purpose and structure of Big Data architecture

One of the fundamental design principles of the Enterprise Big Data Framework is that it provides vendor independent capabilities to set up and structure Big Data solutions. Of all the macro-capabilities discussed in this publication, the Big Data architecture section is most likely the most difficult chapter to discuss from a vendor-independent point of view. Almost every corporate solution will be based on propriety technology from vendors.

To overcome this challenge, we will introduce Big Data architecture, and its corresponding design principles, based on the high-level design principles of a **reference architecture**. A reference architecture is a document or set of documents that provides recommended structures and integrations of IT products and services to form a solution. The reference architecture embodies accepted industry best practices, typically suggesting the optimal delivery method for specific technologies.[3] The reference architecture that will be used as the main structure in this publication is the **NIST Big Data Reference Architecture (NBDRA)**.

The NBDRA, which will be discussed in detail in the following section, provides a uniform design of all the components that are necessary to set up a Big Data environment. Some of the benefits of using a reference architecture include:

- A reference architecture is vendor independent. We can discuss the components, and technical requirement of each component, without a specific vendor solution in mind. When we discuss storage mechanisms, for example, we can focus on database design choices without pre-selecting a proprietary solution.

- A reference architecture is based on best practices, and knowledge that has been acquired over many years. For any enterprise, with strict governance and security requirements, it would be unwise to make a design 'from scratch'. Building on established best practices and experiences from other organizations (especially from internationally recognized institutions such as NIST) reduces design risk.

- A reference architecture is enduring. Whereas technologies and tools change frequently to stay competitive, their underlying function remains the same. Regardless of which technology you choose for data processing, its purpose is to execute an algorithm on an underlying data set. A sound reference architecture is therefore enduring and brings stability to the ever-changing landscape of Big Data tools.

Figure 13.2   The micro-capabilities of Big Data architecture

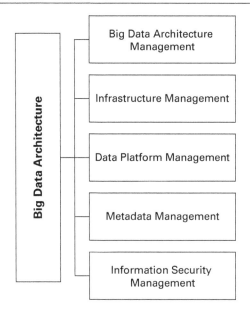

Because of the benefits listed above, we will largely base the capability discussion about Big Data architecture on the coherent design of a Big Data Reference Architecture. This architecture needs to provide the underlying technology to enable enterprise organizations to retrieve value from massive data sets.

The Big Data architecture capability is defined as an organization's ability to effectively design and manage an IT environment that allows the organization to ingest, store and process data in a fast, secure and cost-efficient way.

As with the other capabilities, maturity towards higher levels for this capability can develop over time. With the introduction of tools and new solutions, organizations can make their IT infrastructure more robust, secure or available. The various micro-capabilities, outlined in Figure 13.2, provide core focus areas that build a robust architecture. Beside the micro-capabilities that are an integral part of the reference architecture (and which every Big Data organization needs in some form), privacy and security are also an essential micro-capability that is part of a sound design.

13.4 The NIST Big Data Reference Architecture

The National Institute of Standards and Technology (NIST) is a physical sciences laboratory and non-regulatory agency of the United States Department of Commerce. Its mission is to promote American innovation and industrial competitiveness. NIST is internationally renowned for its standards and publications.[4]

The NBDRA was created, following a highly structured process, through a working group that analysed different use cases, and the way successful organizations structure their Big Data environment.[5] More importantly, the NBDRA is an **open standard**, in line with the vendor-independent approach of the Enterprise Big Data Framework.

In the rest of this chapter, we will use the guidelines from the NBDRA to define which capabilities organizations can develop to build a fast, secure and cost-efficient Big Data architecture. Besides the general benefits of using a reference architecture in general (outlined in section 13.3), the NBDRA will bring organizations the following benefits:

- The use of a Big Data Reference Architecture will bring standardization in terms of common language and taxonomies in every organization that uses it.
- The use of a Big Data Reference Architecture separates the discussion of 'design' from the discussion about tools and products. Whereas tools change over time, or can be upgraded, the reference architecture remains consistent.
- It improves your understanding about the way Big Data environments are structured conceptually, and from a best practice design.

The adoption of the NBDRA model provides organizations with the possibility to constantly evolve their technical Big Data environment, without changing the underlying structure and design of their architecture.

A high-level overview of the NBDRA is provided in Figure 13.3. It provides the basis for the way in which an organization can design its capabilities. It can be used as a blueprint, to support organizations to enhance their understanding (and hence capability) of Big Data architectures. In this section, we will first provide an overview of the core components of the reference architecture. In Chapters 14 to 18, we will subsequently examine different capabilities in further detail.

13.5 Value chains of the NBDRA

The NIST Big Data Reference Architecture is structured around five critical roles, multiple sub-roles and is aligned along two value chains: the **Information Value Chain** (displayed horizontally) and the **Information Technology Value Chain** (displayed vertically).

With the use of the two value chains, it immediately becomes clear that the goal of the Big Data architecture is to provide value and decision-making capability, by moving towards the top-right corner. Centrally located, in the middle of the two axes, is the Big Data Application Provider. This role indicates that data analytics (and

Figure 13.3 The NIST Big Data Reference Architecture (NBDRA)

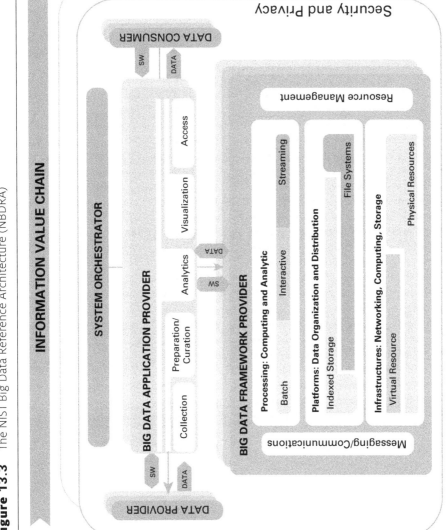

Table 13.1   Value chains in the NBDRA

Value Chains	Description
Information Value Chain	The Information Value Chain showcases that every step in the processing of data is adding additional value to an enterprise. As we move from left to right in the information value chain, every step adds value. The input (data provider) consists of raw data, which has limited value to organizations, whereas the output (data consumer) provides information upon which organizations can base their decisions.
Information Technology Value Chain	The Information Technology Value Chain showcases that every step in an organization's IT infrastructure is adding value to the enterprise. As we move from the bottom to the top, value is created by providing networking, infrastructure, platforms and applications. This infrastructure ultimately supports the Big Data applications that are used by business users.

its implementation) provide value to both business stakeholders (information value chain) and technology stakeholders (IT value chain).

13.6 The five main roles of the NBDRA

The NBDRA is structured around five critical Big Data roles. As shown in Figure 13.3, these roles represent the core of the NBDRA, and represent the technical roles that need to exist in every Big Data ecosystem. Data will flow between each of these five different roles with the objective to create more value for the organization. Data can physically move between the roles or through software tools. The third option of data transfer and communication indicates software programmable interfaces. Through these three forms of dynamic communication, an ecosystem can be structured in which data flows through the organization, based on enterprise needs.

Note that there might be multiple instances of one role. For example, in almost all cases there will be multiple input data sources, which all have the role of a Data Provider. These multiple instances create a dynamic network of information, creating a **Big Data ecosystem** that requires continuous updates and care.

1 Data Provider

The **Data Provider** role represents the start of the Information Value Chain and introduces new data into the Big Data ecosystem. As such, the Data Provider provides the data sources that an enterprise would like to have under management and introduces new data sources in the organization. Every new data source can (potentially) be used by the organization to obtain value. There are various systems that can function as a data provider, depending on the nature of the organization. As discussed in section 3.2, these are known as data generators. The two most common data generators are human-generated data and machine-generated data. Every data source or **data generator** will (from an architecture point of view) have the role of a data provider. For example, a sensor that detects and logs information in a jet engine is a data generator, functioning in the role of Data Provider.

One of the key characteristics of Big Data environment is the ability to import and use data from a variety of different sources (the variability characteristic, discussed in Chapter 2 section 2.2). The sources can have all types of formats, like text, images videos, sensory data or other types of data. Because there are potentially endless different data sources, the Data Provider role provides an abstraction from the actual data source. Even if the data source is not actively managed by the organization itself (for instance Twitter data, residing on Twitter servers), it is still fulfilling the role of Data Provider. This abstraction makes it easy and understandable to consider any data input into the Big Data Ecosystem a data provider.

Most enterprises will have hundreds, if not thousands, of instances which will function in the role of Data Provider. To keep a broad oversight, most enterprises structure their collection of input data sets (source data) into a **data lake**. A data lake is a technical storage solution (and therefore part of the Big Data Framework Provider role), with vast amounts of raw data in its native format until it needs to be processed by Big Data applications or solutions. A data lake additionally makes it easy to search and order data in systematic ways into different **data catalogues**.

2 Big Data Framework Provider

The **Big Data Framework Provider** role consists of all the IT components that are necessary to store, manage and process data. It provides the core functionality and IT infrastructure to operate a Big Data environment. The Big Data Framework provider role is therefore fully integrated in the enterprise IT environment of an organization. It consists of servers, networking, storage solutions and processors that form the core of any IT environment. In most enterprise organizations, these resources and instances are frequently managed in a cloud environment (see Chapter 3 section 3.3)

The benefit of the abstract role of the Big Data Framework Provider is that there are no requirements for technology, and organizations can select solutions (and vendors) based on their own requirements. A database solution, for example, will, from an architecture point of view, fulfill the role of Big Data Framework Provider, regardless of whether these databases are sourced from Microsoft or AWS. In fact, most enterprise organizations have hybrid environments that consist of multiple solutions and multiple IT vendors.

As demonstrated in Figure 13.3, the Big Data Framework Provider consists of three sub-roles, which each focus on a different infrastructure domain:

• Processing: Computing and Analytics
• Platforms: Data Organization and Distribution
• Infrastructure: Networking, Computing and Storage

Each of these sub-roles will be discussed in more detail in the following chapters.

3 Big Data Application Provider

The Big Data Application Provider role is the architecture component that contains all the business logic (i.e. algorithms) that are necessary to extract value from data. It is located at the centre of the NBDRA and connects all data flows across both value streams. The Big Data Application Provider ensures that the enterprise is able to process data that is high-volume, high-velocity and from disparate data sources (i.e. the Data Provider). Because of these characteristics, 'traditional' data processing implementations and algorithms need to be optimized to accommodate Big Data sets.

The various instances of applications execute functionality that is focused on any of the following activities:

• **Collection:** Applications that collect data (and integrate with the Data Provider)
• **Preparation:** Data cleaning and data wrangling activities that prepare data for more detailed and analysis
• **Analytics:** Applications that run statistical or machine learning algorithms to produce future results
• **Visualization:** Applications that transform the results of data analysis or analytics into graphical visualizations that provide decision-making information
• **Access:** The solutions that provide access to results (and integrate with the Data Consumers)

The collection, or instances, of applications that are part of the Big Data Application Provider role is referred to as the **Big Data Application Stack**. As data moves through the Big Data ecosystem, it is sorted, prepared and optimized, so that it can ultimately lead to valuable results. Organizations can have one integrated toolset that will execute all these activities, or they can have stand-alone applications for each of these activities. In most enterprise organizations, the Big Data Application Stack is frequently complex, consisting of dozens of industry-specific applications. Some research suggests that enterprises require more than 30 applications to operate their Big Data Application Stack.[6]

The Big Data Application Provider is situated at the centre of the NBDRA because it needs to interact with all the other four roles on an ongoing and consistent basis. The applications that are part of the stack need to interact with the underlying Big Data Framework provider to store and process data. Additionally, the applications require interactions with the Data Providers (for input data) and with the Data Consumers (who utilize the data). Lastly, because there are typically many instances of these applications, some form of coordination in the data processing pipelines is required. For that reason, the applications that are fulfilling the role of Big Data Application Provider need to interact with the System Orchestrator.

4 Data Consumer

The **Data Consumer** role is situated at the end the end of the Information Value Chain and represents the role that consumes the output (frequently data) of the value chain. The Data Consumer can either be a person that requires a specific outcome of the process, or it can be another system that requests data for other purposes. Note that the Data Consumer can also function as a 'new' Data Provider for a next step. In summary, we could say that the Data Consumer role represents the final output of the NBDRA.

The Data Consumer role will use the interfaces and applications (which are part of the Big Data Application Provider) to get access to the information of interest. The common activities that will be performed by the Data Consumer are:

- Search and retrieve
- Download
- Analyse locally
- Reporting
- Visualization
- Use data for own process

The role of the Data Consumer is analogous to demand. The whole reason that Big Data analytics and processing are done in the first place is because something or someone in the organization would like to retrieve value from data. In other words, it establishes the demand side of the Big Data value chain.

5 System Orchestrator

The System Orchestrator is the role that coordinates activities, workflows and processes of all underlying components or the NBDRA. As we have seen in the previous sections, Big Data ecosystems consists of multiple instances of each role. As a result, Big Data ecosystems can become complex quite quickly, with multiple data processing requests on various data sets at the same time. The System Orchestrator brings order, by coordinating activities and sequences, and providing a uniform and structured overview of the Big Data environment.

Like a conductor that ensures all instruments play in sync to create a beautiful symphony, the System Orchestrator ensures all instances of the NBDRA operate in sync to retrieve value from Big Data.

The function of the System Orchestrator role is to configure and manage all the other components of the Big Data ecosystem. It directs workloads, processes jobs and provides additional storage and compute resources when required. Alongside its active role of managing the resources in the Big Data environment, the System Orchestrator also has a passive role in enabling monitoring and auditing activities, enabling the capability of Big Data Governance (as discussed in chapter 6 section 6.3).

13.7 The two fabrics of the NBDRA

In addition to the five key roles of the NBDRA, Figure 13.3 reveals two fabric roles that encompass the five main roles: **Management** and **Security and Privacy**. These two fabric roles provide service and functionality to all of the five roles and enable a Big Data ecosystem to function properly, and within the governance requirements of the organization.

The five main roles and two fabrics that we outlined in this section form the fundamental basis of a vendor-independent Big Data Reference Architecture, based on

Table 13.2   The two fabrics of the NBDRA

Fabric	Description
Management	The Management fabric of the NBDRA ensures that organizations stay in control of their Big Data environment. It contains all the activities that relate to systems management (provisioning, configuration, package management, resource management, etc.) as well as Big Data Lifecycle Management. Big Data Lifecycle Management is primarily responsible for the activities surrounding the collection, preparation, visualization and access of data.
Security & Privacy	Security and privacy are an integral part of every Big Data environment. Just as with the management fabric, security and privacy considerations encompass all the other five roles, and are a fundamental part of any Big Data architecture. Since the importance of security and privacy is becoming more and more important every day, this fabric has grown to become a separate micro-capability within the Enterprise Big Data Framework. The security and privacy micro-capability will be explored further in Chapter 18.

best practices and established technology in the enterprise domain. It helps organizations to understand how their Big Data technology is built, and which **role** every component fulfills. As such, the NBDRA provides a comprehensive overview of the technical and functional components that are necessary to set up or maintain a Big Data architecture. Since the structure of the NBDRA is abstract, we will next focus on the practical capabilities that organizations can develop to build a maturity Big Data architecture, based on essential micro-capabilities.

13.8 Other Big Data architecture standards

In this chapter, we have solely focused on the NBRDA as a model for a proper Big Data architecture design. Besides the NBDRA, there are many other Big Data Reference Architectures available.[7] Some are driven by technology vendors, other were predecessors of contributors to the NBDRA. Another notable Big Data Reference Architecture to reference is ISO/IEC 20547, the Big Data Reference Architecture of the International Standards Organization (ISO).[8] In the rest of the Enterprise Big Data Framework, we will be building on the NBDRA, because it is vendor-independent, can be used freely (open source) and was created by an international panel of experts.

Notes

1   E Curry (2016) The big data value chain: definitions, concepts, and theoretical approaches. In *New horizons for a data-driven economy*, Cham, Springer, 29–37

2   P Sawadogo and J Darmont. On data lake architectures and metadata management, *Journal of Intelligent Information Systems*, 2021 56 (1), 97–120

3   M van Geest, B Tekinerdogan and C Catal. Design of a reference architecture for developing smart warehouses in industry 4.0, *Computers in Industry*, 2021 124, 103343

4   P Mell and T Grance (2011) The NIST definition of cloud computing, https://scholar.google.com/scholar?hl=en&as_sdt=0%2C5&q=P+Mell+and+T+Grance+%282011%29+The+NIST+definition+of+cloud+computing&btnG= (archived at https://perma.cc/XAM6-P2FR)

5   W L Chang, D Boyd and O Levin (2019) NIST Big Data Interoperability Framework, vol 6, Reference Architecture, www.nist.gov/publications/nist-big-data-interoperability-framework-volume-6-reference-architecture?pub_id=918936 (archived at https://perma.cc/ZU4M-4Y2M)

6   J Qiu, S Jha, A Luckow and G C Fox. Towards hpc-abds: An initial high-performance big data stack, *Building Robust Big Data Ecosystem ISO/IEC JTC*, 2014 1, 18–21

7   M Volk, S Bosse, D Bischoff and K Turowski 2019, June. Decision-support for selecting big data reference architectures. In International Conference on Business Information Systems (pp. 3–17). Springer, Cham.

8   Q Li, Z Xu, I Chan, S Yang, Y Pu, H Wei and C Yu 2018, October. Big data architecture and reference models. In OTM Confederated International Conferences "On the Move to Meaningful Internet Systems" (pp. 15–24). Springer, Cham.

Big Data Architecture Management

14

14.1 Introduction to Big Data architecture management

Big Data architecture management is the process of designing, implementing and maintaining the infrastructure and systems required to store, process and analyse large amounts of data. This includes designing and implementing data storage systems such as Hadoop and NoSQL databases, setting up data processing frameworks like Apache Spark and Apache Storm, and selecting and configuring tools for data analysis and visualization. It also includes management of the overall enterprise IT architecture, scaling the architecture to handle more data and users, and ensuring data security, reliability and performance.

Architecting a Big Data environment is a complex task, which requires a careful design approach, and careful trade-off between the costs and benefits of different solutions. There is not just one way to design a sound architecture. The reason this capability is crucial for most organizations is twofold:

- **Increased efficiency and cost control:** With the right Big Data architecture in place, organizations can process and analyse data more quickly and efficiently, resulting in cost savings and improved productivity. The decisions that are made in the architecture of the Big Data environment contribute to a significant extent towards the overall cost structure of the Big Data organization.

- **Improved scalability:** By designing a Big Data architecture that can scale to handle more data and more users, organizations can ensure that their systems can grow and evolve as needed.

Designing a Big Data architecture is the primary role of the **Enterprise Big Data Architect.** The Enterprise Big Data Architect is responsible for designing, implementing and maintaining the Big Data architecture for an organization, and is therefore a complex job. Big Data Architects need to be familiar with the data management and governance best practices and regulations (discussed further in Part 6). Additionally, they need to work closely with other IT and business teams to understand their needs, goals and objectives and translate them into a Big Data architecture and solution. They also work with the team to develop and implement a data governance strategy and ensure compliance with relevant regulations.

14.2 Purpose and maturity levels of Big Data architecture management

Purpose

Big Data architecture is a critical capability for any organizations. Besides the efficiency, cost and scalability considerations mentioned in the previous section, it is clear that the design choices that are made in this stage contribute – to a significant extent – to the success of a Big Data programme. The right combination of technologies and tools will accelerate the adoption of Big Data and data-driven decision-making in organizations. A poor design, on the other hand, typically leads to outages, wrong predictions and can ultimately undermine the trust in Enterprise Big Data.

The purpose of having a sound enterprise Big Data architecture capability is to provide a comprehensive and efficient infrastructure and system that can store, process and analyse large amounts of data in a way that meets the organization's needs.

As we outlined in Chapter 13, Big Data architectures can be efficiently designed (or fast-tracked) with the help of the Big Data Reference Architecture. The NIST Big Data Reference Architecture provides a good conceptualization that any organization can use to start building this capability. It provides a high-level view of the key components and interactions involved in a Big Data system, as well as best practices for designing, deploying and managing such systems. The NBDRA is intended to be a flexible and extensible architecture that can be adapted to meet the specific needs of different organizations.

Table 14.1   The purpose of the Big Data architecture management capability

Capability	Purpose
Big Data architecture management	Defines the ability to plan, design, manage and control the conceptualization of Big Data systems and processes, and the relationships between them.

Big Data architecture management maturity levels

To develop capability in Big Data architecture management, organizations need to set up a sound process that continually assesses the overall design and efficiency of the Big Data technology stack. The Big Data technology stack refers to the collection of software and technologies that are used to store, process and analyse large amounts of data. In most organizations, a Big Data technology stack typically includes a combination of open-source and commercial technologies that work together in a comprehensive architecture.

The extent to which an organization can guide their Big Data architecture management is reflected in their maturity levels. Table 14.2 outlines the five maturity levels of the Big Data architecture management capability.

An organization that operates at a high capability level (level 4–5) has a well-designed and well-implemented Big Data architecture that can handle large amounts of data and can scale to meet the organization's needs. This architecture would likely include distributed storage systems, data processing frameworks and data analysis and visualization tools. We will discuss some of these components in the next section.

Table 14.2   Big Data architecture management maturity levels

Maturity Level	Description
Level 1 – Initial	Big Data architecture management is conducted within the context of individual Big Data projects, by applying one-off principles and methods within those projects. There is no overarching or guiding strategy for how Big Data tools and technologies will be used.
Level 2 – Managed	A limited number of basic architecture design principles and practices are emerging in certain IT domains or key projects. There is some consistency about the use of Big Data tools and technology across the enterprise.
Level 3 – Defined	There exists an overall design that outlines the structure of Big Data technologies and tools, and this design is actively followed in the procurement and integration of new Big Data technology.
Level 4 – Controlled	Based on the overall Big Data architecture design and corresponding blueprints, the organization periodically assesses the suitability, efficiency and merits of the Big Data technology stack. Based on this evaluation, tools are optimized or replaced.
Level 5 – Optimized	The Big Data architecture accelerates the performance of the company, and enables the organization to innovate, which leads to direct and tangible business benefits.

14.3 Structuring Big Data architecture management

An enterprise Big Data architecture is designed to handle the ingestion, processing and analysis of data that has too large or too complex data sets for traditional database systems. Conceptually, an enterprise Big Data architecture can be based on the following structural components.

The components of the Big Data architecture in Figure 14.1 are based on the NIST Big Data Reference Architecture (discussed in Chapter 13), and specifically includes both batch and streaming options (discussed in Chapter 2 section 2.3). Each of the components is briefly outlined below, providing Big Data architects with an indication of which technology and tools can be used to cover all architecture components.

Data sources

Data sources refer to the origin or location from which data is obtained. As discussed in Chapter 2 section 2.4, they can be broadly categorized into three types: structured, semi-structured and unstructured data sets. All Big Data solutions start with one or more data sources.

Big Data storage solutions

Data storage solutions is the architecture component that considers the solutions where data is being stored. The purpose of Big Data storage is to provide a system

Figure 14.1   Components of a Big Data architecture

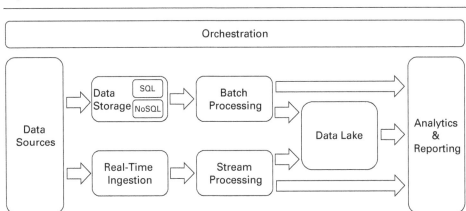

that can handle the large volume, velocity and variety of data that is generated by organizations.

A common practice in Big Data environments is to separate SQL (i.e. relational) and NoSQL (non-relational) databases. Common non-relational databases were discussed in Chapter 2 section 2.5. Big Data storage solutions are used to store and manage large amounts of structured and unstructured data, including data from various sources such as social media, IoT devices and transactional systems. These solutions enable organizations to store, process and analyse this data to gain insights and make more informed decisions.

Batch processing

Batch processing is the execution of a series of jobs, without human intervention, on a computer or group of computers. These jobs are typically executed in a predefined order and are executed as a single unit, or 'batch', rather than one at a time. Batch processing in Big Data environments is used for tasks such as data processing, data integration and data analysis, which need to be performed frequently or on a repetitive basis.

Batch processing jobs are usually run at a specific time, such as overnight or during non-peak hours, when the system is less busy and resources are more available. This way, the system can process large amounts of data in a relatively short period of time, without impacting the performance of the system during peak usage hours.

Example of common Big Data batch processing jobs are:

- **Data integration:** Combining data from multiple sources into a single data repository

- **Data transformation:** Modifying data from one format to another, or from one structure to another

- **Data archiving:** Moving old data from primary storage to a secondary storage device

- **Data backup:** Copying data from primary storage to a secondary storage device for disaster recovery

- **Data analysis:** Running complex queries on large volumes of data to extract insights or generate reports

Batch processing is useful for executing long-running jobs that can be run at a specific time and don't require real-time processing. That also means it is more cost-efficient than streaming processing. It is also a good fit for high-throughput data processing, where large amounts of data need to be processed quickly and efficiently. Some examples and technologies of batch processing were discussed in detail in Chapter 2 section 2.3.

Real-time ingestion

Most Big Data environments require forms of real-time ingestions, and therefore need architecture components that are able to support this. This means the Big Data architecture must include a way to capture and store real-time messages for stream processing. This might be a simple data store, where incoming messages are dropped into a folder for processing. However, more complex examples require a **message ingestion store** to act as a buffer for messages, and to support scale-out processing, reliable delivery and other message queuing semantics. The most commonly used solutions for this architecture component is Kafka.

Kafka is a publish-subscribe messaging system, which means that it allows multiple systems to send and receive streams of data in real-time.[1] It achieves this by using a publish-subscribe model where producers write data to topics and consumers read from those topics. This allows for a decoupled architecture where the producers and consumers can evolve independently.

Stream processing

Stream processing (as discussed in Chapter 2 section 2.3) is a method of analysing and processing data in real-time as it is generated, rather than processing it in batches. It is a way to process and analyse large volumes of data in real-time, as it is generated, rather than waiting for all the data to be collected and then processing it in batches.

The data streams are generated from various sources such as social media, IoT devices, financial transactions and other online and offline systems. The data streams are then processed and analyzed as they are generated, rather than waiting for all the data to be collected and then processing it in batches.

Data lake

A data lake is a centralized repository that allows organizations to store, process and analyse large volumes of structured and unstructured data. The data stored in the data lake can be raw and in its original format, allowing for more flexible and efficient processing and analysis.

A data lake is designed to handle Big Data, and it can store data from various sources such as transactional systems, social media, IoT devices and log files. The data is stored in its raw format, which makes it easier to access and analyse. Examples of Big Data lakes and solutions are further discussed in the next chapter.

Analytics and reporting

Analytics and reporting represents the architecture component that concerns itself with data analysis, analytics and data visualization. In most cases, different applications are necessary to support this. The goal of most Big Data solutions is to provide insights into the data through analysis and reporting. To empower users to analyse Big Data, the architecture must include a data modelling layer that gives users the ability to request and visualize data.

The analytics and reporting component in Figure 14.1 is similar to the **data consumer** function discussed in Chapter 13. Which analytics and reporting engines an organization requires is greatly dependent on the nature and purpose of an organization. The Enterprise Big Data architect therefore requires domain knowledge to architect the best solution.

Orchestration

The orchestration component in a Big Data architecture is the process of managing and coordinating the execution of complex data pipelines and workflows. It involves automating the execution of tasks and processes, scheduling jobs and managing their dependencies, and monitoring the status of the jobs and the entire workflow. The role of orchestration is the same as the orchestration role in the NBDRA.

14.4 Big Data architecture management summary

In this chapter, we looked in detail at the importance of the Big Data architecture management capability. We have seen that Big Data architecture management is critical for organizations to ensure that their Big Data infrastructure is designed to meet their specific needs and requirements, and that it can handle the volume, velocity and variety of data that is generated by the organization.

In section 14.3, we looked at the main architectural components of a Big Data architecture. The architecture components discussed in this section build upon the NIST Big Data Reference Architecture and help Big Data architects to structurally consider all components necessary to help ensure that the data is stored, processed and analysed in a timely and accurate manner, and that the organization can extract value from its Big Data.

Note

1 H Wu, Z Shang and K Wolter (2019) Performance prediction for the Apache Kafka messaging system. In 2019 IEEE 21st International Conference on High Performance Computing and Communications; IEEE 17th International Conference on Smart City; IEEE 5th International Conference on Data Science and Systems (HPCC/SmartCity/DSS), August, 154–61. IEEE

Infrastructure Management   15

15.1 Introduction to infrastructure management

In the previous paragraph, we considered the Architecture Management capability. The Architecture Management capability is necessary in any enterprise, because it safeguards a proper design of the Big Data environment. Based on this design, organizations will purchase tools and infrastructure to support its solutions. After the design and implementation, these components will need to be managed on a day-to-day basis; this is where infrastructure management comes in.

The infrastructure management capability is the process of managing and maintaining the hardware, software and network resources that are used to store, process and analyse large volumes of data. It includes tasks such as installing, configuring and maintaining the various components of the Big Data infrastructure, such as servers, storage systems and software tools.

The infrastructure management capability is important for several reasons:

- **Scalability:** ensures that the infrastructure can handle large volumes of data and can scale to meet the growing data needs of an organization.
- **Performance:** ensures that the infrastructure is optimized for performance and can handle high-velocity data streams and process data in real-time.
- **Security:** ensures that the infrastructure is secure and can protect sensitive data and comply with data privacy regulations.
- **High availability:** ensures that the infrastructure is highly available and can handle failures and provide continuous service.
- **Monitoring and maintenance:** includes monitoring the infrastructure and performing maintenance tasks such as software updates, backups and disaster recovery.
- **Monitoring and optimization:** includes monitoring the infrastructure and optimizing the performance of the system, such as managing resources and fine-tuning configurations.

The infrastructure management capability is critical for organizations to ensure that their Big Data infrastructure is running efficiently, securely and reliably. It's essential to ensure that data is stored, processed and analysed in a timely and accurate manner, and that the organization can extract value from its Big Data. Additionally, it's important to have a proper monitoring and management system to have visibility and control over the infrastructure, which is crucial for troubleshooting, managing and scaling the Big Data systems. In this section, we will consider some of the most important components of managing a Big Data infrastructure and how organizations can grow their capability.

15.2 Purpose and maturity levels of infrastructure management

Purpose

The purpose of infrastructure management is simple and straightforward: at any moment, an organization can be in control of their IT infrastructure (and all their underlying components). The infrastructure management capability aims to ensure that the hardware, software and network resources used to store, process and analyse massive quantities of data are properly installed, configured and maintained. It aims to provide a stable, secure, and high-performing Big Data infrastructure that can handle the large volume, velocity, and variety of data that is generated by organizations today.

The purpose of the infrastructure management capability is outlined in Table 15.1.

The purpose of infrastructure management is closely related to some of the objectives of IT Service Management. Organizations that have a high maturity of IT Service Management in their organization will therefore be able to achieve high maturity levels in this capability as well. By structuring the infrastructure management capability, organizations have the ability:

- To ensure the **stability and availability** of the Big Data infrastructure
- To ensure the **security and compliance** of the Big Data infrastructure
- To ensure the **performance and scalability** of the Big Data infrastructure

Table 15.1 The purpose of the infrastructure management capability

Capability	Purpose
Infrastructure management	Defines the ability to manage all physical and virtual components of the IT infrastructure to support the introduction, maintenance and retirement of Big Data services.

- To support the proper functioning of the Big Data **pipeline and workflows**
- To ensure **data governance** and compliance with **data privacy** regulations
- To **monitor and maintain the infrastructure** and ensure the smooth operation of the system

Infrastructure management maturity levels

A high maturity of the infrastructure management capability would be characterized by a well-designed, stable, secure, highly available and highly scalable infrastructure that is continuously monitored. Alongside the IT operations function that is necessary to achieve this, it means that organizations need to establish sound monitoring and control processes.

Table 15.2 outlines the five maturity levels of the infrastructure management capability.

A high maturity level of infrastructure management refers to the level of organization, automation and optimization of the hardware, software and network resources

Table 15.2 Infrastructure management maturity levels

Maturity Level	Description
Level 1 – Initial	Management of the Big Data infrastructure is reactive or ad hoc.
Level 2 – Managed	Documented policies exist that outline procedures for the management of the Big Data infrastructure. However, these procedures, which are predominantly manual, are used for IT infrastructure management. Visibility of capacity and utilization across infrastructure components is limited.
Level 3 – Defined	Approaches for IT operations and infrastructure management are standardized across the IT infrastructure, providing management with an end-to-end view across various infrastructure components. Infrastructure management is automated, scalable and monitored continuously.
Level 4 – Controlled	Information is shared between the Big Data function and the rest of the business based on monitoring practices, and this helps ensure that the IT infrastructure is managed effectively and with virtually no disruption to business operations. Infrastructure management utilizes industry standard best practices.
Level 5 – Optimized	Approaches for infrastructure management are continually reviewed, updated and improved, and the organization actively contributes to the continual improvement of best practices.

used in an organization. Since the IT infrastructure is the 'beating heart' of the Big Data function, this capability is critical to achieve long-term success.

15.3 Structuring infrastructure management

A high maturity level of infrastructure management for Big Data would be characterized by a well-planned, organized and automated approach to managing the hardware, software and network resources that are used to store, process and analyse large volumes of data. It would be designed to handle the large volume, velocity and variety of data that is generated by organizations today, while also ensuring security, availability and performance.

Infrastructure automation

Automation is a key aspect of high maturity infrastructure management for Big Data. Automation tools such as Ansible, Puppet and Chef can be used to automate the deployment, configuration and scaling of Big Data clusters. This reduces the need for manual intervention and minimizes the risk of human error, which is crucial for managing large and complex Big Data infrastructures.

In a mature organization, the infrastructure management process is automated to the greatest extent possible, with tasks such as installation, configuration and maintenance being performed automatically, reducing the need for manual intervention, and minimizing the risk of human error.

Automation of infrastructure management leads to reduced errors and improved accuracy: automating tasks such as installation, configuration and maintenance can reduce the risk of human error and improve the accuracy of the process. This can lead to fewer issues and improved system performance. Since demand for Big Data storage and processing jobs is never static, infrastructure automation can help significantly in achieving stable performance.

Scalability

Scalability is also an important aspect of high maturity infrastructure management for Big Data. The infrastructure should be designed to handle large volumes of data and be able to scale to meet the growing data needs of an organization. Technologies such as Hadoop and Spark can be used to handle large data sets and scale out to handle increasing data volumes. This allows for more efficient and cost-effective management of large and growing data sets.

Automation and scalability reinforce each other. Automating the process of scaling infrastructure can make it easier to handle large volumes of data and respond to changing needs. This can help to ensure that the infrastructure can handle the volume, velocity and variety of data that is generated by organizations today.

Monitoring and event management

Monitoring the infrastructure can provide insights into the performance of the system, including system utilization, resource consumption and throughput. This can help to identify any performance bottlenecks and ensure that the infrastructure can handle the volume, velocity and variety of data that is generated by the organization.

In addition, monitoring and event management are important for several practical reasons. Monitoring the infrastructure can provide information about the usage of the system, including the storage and processing capacity, which can help in capacity planning and forecasting the future needs.

Monitoring the Big Data infrastructure is important to ensure that the infrastructure is running efficiently, securely and reliably. It provides visibility into the system and can help to identify and resolve issues, improve performance and availability, and ensure compliance with relevant regulations and standards.

Best practice

Finally, there are several standards and best practices that can help with structuring infrastructure management. Although some of the challenges for Big Data infrastructure are unique, enterprises have been confronting the challenges of large-scale infrastructure for many years. Many IT infrastructure frameworks and best practices exist, which can expedite the maturity for Big Data organizations. The most popular best practices for infrastructure management are the Information Technology Infrastructure Library (ITIL) and the Control Objectives for IT-Related Technologies (COBIT). These best practices can be adopted and adapted for use in Big Data infrastructure management.

Table 15.3 outlines some important guidance and lessons from these frameworks that will drive the maturity of the infrastructure management capability.

This list in Table 15.3 is not exhaustive, but it includes some of the main best practices of IT infrastructure management. These best practices are beneficial to Big Data infrastructure management because they help organizations to manage and maintain the hardware, software and network resources that are used to store, process and analyse large volumes of data efficiently and effectively.

Table 15.3   Infrastructure management best practices

Best Practice	Description
Develop infrastructure management strategy	This includes identifying the key components of the infrastructure, such as servers, storage and networking, and developing a plan for managing, maintaining and upgrading these components over time.
Automate repetitive tasks	Automating repetitive tasks such as software updates, backups and disaster recovery can improve efficiency and reduce the risk of human error.
Establish monitoring and management tools	Implementing monitoring and management tools can help to improve visibility into the infrastructure, and make it easier to identify and resolve issues. This includes using monitoring tools to track resource usage, network performance and security events, and management tools to automate the process of scaling, provisioning and deprovisioning resources.
Implement security best practices	Implementing security best practices, such as encryption and authentication, can help to protect sensitive data and ensure compliance with data privacy regulations.
Implement disaster recovery	Implementing disaster recovery and business continuity plans can help to ensure that the infrastructure can handle failures and provide continuity of service.
Establish continual improvement	Continuously reviewing and improving the infrastructure can help to ensure that the infrastructure is well-planned, organized and optimized to meet the needs of the organization.
Keep current with technology	Keeping up with the latest technologies can help to ensure that the infrastructure is optimized for performance, is secure and can handle the volume, velocity and variety of data that is generated by organizations today.
Establish training plans for staff	Training IT staff on best practices of infrastructure management and the technologies used can help to ensure that the infrastructure is managed and maintained effectively.
Establish a culture of collaboration	Building a culture of collaboration between different teams and departments can help to ensure that the infrastructure is aligned with the business goals and objectives of the organization.

15.4 Infrastructure management summary

The storage and processing of Big Data ultimately happens within IT infrastructure. Even with the best data scientists, algorithms and strategy, there is still a large dependency on the underlying IT infrastructure. An underlying IT infrastructure which experiences frequent outages or poses security risks will have a significant impact on the success of any Big Data programme.

The infrastructure management capability establishes the processes and best practices to operate a secure and scalable Big Data environment. Through proper **infrastructure automation, scalability, monitoring and event management, and infrastructure best practices,** organizations can create an IT environment that is under control, dependable and which will support the overall business objectives of the organization.

Data Platform Management

16

16.1 Introduction to data platform management

A **data platform** collects, organizes and activates first-, second- and third-party audience data from various online, offline and mobile sources. It then uses that data for various use cases across the enterprise. **Data platform management** is the capability that establishes the processes to import, monitor and control enterprise data. With effective data platform management, organizations have control over their enterprise data, and decision-makers can trust the data within these platforms. Effective data platform management therefore leads to enterprise trusted data.

Whilst enterprise data platforms are technically infrastructure components (and could therefore be considered as a subset of infrastructure management), the importance of data platforms in enterprises is so significant that it warrants its own micro-capability.

A data platform is a comprehensive infrastructure, software and tool that enables any organization to collect, store, process and analyse large volumes of data. It is designed to support the data management (discussed further in Part 6) and data governance objectives of an enterprise. The data platform itself is the technical infrastructure component – an integral part of an enterprise Big Data architecture – that stores all the data. Although most data platforms integrate with processing, and analytics solutions, the primary function of the data platform is data storage. A modern data platform includes databases, data lakes and data warehouses that are used to store and manage large volumes of data.

An important feature of data platforms is that they frequently allow for self-service data access and analysis, enabling business users and data scientists to access and analyse data without relying on IT, and it is designed to be highly available, secure and scalable to handle growing data needs. This feature is better known as the **data catalogue**, which we will discuss in more detail in the next section.

The data platform – when established properly – provides one single source of truth of enterprise data. This capability is therefore critical to the success of any Big Data programme. Without the proper controls in place with data platform management, organizations will face scepticism as to how much the enterprise data can be trusted.

16.2 Purpose and maturity levels of data platform management

Purpose

The purpose of a data platform is to provide a centralized, unified and well-governed infrastructure to collect and store enterprise data. It enables organizations to make data-driven decisions by providing a **single source of truth** for data that can be accessed and analysed by various teams and departments.

A modern data platform ensures data is accessible to relevant data users based on their unique workflows. Well-designed data platforms simplify data access in an organization and facilitates self-service data consumption through a data catalogue. Teams can use the data platform to automate data discovery, governance and consumption, through its integrated end-to-end data management capabilities. Through the assignment of roles and responsibilities, different data sets can be made available to different users.

Data platform management is the capability that any organization needs to set up and control their data platforms. Data platform management includes processes, policies, measurement and control activities. The purpose of data platform management is outlined in Table 16.1.

Data platform management might seem an easy capability at a first. Yet many organizations find it difficult to structure it properly. The most cited concerns that make this capability difficult to master are:

- **Complexity:** Data platforms typically include a wide range of technologies and tools, such as databases, data lakes, data warehouses, Big Data processing frameworks, and data visualization and reporting tools. Managing and maintaining these different components can be complex and time-consuming.

- **Scale:** Data platforms are designed to handle large volumes of data, which can require significant resources, including storage, processing power and networking bandwidth. Managing these resources at scale can be challenging.

- **Data variety:** Data platforms need to handle a wide variety of data types, such as structured, semi-structured and unstructured data, and different data formats,

Table 16.1   The purpose of the data platform management capability

Capability	Purpose
Data platform management	Defines the ability to control enterprise data in line with the enterprise data strategy so that data is safeguarded as a corporate asset.

such as text, images and video. Managing and processing such a diverse set of data can be difficult.

- **Security:** Data platforms often handle sensitive data and need to comply with data privacy regulations, which can be challenging to ensure and maintain.

- **Governance:** Data platforms need to ensure data quality, data lineage, data security and data compliance, which can be difficult to implement and maintain.

- **High availability:** Data platforms need to be highly available, which can be challenging to achieve, especially in the case of large data sets and high traffic.

- **Keeping up with new technologies:** Data platforms are constantly evolving, with new technologies, tools and best practices being developed all the time. Keeping up with these developments can be difficult and time-consuming.

- **Collaboration:** Data platforms often need to support different use cases and business requirements, which can be challenging to align and collaborate on.

Data platform management is a complex and dynamic capability that requires a deep understanding of the technologies and tools involved, as well as the ability to adapt to changing business needs and new technologies. It requires a combination of technical and domain expertise, as well as a well-defined data governance and management strategy to be successful.

Data platform management maturity levels

Achieving a high level of data platform management maturity requires a combination of technical and organizational capability. It requires a strong focus to continually update the data platform to the latest standards, and to keep up with changes in legislation and technology. To measure data platform management maturity, the five levels that are depicted in Table 16.2 can be used.

The main benefit of having a high data platform management maturity, compared to having a low data platform management maturity, is that a high level of maturity allows organizations to manage and maintain the data platform in a more efficient, effective and secure way. Organizations that have high levels of maturity typically have **enterprise trusted data,** upon which they base their day-to-day decision-making process.

16.3 Structuring data platform management

Structuring the data platform management capability will require focus on the creation of proper processes and policies, which can be implemented through technology. Because there are many facets to data platform management, this section will

Table 16.2   Data platform management maturity levels

Maturity Level	Description
Level 1 – Initial	Data platform management is ad hoc and reactive, with little or no formal processes or procedures in place. There is a lack of visibility of the infrastructure and data, and little or no automation or monitoring in place.
Level 2 – Managed	Data platform management is more structured and formalized, with processes and procedures in place to manage and maintain the infrastructure and data. There is some automation and monitoring in place, but it is limited in scope.
Level 3 – Defined	Data platform management is more strategic, with a well-defined and comprehensive data platform management strategy in place. There is a higher degree of automation and monitoring in place, and the infrastructure and data are more tightly integrated.
Level 4 – Controlled	Data platform management is more quantitative, with a focus on measuring and analysing performance to continuously improve the infrastructure and data. There is a high degree of automation and monitoring in place, and the infrastructure and data are closely aligned with business objectives.
Level 5 – Optimized	Data platform management is highly optimized and continuously improving, with a focus on innovation and the use of advanced technologies and best practices. The infrastructure and data are closely aligned with business objectives, and there is a high degree of automation, monitoring and security in place

outline some of the main technological considerations. Data management processes and data governance processes (which are implemented through enterprise data platforms) will be discussed in more detail in Part 6.

Databases design

The core of any data platform is a collection of databases. Databases are one of the key components of a data platform and are used to store and manage structured data, such as transactional data, master data and metadata. Transactional data, master data and metadata are different types of data commonly used in modern data platforms:

- **Transactional data:** This is the data generated from the core business operations of an organization. It is typically used to record and track business transactions, such as sales, purchases and financial transactions. This type of data is also referred to as operational data and is usually stored in transactional databases.

- **Master data:** This is the data used to define the key entities in an organization, such as customers, products, suppliers and employees. This data is usually stored in a master data management (MDM) system and is used to provide a single, consistent view of key entities across the organization. Master data is also used to provide context and meaning to transactional data.

- **Metadata:** This is data that describes other data. It provides information about the data, such as its structure, format, quality and lineage. Metadata is used to help understand, manage and govern the data in a data platform. It is also used to improve the discoverability and usability of the data.

Whereas the transactional data typically 'organically' grows in data platforms, depending on the data that is imported, master data management and metadata management require design and implementation. This is the job of data stewards, who safeguard the quality of the enterprise data. Given its importance, master and metadata management are discussed in more detail in Chapter 17.

Data warehouses

Most data platforms have the ability to design and create one (or more) data warehouses. A **data warehouse** is a system designed to store and manage large amounts of historical data in a **structured way**, with the purpose of supporting business intelligence and reporting needs.

A data warehouse typically stores data that is cleaned, transformed and integrated from various sources, such as transactional systems, log files and external data feeds. This data is then made available to analysts and business users in a form that can be easily queried and analysed. The data is typically stored in a relational database management system, and optimized for reading and querying, rather than for writing or transactional processing.

The data in a data warehouse is stored in a multidimensional data model; that is, data is organized into facts and dimensions. A fact represents a measurable event or a piece of data that can be quantified, such as sales, revenue or inventory. A dimension represents a set of attributes that can be used to describe or filter the facts, such as time, location and product. This multidimensional data model allows for easy and fast querying of data and enables the creation of complex and detailed reports.

Data warehousing is an important part of a data platform, but it's not the only component. Most modern data platforms can create or manage multiple internal and external data warehouses.

Data lakes

A data lake is a centralized, large-scale data repository that stores Big Data in its **native format**, with minimal transformation or processing. A data lake is designed to handle a wide variety of data types and sources, including **structured, semi-structured and unstructured** data, and allows data to be stored in its native format, without the need for pre-processing. This flexibility enables organizations to store all their data, structured and unstructured, in one place, making it easier to discover, process and analyse.

Data lakes are typically built on a distributed file system, such as Hadoop Distributed File System (HDFS), which allows for the storage of large volumes of data at a lower cost. Data is stored in the data lake in its raw form, without any specific schema or structure, and can be easily ingested, stored and accessed by different departments, applications and tools. Data can be stored in its raw format and can be processed, analysed and queried in a variety of ways, using a variety of tools and technologies, including SQL, Spark and Hive.

Most modern data platforms allow for the creation of data lakes. Data platform management requires the creation of policies, design choices and processes that explain how the data lake will be structured.

Data catalogues

A data catalogue in a data platform allows users to browse and search the enterprise data. Technically, a data catalogue is a metadata management tool that enables organizations to discover, understand and govern their data assets. It provides a centralized and easily searchable repository of data assets, including data sources, data structures, data quality and data lineage information. With a data catalogue, a business user can easily find and retrieve data. For examples, if a marketing executive needs to obtain data about successful marketing campaign per region, the executive can go to the centralized repository, query the search and then (depending on the role and authorizations) view and export the data set for further analysis.

A data catalogue enables organizations to:

- **Discover data assets:** It allows business users and data scientists to discover the data they need without relying on IT. It also enables organizations to identify and remove redundant, obsolete or low-value data.

- **Understand data assets:** It provides detailed information about the data assets, including their structure, format, quality and lineage, which makes it easier to understand the data and determine its suitability for a particular use case.

- **Govern data assets:** It provides a set of governance controls, including data quality, data lineage, data security and data compliance, to ensure that the data is trustworthy, accurate and compliant with data privacy regulations.

The creation of a data catalogue can be a complex and time-consuming process, depending on the size and complexity of an organization's data landscape. Some of the challenges that organizations may face when creating a data catalogue include: searchability of data sets, metadata descriptions and determining the quality of the data set. The master and metadata management capability (discussed in Chapter 17) can help to ease this process.

16.4 Data masking

A new and increasingly more important design aspect of the data platform management capability is how the enterprise sets up rules for data masking. **Data masking**, also known as **data obfuscation**, is the process of hiding sensitive data by replacing it with fictitious but realistic data, while still preserving its original format and structure. The purpose of data masking is to protect sensitive data from unauthorized access and to comply with data privacy regulations.

Data masking can be applied to various types of data, including personal identifiable information (PII), financial data and confidential business information. In more and more countries, new regulations are prepared that requires organizations (by law) to apply data masking rules to safeguard data privacy. The most common methods of data masking include:

- **Substitution:** Replacing sensitive data with fictitious but realistic data, such as using fake names and addresses in place of real ones.
- **Tokenization:** Replacing sensitive data with a token or a reference number that can be used to retrieve the original data when needed.
- **Encryption:** Encrypting sensitive data so that it cannot be read or understood by unauthorized users.
- **Masking:** Replacing sensitive data with a masking character, such as asterisks or Xs, so that it is not readable.

Data masking can be applied to both structured and unstructured data, and can be done at various levels, including field level, file level and database level. As part of creating a mature data platform management capability, every organization will need to establish **a data masking policy**. Data masking is often used in combination with other data security techniques, such as data encryption, data access controls and data auditing, to provide a comprehensive data security solution. These data security techniques for Big Data will be discussed further in Chapter 18.

16.5 Data platform management summary

The data platform management capability considers all technical components that an organization needs to manage its enterprise data. Since data is as trategic asset, and Big Data has significant value, this is a critical capability to enable long-term Big Data success.

Structuring the data platform management capability will require focus on the creation of proper processes and policies, as well as several common design choices that the organization needs to consider. In this chapter, we discussed a number of design aspects that an organization need to consider to establishing a mature data platform management capability.

Through the proper design of databases, data warehouses and data lakes, an organization can establish the proper storage mechanisms to safeguard enterprise data and ensure that this data can be trusted. By establishing a data catalogue, the enterprise data can be made available to the rest of the organization. And finally, through the establishment of data masking rules, data platform management ensures that the right data is accessible to the right persons, following proper rules and regulations.

Master and Metadata Management

17

17.1 Introduction to master and metadata management

Master and metadata management is the process of organizing, storing and maintaining information about data assets within an organization. With the enormous amounts of data that exist in any organization, it is critical to set up a suitable (technical) structure that enables an organization to manage its data assets.

Master data management is the process of managing the data that is used as a reference point for an organization, such as customer or product data. Metadata management is the process of managing data about data, such as information about the structure, format and lineage of data assets. Together, master and metadata management help organizations ensure that their data is accurate, consistent and can be easily accessed and understood by those who need it.

Master and metadata management is a critical (architecture) capability, which requires a sound and tested design. Organizations who have structured this capability adequately will experience **improved data quality**. A properly architected master and metadata management design ensures that the data assets within an organization are accurate, consistent and complete, which can improve the overall quality of the data and allow better use of it. This can lead to more accurate insights and predictions, and less risk of errors and inconsistencies in data-driven decisions.

Second, an adequately structured master and metadata management design will lead to enterprise-wide increased efficiency. By having a centralized repository for master data and metadata, organizations can reduce the time and effort required to access and understand data. This leads to **increased efficiency** in decision-making and operations, as users can easily find the data they need and trust that it is accurate and up to date. This can also help organizations avoid duplication of data, which can save time and resources.

Building on top of increased efficiency, organizations with a properly structured master and metadata management structure frequently experience **better decision-making**. With accurate and complete data, organizations can make better decisions, which can give them a competitive advantage in their industry (as discussed in Part 3). By having good master and metadata management, organizations can ensure that data is accurate and consistent, which can lead to better insights and predictions. This can help organizations make more informed decisions and improve their overall performance.

Finally, there is a strong business case for master and metadata management from a **cost perspective**. By automating data management processes and reducing errors, organizations can lower the costs associated with data management and maintenance. By having good master and metadata management, organizations can ensure that data is accurate and consistent, which can reduce the need for data cleaning and validation. This can also help organizations avoid duplication of data and improve data quality, which can save time and resources. Additionally, having a centralized repository for master data and metadata can reduce the cost of maintaining multiple systems and data silos.

From the four listed benefits above, it is easy to see that master and metadata management is a critical capability, which requires proper design. Although many tools and technologies offer the features to set master and metadata, very few organizations have properly structured this. Yet, it is a fundamental aspect of proper design of a Big Data organization. The bigger the data an organization collects, the stronger the need for master and metadata management. In the next few sections, we will discuss the purpose and capability levels of this capability, as well as some fundamental design approaches.

17.2 Purpose and maturity levels of master and metadata management

Purpose

The fundamental purpose of the master and metadata management capability for any organization is to exercise control – control over the data that enters the organization, and over the data that is stored. By establishing master and metadata management, organizations can work towards standardization of data assets. Ultimately, the purpose of master and metadata management is to ensure that data is accurate, consistent and can be easily accessed and understood by those who need it.

The master data management part of this capability ensures **consistency**. With master data management, organizations determine a schema for the way data should be stored, together with the relevant naming conventions. Master data management is, in that regard, similar to the schema definitions in database design (for those who have a background in database design), but then at scale. The schemas are not just determined for individual tables, but for all information across the enterprise.

The purpose of master data management is to ensure that this schema or reference data is accurate and consistent across the organization, and that it can be easily accessed and understood by those who need it. This can include data such as customer names, product codes and account numbers. Master data is often shared across multiple systems and departments, so it is important that it is accurate and consistent to avoid errors and confusion. Master data management requires proper design, and the making of choices. In a multinational enterprise, for example, a decision will need to be made about the language (and therefore spelling) of master data. Will the organization have tables with 'organizations' or 'organisations'? A simple decision, but one with potentially far-reaching implications for the storage and usage of data.

The metadata part of this capability concerns itself with the **searchability** of data sets. Metadata management is the process of managing data about data, such as information about the structure, format and lineage of data assets. The purpose of metadata management is to ensure that data assets are properly understood and can be easily accessed and understood by those who need it. Most search algorithms (and data catalogues, which were discussed in Chapter 16) work based on metadata. Therefore, the organization needs to determine what data it will store about other data sets. This can include information such as data types, data relationships and data sources. Metadata is essential for understanding data assets and how they are used within an organization.

The purpose of master and metadata management is outlined in Table 17.1.

A key characteristic of an organization that has structured master and metadata management well is that it has a **centralized, unified view of its data assets**. This means that master data and metadata is stored in a single, centralized repository, which can be easily accessed and understood by those who need it. This can help ensure data consistency and searchability across the organization, and can make it easier for users to find the data they need.

Additionally, an organization with well-structured master and metadata management typically has a robust data governance framework in place. This includes clear roles, responsibilities and processes for managing data assets, and can help ensure that data is of high quality and that data breaches are prevented. We will discuss the

Table 17.1 The purpose of the data platform management capability

Capability	Purpose
Master and metadata management	Defines the ability to establish infrastructure and processes for specifying and extending clear and organized information about the enterprise data assets under management.

relationship between the master and metadata management capability and the data governance process further in Part 6.

Master and metadata management maturity levels

Master and metadata management is a clear capability, since it is easy to determine how well this has been put in place. Since it is very factual and operational (it is either in place or not), it is relatively straightforward to determine the maturity at which any enterprise is operating. An organization that has a high maturity level in this capability has structured master and metadata management well, and is characterized by its ability to effectively organize, store and maintain information about its data assets, while ensuring data consistency, accuracy, security and compliance. These organizations have implemented best practices and processes to maintain high quality data and have a centralized, unified view of their data assets, which makes it easy to access, understand and make use of it.

Table 17.2 Master and metadata management maturity levels

Maturity Level	Description
Level 1 – Initial	Master and metadata management is done based on 'best effort' with limited formal processes in place. Data is often stored in silos and there is little governance or oversight of data quality.
Level 2 – Managed	There are some basic processes in place, and master and metadata management are recognized as a requirement in the organization. Data is still stored in silos, but there is more oversight and control over data quality.
Level 3 – Defined	Master and metadata management is more centralized, with formalized processes in place for data governance, data quality management and metadata management. Data is integrated across different systems and departments, and there is better oversight and control over data quality.
Level 4 – Controlled	Master and metadata management is highly centralized, with formalized processes and metrics in place for data governance, data quality management and metadata management. Data is integrated across different systems and departments, and there is a high level of oversight and control over data quality. Automation is used to improve data quality, and data governance and metadata.
Level 5 – Optimized	Master and metadata management is continuously improved using metrics, and automation is used to improve data quality and data governance. The organization can optimize the use of data and the management of data assets.

An organization that lacks master and metadata management, on the other hand, may face several consequences such as inaccurate or inconsistent data, difficulty in accessing and understanding data and unpredictable cost patterns.

Effective master and metadata management starts with a proper design. Without this design, the management aspect of this capability will become infeasible. The different maturity levels in Table 17.2 clearly indicate the impact of this design, and what organizations can do to grow or elevate their maturity. This design is subsequently translated into a proper architecture, which can be implemented through various tools and technologies.

17.3 Structuring master and metadata management

Designing master and metadata management in an enterprise can be a complex and challenging task, as it involves integrating and managing a large amount of data from different systems and departments. In this section, we will consider some of the main approaches and considerations that will help determine where to start.

Identification of critical master and metadata

The first step in setting up proper master data management is to identify **critical master and metadata,** which are the key data elements that are used as reference data throughout an organization. Identifying critical master data is an essential first step in setting up master data management, as it helps organizations prioritize which data elements to focus on and ensures that master data management is aligned with the organization's goals and objectives.

To identify critical master data, organizations can take the following steps.

1 **Conduct a data inventory:** Conduct a thorough inventory of all data assets within the organization, including data stored in different systems and departments. This can help organizations understand the breadth and depth of their data assets and identify which data elements are used as reference data.

2 **Analyse data usage:** Analyse how data is used within the organization, including which data elements are used most frequently and which ones are critical for different business processes. This can help organizations understand which data elements are most important and prioritize them accordingly.

3 **Identify data duplication:** Identify data elements that are duplicated across different systems and departments, as these are likely to be critical master data.

4 **Consult with stakeholders:** Consult with stakeholders, such as business users and department heads, to understand their data needs and identify which data elements are critical for their specific roles and responsibilities.

5 **Assess the impact of data quality issues:** Assess the impact of data quality issues on the business processes; this can help identify which data elements are critical to the business and need to be prioritized.

In most organizations, the role that typically performs the step to identify critical master data is that of the **Data Governance Team** or **data steward**. The Data Governance Team is responsible for the overall management of data assets within an organization and typically includes members from different departments, such as IT, operations and business units. The data steward is a role within the Data Governance Team, and is usually someone with domain knowledge, and for that reason is one of the most suitable roles to help identify which data should be considered master data.

Create a centralized repository

Since master data is enterprise wide, it should be stored in a centralized repository. Creating a centralized repository for master data management is a critical step in ensuring that data is accurate, consistent and accessible across different systems and departments. By storing master data in a single location, organizations can ensure that data is consistent and accurate, which can help improve data quality and reduce errors. It is generally considered best practice to have just a single tool that determines the master data schema across the entire enterprise.

An additional benefit is that data governance (which we will discuss in more detail in Part 6) is also improved by having a centralized repository, as it provides a clear structure of the master data and its lineage, which can help ensure that data is being used ethically and responsibly, and that data breaches are prevented. The centralized repository also allows for better control and monitoring of data access, which can help improve data security and protect sensitive data from unauthorized access. A centralized repository makes it easier to integrate master data with other data sources and systems, which can help improve data integration and support business intelligence, analytics and reporting.

A common mistake about the centralized master data management repository is that organizations consider it the same as a data lake. Most data lakes (discussed in Chapter 14) can support master data management by providing a centralized repository for storing and managing large amounts of data. Data lakes are designed to handle Big Data and support a wide variety of data types and formats, which can be useful for storing master data. However, note that data lakes are not specifically designed for master data management, but can be used in conjunction with master data management tools to provide an efficient way to store and manage master data.

Enable automated data integration

Establishing proper master and metadata schemas and definitions is of no use if data is subsequently not properly stored in the required format, or if the required metadata is not properly added. Establishing automated data integration is crucial to establishing a high level of maturity in this capability.

Automated data integration helps to collect data from different sources, and takes the appropriate steps to ensure that only the correct data (as determined by the master data managements schema) is integrated by different systems and sources into the centralized repository. This centralized repository will therefore only contain the master data.

To enable automated data integration towards a single repository requires some advance forms of data engineering. For static data, it is common to use Extract-Transform-Load (ETL) operations to change data (frequently referred to as **data wrangling**) to the required format. For streaming data, it requires the design and establishment of data pipelines to govern this process. In Big Data organizations, it will be close to impossible to do this process manually, so the integration and transformation toward master data must be supported by automated tools and workflows.

17.4 Master and metadata management summary

As we have seen throughout this chapter, establishing master and metadata management is a critical design capability. A proper design will ensure enterprise data sets are properly structured and easy to search. However, it is a capability that requires significant effort.

As we have seen in this chapter, setting up high maturity master and metadata management can be a complex and multi-step process. The process starts with the proper identification of the master and metadata an organization wants to collect. What master data does the organization want to keep, and which metadata needs to be added to existing and new data sets?

The second key objective is to create a centralized repository. By creating a centralized repository for master data and metadata, data can be easily accessed and understood by those who need it. This repository should be integrated with other systems and departments to ensure data consistency and accuracy across the organization.

Lastly, organizations need to make sure that data is integrated based on the master and metadata requirements that have been defined. A highly mature organization needs to enable data integration capabilities, such as data mapping and data trans-formation, to ensure that master data and metadata can be easily integrated with other data sources and systems.

The ultimate benefit of master and metadata management is the ability to make better, more informed decisions. Master data management ensures that the reference data that is used throughout the organization is searchable and consistent. This can help improve data quality, reduce errors and make data more actionable. Metadata management ensures that data is well-described, properly classified and related to other data, making it more findable, understandable and usable.

Information Security Management 18

18.1 Introduction to information security management

The last critical capability in Big Data is information security management. It is an all-encompassing capability that is applicable to an organization's entire Big Data architecture. Information security management is, and should be, interwoven with all the other capabilities that were discussed in this section.

Because of its importance, we have seen the Information Security capability also in the NIST Big Data Reference Architecture, which was presented in Chapter 13 section 13.4. Security in this context was defined as a 'fundamental aspect of the NBDRA', which is similar to our definition of a critical capability.

The information security management capability has become of increased importance, since most organizations' value today can be expressed in data. And large data sets can contain a potential significant amount of value. Information about customers, bank account details, production recipes and product blueprints are now all stored in digital format. For people or organizations with malicious intentions, these records can have a significant amount of value. Even if hackers don't intend to exploit information themselves, the data alone can have significant value for people who are willing to pay the price.

With the increasing volume of data that is being collected, the value that has been captured in enterprise data has grown. As a result, the number of cybersecurity attacks has also increased. Hackers today are no longer just kids in the attic trying to see if they can access a system for fun. Rather, most cybercrime is perpetrated by professional criminal organizations. These organizations have the resources, teams and money to launch advanced attacks, and they typically go after organizations that have Big Data sets. As a multinational organization today, it is no longer a question of whether you will be targeted by these groups, but when. The fact that we still, unfortunately, read about data leaks or stolen records on a daily basis in the newspapers is a testament to the criminals' success.

The information security management capability is therefore critical, and any Big Data architecture should be designed from a security point of view. In this section, we will take a closer look at some of the main threats to Big Data organizations, and what measures and structures organizations can put in place to safeguard their enterprise data.

18.2 Purpose and maturity levels of information security management

Purpose

The main objective of the information security management capability is to ensure that enterprise data is safe. With safe data, organizations can safeguard the confidentiality, integrity, availability and non-repudiation of data. In more simple terms, information security management needs to ensure that enterprise data is only accessible by those in the enterprise who should have access to it, and that everyone can trust the data that they are looking at.

Whereas in the early days of cybersecurity, the focus was primarily on confidentiality and integrity, more advanced security threats now target the validity and accuracy of models and machine learning algorithms, which are significant risks for Big Data organizations. We will consider these types of attacks further in section 18.3.

The purpose of information security management is outlined in Table 18.1.

Ultimately, the information security management capability aims to protect the enterprise data held by the organization from damage, to prevent its harmful, illegal or inappropriate use (to people or organizations), and to facilitate its legitimate operational and business use.

Information security management maturity levels

Building high levels of maturity in information security management is a lengthy but worthwhile exercise. More than any other capability in the Enterprise Big Data Framework, the lack of maturity in this capability has the potential to significantly harm an organization. Besides the obvious financial damage that is caused by

Table 18.1   The purpose of the information security management capability

Capability	Purpose
Information security management	Defines the ability to protect enterprise data and information from damage, theft or inappropriate use.

Table 18.2   Information security management maturity levels

Maturity Level	Description
Level 1 – Initial	The approach to information security management tends to be localized. Incidents are typically not responded to in a timely manner.
Level 2 – Managed	The organization has defined security approaches, policies and controls, but these controls are primarily focused on complying with regulations or meeting certain external security standards.
Level 3 – Defined	Standardized security approaches, policies and controls are in place across the Big Data organization, dealing with access rights, business continuity, budgets, toolsets, incident response management, audits, non-compliance and management controls.
Level 4 – Controlled	Comprehensive security approaches, policies and controls are in place and are fully integrated across the organization. The organization has an effective security strategy, technical security measures, security data administration and data model security.
Level 5 – Optimized	Security approaches, policies and controls are regularly reviewed to maintain proactivity in preventing security breaches. The organization is considered to be a leader in safeguarding enterprise data.

cybersecurity threats and stolen data, there is also the reputational damage from which it might take years to recover.

For any organization that processes Big Data at scale, and which is dependent on Big Data for its day-to-day strategic and operational decision-making, it is therefore recommended to set a high, ambitious target for maturity in information security management.

An overview of the different maturity levels is outlined in Table 18.2.

In a mature organization, there is awareness and understanding across the organization of the role that effective information security plays in business success – security is recognized as an enabler rather than a disabler.

18.3 Structuring information security management

The information security management capability concerns itself with the information and data protection of Big Data environments from unauthorized tampering with regards to different users and the authorization they have. The security of Big

Data architecture builds on the extensive domain of cybersecurity, and is characterized by confidentiality, integrity, availability, accountability and authenticity.

To structure an information security management capability, many good standards and best practices exist. An effective management structure will always consider multiple points of view, and focus on a combination of technical, process, people and vendor security measures. To build an effective capability, organizations will need to consider:

- Security strategy and governance
- Technical security measures
- Security data administration
- Data model security

Whereas the first three components are applicable for all IT organizations that process data, the last components is more specialized specifically to the processing of Big Data sets.

Security strategy and governance

Security strategy and governance means that an organization should have the information security management capability on its strategic agenda. Any organization that processes Big Data should develop, communicate and make resources available to **define security objectives**. This starts with identifying which data has value for the enterprise, and cascaded down to different security measures, based on the importance (and dependence) on these enterprise data sets.

This strategy needs to be expressed in information security policies and controls. These controls determine on what the organization should focus, and what investments are required to meet the strategic objectives. Most organizations will base their security strategy, governance and policies on international standards and best practices, such as the ISO/IEC 27001:2018 standard for information security management.

As part of these controls, procedures and policies, it is important not to forget about the largest threat to security in any enterprise: employees. In order to make security a priority, people should be aware about the nature of attacks, common threat mechanisms and what they can to personally contribute to safeguard security. This means that organizations need to disseminate security policies, organize **security awareness training** and develop security skills across the enterprise.

Technical security measures

Besides management controls, Big Data architecture obviously requires a variety of technical security measure. This measure will safeguard the networks, storage solutions and processing capabilities across the enterprise. A sound design for technical security measures begins with a security architecture, then needs be integrated within the enterprise Big Data architecture. This means that security already needs to be 'built in' the design of Big Data environments, like, for example, by defining coding protocols, depth of defense and configuration of security resources.

As part of this infrastructure, is important to secure all end points and potential locations where malicious intermediaries can get access to enterprise data. **IT endpoint security** implements measures to protect all IT components, both physical and virtual, such as servers, networks and storage devices. Through end-point security, organizations can limit the possibilities of potential attacks by minimizing the number of locations attackers can access the Big Data environment.

Technical security measures additionally include all the 'standard' security techniques and best practices that are, or should be, part of any professional IT organization. Examples include the encryption of sensitive data, establishing secure communication protocols and protection enterprise network traffic.

Security data administration

Since data sets or files contain value, they are the main target and object of interest for any attackers. In Big Data environments, special consideration should therefore be taken to protect the data sets themselves. This starts with establishing a proper **data identification and classification programme**, which categorizes and ranks enterprise data into different security classes. Common classification schemes vary from 'top secret' to 'public', with a number of different security classifications in between. Based on this classification, organizations can subsequently define roles and permissions based on different departments and job roles. Data identification and classification is an integral topic in the data management process, a capability that we will explore further in Part 6.

Based on the data classification, individual employees should be granted appropriate access rights, which is better known as identity and access management (IAM). Identity and access management manages user access rights to information throughout its life cycle, including granting, denying and revoking access privileges. For any organization with a significant number of employees, this is a day-to-day operational function.

Lastly, security data administration also includes the proactive monitoring of enterprise data. Is a particular employee trying to access data for which they lack the proper security clearance? Or is an employee downloading large amounts of data that appears to be unrelated to their job role? If one of these situations happens it is likely that there will be a security leak. Although the topic of **proactive monitoring** is subject to debate (especially with regards to privacy), it is nowadays a must-have requirement for organizations. If something malicious is transpiring, it is important that an organization acts immediately, instead of after a few hours. Only through proactive, round-the-clock monitoring can this goal be accomplished.

Data model security

The last category that can help to build information security management in organizations is specifically related to Big Data, and includes a new set of threats that are especially relevant to organizations that use models and algorithms to make predications. Most of these threats are aimed at deliberately tricking algorithms or models into making false predictions,

Adversarial examples or data poisoning techniques aim to inject small sets of erroneous or deliberately false data into enterprise databases, so that predictive machine learning models make the wrong conclusions. With adversarial examples, the alterations are typically small, and therefore frequently go undetected. Data poisoning attacks are usually a bit more extreme and have the goal of undermining trust. If an organization no longer knows which data they can trust, it becomes very hard to make adequate decisions. Especially if data poisoning goes undetected for longer periods of time, which can have a significant impact.

There are many techniques nowadays to deal with adversarial examples of data poisoning, like adversarial example detection, hashing, data encryption and ensemble analysis. However, most organizations are unaware that attacks exist that specifically target machine learning models or data analysis processes. To structure a proper information security management system, it is therefore critical to also consider data model security.

18.4 Information security management summary

Information security management is the last critical capability of Enterprise Big Data architecture. We have deliberately chosen to consider this topic as the last capability since it encompasses all the other topics we have discussed throughout this section.

Information security management is critical and crucial to any Big Data organization. Since value is nowadays in data, protecting this value has become a core objective. As we have seen throughout this chapter, the risks for cybersecurity attacks have grown significantly, and most attacks today are professionally organized.

In order to protect enterprise data, it is important that organizations safeguard the confidentiality, integrity and non-repudiation of the data. Protecting the enterprise data starts with the establishment of a sound security strategy, and adequate governance measures. These measures subsequently need to be translated into policies, procedure and processes, which will safeguard security controls throughout the organization. Here, it is important not to forget about the human aspect, and organize appropriate security awareness and information campaigns.

It is imperative that an organization also protects its direct assets and limits the way it can become vulnerable to cybersecurity attacks. Through the implementation of technical security measures, the organization needs to protect its devices, servers and databases. Through data security administration, the organization can put in place additional controls to establish a system of data classification and data access.

We concluded the chapter by looking at more advanced security concerns, especially for Big Data organizations that use predictive models and algorithms. Organizations that rely on these algorithms for day-to-day operations need to establish a proper data model security.

Big Data Architecture Maturity Assessment

19

Please respond to the following questions by indicating the relevant level of maturity for each activity and its importance to your organization.

The Capability Maturity Model levels are shown in Table 19.1.

Please note that responses to this survey should reflect how the organization performs the task today, not how you would like to see the organization perform the task in the future. Your choices should be based on your opinion of the organization, not just the way the task is performed in your own workgroup.

Table 19.1 Capability Maturity Model levels

Score	Description
0 – Non-existent	Describes a total lack of activity or lack of recognition that the activity exists.
1 – Initial	Describes evidence that the organization recognizes issues exist and need to be addressed.
2 – Managed	Describes activities designed so that similar procedures are followed by individuals. There is a high reliance on individual knowledge and skill level.
3 – Defined	Describes a standardized and documented level of activities which is being communicated through training, processes and tools.
4 – Controlled	Describes activities that are good practice and under constant improvement. Automation and tools are used to support the activities.
5 – Optimized	Describes activities that are considered leading and best practice and can be considered an example to other organizations.

Table 19.2   Big Data Architecture Maturity Assessment

#	Big Data Architecture Management	Score
7.1	Our Big Data architecture is based on an international standard and reference architecture.	
7.2	We have a comprehensive, accurate and documented view of our Big Data architecture, including all components that make up this architecture.	
7.3	We have a modular Big Data architecture, where we can update individual components or applications on a periodic basis.	
7.4	We periodically review our Big Data architecture and take actions to improve the overall architecture.	
7.5	Our IT architecture supports both batch processing and stream processing, and the establishment of data pipelines.	
7.6	We have appointed dedicated Big Data architect roles, who manage and strategically lead the development and maintenance of the Big Data architecture.	
	Infrastructure Management	**Score**
8.1	Our organization's Big Data infrastructure ensures stability and availability of data sets through robust infrastructure solutions.	
8.2	Our organization's infrastructure solutions ensure that our environment is in line with security best practices and always compliant to internal and external audit requirements.	
8.3	The infrastructure of our Big Data organization meets performance and scalability requirements through automated provisioning of IT services.	
8.4	Our Big Data infrastructure supports the proper functioning of Big Data pipelines and workflows to appropriately manage high-volume, high-velocity requests.	
8.5	Our Big Data infrastructure is designed in line with data governance standards and meets required data privacy regulations.	
8.6	Our organization has real-time monitoring and response procedures in place to monitor and maintain the Big Data infrastructure and ensure the smooth operation of the system.	
	Data Platform Management	**Score**
9.1	Our data platform can differentiate between transactional data, master data and metadata.	
9.2	Our organization's data warehouse is stored in a multidimensional data model.	
9.3	Our organization's data platform is designed to handle a wide variety of data types and sources, including structured, semi-structured and unstructured data.	

(continued)

Table 19.2   (Continued)

9.4	Our enterprise data platform has the ability to create profile-based data catalogues, allowing users to browse and search the enterprise data
9.5	Our data management platform has capabilities for data masking, to obfuscate or hide confidential or personal information.
9.6	Our organization has defined adequate processes to validate the quality of data entering the data platform and enforces these processes.

Master and Metadata Management	**Score**
10.1	Our organization's data catalogue and metadata repository are maintained and proactively updated.
10.2	We have defined adequate master and metadata management procedures, particularly regarding data definitions, standards and policies, and these procedures are adequately enforced.
10.3	Our organization has developed data lineage and impact capabilities that are actively used.
10.4	Our organization has defined and implemented master data management (MDM), particularly about data quality, consistency and accessibility.
10.5	Our metadata management processes are integrated with our Big Data architecture and management systems.
10.6	Our organization utilizes metadata to support data discovery, exploration and analytics.

Information Security Management	**Score**
11.1	Our organization's information security strategy is aligned with industry best practices and standards, such as ISO/IEC 27001 and NIST.
11.2	Our organization's big data infrastructure is secured against external and internal threats, such as cyber-attacks and unauthorized access.
11.3	Our organization's data encryption, access control and identity and access management (IAM) policies and technologies have been properly implemented and are suitably enforced.
11.4	Our organization's data privacy policies and procedure are compliant with relevant regulations.
11.5	Our organization's Big Data environment is proactively monitored, audited and tested for vulnerabilities and potential security breaches.
11.6	Our organization has measures in place to safeguard the quality of the predictions of algorithms and has measures to safeguard against adversarial examples or data poisoning techniques.

PART FIVE
Big Data
Algorithms

Big Data Algorithms

20

20.1 Introduction to Big Data algorithms

The potential applications of Big Data are vast and numerous. Big Data can be used to predict stock prices, identify fraudulent transactions or find cures to new diseases. To build successful solutions or use cases, data scientists need to find a way to retrieve value from massive data sets.

To accomplish this objective, data needs to be queried or analysed with the help of algorithms. Some of these algorithms will be very simple, like finding the averages in historical sales records. Other algorithms will be extremely complex, like Google's search algorithm to determine the most 'suitable' search results based on a few keywords.

No matter how simple or complex the problem, a basic tenet of Big Data is that there will always be some form of algorithm that will need to run, to obtain a specific result. We could even go as far as to say that Big Data would not exist without algorithms. To benefit from data analysis, analytics and Big Data, it is therefore a requirement that organizations build up knowledge in the proper design and application of algorithms. Which algorithms need to be used? How will these algorithms be selected? And who develops (and maintains) these algorithms? Building capabilities in this area is a key characteristic of successful Big Data organizations.

In this section of the book, we will first start with providing a comprehensive overview of the world of Big Data algorithms and explain the main differences between different classes of algorithms and their main purposes. After this overview, we will dive into the capabilities that organizations can build up to properly design, develop, store and maintain algorithms within an enterprise environment.

Building knowledge about the development of algorithms is a task that is frequently referred to as the domain of data science: the scientific approach of looking at data. This section of the book can be considered the 'data science part' of the Enterprise Big Data Framework. There is, however, one fundamental difference compared with the traditional views in data science. We strongly believe that knowledge about algorithms (i.e. data science) is just one essential capability within the framework. You can have all the knowledge in the world about algorithms but still not be able to set up a successful Big Data organization if you are lacking the proper direction (strategy), sound underlying technology (architecture) or suitable structures and processes (discussed in the next few sections). It is therefore important to consider algorithms as a part – a very important part – of Big Data, but not as a standalone capability.

The ability to design and develop algorithms is a skill that requires years to master, and which is a process of trial and error (with mostly errors). An organization needs to create an environment in which this skill can flourish, and in which people can learn this skill from colleagues and other peers. In Part 7 of this book, we will further expand on organizational capabilities that are necessary to create such an environment.

20.2 Classes of Big Data algorithms

To retrieve value from data sets, there are potentially hundreds, if not thousands, of approaches that data analysts or data scientists can take. Some of these problems would simply require the use of pre-programmed, readily available algorithms (in standardized R or Python libraries). Other problems would require a data scientist to develop an algorithm from scratch, creatively combining multiple mathematical rules together.

To bring some structure to the large topic of Big Data algorithms, it is first necessary to bring some structure to the types of algorithms that exist. A functional approach is to categorize algorithms by their business purpose. What problem is the algorithm trying to solve? And what is the main question that the algorithm needs to answer?[1]

A functional classification of the types of algorithms that can used to solve Big Data business problems is depicted in Figure 20.1.

For functional purposes in business environments, the five classes of algorithms above will cover most enterprise problems. For example, a bank that needs to make a prediction about which customers will default on loans is dealing with a machine learning problem and will need to select a machine learning algorithm to solve this problem. In another example, a transportation company trying to optimize its delivery routes is dealing with a search problem and needs to apply a search algorithm.

Most algorithms that are used or developed in an enterprise context will be used to solve a business problem. By understanding some of the most common and important algorithms in each class, organizations can prepare themselves (i.e. build the capability to become more proficient) in solving problems.

To complete the picture above, there is a sixth class of algorithms that is more advanced, and which aims to mimic human decision-making in a computer. This class of algorithms – better known as artificial intelligence – has been omitted from Figure 20.1 on purpose, because it will be discussed in further detail in Part 8.

Figure 20.1   Common classes of algorithms based on their business purpose

Descriptive Analysis	Data Mining	Searching	Machine Learning	Reasoning
Do you need to report summary information about a data set?	Are you trying to uncover unknown patterns in a data set?	Are you trying to find the best design or solution amongst a variety of options?	Are you trying to predict a future value or class based on input data?	Are you trying to find a causal relationship between two or more variables?

20.3 Algorithm design and Big Data programming languages

To develop or design algorithms requires creativity, analytical capabilities and – above all else – some fundamental knowledge about the ways in which data is processed by a computer. Although many excellent Big Data tools exist, with many good pre-built algorithms, there is never a one-size-fits-all kind of application, and data analysts and scientists will need to be able to read code and master a programming language.

In the domain of Big Data, there are two programming languages that are most widely used: Python and R. Each language has its own advocates, and its own benefits and disadvantages. People who have learned Big Data in the academic domain were most likely taught to design algorithms in the R programming language. Data analysts or scientists who were trained at software development companies will likely have more experience – and hence be advocates of – Python.

Python

Whilst is recommended to learn both, in most enterprise organizations Python is the dominant language for solving business problems (R is still the most dominant language in the academic domain). Python is a high-level, interpreted, general-purpose programming language. Its design philosophy emphasizes code readability with the use of significant indentation.[2] It was originally released in 1991 by Guido van Rossum, a Dutch researcher at the Dutch Mathematical Institute.[3]

What makes Python a strong language, especially for solving Big Data problems, is that it is relatively simple to read and therefore can be shared amongst team members. Additionally, Python has a design that is highly modular, and which allows for easy integration of third-party solutions or algorithms. In Python, these modular components are called packages. The fact that any person or any organization can create packages to 'plug' into Python makes the support and community for this language very strong. For enterprise organizations, who frequently don't have the time or knowledge to develop and maintain solutions from scratch, working with Python-based solutions provides a comprehensive way to enable their Big Data solutions.

For that reason, we will illustrate algorithms in this section in the Python language, whenever this necessary or applicable. The purpose of this book is not to provide a comprehensive overview of Python, or to teach you how to code. There are numerous very good resources available to support this purpose. However, we do think it is important to be able to relate conceptual capabilities into practical solutions. In Chapter 22, for example, we will discuss the Data Cleaning and Wrangling capability. Everyone will understand that clean data is important for data analysis. We will also discuss in more detail how this capability can be built, which is where some basic Python scripts will be necessary.

R

The second dominant language in the design and development of Big Data algorithms is the R programming language, simply known as 'R'. The R language is based on the proprietary 'S' language, which was developed at Bell Labs in 1976. R has a strong history in the statistics domain, and is a language devised by statisticians for statisticians. Because of this reason, R has many comprehensive and high-quality packages for advanced statistical operations.[4]

A second reason – besides its strong statistical capabilities – the R language has many fans and advocates is its strong graphical capabilities and visualizations. R has the ability to easily create high-quality graphs and images, which many people use to explain complicated research results, or to explain the steps in more advanced algorithms. These two features combined make R the second most popular language in the Big Data domain.

So which language is best to learn? Since this book is called *The Enterprise Big Data Framework*, and therefore focuses on Big Data in corporate environments, the answer to this question would be Python. However, to become a 'well-rounded' and capable data analyst or data scientist, it is strongly advisable to have more tools in your toolbox and learn R as well. Just like a good politician or businessman can converse in multiple languages, knowing multiple programming languages will give you a better understanding of the best way to design or create Big Data algorithms.

Jupyter Notebooks

The main thing that developers in Python and developers in R have in common is that they will frequently use Jupyter Notebooks. The Jupyter Project is a non-profit organization that develops open-source software, open-standards and services for interactive computing across dozens of programming languages.[5] In a simpler explanation, Jupyter Notebooks provides you with the ability to embed interactive scripts in between written texts. The text can explain the reasoning or design choices that have been made, whereas the scripts can be activated from within the document.

More importantly, Jupyter notebooks support scripts in Python and R (and even some other languages). So no matter which programming language is used in a project, understanding how to read and use a Jupyter Notebook is a fundamental skill in the use and development of Big Data algorithms. As we will discuss further in Chapter 25 on reproducible research, one of the main capabilities that organizations will need to build is the ability to share and distribute information between teams and groups of people. It is therefore imperative that choices with regards to data, design and algorithm development are properly documented and supported. Jupyter Notebooks provide a comprehensive way in which this documentation can be created and is therefore a technology to understand.

20.4 Building Big Data algorithms capabilities

What does it mean to be capable in Big Data algorithms? And if these capabilities exist, how can an organization build them? Many organizations struggle with these questions. Fundamentally, Big Data algorithms answer the question of how an organization can retrieve value from its Big Data sets. This can be through very simple queries that showcase summary statistics, like historic sales record, or the algorithms can be very complex, like automated facial recognition.

Understanding how algorithms work requires logical thinking and a fundamental understanding of how computer programs execute code to generate results. Whereas minor performance issues might be irrelevant for small data sets, Big Data requires data scientists to also think about performance issues. If you need to analyse terabytes of data in real-time, it does matter how your algorithms execute their code. And to understand this requires a 'beyond-average' understanding of some of the basic computer processing and storage techniques. Big Data problems require skills in software engineering that traditional statisticians or data analyst typically don't have. In more simple words, it requires skills that make you understand what happens 'under the hood' of an algorithm.

To define capabilities for sound Big Data algorithms, we therefore need to look at the competencies of the people who need to understand and build these algorithms. Any organization that wants to obtain value from large data sets therefore needs to have fundamental knowledge about how to apply algorithms to solve real-world problems. As with most of the capabilities discussed throughout this book, this requires knowledge and experience that organizations can build up over years.

Besides the **software engineering** capabilities that we mentioned above, it is also important to understand which algorithms can be used to solve business problems.

Before any organization can, for example, build a recommendation engine to increase their sales processes, they first need to know which types of recommendation engines exists. And from the half-dozen recommended, commonly used engines, a data scientist would need to choose the most suitable option, based on the characteristics of the input data and the performance (i.e. computational speed) of the algorithms. Since it is important to 'know your algorithms', this section will consider **data cleaning and wrangling, descriptive data analysis** and **machine learning** fundamental capabilities required for creating a Big Data organization. Although data cleaning, descriptive data analysis and machine learning all use algorithms, they all use distinct (and different) sets of algorithms, so it is more practical to consider these as three separate capabilities.

The last capability that organizations need to retrieve long-term value from data is concerned with the ability to communicate about the technology. And in many cases this is where even the most experienced data scientists struggle. Algorithms may contain tremendous value, but if they cannot be properly explained to senior managers or boardrooms, they have little impact. The capability of **reproducible research** is therefore equally crucial. A complete overview of all five capabilities that make up the Big Data algorithms capability is shown in Figure 20.2.

20.5 Big Data algorithms and data science

The terms Big Data and data science are frequently used interchangeably, and there is a significant amount of overlap between these domains. Data science, as per the

Figure 20.2 Big Data algorithms capabilities

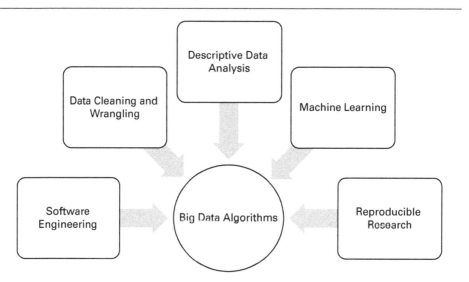

definition from NIST, is the empirical synthesis of actionable knowledge from raw data through the complete data lifecycle process.[6] As such, data science focuses primarily on the process from data ingestion to actionable insights. However, the domain of data science does not say anything about the size of the data sets that need to be processed. Building machine learning on a small data set would fall under the data science domain, but would be considered Big Data.

In the Enterprise Big Data Framework the primary focus is retrieving value by analysing data sets that are large in volume, velocity and variety. In the modern world, and in most enterprises or other large organizations, the data sets will be large. And as we have seen in the preceding chapters, this requires additional considerations in terms of strategy and technology. For that reason we have chosen not to use the word 'data science' to indicate the development of algorithms, but to consistently use the term 'Big Data algorithms'. We feel this term more adequately reflects the technical knowledge required to retrieve value from Big Data, and that it might contribute to a reduction in the confusion between the two terms.

In the next five chapters, we will focus on the five micro-capabilities that help organizations understand *how* value is retrieved from large data sets, and which capabilities are necessary to achieve this. Although the algorithms that organizations will need to use will be different from business problem to business problem, these six capabilities are universal.

Notes

1 J T Leek. and R D Peng. What is the question?, *Science*, 2015 347 (6228), 1314–15
2 D Cielen and A Meysman (2016) *Introducing Data Science: Big data, machine learning, and more, using Python tools*. Simon and Schuster
3 G Van Rossum (1995) Python reference manual. Department of Computer Science [CS], (R 9525)
4 N Matloff (2011) *The Art of R Programming: A tour of statistical software design*. No Starch Press
5 F Perez and B E Granger. Project Jupyter: Computational narratives as the engine of collaborative data science, 2015 11 (207) 108, https://scholar.google.com/scholar?hl=en&as_sdt=0%2C5&q=F+Perez+and+B+E+Granger.+Project+Jupyter%3A+Computational+narratives+as+the+engine+of+collaborative+data+science.+Retrieved+September%2C+2015+11+%28207%29+108&btnG= (archived at https://perma.cc/4SSL-D7Y3)
6 B J Dorr, C S Greenberg, P Fontana, M Przybocki, M Le Bras, C Ploehn, O Aulov, M Michel, E J Golden and W Chang (2015) The NIST data science initiative. In 2015 IEEE International Conference on Data Science and Advanced Analytics (DSAA), October, 1–10. IEEE

Software Engineering 21

21.1 Introduction to software engineering

Designing or building an algorithm requires a fundamental understanding of computer science and the way that computers execute code by processing instructions. Ultimately, processing a Big Data set is nothing more than a number of computer instructions executed by a software program. And this means that, as a data analyst or scientist, it is necessary to have knowledge and skills around software engineering. As an organization, it means that you require software engineering capabilities.

Algorithms that are poorly designed may cause significant risks from a performance (and therefore monetary) aspect but can also have a significant impact from a security perspective. As data is becoming more and more valuable to power decision-making, it also means that there will be more and more people trying to get access to this data and exploit it. Most malicious attackers will look for weaknesses in software programs, which is another reason it is important to have a sound software engineering capability in your data organization.

Software engineering is the capability of an organization to create and maintain standardized and coherent code across the organization. In practice, this means a coherent way in which the hundreds of lines of code that are created across multiple Big Data projects are maintained, annotated and formatted in a clear and manageable way.

In many cases, the creation of an algorithm or Big Data system is similar to the creation of software, and it would be advisable to adhere to software engineering best practices, which have been around for many decades. Yet, many large organizations fail to do this. It might be the case that most data scientists come from the mathematical or statical domain, instead of computer science. Or it might be that this has always been an undervalued area for an organization, whose primary business is not software development. Whatever the reason, the fact remains that many companies lack clear standards on how code should be written and maintained, what the formatting requirements are and how it should be properly documented. For algorithms to remain enduring value, after the initial data scientist has created it, it is important that they (and their underlying code) are clean and maintainable by others.

A second reason that this capability is highlighted in the Big Data algorithms section is that – once an organization's Big Data maturity grows – companies would like to re-use work across multiple divisions or countries. In practice, this means that algorithms are translated into packages (in Python or R) that can be re-used in other parts of the organization. To take this step, it is even more important for organizations to adhere to clean and clear ways of developing algorithms. For this capability, we will also look at the ways in which organizations can grow maturity in software engineering, and which software engineering best practices will improve the capability of individual data engineers or scientists, and hence the capability of the entire organization.

21.2 Purpose and maturity levels of software engineering

Purpose

Ultimately, every algorithm is encoded into a number of lines of code. These lines of code will be executed on large data sets, in most cases numerous times. As organizations start benefitting from their data-driven decisions, the number of use cases (see Chapter 6) will further expand, leading to even more lines of code.

In most enterprise organizations, multiple people will work on Big Data projects and, over time and due to normal attrition, new people will join the organization and some people might leave. Each of these people will need to be able to read the code that colleagues created, in order to maintain and understand it over longer periods of time. The more the organization follows software engineering best practices, the easier it will be to maintain the algorithm's code base, and the less likely it will be that certain analysis might fail in case of any updates. Within the context of Big Data, the purpose of software engineering is defined as follows.

You might wonder to what degree maintenance of algorithms will be necessary in an organization. Algorithms that will summarize sales, for example, will always remain the same. Similarly, common machine learning algorithms (discussed in Chapters 23 and 24) rely on statistical principles, which are static. These algorithms, or the Python or R software packages in which they are encoded, rarely change.

Table 21.1   The purpose of the software engineering capability

Capability	Purpose
Software engineering	Defines the ability of an organization to maintain a structured and reliable code base of algorithms, which can be easily maintained.

Yet the element that in our experience is subject to change is either the input data or the output analysis. Over time, organizations have started utilizing new technology, which might generate new input data or input data in a different format. A company that upgrades their cameras, for example, will typically be confronted with newer, higher-quality videos. The algorithm that analyses these videos, for example for facial recognition, will need to be adjusted to these new input sources.

Similarly, organizations might change their requirements about the results of data analysis. If results are displayed in a particular graph, for example, it might be the case that management decides that they require a different, or more in-depth, visualization. In this case, the data scientist will equally need to be able to read and understand the code base, to accomplish this task.

A third and final category in which software engineering best practices are required for proper maintenance is for companies that develop and maintain Big Data algorithms. Take for example the Google search algorithm, which is probably the most famous (and most valuable) Big Data algorithm on the planet. This algorithm, which matches web page search results to an input phrase, has been frequently updated to make the search results users more relevant. Having the ability to easily read and understand the code base is in this case paramount to success. Although most enterprise companies will just use 'standardized' Big Data algorithms, instead of developing their own, it does illustrate why software engineering best practices are a critical capability for every organization that aims to get long-term value from the algorithms they utilize.

Maturity levels

The software engineering capability is one of the more straightforward capabilities that organizations can grow. Maturity of this capability mostly depends on the discipline amongst data scientists to adhere to an agreed corporate standard, and the quality control processes that an organization has in place to safeguard the quality of code. For example, an organization that has processes of peer-to-peer review before updated algorithms are put into production will operate at a higher maturity level than an organization where each data scientist can create algorithms based on their own preferences.

The five levels that define the software engineering capability are listed in Table 21.2.

As you identify the different levels of the software engineering capability, as outlined in Table 21.2, you will see that growing maturity in this capability is not tremendously difficult. Rather, it is a process of installing a structured and best practice discipline amongst the team of data scientists and data engineers. In the following section, we will consider some subsequent best practices to achieve this.

Table 21.2   Maturity levels of the software engineering capability

Maturity Level	Description
Level 1 – Initial	There is little or no standard when it comes to software engineering. Every data scientist will create, maintain and update code, based on their personal experience and personal preferences.
Level 2 – Managed	There is some level of collaboration and quality control between different colleagues (data scientists), but only on an informal and ad hoc basis. There is no uniform software development standard for the organization.
Level 3 – Defined	The organization has a defined software engineering standard for the creation and maintenance of big data algorithms, which is known and shared by the data scientist in the organization.
Level 4 – Controlled	The organization has quality control processes in place to check and identify whether code in algorithms adhere to the software engineering standards. These quality control processes can be formalized in human peer-to-peer review, or through automated tools. Any deviations from the standard are corrected or updated accordingly.
Level 5 – Optimized	Software engineering best practices are ingrained in the organization. The organization hosts frequent knowledge-sharing sessions about how the software engineering standards should be used, and has a quality review process in place to ensure that these standards are updated.

21.3 Structuring software engineering

In the previous section, we saw that the main purpose of the software engineering capability is to create, develop and maintain the code of Big Data algorithms in a way that is easy to understand and comprehend for all stakeholders involved.

Sound and mature software engineering practices will increase collaboration between teams, create a culture in which people motivate each other to improve and create an environment where people can learn from peers. More importantly, it will significantly reduce the time that people need to find and correct bugs and, significantly correlated with this, reduce frustrations. Poorly written code is one of the main reason people spend hours and hours trying to understand what is happening, before they can even try to come up with a solution. If you have any background in computer science or programming, this will sound familiar, because the problem is not unique to Big Data. All the more reason why the Big Data function should be leading the way in developing this capability.

In the next few sections, we will look at some of the best practices in software engineering that answer the question as to how an organization can build this capability. We will consider **coding standards, version control, testing best practices** and finally the development methodology of **Agile and Scrum**. Please note that these topics are not discussed in a particular order of importance, but all contribute to sound software engineering.

Coding standards

A first and simple step to take is to create a coding standard (or policy) for everyone that is working on creating, developing and maintaining the code for Big Data algorithms. This standard should outline choices that the company makes with regards to the way they develop. The whole purpose of a coding standard it to provide standardization, which becomes especially relevant in large organizations. It sounds trivial, but it greatly helps if everyone speaks the same language.

Let's take, for example, a very simple example as variable declaration, which should be part of every standard. Suppose we are building a customer credit rating system, and we would like to assign a numeric value (i.e. the credit rating to a variable). Below are five different ways in which the variable can be declared.

Although this example is trivial (and all the five different options will work in practice), it becomes messy if five different data scientists all use a different version. In algorithms, variables will form the input or output to other functions, which might be developed or maintained by other teams. And if the variables don't match, there will likely be errors. This is why standardization and a coding standard is important.

The way to specify variables is just one aspect that should be in a coding standard. Other aspects that need to be considered are:

- Commenting: the way in which comments are embedded in scripts
- Indentation: standardization in the indentation of scripts

Table 21.3   Variable declaration

Credit Rating =	0.96
Credit Rating =	0.96
Credit Rating =	0.96
Credit Rating =	0.96
CREDIT RATING =	0.96

- Function names: similar to variable names, a standard way in which functions are expressed

- Modularity: guidance on how large a single script should be or when a script should be broken down into individual modules.

All of the points listed above are straightforward and simple, and you will probably have your own preferences. But you will also have seen scripts created by others that you found more difficult to read or interpret because that author used different conventions. And that is exactly the point of defining a coding standard: to facilitate an easy and understandable way of working on Big Data algorithms.

Even though it sounds very easy to create a coding standard, the reality is that very few organizations have one in place. Not amongst data scientists or other IT staff in the organization. It is therefore recommended not to isolate the coding standard just to the Big Data function (and the data analysts and scientists working on Big Data algorithms), but to have a wider discussion about the desired coding standard in the entire organization. This will not only benefit the Big Data function but the entire IT department in general.

Version control

In the development of algorithms, and especially the maintenance over time, version control is a must-have requirement. As code gets updated, it is imperative that different people know what the latest version of a particular algorithms is, or who made changes at what moment in time. As complexity grows, and the adoption of Big Data solutions increases, the need for adequate version control becomes a necessity.

The need for version control in in Big Data algorithms can be summarized in the following three points:

- Collaboration – through version control, everyone in the team always knows the latest version of algorithms and scripts, and who has made changes to the code

- Backup – in case any work gets lost due to unforeseen circumstances (machine crash, laptop stolen), the organization can always revert to the latest version

- Rollback – if for whatever reason a new script or algorithm gives problems or errors in a production environment, the organization can always revert back to the latest version

Like coding standards, version control is a cornerstone in building capability in the software engineering domain. Although there are many good version control systems in the world, and most technology solutions come with a framework, the industry standard for algorithm version control is Git.

Git is a distributed version control system that allows users to efficiently download code bases and scripts (i.e. the code that describes your algorithms) from a centralized repository to a directory on your computer (for people familiar with Git, this process in known as 'cloning'). Individual users can then make edits or changes to the algorithms on their machines, and subsequently sync these changes back to the repo. Git will automatically keep track of any changes you made to script, add appropriate version numbering, and store it back in the repository.

A good analogy is to think about Git as system that automatically keeps track of different versions that you are writing, for example a Word document. Every time your open and edit the document, Git keeps track of the changes that you have written. But, unlike Word, you can also revert back to all the previous versions you have ever written, and it keeps track of every edit that has ever been made by anyone.

Note that Git is the distributed version control 'language', which can be used as open-source methodology by everyone. However, the repos (i.e. the centralized storage) are typically cloud-based storage, which is hosted by commercial companies. The most popular companies in this space are GitHub and Gitlab, which both have a similar offering to store version-controlled scripts based on Git version control.

Testing

Building capability in software engineering requires not just the writing and storage of algorithms and scripts but also the process to ensure that these algorithms work correctly. In other words, algorithms need to be tested to ensure that the work in the correct way. The primary purpose of creating tests is to ensure there are adequate checks in place that safeguard the algorithm to perform in the way it should, and that that the algorithm does not crash whenever it needs to process data for which it is not optimized, i.e. dealing with an exception.

Writing and maintaining good test scripts is a sign of high maturity in the software engineering capability and showcases that an organization has control over (and has thought about) the algorithms it develops. Building adequate testing methods is, however, a difficult skill to master. It requires significant time to think about what the algorithm should be doing and, maybe even more importantly, what the algorithm should not be doing. Within the software engineering domain, there are various best practices that help with building testing capability: **unit tests**, **integration tests**, and **test-driven development (TDD)**.

Unit tests, and more specifically the practice of creating unit tests, deals with establishing whether small, independent pieces of your Big Data algorithm work and perform the way they should. Unit testing is a software engineering method by which individual units of source code are tested to determine whether they are fit for use.[1] The scope of unit testing is therefore always on individual modules, which typically test whether an individual script is working. Unit tests are very useful to check whether a particular algorithm produces the 'right' output.

Unit testing is a crucial practice in the design of Big Data algorithms. Since most Big Data algorithms are complex and evolve over time by data scientists who develop the algorithm further, the unit tests provide strong controls to ensure the algorithms keep working. By setting up several simple tests (in the testing world, these are called cases), you can build the appropriate checks and balances to see whether the algorithm still creates the desired results. If changes to an algorithm are made, and the unit tests fail, it immediately showcases that the change created some undesired side effect. As a result, unit testing puts controls into place that continually check whether the algorithm still functions adequately.

The only limitation about unit testing is that the scope of the test limits itself to a small, independent script. In many cases, Big Data algorithms are modules made up of several modules that need to work in sync. A Big Data search algorithm, for example, will combine your search query with your search history, your location or your type of device to showcase the optimal search result. It is likely that each of these factors will be determined or calculated in a different script. For this reason, a second key practice is **integration testing**.

Integration testing – as the name suggests – considers the integration between different parts of an algorithm. It considers multiple components together and tests the system as a whole.[2] Even though all unit tests might function perfectly, the integration test might highlight new problems. In practice, in Big Data environments, integration tests fail if data is not adequately transferred between different modules, or that the process is taking too long.

The element of time is particularly crucial in the design and development of Big Data algorithms. Algorithms might be technically sound, but if they take too long to process data, they can be effectively worthless. Think for example about a prediction that calculates which stock to purchase or sell. These predictions need to be almost real-time because stock prices fluctuate. If the algorithm took two hours to calculate the prediction, the results might be outdated again. Testing for time in integration testing therefore requires special attention.

The last key testing concept that showcases significant maturity in the Big Data algorithms capability is if an organization applies **test-driven development** (TDD). Test-driven development is the reverse engineering of the algorithm design process. Instead of creating the code, and subsequently testing the script, TDD starts with the development of the test script. In other words, TDD forces data scientists to think about which tests their algorithms need to pass in the first place. Only after these tests have been defined and developed will the development process start.[3] The benefits of this approach are apparent: with TDD, there is a clear goal of what the algorithms should do, and which key constraints to take into consideration. Additionally, using TDD will provide focus to the development of the project, because once all the tests have been successfully passed, the development of the algorithm is done. TDD will therefore create focus and helps to determine when an algorithm is 'done'.

Agile and Scrum

Software development, and equally the process of developing Big Data algorithms, is an iterative, incremental process. In reality, it will almost never be the case that a correct and working algorithm is developed from scratch. Rather, it is a process of trial and error, in which a data scientist or team finds the best possible solution in a few iterations.

The Scrum methodology, which is one of the most famous Agile methodologies, is therefore a proper methodology to develop Big Data algorithms. Scrum is a light-weight framework that helps people, teams and organizations generate value through adaptive solutions for complex problems.[4] Most of all, it is a practical approach, in which data scientists can use insight from one development iteration to make changes in the next development cycle. In Scrum, it is perfectly fine not to have all the answers up front, but to add more details later.

The structure of Scrum, and the Scrum way of working, is inherently simple. In Scrum teams, work is broken down into several iterative cycles, which are called sprints. These sprints typically take two to three weeks in duration and are self-contained development cycles. During each sprint, a team of developers works together to create a next 'working version' of the Big Data algorithms, which can be tested toward the end of the sprint. A high-level breakdown of working in sprints is depicted in Figure 21.1.

Figure 21.1   High-level overview of Scrum

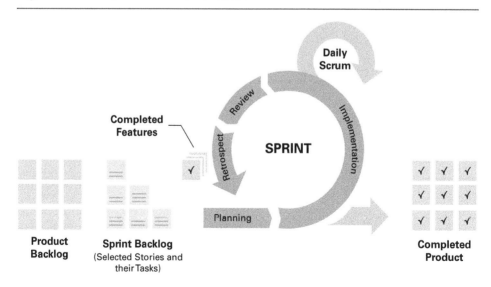

There are numerous benefits in working in an agile manner in developing enterprise Big Data solutions. Most importantly, Scrum allows development teams to leverage insights from previous iterations into the new planning cycle (i.e. sprint planning). Since it is very hard to predict the exact behaviour of algorithms from the start, data scientists can test numerous options and proceed with the most optimal design. Insights that are obtained during the creation or development process can therefore be used in subsequent development cycles.

Scrum is an Agile framework, which builds on the larger 'Agile' movement. The term 'Agile' is used to indicate a working philosophy that is flexible, and a culture in which there is strong collaboration between team members and the individual customers. Agile is not just relevant in the software engineering capability practice discussed in this chapter, it is a culture through which Big Data teams thrive, and a mindset that enables the rapid delivery of results. We will therefore discuss agile in more detail in Part 6 (Big Data Processes).

21.4 Software engineering summary

The software engineering capability enables organizations to create Big Data algorithms in proven, sound and process-oriented ways. Since the development of algorithms is ultimately a software development exercise, there are important lessons from the software engineering domain that can be used in the development of algorithms.

In this section, we reviewed some of the software engineering best practices, and discussed how they can be applied to the Big Data domain to build robust algorithms that function as expected, and that are easy to maintain. Coding standards and version control gives organizations the ability to collaborate effectively, and always have the opportunity to return to previous versions in case of any mistake or bug. Proper testing techniques will help teams to ensure that an algorithm is producing the required results, and that it is effective to process large quantities of data within the required time sets. Lastly, we discussed how Scrum methodology can empower development teams to work together effectively.

Although software engineering is a more technical capability, its importance in the creation of Big Data algorithms should not be underestimated. Organizations that have a strong software engineering capability will see their Big Data solutions work effectively, with fewer errors, and in a way that is way easier to maintain. To build this capability will require some discipline and a considerable time effort, but the result is worth it.

Notes

1 V Khorikov (2020) *Unit Testing Principles, Practices, and Patterns*. Simon and Schuster

2 V Garousi, A Rainer, P Lauvås Jr, and A Arcuri. Software-testing education: A systematic literature mapping, *Journal of Systems and Software*, 2020 165, 110570

3 K Beck (2003) *Test-driven development: By example*. Addison-Wesley Professional

4 K Schwaber and J Sutherland. The scrum guide, *Scrum Alliance*, 2011 21 (19), 1

Data Cleaning and Wrangling

22

22.1 Introduction to data cleaning and wrangling

Even with the best and most sophisticated algorithm in the world, the outcome of any analysis will be worthless if the input data is incorrect, skewed or otherwise invalid. In Big Data, the old saying of garbage in, garbage out is very appropriate. In Big Data environments, the volumes of data are large, and so is the possibility for mistakes.

Most Big Data sets contain data that is duplicate, erroneous or even plain missing. Frequently, data sets have been built up over years and years, during which time fields in databases have changed, were renamed or simply ignored. As a result, most organizations have databases and data sets that are far from perfect in terms of their accuracy or preciseness.

A large part of the Big Data analyst's job is therefore to evaluate and clean up the data sets, before they can be processed. Research figures vary, but according to some interviews, data analysts spend 50 to 80 per cent of their time on data cleaning and data wrangling activities, something that the *New York Times* has famously called the 'Janitor's Job' of data science.[1] Indeed the activities that are necessary to clean and wrangle data will sometimes feel like a never-ending task of filtering, cleaning and scrubbing data, words that are similarly used by janitors. But organizations who can build sound capability in this domain will see accurate predictions, and more reliable decision-making.

In this section, we take a closer look at the capabilities that organizations can build to clean and wrangle data. It is important to note that data cleaning and data wrangling typically happen **before** the main algorithm will run. The purpose of data cleaning and data wrangling is to ensure that the **input data** will have significant **data quality** and, maybe even more importantly, that an organization can prove that its data has a certain level of quality.

Before we discuss different data cleaning and data wrangling techniques, let's first quickly review the difference between the two terms.[2]

In summary, data cleaning is the act of altering existing records, whereas data wrangling concerns itself with creating new records.[3] Obviously, there is a grey area between these two domains and many tools are available that combine elements of

Figure 22.1   Difference between data cleaning and data wrangling

Data Cleaning	Data Wrangling
Data cleaning is the process of detecting and correcting (or removing) corrupt or inaccurate records from a record set, table or database. It refers to identifying incomplete, incorrect, inaccurate or irrelevant parts of the data and then replacing, modifying or deleting the dirty or coarse data.	Data wrangling, sometimes referred to as data munging, is the process of transforming and mapping data from one 'raw' data form into another format with the intent of making it more appropriate and valuable for a variety of downstream purposes such as analytics.

both approaches. In the end, both data cleaning and data wrangling have the same objective – to ensure that correct and accurate data is being processed.

There is one aspect that makes data cleaning and data wrangling significantly distinct in a Big Data environment, compared to other forms of data analysis. Due to the volume and velocity characteristics of Big Data, it become impossible (or at least highly impractical) to do data cleaning and data wrangling manually. In a Big Data environment, the process of data cleaning and data wrangling needs to be standardized and automated.

In this chapter, we will not focus on the skills necessary to inspect an individual data set or table, or to determine whether it has missing values, but instead look at the capabilities necessary to set up an enterprise data cleaning and wrangling programme, which **continuously** cleans and wrangles incoming data sets, and can put measures in place to the extent in which an organization has quality data in place that can be trusted.

22.2 Purpose and maturity levels of data cleaning and wrangling

Purpose

Organizations need to be able to trust the predictions that are made by algorithms. And in order to generate this, having a high trust in the data quality is of paramount importance. Data cleaning and data wrangling practices enable an organization to safeguard **data quality**, transforming it into **trusted data**.

To further illustrate the importance of data cleaning and wrangling, let us compare an organization with a low maturity level with an organization with a high maturity level in this capability. In organizations with a low maturity level, there is constant discussion about the validity of predictions, and data scientists are continuously challenged by management as to how they arrived at a prediction. There is an ongoing discussion about the input data, and you frequently hear phrases such as 'I know the data predicts this, but my experience tells me that can't be right.' In other words, low levels of data cleaning and data maturity undermine the complete validity of data-driven decision-making.

Organizations with high levels of data cleaning and wrangling maturity, on the other hand, inherently trust the enterprise data. In these organizations there might also be challenges, but they are focused on the design of the algorithm, and not on whether the enterprise data can be trusted. A high maturity level leads to more trust in enterprise data.

Most organizations underestimate the importance of this capability and overestimate the extent to which they have quality data. As a result, data cleaning and data wrangling are frequently considered operational activities, without clear measurements or defined goals. Efforts are concentrated on technical tools for database management, rather than processes for the continuous improvement (i.e. cleaning and wrangling) of enterprise data.

Maturity levels

The data cleaning and wrangling capability provides a path to trusted data. At the highest level of maturity, organizations use automated approaches to data acquisition, cleaning, transformation, integration and aggregation. Data is continuously assessed and validated for errors, and automatically updated whenever mistakes or inconsistencies are found. At the highest level of maturity, the enterprise data becomes a single source of truth, which is constantly evolving and ever updating.[4]

The five levels that define the data cleaning and wrangling capability are listed in Table 22.2.

Big Data solutions and technologies can generate and store massive amounts of data. The data cleaning and wrangling capability is therefore becoming increasingly

Table 22.1 The purpose of the data cleaning and wrangling capability

Capability	Purpose
Data cleaning and wrangling	Defines the ability of an organization to structurally deal with missing, incomplete, inconsistent, inaccurate, duplicate and dated enterprise data, in order establish quality data that stakeholders trust.

Table 22.2   Maturity levels of the data cleaning and wrangling capability

Maturity Level	Description
Level 1 – Initial	Data cleaning and wrangling is done manually, ad hoc and on a project-by-project basis. There are no documented procedures, data dictionaries or reference and metadata management procedures.
Level 2 – Managed	There is some level of structured data cleaning and wrangling, but without a centralized coordinated effort. Some automated data cleaning tools are used, but there is no overall data cleaning and wrangling strategy.
Level 3 – Defined	The organization has a defined automated process for data acquisition and semantics generation. All datasets entering the organization (input data) is cleaned according to this process.
Level 4 – Controlled	There are automated and ongoing procedures in place to clean and wrangle data continuously. Data is not just cleaned, updated and validated when it enters the organization, but on an ongoing basis.
Level 5 – Optimized	Data cleaning and wrangling uses analytic functions and algorithms to automatically detect inconsistencies in data, and update data sets. Data quality is actively monitored, improved and optimized, and cleaning procedures are continuously improved.

more important in recent years to safeguard the accuracy of Big Data predictions and algorithms.

22.3 Structuring data cleaning and wrangling

As we established in the previous section, the data cleaning and wrangling capabilities are inherently linked. Organizations that have a higher level of maturity have a higher level of data quality, enabling them to make more trusted decisions. There is therefore a significant incentive for any organization to start investing time, energy and financial resources to improve this capability.

In this section, we will discuss the approaches organizations can take to set up or improve their data cleaning and wrangling capability. We will first outline the major issues that data cleaning and data wrangling need to overcome, and subsequently explain which techniques can be used to structure data in an automated and efficient way.

Challenges in Big Data sets

It is hardly a surprise that most Big Data sets are messy and convoluted. Most data sets build up over large periods of time, they are rarely documented. In many cases, database are created and populated based on the decisions of software developers, who are adding rows and columns in the order in which they develop their applications, and without a proper database design. You might not necessarily like this, but the job of any data scientist is to deal with data sets as they come. In most cases, the way that data sets are created is outside your scope of control.

There can be many issues with Big Data sets that make them difficult or inaccurate to analyse. Before we discuss various data cleaning and wrangling techniques and approaches, it is therefore first important to understand the common challenges with data sets. Table 22.3 provides an overview of the most common challenges in Big Data sets.

As can be seen in Table 22.3, the number of challenges in Big Data sets is vast and significant. Data cleaning and wrangling techniques will be able to address these challenges, but unfortunately there is not a one-size-fits-all solution. The amount of duplicate, missing or erroneous data that any organization has will depend on its history, collection process, culture and tools. Although these challenges exist for any organization, there are several data cleaning and wrangling techniques that can be considered best practice, and which will make an organization's maturity higher, compared to an organization that doesn't have this in place. A summary overview of these techniques is provided in Figure 22.2.

Acquisition and semantics

The first opportunity that an organization has to clean and wrangle data is the moment it is collected and entering the organization. Organizations who have proper procedures for **acquisition and semantics** of input data will need to spend less time and energy later to correct erroneous data sets. For that reason, acquisition and semantics have a strong gatekeeper function.

Filtering and sampling input data is a straightforward technique that sets rules with regards to the amount of information that is collected and stored. Out of all the data that a sensor generates, for example, it might not be necessary or valuable to store all features or observations. By providing a filter or sample only, organizations can already control which information actively enters the company.

Filtering and sampling are especially relevant for streaming data that is high volume and high velocity. A good example would be the filtering and sampling of social

Table 22.3 Common challenges in Big Data sets

Challenge	Description
Dealing with missing data	Missing data is the most common challenge in Big Data sets. Missing data is frequently the results of errors in sensors, data transfer mistakes or simply because values were deliberately not completed. Missing data requires significant attention because it can skew or bias datasets.
	There are various techniques for dealing with missing data. The simplest solution is to eliminate rows with missing data, but the downside is that other values might get lost. Other approaches include filling data with values from nearby observations, or predicting missing values based on some form of simulation.
Dealing with duplicate data	After missing data, dealing with duplicate data is the most common challenge in Big Data sets. Duplicate records can be created for a variety of different reasons. People can, for example, fill a particular CRM record multiple times by clicking the enter button many times. A second common scenario is a sensor that malfunctions, and that writes data into a database more than once.
	To clean duplicate data, the main challenge is to find a unique identifier in the dataset. For user accounts (for example for social media profiles), this could be a person's email address, since a person that uses the same email address will likely be the same person. Once the unique identifier has been selected, the cleaning tool needs to select which records will be kept or automatically merged.
Dealing with data variety	Big Data is characterized by the four Vs. Out of these characteristics (see Part 1), the variety aspect is the most difficult to deal with. Data variety leads to datasets that structured, semi-structured or unstructured, and might be dispersed at different locations across the enterprise. With unstructured data (video, audio) becoming more important every day, this poses new data cleaning and wrangling challenges.
	To clean and wrangle a variety of data sources, the information extraction (IE) technique has emerged as the most successful approach. Information extraction (IE) refers to synthesizing structured information such as entities, attributes of entities and relationships among the entities from unstructured sources.[1] Through IE techniques, it is possible to extract key information from, for example, video, and to order information and data based on these extracted features.

(continued)

Table 22.3 (Continued)

Challenge	Description
Dealing with bias and variance	A last category that makes data cleaning and wrangling increasingly more challenging is the inherent quality of the data. The data might be complete, without and any duplicates, and exactly in the same format (the three previous challenges), but still lead to incorrect predictions when used in a Big Data algorithm due to bias or variance. High bias and variance are typically caused by the fact that available data collection processes can only capture a subset of reality.
	Bias and variance are competing characteristics of data, and minimizing both is therefore impossible. Automated data cleaning and wrangling solutions would therefore need to identify adequate thresholds that will lead to the most adequate predictions.

1 S Sarawagi. Information extraction, Foundations and Trends® in Databases, 2008 1 (3), 261–377

Figure 22.2 Overview of data cleaning and wrangling techniques

Acquisition and Semantics	Transformation, Integration and Aggregation	Quality Monitoring and Review
• Filtering and sampling • Cleaning and enrichment • Semantics and metadata generation	• Transformation • Integration • Aggregation and semantics generation	• Dashboards • Thresholds and triggers • Profiling and auditing • Issue management

media data. At any given moment of the day, there is so much new data generated that is impossible (or unaffordable) for any company to collect and store these massive new input streams. Rather, an organization will be interested particularly in certain keywords, product names or brands that have value for their particular interest. It is therefore necessary to create and set adequate filters right from the start.

Another good practice, after filtering and sampling, is to clean and enrich the data before it enters the company databases. **Cleaning and enrichment** of data is the process that ensures that only validated data enters the organization. This process includes activities for data standardization, the detection and removal of duplicates, and the imputation for missing data. This process is the most traditional form of 'data cleaning', and focuses the configuration of algorithms that automatically address the challenges that are listed in Table 22.2. In the same example of collecting and storing social media data, this process would ensure that duplicate posts are eliminated, and that social media posts that only consist of one character would be automatically discarded. The cleaning and enrichment process typically uses automated algorithms and tools to execute this process.

The last stage in the data collection process to clean and wrangle data is **semantics and metadata generation**. These activities refer to the steps taken to add information to incoming data sets, which might be used at later moments in time, or to easily retrieve and restore key information. For example, a company might want to add a timestamp when the cleaning process was executed or to add some keywords to a particular data set. These additional labels about a data set are called metadata and give a particular meaning to the data sets (i.e. semantics).

Semantics and metadata generation provide an opportunity for organizations to structurally describe data, and to retrieve and use that data a later stage very effectively. It does, however, only work if this process is executed consistently, and with are certain amount of rigour. It is therefore important that organizations think beforehand about how the metadata will be used, and to what extent semantics are adding value that will be used. Establishing some form of metadata and semantics strategy (however simple it may be) can therefore significantly help to accomplish this objective.

Transformation, integration and aggregation

Transformation, integration and aggregation are steps taken to clean and wrangle data on a periodic basis, after it has entered the organization. **Data transformation** is a step in which data is altered or adjusted so that it conforms to a standard enterprise structure. For example, an organization that collects and processes financial information wants to ensure that currency numbers adhere to the exact same format. Data transformation is an automated process that typically focuses on improving data normality and equalizing variance, and for that reason is more complex than the operations performed under acquisition and semantics.

Modern enterprises have a diverse number of data sets that originate from different sources and have different file formats. **Data integration** is the automated step with which these disparate data sources are combined into one uniform data source, which is typically the enterprise data lake or data store. Data integration encourages collaboration between internal as well as external users. The data being integrated must be received from a heterogeneous database system and transformed to a single coherent data store that provides synchronous data across a network of files for clients.[5] Since data integration is on ongoing process (especially for streaming data), automated tools are required to perform this activity.

Data aggregation is the compiling of information from different databases (which were just aggregated) with the intention of preparing combined datasets for data processing. Besides the fact that data aggregations make it easier to run analysis (i.e. there is one aggregated view), there is a second important goal in the context of Big Data. It is less compute- and time-intensive to run analysis on aggregated data than on data stored in different locations. Data aggregation therefore speeds up the data analysis task.

Data transformation, integration and aggregation are fundamental in the cleaning and wrangling of data on an ongoing basis and safeguard the quality of data. All three activities highly depend on the set-up and structuring of automated tools, because these activities need to be performed on an ongoing basis. During these activities, a significant amount of metadata and semantics are generated, which has additional value for the organization.

Quality monitoring and review

The last set of techniques that are an integral part of data cleaning and wrangling is quality monitoring and review. Since data cleaning and data wrangling is an ongoing activity (which never stops), it is imperative to set up a cycle of continual data improvement. Quality monitoring and review provides the knowledge and insights data needs to be further cleaned or improved, or where there are potential weaknesses. Paradoxically, you could say that this activity is about structuring data analytics for the analytics function.

Quality monitoring and review can be executed by the standard processes and tools for continual improvement. **Dashboards and visualizations** provide a uniform and standardized overview of the current state of the data quality, and where there are areas that can likely benefit from data cleaning and wrangling. These dashboards are established by setting KPIs (key performance indicators) and targets for data quality (these KPIs will be discussed in Part 6).

After KPIs have been established, **automated triggers** can be set up. For example, if it is detected that the number of duplicate entries reaches above a certain threshold in a database, a filtering process might be triggered to eliminate the duplicate values. Similarly, time triggers can be set up so that data sets will be cleaned at periodic intervals, for instance every week.

More advanced forms of quality monitoring and review (and hence indicating a higher capability in this domain) include profiling, auditing and issue management. With **data profiling**, an organization starts to include an internal rating system for data, with a quality label that indicates how reliable or trustworthy a data set is. For data sets at the highest level, executives can be certain that the input data is completely correct, because it is, for example, data that is generated by the organization itself. Data that is rated at lower levels might on the other hand originate from partners or third-party sources, for which it is more difficult to check the provenance.

Auditing and issue management are more formalized procedures to periodically review the performance of data cleaning and data wrangling, and to act on issues that might arise during such an audit. An organization might, for example conduct an audit every six months, to review formally (and frequently externally) what data cleaning and wrangling activities are working well, or where further improvements need to be made. The benefit of conducting more formal audits is that they are frequently more independent and provide an unbiased scheduled review of the organization's performance. The downside is that it is obviously an additional expense.

22.4 Data cleaning and wrangling summary

Data cleaning and data wrangling are integral activities that lead to more trusted data, and therefore more adequate decision-making. Because almost all data cleaning and wrangling activities are performed by (automated) algorithms, this micro-capability will support all other algorithms that are discussed in this section. Without sound data cleaning and wrangling, organizations cannot be sure whether the input data is valid and unbiased.

In this section, we discussed three major techniques that organization can use to grow capability in this domain. Establishing sound acquisition and semantics algorithms and procedures enables an organization to safeguard which data will enter the organization. The primary focus of this activity is to keep invalid, missing or duplicate data outside the enterprise domain.

Secondly, we discussed techniques for ongoing operational data transformation, integrations and aggregation. With these techniques, enterprises ensure data sets are reviewed on a periodic basis and are improved where necessary. Lastly, we discussed some quality monitoring and review techniques, which enable an organization to review the quality of its data sets periodically, and to indicate opportunities for future improvement.

Data cleaning and data wrangling have a significant connection with data governance and data management practices, which will be further discussed in Part 6.

Notes

1 S Lohr. For big-data scientists, 'janitor work' is key hurdle to insights, *New York Times*, 2014 17, B4
2 W McKinney (2012) *Python for data analysis: Data wrangling with Pandas, NumPy, and IPython*. O'Reilly Media, Inc.
3 S Wu. A review on coarse warranty data and analysis, *Reliability Engineering & System Safety*, 2013 114, 1–11

4 V Gudivada, A Apon and J Ding. Data quality considerations for big data and machine learning: Going beyond data cleaning and transformations, *International Journal on Advances in Software*, 2017 10 (1), 1–20

5 P T Chung and S H Chung (2013) On data integration and data mining for developing business intelligence. In 2013 IEEE Long Island Systems, Applications and Technology Conference (LISAT), May, 1–6. IEEE

Descriptive Data Analysis   23

23.1 Introduction to descriptive data analysis

The next critical capability that every organization should master to benefit from Big Data is the **descriptive data analysis** capability. With descriptive data analysis, organizations can summarize large amounts of data across multiple datasets. Although this capability is sometimes mistakenly characterized as 'simple', it is important to note that the vast majority of information used for enterprise decision-making is descriptive in nature.

Questions like, what are the consolidated sales figures from all subsidiaries across the globe? What is the value of our inventory? And what it the average salary of our employees? All these questions are descriptive in nature. The challenge with these questions is not so much that they are computationally challenging, but the consolidation of various datasets.

The descriptive data analysis capability is the ability of an enterprise to summarize and describe characteristics of a dataset. The key objective involves the use of various techniques, such as statistical summaries, charts and plots, to help understand the distribution and patterns in the data. The goal of descriptive data analysis is to provide a **general understanding** of the data, rather than making inferences or predictions about it.

Descriptive data analysis is important for organizations because it can help them to gain a better understanding of their data and make informed decisions. For example, by summarizing the key characteristics of customer data, an organization may be able to identify key demographics or buying patterns that can be used to improve marketing efforts or product development.

Second, descriptive data analysis can also be useful for identifying outliers, errors or inconsistencies in data, which can help organizations to improve the quality of their data and ensure that it is accurate and reliable.

Finally, descriptive data analysis is a cost-effective and efficient way to explore data before applying more advanced and complex methods. It can help organizations to identify the most important questions to be addressed, and to identify the appropriate methods for answering those questions.

Descriptive data analysis is the process of describing the enterprise data. In order to meet this objective, information is typically displayed in graphs and dashboards. The descriptive data analysis capability is therefore most linked with what traditionally has been called business intelligence. Although descriptive data analysis and business intelligence are technically not the same, there is a large overlap. **Business intelligence (BI)** is generally considered a broader concept that involves the use of technology, tools and in most cases BI discussions are based around the structuring and appropriate configuration of tools. Since the Enterprise Big Data Framework is vendor-independent, our aim is to focus more on the techniques that help describe datasets. For this reason, we have chosen to label this capability descriptive data analysis. In the following sections we will consider the main techniques and knowledge necessary to describe Big Data sets.

23.2 Purpose and maturity levels of descriptive data analysis

Purpose

The purpose of descriptive data analysis is to summarize and describe the characteristics of enterprise data. It is used to understand the distribution and patterns in the data, and to provide a general understanding of the data. This understanding can be used to identify trends, outliers and unusual patterns in the data, and to gain insights into the data that can inform decision-making and strategic planning.

Some specific purposes of the descriptive data analysis capability is:

- Summarizing the key characteristics of a dataset, such as the mean, median and standard deviation.
- Identifying patterns and trends in the data, such as changes over time or differences between groups.
- Identifying outliers or unusual observations in the data that may indicate errors or inconsistencies.
- Providing a visual representation of the data, such as through charts and plots, to make it easier to understand and interpret.
- Exploring the data to identify the most important questions to be addressed, and to identify the appropriate methods for answering those questions.

The main goal of descriptive data analysis is to provide a general understanding of the enterprise data, which can be used to inform decision-making and strategic planning, as outlined in Table 23.1.

Table 23.1　The purpose of the descriptive data analysis capability

Capability	Purpose
Descriptive data analysis	Defines the ability of an organization to summarize internal and external enterprise data to support decision-making.

The results of descriptive data analysis are frequently used by senior management in a variety of ways to inform decision-making and strategic planning. They are used to identify key trends and patterns in the data, to identify potential issues and opportunities, and to communicate the key findings to stakeholders.

The activity of conducting descriptive data analysis is mostly done by data analysist, who focus on summarizing datasets and create summary information. It is important to differentiate between the role of the data analyst (who is involved in this capability) and the role of the data scientist, who is frequently more involved with model building and machine learning. We will discuss machine learning in more detail in Chapters 24 and 25.

Maturity levels

There are clear and easily identifiable differences between different maturity levels in descriptive data analysis. An organization that is low in maturity in descriptive data analysis may face several challenges that can make it difficult for them to effectively analyse and understand their data.

The main challenge will be the enterprise's limited data collection and management capabilities. Organizations that are low in maturity in descriptive data analysis may have difficulty in collecting, storing and managing large amounts of data. This can make it difficult to perform descriptive analysis and can lead to a lack of comprehensive data that can be used to inform decision-making and strategic planning.

An organization that is high in maturity in descriptive data analysis, on the other hand, is typically one that effectively uses descriptive data analysis to inform decision-making and strategic planning. They experience day-to-day value from the summarized data, and it guides decision-making for senior management. Having a high maturity in the descriptive data analysis capability is therefore crucial in becoming a data-driven organization.

The five levels that define the descriptive data analysis capability are listed in Table 23.2.

Like the other capabilities discussed in this section, the descriptive data analysis capability is strongly linked (or dependent on) other capabilities. For example, an

Table 23.2   Maturity levels of the descriptive data analysis capability

Maturity Level	Description
Level 1 – Initial	The organization has limited data analysis capabilities and lacks skilled personnel or data visualization tools. They may only be able to perform basic data analysis and may not have a clear understanding of the data.
Level 2 – Managed	The organization has begun to establish processes for descriptive data analysis and may have some basic data visualization tools. They may have a general understanding of the data but may not be able to gain deep insights from it.
Level 3 – Defined	The organization has established more data analysis processes, and has a team of skilled personnel with expertise in data analysis and visualization. This team has a deeper understanding of the data and can use more advanced data analysis techniques to gain insights from it.
Level 4 – Controlled	The organization has a highly skilled team of data analysts, uses a variety of advanced data visualization and analysis techniques, and has a deep understanding of the data. They can use data to inform decision-making and strategic planning and can identify areas for further research and analysis.
Level 5 – Optimized	The organization has fully integrated data analysis into their decision-making processes and share and use data in a collaborative way across the organization. They have achieved a high level of data-driven insights and can use data to continuously improve their operations and performance.

organization with very limited capability in data cleaning and data wrangling (discussed in Chapter 22), will find it quite difficult to achieve a high capability level in descriptive data analysis.

23.3 Structuring descriptive data analysis

There are several capabilities that are necessary to structure descriptive data analysis in an organization. Most importantly, the organization needs to have the ability to perform descriptive data analysis, including statistical techniques and data mining. This includes capabilities such as the ability to describe data in summary statistics, the detection of patterns and trend, the ability to detect unusual data (outliers) as well as the ability to neatly present summary data with adequate graphs and visualizations.

Summary statistics

Descriptive data analysis starts with mastering descriptive summary statistics. Summary statistics are a set of mathematical measures that are used to describe the characteristics of a dataset in a concise and easy-to-understand format. They are used in descriptive data analysis to provide a quick and general overview of the data, and to identify patterns and trends. Common examples of summary statistics that form the fundament of decision-making are:

- **Mean:** The average value of a dataset. It's calculated by adding up all the values in the dataset and dividing by the number of values.
- **Median:** The middle value of a dataset when it is arranged in ascending or descending order.
- **Mode:** The most frequently occurring value in a dataset.
- **Standard deviation:** A measure of the amount of variation or dispersion in a dataset.
- **Variance:** A measure of the spread between numbers in a dataset, like standard deviation but it's squared.
- **Count and percent:** The number and percentage of observations in a dataset that have a certain characteristic.

Summary statistics are important for organizations because they can provide valuable insights into the data that can inform decision-making and strategic planning. For example, if an organization is trying to understand how its customers rate its products, summary statistics such as mean, median and standard deviation can be used to quickly identify patterns and trends in the data, such as the overall satisfaction level of customers, the most common issues customers have and how much variation there is in the data.

A common and insightful way to depict summary statistics is with the help of charts. A boxplot is a common visualization that quickly depicts the summary statistics of data features. A boxplot, also known as a box-and-whisker plot, is a type of graph that is used to display the distribution of a dataset. It is particularly useful for comparing multiple datasets or groups of data.

A boxplot consists of a box that represents the middle 50 per cent of the data (the interquartile range), a line inside the box that represents the median value, and 'whiskers' that extend out from the box to show the minimum and maximum values (excluding outliers). The boxplot also can display the outliers, which are the data points that are beyond the whiskers.

The boxplot provides a quick and easy way to visualize the distribution of a dataset, including the median, quartiles and outliers. It can be used to quickly identify

Figure 23.1   Example of a boxplot, used for descriptive data analysis

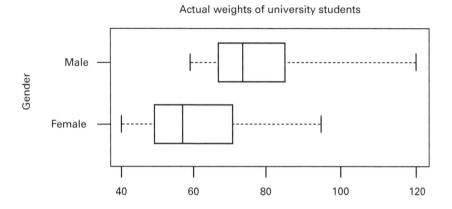

patterns and trends in the data, such as skewness, and to compare multiple datasets or groups of data. An example of a boxplot is outlined in Figure 23.1.

To grow capability in descriptive data analysis, it is important that the organization's data analysts have a sound understanding of summary statistics. Setting up appropriate training courses can help to increase this capability.

Pattern and trend analysis

Pattern and trend analysis is a technique used to identify patterns and trends in data over time. It involves identifying patterns and trends in a dataset by analysing the data over a period of time, such as weeks, months or years. These patterns and trends can then be used to make predictions about future data, or to identify opportunities for improvement.

There are several types of pattern and trend analysis, including time series analysis, trend analysis and seasonal analysis.

Pattern and trend analysis is important in data analysis because it helps organizations to understand their data better, and to make informed decisions based on that data. For example, an organization might use pattern and trend analysis to identify patterns in customer behaviour, such as when customers are most likely to make purchases, or to identify trends in sales data, such as which products are becoming more popular over time. This information can then be used to inform marketing strategies, product development and other business decisions. Additionally, pattern and trend analysis can also help organizations to identify potential problems or opportunities early on, so that they can act before those problems or opportunities become critical.

Table 23.3   Different forms of trend analysis

Trending Type	Description
Time series analysis	Time series analysis is a method of analysing data over a period of time, such as weeks, months or years. It involves identifying patterns and trends in the data, such as seasonality, cyclical patterns and trends in the mean and variance. Time series analysis is commonly used in fields such as finance, economics and engineering to analyse data such as stock prices, sales data and weather data.
Trend analysis	Trend analysis is a method of identifying the direction and rate of change in a dataset over time. It involves analysing the data to identify upward or downward trends, and to determine whether the trend is increasing, decreasing or stable. Trend analysis is commonly used in fields such as finance, economics and marketing to analyse, for example, sales data, stock prices and consumer behaviour.
Seasonal analysis	Seasonal analysis is a method of analysing data to identify patterns and trends that occur at specific times of the year, such as holidays or seasons. It involves analysing data over multiple years to identify patterns and trends that repeat at the same time each year. Seasonal analysis is commonly used in fields such as retail, tourism and weather forecasting to analyse, for example, sales data, temperature data and weather data.

Outlier detection

Outlier detection is the process of identifying data points that are significantly different from the rest of the data in a dataset. These points are also known as 'outliers' or 'anomalies'. Outliers can be caused by measurement errors, data entry errors or they can indicate a real-world phenomenon that is worth further investigation.

Outlier detection is important for organizations because outliers can have a significant impact on the analysis and interpretation of the data. For example, if an outlier is present in a dataset, it can skew the mean, median and other statistical measures, leading to incorrect conclusions about the data. Outliers can also affect the performance of predictive models, leading to inaccurate predictions. Additionally, outliers can also indicate a problem or an opportunity that could be worth investigating further.

There are several methods for detecting outliers, including:

- Visual methods, such as boxplots, scatter plots and histograms
- Statistical methods, such as the Z-score and the interquartile range (IQR)

Figure 23.2   Example of outlier detection

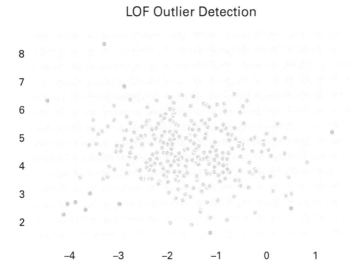

- Machine learning methods, such as clustering and anomaly detection algorithms. These will be discussed in the next chapter.

Not all outliers are necessarily bad or errors, it depends on the context and the problem that the data is trying to solve. It's important to evaluate outliers carefully and not to automatically exclude them from the analysis.

Outlier detection is a crucial step in data analysis, and it helps organizations to identify and understand unusual or unexpected data points that could impact the interpretation of the data. Building capability in this area can ultimately help organizations to make better decisions and to identify potential problems or opportunities that might otherwise be overlooked.

Data visualization

A good picture is worth a 1,000 words. By nature, people are visually included, and they memorize and interpret images and graphs better than written texts. Data visualization is therefore an important component of descriptive data analysis to identify patterns and trends in the data that could be used to make decisions or predictions.

For example, a scatter plot can be used to identify relationships between two variables, such as the correlation between the price of a stock and its volatility. This type of analysis can help investment agencies make informed decisions about when to buy or sell a stock. Similarly, data visualization can be used to identify trends in customer spending habits over time, helping businesses make decisions about which products to promote and how to adjust pricing.

Data visualization can also be used to find insights from the data that might inform marketing decisions. For example, a heatmap can be used to identify which areas of a website are the most popular among visitors, allowing marketers to optimize the user experience. Additionally, visualizations can be used to identify correlations between different variables and uncover relationships between variables that may not be immediately apparent. For example, a visualization can reveal correlations between customer reviews of a product and its sales, helping businesses understand what factors are driving customer purchases.

Finally, data visualization is useful for presenting data to stakeholders clearly and in an easy to understand way. Visualizing data can make it easier for people to digest and interpret it, allowing them to quickly draw conclusions and make decisions based on it. Additionally, data visualizations can be used to communicate complex ideas and to illustrate the impact of decisions made using the data in a clear and concise manner.

The most common visualizations used in descriptive data analysis are:

- Bar charts: a type of graph that is used to compare different categories of data. They are one of the most common visualizations used in descriptive data analysis.

- Histograms: show the distribution of data over a continuous interval or certain time. They are used to identify trends or patterns in data.

- Scatter plots: demonstrate the relationship between two variables. They can identify correlations between variables or to identify outliers.

- Pie charts: compare proportions or percentages of data. They are useful for understanding the relative sizes of different categories of data.

- Line graphs: identify changes in data over time. They are useful for understanding trends and patterns in data.

Mastering adequate data visualization techniques is crucial for any organization that aims to build capability in descriptive data analysis. Understanding how to create effective visualizations to convey critical information is important for every data analyst. Through training, practice and experience, this capability can be increased significantly.

23.4 Descriptive data analysis summary

In this chapter, we have seen that descriptive data analysis is a crucial capability for summarizing information. Particularly with Big Data sets, it is important for organizations to consolidate information, so that it can support day-to-day decision-making.

Descriptive data analysis algorithms aggregate and summarize datasets. In many cases this data is then displayed in graphs and visualizations and made available to the rest of the enterprise through dashboards. There are many descriptive data analysis algorithms and functions that exists. In this chapter, we covered some of the main elements that data analysts need to understand and master to grow capability in the organization. We discussed summary statistics for summarizing datasets, pattern and trend analysis to detect changes over time and outlier detection to look for irregularities or anomalies. Finally, we considered the importance of data visualization techniques to enhance this capability.

Descriptive data analysis algorithms are the cornerstone of any Big Data organization. Although they might not necessarily be complex or require complex computations, most enterprises rely on summarized data and aggregations for their decision-making process. More complex algorithms typically belong to the domain of machine learning, which we will cover in the next two chapters.

Machine Learning 24

24.1 Introduction to machine learning

The value that any organization can retrieve from data is directly proportional to the accuracy of its predictions. In uncertain markets, more accurate predictions lead to better business decisions and, ultimately, a competitive advantage. An organization that is better able to predict its inventory levels will have less wasted stock than a competitor. And an organization that is better able to predict which mix of marketing channels will lead to higher conversion will have more sales (for the same marketing budget) than a competitor. In business, the ability to accurately to predict the future gives organizations a financial advantage.

The technical ability to predict is brought by machine learning algorithms. We have deliberately chosen to use the phrase 'technical ability' because (as you probably now realize at this stage in the book) other capabilities are equally important. The best machine learning algorithm in the world will make inadequate predictions without business understanding or trustworthy input data. Nevertheless, it is also true that these predictions cannot be made without machine learning algorithms, a critical capability in Big Data.

Broadly speaking, the domain of machine learning can be subdivided into two main categories: supervised machine learning and unsupervised machine learning. Each domain has a different objective, but, more importantly, consists of different techniques and featured algorithms. For this reason, we have decided to treat each domain as an individual capability. Ultimately, any Big Data organization will need to have maturity in both domains to be successful. In this chapter, we will discuss common supervised machine learning techniques and approaches. In the next chapter (Chapter 24), we will move to unsupervised machine learning. The difference can be explained as follows:

- **Supervised learning:** type of machine learning where the algorithm uses labelled input data, to learn the pattern and be able to predict the values or labels of outputs for new unseen input data.

- **Unsupervised learning:** type of machine learning, in which unlabelled data is used to train the algorithm, and the purpose is to explore the data and find some structure within the dataset.

A third domain that is rising quickly is **reinforcement learning,** where no raw data is given as input and instead the algorithm must learn by means of reward to its actions. Since this is a more advanced subject, we will discuss reinforcement learning in Part 8.

The world of machine learning is complex, and requires years of practice to fully understand, and could easily fill an entire book. For that reason, we will not go into technical discussions (or code) of supervised machine learning. Instead, we will provide a comprehensive overview that defines this capability and showcases how to structure supervised machine learning in the enterprise.

24.2 Purpose and maturity levels of machine learning

Purpose

Machine learning algorithms are used to build models that can be used to predict future outcomes and patterns. For that reason, these algorithms have significant business value, and building this capability can strongly increase the benefits of Big Data to any enterprise.

Machine learning algorithms are the most used type of artificial intelligence algorithms, and they are used in many industries, such as finance, healthcare and marketing. Supervised machine learning algorithms are beneficial for organizations because they can help them to make better decisions and to improve the efficiency of their operations. The purpose of machine learning algorithms is to build models which can be used to predict future outcomes and patterns, as outlined in Table 24.1.

Machine learning algorithms use data from the past to learn patterns which can then be used to make predictions about the future. These models are trained on **labelled data** (supervised), where the labels indicate a `correct' output has already been assigned, or **unlabelled data** (unsupervised). Through supervised learning and unsupervised learning, the machine learning algorithms can learn from past data and make predictions about future data.

Table 24.1 The purpose of the supervised machine learning capability

Capability	Purpose
Machine learning	Defines the ability of an organization to use machine learning algorithms for predictive decision-making.

The benefit of machine learning algorithms for organizations is that they can help organizations to make better decisions and improve the efficiency of their operations. By using machine learning algorithms, organizations can automate certain tasks and processes, as well as reduce costs and improve accuracy.

For example, a company can use supervised machine learning algorithms to analyse customer data and identify patterns which can be used to target customers with more relevant ads and offers. This can help the company maximize its profits and optimize its marketing campaigns.

Another benefit of machine learning algorithms is that they can help organizations to improve their customer service. By using machine learning algorithms, organizations can develop models which can be used to predict customer preferences, needs and behaviours. This can help organizations to better understand their customers, and to provide more personalized services which will improve customer satisfaction.

Maturity levels

The level of maturity at which an organization use machine learning algorithms is dependent on the actual adoption of machine learning in the organization. Are these algorithms used to actually make and support decisions?

An organization that has mature machine learning algorithms should have a structure in place to develop and maintain supervised machine learning algorithms, and these algorithms should drive the day-to-day business. In these mature organizations, experienced data scientists should be able to develop, test, deploy and maintain supervised machine learning algorithms. Automated modelling tools should be available to quickly develop and deploy supervised learning models, and a robust infrastructure should be in place to support data storage, model training and deployment, and model evaluation. Finally, the organization should have a system in place to continuously improve their supervised learning algorithms based on model performance and feedback from users.

The five levels that define the supervised machine learning capability are listed in Table 24.2.

Unlike some of the other capabilities discussed in this book, maturity in machine learning is, to a significant extent, determined by the way an organization can automatically manage its machine learning algorithms. Since supervised machine learning is greatly dependent on the knowledge and skills of the data scientists working in the organization, this capability (and the extent to which automations can be managed) is significantly correlated with the level and skills of the data science team.

Table 24.2   Maturity levels of the machine learning capability

Maturity Level	Description
Level 1 – Initial	The organization is experimenting with machine learning and may have a small number of proof-of-concept projects.
Level 2 – Managed	The organization has a dedicated team and resources for developing machine learning models, but they are not yet being used in production.
Level 3 – Defined	The organization has deployed machine learning models in production and is using them to support business operations
Level 4 – Controlled	The organization is continuously monitoring and optimizing its machine learning models to improve their performance and drive business value.
Level 5 – Optimized	The organization is using machine learning to make decisions without human intervention.

24.3 Structuring machine learning

Understanding supervised machine learning

With machine learning algorithms, it has become possible for computers to predict the best possible course of action, based on input enterprise data. Machine learning algorithms (regardless of which domain) therefore always have three components: input data, a learning algorithm and output data, as shown in Figure 24.1.

For any machine learning algorithm to create accurate predictions, it needs to solve three problems. First, from the input data, the algorithm needs to determine which features say something meaningful for a prediction, a process known as **feature selection**. For example, if we are trying to predict whether a website customer will convert to a purchase, the number of times that person visited the website

Figure 24.1   Supervised machine learning

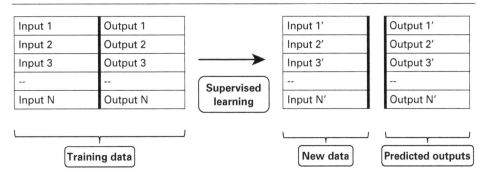

before is a useful feature (people who are serious about buying a product typically look at it multiple times). Similarly, the hair colour of a person might be a less interesting feature to predict sales (unless you are selling shampoo or something similar). Determining which input data is relevant for making a prediction is a crucial first step.

Secondly, as soon as the machine learning model made its predictions, we need to determine how accurate or valid these predictions are. Finding the answer to this question is called **model evaluation** and looks at the number of predictions that has been adequately made. For example, a bank that is able to predict with 95 per cent accuracy whether people will pay back their mortgages uses a (supervised) machine learning algorithm that has 95 per cent of its prediction (extend a mortgage or decline a mortgage) correct.

The third and final step in machine learning is subsequently **model optimization**, to make the predictions more accurate over time. Because of their structure, machine learning models become more accurate over time. If a model made a correct (or wrong) prediction in the past, this output data is now converted into input, which provides the algorithm with 'new' information to base decisions on. To illustrate this, let's consider a very simple example. Suppose that a machine learning model makes predictions on mortgage applications for 5,000 new customers, based on 500,000 previous records from customers. After these predictions have been made, these 5,000 predictions are added to the 'previous records'. So, for the next set of 5,000 customer predictions, the algorithm can use 505,000 records to make the predictions. If the last 5,000 predictions were already highly accurate, the model improves with every new customer evaluation.

The three challenges that are addressed above (feature selection, model evaluation and model optimization) are generic for all machine learning domains. Where supervised machine learning is different is that we know the input data and can actively evaluate this input data. In most enterprise data, the input data is known or can very easily be labelled. Out of all the machine learning algorithms that exist, we therefore see that **supervised machine learning techniques** have the most common enterprise applications.

There are many examples where supervised machine learning can be useful for organizations. Some of the most popular use cases include:

- **Fraud detection:** Identifying fraudulent transactions or suspicious activity by analysing patterns in historical data.

- **Customer churn prediction:** Identifying customers at risk of leaving a company by analysing their behaviour and demographics.

- **Sales forecasting:** Predicting future sales by analysing historical sales data, demographic information and other relevant factors.

- **Image and speech recognition:** Identifying objects, faces or transcribing speech within images or audio files.

- **Natural language processing (NLP) and text classification:** Identifying sentiment, topics or classifying text such as emails, chat and social media posts, etc.

- **Predictive maintenance:** Identifying equipment that is likely to fail by analysing sensor data and historical maintenance records.

- **Marketing and advertising:** Identifying target customers and optimizing marketing campaigns by analysing demographics, purchase history and other relevant information.

- **Supply chain optimization:** Optimizing the flow of goods and services by analysing data on inventory levels, delivery times and other logistics information.

- **Risk management:** Identifying and mitigating risks by analysing financial data and other relevant information.

- **Healthcare:** Identifying patients at risk of certain conditions or predicting the effectiveness of treatment by analysing patient data such as electronic health records.

Although these use cases are all different, most work on the same underlying principles of classification or regression algorithms. To build capability in supervised machine learning, organizations can actively work to master the following topics.

Supervised machine learning algorithms

There are several ways to increase the maturity of supervised machine learning in an organization. One of the most important ones is to develop a strong data science team. Having a team of experienced data scientists and engineers who can implement and maintain the machine learning models is essential.

Data science teams need to have a clear understanding of the different types of supervised machine learning algorithms that exist, and how they can be utilized to solve business problems. The sheer number of supervised machine learning algorithms that exist is far beyond the scope of this book, but it is important to be able to differentiate between the different purposes of machine learning algorithms.

An overview of the most common supervised machine learning algorithms is outlined in Table 24.3.

One of the classes of algorithms listed in Table 24.3 – regression and classification – is by far the most popular and widely used groups of algorithms. Each algorithm has its own strengths and weaknesses and is suitable for specific types of problems. Choosing the right algorithm for a specific task typically requires a combination of domain knowledge and experimentation.

Table 24.3   Different classes of supervised machine learning algorithms

Algorithm Class	Description
Regression algorithms	These algorithms are used to predict a continuous numerical output value (e.g. price, temperature, weight, etc.) based on input features. Examples of regression algorithms include linear regression, polynomial regression, decision tree regression and random forest regression.
Classification algorithms	These algorithms are used to predict a categorical output value (e.g. yes/no, A/B/C, spam/not spam, etc.) based on input features. Examples of classification algorithms include logistic regression, k-nearest neighbours, decision tree classification and support vector machines.
Neural networks	These algorithms are based on the structure and function of biological neural networks and can be used for a variety of tasks such as image and speech recognition, natural language processing and prediction.
Bayesian algorithms	These algorithms are based on Bayesian probability theory and are often used for problems such as text classification, image recognition and natural language processing.
Ensemble methods	These algorithms combine multiple models to produce more accurate or robust predictions. Examples of ensemble methods include random forests, gradient boosting and bagging.
Time series algorithms	These algorithms are used to analyse and make predictions based on time-stamped data. Examples include ARIMA and Exponential Smoothing.

Understanding unsupervised learning

Unsupervised learning is a type of machine learning that is used to find patterns and relationships in data, **without the need for labelled data**. In contrast to supervised learning, where the model is given labelled data and is trained to make predictions based on that data, unsupervised learning is used to identify underlying structure in the data and to uncover hidden patterns.

Figure 24.2 graphically displays the process of unsupervised machine learning. When compared with the process of supervised machine learning, it is clear that unsupervised learning does not require any labelled data. Instead, it relies on its internal algorithms to find similarities in the data sets. For that reason, unsupervised learning is frequently used for data mining. Data mining is the process of discovering patterns and relationships in large datasets. It involves using techniques from machine learning (and statistics) to extract valuable insights from data. The goal of data mining is to identify useful information and knowledge that can be used to improve decision-making and to gain a competitive advantage.

Figure 24.2   Unsupervised machine learning

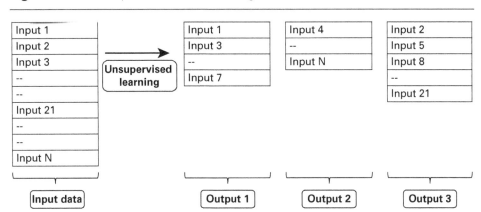

Unsupervised learning has a wide range of applications, including natural language processing, image processing, genomics and customer segmentation. It can be used to discover hidden patterns and relationships in data, to reduce the dimensionality of data and to identify unusual or anomalous data points.

One of the main advantages of unsupervised learning is that it can be used in situations where labelled data is scarce or expensive to obtain. Additionally, it can be used to uncover patterns and relationships that would be difficult or impossible to discover through other means. However, unsupervised learning can also be more challenging than supervised learning, as it can be difficult to evaluate the quality of the results and to interpret the patterns and relationships that are discovered.

Unsupervised learning can also be used in combination with supervised learning, in a technique known as **semi-supervised learning**. In semi-supervised learning, a small amount of labelled data is used to guide the unsupervised learning process, and the resulting model can then be used for supervised learning tasks.

Unsupervised machine learning algorithms

Similar to the way there are a number of algorithms that define supervised machine learning, there are a number of common groups of algorithms that are used in unsupervised machine learning. An effective team of data scientists should have knowledge about these algorithms and how they can be used to solve business problems.

There are several different techniques that can be used for unsupervised learning, including clustering, dimensionality reduction and anomaly detection, as outlined in Table 24.4.

Out of all the techniques outlined in Table 24.4, clustering is considered the most common technique in unsupervised machine learning. It involves clustering algorithm

Table 24.4   Different classes of supervised machine learning algorithms

Algorithm Class	Description
Clustering algorithms	Clustering is a technique that groups similar data points together. The goal is to discover natural groupings or patterns in the data. K-means, hierarchical clustering and DBSCAN are examples of clustering algorithms.
Dimensionality reduction	Dimensionality reduction is a technique that reduces the number of features in a dataset while preserving as much information as possible. Principal Component Analysis (PCA) and Linear Discriminant Analysis (LDA) are examples of dimensionality reduction techniques.
Anomaly detection	Anomaly detection is a technique that identifies data points that are unusual or different from the norm. It can be used to detect outliers, fraud or other abnormal behaviour.
Association rule mining	Association rule mining is a technique that finds associations and correlations among variables in large datasets. It is commonly used in market basket analysis, to understand what products are commonly bought together.
Autoencoders	Autoencoders are neural networks that are trained to reconstruct their inputs. They can be used for dimensionality reduction, anomaly detection and feature learning.
Time series algorithms	Generative models are unsupervised learning models that learn the probability distribution of the data, and can generate new data points that are similar to the ones in the training set. Examples are Variational Autoencoder (VAE) and Generative Adversarial Networks (GAN).

group similar data points together based on similar criteria. It helps to discover natural groupings or patterns in the data and understand the underlying structure of the data.

The machine learning development process

One of the main objectives in growing maturity is machine learning (as discussed in the previous section) is the ability of an organization to automate elements of the machine learning process. Through automation, these algorithms are no longer dependent on 'individual' data scientists but can start to bring benefits to the entire organization.

Before we dive into the ways in which automation can help or expedite, it is important to first understand the process of developing a machine learning algorithm.

The steps in developing a machine learning model typically include:

1 **Define the problem and gather data:** Understand the problem you are trying to solve and gather the necessary data to train and test the model. This includes identifying the target variable (also known as the dependent variable) and the input features (also known as the independent variables).

2 **Data pre-processing:** Prepare the data for modelling by cleaning, transforming and normalizing it. This may include handling missing values, dealing with outliers and encoding categorical variables.

3 **Feature engineering:** Create new features that can be used to train the model by combining or transforming existing features. This can involve creating interaction terms, performing dimensionality reduction and extracting features from text or images.

4 **Model selection:** Select a model or set of models that can be used to solve the problem. This may involve experimenting with different algorithms and comparing their performance using techniques such as cross-validation.

5 **Model training and evaluation:** Train the model using the preprocessed and engineered data and evaluate its performance using metrics such as accuracy, precision, recall and F1 score.

6 **Model tuning and selection:** Fine tune the hyperparameters of the model to optimize its performance and select the best performing model(s) for deployment.

7 **Model deployment and monitoring:** Deploy the model in a production environment and monitor its performance over time. This may involve implementing a feedback loop to gather predictions and true outcomes, and using the feedback to refine the model.

8 **Model maintenance:** Regularly update the model with new data and re-evaluate its performance to ensure that it continues to perform well over time.

These steps may vary slightly depending on the specifics of the problem and the data, but they provide a general framework for developing supervised machine learning models.

As depicted in Figure 24.3, the steps in this process are iterative, such as feature engineering, model selection and model tuning, so it's normal to go back and forth between those steps, testing different approaches and techniques until you have found the best possible solution.

Figure 24.3   Steps in the development of supervised machine learning

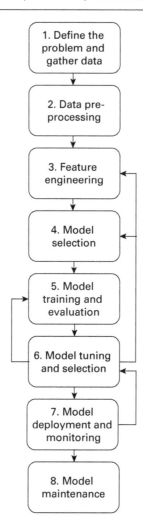

Automating the machine learning process

The benefits of automating the machine learning process cannot be overstated. Keeping everything manual is impractical and time-consuming. Organizations can significantly increase their maturity by automating (parts of) the machine learning development process.

There are several ways to automate machine learning algorithms:

- **Automated model selection:** involves using algorithms that can systematically search through a set of possible models and select the best one for a given task. This can be done using techniques such as grid search, random search and Bayesian optimization.

- **Automated feature engineering:** using algorithms that can automatically extract relevant features from the data and create new features that are useful for the task at hand. This can be done using techniques such as principal component analysis (PCA), independent component analysis (ICA) and feature extraction.

- **Automated hyperparameter tuning:** involves using algorithms that can automatically search for the optimal combination of hyperparameters for a given model. This can be done using techniques such as grid search, random search and Bayesian optimization.

- **Pipeline automation:** Automating the pipeline of data preprocessing, feature engineering, model selection, training, evaluating and deploying. This can be done using tools such as MLflow, DataRobot and AWS SageMaker

- **Deployment automation:** Automating the process of deploying models in production can be done using tools such as TensorFlow Serving, Seldon and MLflow Model Registry.

By automating these steps, organizations can improve the efficiency and scalability of their machine learning models, and reduce the need for manual intervention. This can lead to more accurate and reliable models, which can be deployed faster and with less risk.

Establishing machine learning data products

An approach that combines some of the best practices describe above is the creation of machine learning data products. A **data product** is a software application or system that uses machine learning or other data-driven techniques to provide a service or solve a problem. It typically takes in data as input, applies a set of algorithms or models to process the data, and produces some form of output, such as a prediction, recommendation or action.

A data product can be a standalone application, such as a recommendation engine for e-commerce websites, a predictive maintenance system for industrial equipment or a fraud detection system for financial transactions. It can also be a component of a larger system, such as a speech recognition module in a virtual assistant or a natural language processing module in a chatbot.

A data product is not just the model itself, it's the whole pipeline that starts by data collection, data preprocessing, feature engineering, model selection, training, evaluating and finally deploying and monitoring the model in a production environment. For external users, this typically means a black box solution, meaning that the users of the product or tool do not know how the underlying algorithms work. A common example of such black box data products are credit scoring applications.

A well-designed data product is able to handle Big Data, is scalable, easy to use and maintain, able to adapt to changes in the input data and provide interpretable and actionable outputs. Organizations that create machine learning data products for their customers therefore typically have a high level of maturity in this capability.

Maintenance

A last topic that helps to structure the machine learning capability is to establish a maintenance function of machine learning algorithms. Model maintenance (depicted as the last step in the creation of machine learning algorithms) is a sign of high maturity in the organization and requires ongoing attention and support.

Structuring maintenance for machine learning models is a critical step in ensuring that the models continue to perform well over time. There are several key steps involved in this process. **Monitoring** is the first step. It involves continuously monitoring the performance of the model in production using metrics such as accuracy, precision, recall and F1 score. By monitoring the model's performance, organizations can detect any issues or degradation in performance early on and take corrective action.

The second step is versioning. This involves keeping track of different versions of the model and their performance over time. **Versioning** allows organizations to roll back to a previous version of the model if necessary and compare the performance of different versions to understand how the model's performance evolves over time.

Retraining is the third and final step. Regularly retraining the model with new data is necessary to ensure that the model continues to perform well over time. This can be done using techniques like online learning, incremental learning and transfer learning. By retraining the model with new data, organizations can ensure that the model continues to perform well in light of changing data distributions.

Setting up maintenance of supervised machine learning algorithms is crucial for enterprise organizations. Particularly for organizations that develop and utilize hundreds of machine learning algorithms, proper maintenance will give your control over the supervised machine learning capability.

24.4 Machine learning summary

Machine learning algorithms are the more complex sets of algorithms (compared to descriptive data analysis) used to achieve value from Big Data. When properly architected, supervised machine learning algorithms have significant business value and can change the course of an organization.

In this chapter we reviewed the foundational components that organizations need to arrange to structure and set up supervised machine learning. Organizations that aim to have a high maturity in this capability need to understand how machine learning models can be used to create business value. They subsequently need to establish a sound process to develop (and maintain) these algorithms, and then leverage the capabilities of automation to effectively use these algorithms across the enterprise.

By building data products and establishing maintenance of machine learning algorithms, organizations can move to higher levels of maturity. Organizations that operate at level 4–5 in this capability typically achieve significant value from their Big Data.

Reproducible Research   25

25.1 Introduction to reproducible research

The final capability that organizations require in Big Data algorithms is the ability to set up and structure reproducible research. Reproducible is the idea that the entire algorithm development and research process, including data, methods and code, should be made available to others, so that the research can be independently verified and replicated. This allows others to check the validity of the algorithms that have been developed and build upon the findings. In practice, reproducible research often involves making data, code and other materials openly available, and providing detailed documentation of the methods used in the research.

The reproducible research capability is especially important in the design, development and maintenance of algorithms. Particularly with algorithms, people are uncomfortable if they don't exactly know how results are generated, and how certain calculations are made. Because algorithms are complex and sometimes difficult to understand, building a reproducible research capability helps organizations in the following ways:

- **Validity and robustness:** allows others to independently verify and replicate the results that algorithms generate, which helps to ensure the validity and robustness of the findings.

- **Progress and innovation:** makes it possible for other data analysts and data scientists to build upon the work and improve upon it, leading to the development of new and better methods and techniques.

- **Transparency and trust:** promotes transparency and trust in the research by making data, methods and code openly available and providing detailed documentation of the research process. Transparency and trust are of paramount importance if algorithms need to be explained to senior executives.

- **Avoiding bias:** helps to avoid bias by making it possible for others to check the data, methods and process that were used to develop the algorithm, which is especially important when the algorithm is going to be used in decision-making or in critical systems.

- **Improving collaboration:** helps to improve collaboration among data scientists by making it easy for others to understand, use and build upon the work, which can lead to more efficient and effective research.

- **Ethics and control:** ensures that the research is conducted in an ethical and responsible manner, and that the findings are accurate and reliable. Especially in the domain of artificial intelligence, the topic of ethics is becoming more and more prevalent, which we will discuss further in Chapter 45.

Reproducible research is also a form of knowledge management (discussed in Chapter 35) because it makes data, methods and code available to others, so that they can use this knowledge to solve new and different problems. This allows for the validation of results, and facilitates collaboration among data scientists, both within and outside the organization.

Organizations that engage in reproducible research are seen as more trustworthy and credible, which can enhance their reputation and attract more customers, partners and investors. Additionally, reproducibility can help organizations meet regulatory requirements for transparency and accountability in research and decision-making. Especially since data privacy and data security laws are becoming more strict, this capability can help to show or 'prove' to regulators that an organization is using algorithms in a fair and sustainable way.

Having the capability to conduct reproducible research can also increase the return on investment in the development of algorithms by making it possible for others to build upon the work and develop new and improved products and services. Moreover, reproducibility can help organizations avoid legal issues by demonstrating that the research was conducted in an ethical and responsible manner, and that the findings are accurate and reliable.

In summary, building reproducible research capability is important for organizations because it can improve decision-making, enhance reputation, facilitate collaboration, meet regulatory requirements, increase return on investment and avoid legal issues. It is a key element to ensure the research being conducted is rigorous, unbiased and fair.

25.2 Purpose and maturity levels of reproducible research

Purpose

The purpose of reproducible research for enterprise organizations is to ensure that research findings are reliable, valid and robust, and that the research is conducted in an ethical and transparent manner. This is critical for organizations that rely on data-driven decision-making, as it allows them to make informed decisions based on sound scientific evidence.

One of the key benefits of reproducible research for enterprise organizations is that it allows for independent verification and replication of research findings. This helps to ensure the validity and robustness of the research, and gives organizations confidence that their decisions are based on sound scientific evidence. Additionally, reproducibility makes it possible for other researchers to build upon the work and improve upon it, which can lead to the development of new and better products and services.

Maturity levels

There are several maturity levels, outlined in Table 25.2, that organizations can reach with regards to the reproducible research capability. These levels can be used as a benchmark for organizations to track their progress and identify areas for improvement.

Table 25.1   The purpose of the reproducible research capability

Capability	Purpose
Reproducible research	Defines the ability of an organization to have a verifiable and auditable trail that outlines how algorithms produce specific results.

Table 25.2   Maturity levels of the reproducible research capability

Maturity Level	Description
Level 1 – Initial	Organizations have few to no formal processes in place for reproducible research. Data scientists develop algorithms in a way that is not easily replicated by others, and there may be little to no documentation or sharing of data, methods and code.
Level 2 – Managed	Organizations have implemented some basic processes for reproducible research, such as data management and documentation best practices. Data scientists may be trained on best practices for reproducible research, but there is limited monitoring and review of research projects.
Level 3 – Defined	Organizations have a dedicated reproducibility team in place and have implemented more advanced processes for reproducible research, such as collaboration and sharing of data, methods and code. The reproducibility team regularly monitors and reviews research projects and provides support and guidance to the Big Data teams.

(continued)

Table 25.2   (Continued)

Maturity Level	Description
Level 4 – Controlled	Organizations have implemented a comprehensive reproducibility framework and have dedicated resources to support reproducible research. The reproducibility team works closely with researchers to ensure that research is conducted in an ethical and transparent manner, and that it can be easily replicated by others. The organization also promotes reproducibility within the organization and with external partners.
Level 5 – Optimized	Organizations not only implement best practices for reproducible research but also actively contribute to the development of new methods and tools in the field. They have implemented a culture of reproducibility, where reproducibility is embedded in the algorithm design and development process, and is a core part of their research strategy.

25.3 Structuring reproducible research

Building capability in reproducible research can be challenging for some organizations as it requires a significant investment of time and resources. It may also require a change in culture and mindset among researchers, as they may need to adjust their workflows and practices to ensure that their research is reproducible.

There are several factors that can make building capability in reproducible research difficult, such as:

- lack of understanding or awareness of the importance and benefits of reproducibility among data analysts and data scientists
- limited resources and funding to invest in data management and documentation practices
- limited expertise and knowledge in using the tools and platforms that support reproducibility
- resistance to change and lack of incentives to adopt new practices

Additionally, the complexity of reproducibility can vary depending on the domain, the data and the methods used. For example, reproducibility in corporate environments may be different from reproducibility in research firms or government organizations.

However, with the right approach and resources, organizations can overcome these challenges and build a strong capability in reproducible research. This can be achieved by providing training, resources and incentives for researchers, implementing best practices for data management and documentation, and using open-source tools and platforms that support reproducibility. Building capability in reproducible research is an ongoing process that requires regular review and monitoring to ensure that reproducibility practices are being followed and to identify areas for improvement.

Building capability in reproducible research in an enterprise involves several steps.

Establish a reproducibility policy

Organizations should establish a clear policy on reproducibility, outlining the expectations for data, methods and code sharing, as well as the procedures for ensuring the reproducibility of algorithm development and its key results.

The components of a data reproducibility policy typically include:

- Guidelines for data management, including data collection, storage, documentation, and sharing. This includes the use of unique identifiers for data, the format in which data should be stored and shared, and the procedures for maintaining the integrity and security of the data.

- Guidelines for sharing code, including the use of version control systems, code sharing platforms and open-source licenses. This also includes the procedures for ensuring that the code is readable, well-documented and understandable by others.

- Guidelines for documenting methods and analysis, including the use of detailed records of the data processing and analysis steps, and the use of standard formats for reporting research results.

- Guidelines for ensuring that algorithm design and development is conducted in an ethical and transparent manner, including guidelines for data protection, privacy and informed consent.

- Procedures for ensuring compliance with the policy, including training, education and incentives for data science teams to follow the policy.

A data reproducibility policy provides a framework for organizations to ensure that their research findings are reliable, valid and robust and that the research is conducted in an ethical and transparent manner. It also helps to promote transparency, accountability and trust in the research process by making data, methods and code available to others for review, replication and reuse.

Data and documentation management

Organizations should implement best practices for data management and documentation, such as using unique identifiers for data and keeping detailed records of the data processing and analysis steps. This will ensure that the data can be easily located and used by other data scientists and other people involved with the development of algorithms.

Organizations should ensure that data is well-documented, including information about the data's origin, format and content. This documentation should be stored in a central location and be easily accessible to others. One of the structured ways to accomplish this is by starting using version control systems, such as Git, to manage and track changes to data and code. This ensures that the data and code are easily accessible to others and that changes can be traced. Version control was discussed in more detail in Chapter 21.

Use open-source tools and platforms

To increase maturity of the reproducible research capability, organizations should use open-source tools and platforms that support reproducibility, such as version

Table 25.3 Objectives of open-source tools

Objective	Description
Collaboration	Open-source tools provide a platform for data analysts and data scientists to collaborate on data, methods and code, regardless of their location or organization. This promotes transparency, accountability and trust in the research process by making data, methods and code available to others for review, replication and reuse.
Code Sharing	Open-source tools provide a way to share code with others, making it easier for other data scientists to understand and replicate the research. Additionally, using open-source tools can help algorithm developers to maintain the integrity of their data and code over time.
Transparency	Open-source tools provide a way for data scientists to document and share their data, methods and code in an open and transparent manner. This allows other data scientists to understand the research process, identify potential issues or errors and replicate the research.
Reusability	Open-source tools provide a way for data scientists to share their data, methods and code, making it available for other developers to reuse in their own research. This helps to promote the efficient use of resources in the design of algorithms.
Community	Open-source tools foster a sense of community among researchers, allowing them to share ideas, collaborate on projects and contribute to the development of the tools.

control systems, data management systems and code sharing platforms. This will make it easy for others to access and use the data, methods and code.

Open-source tools can play a significant role in reproducible research by providing a way to share and collaborate on data, methods and code. Some ways open-source tools can help with the reproducible research capability are listed in Table 25.3.

Reproducibility team

Larger enterprise organizations that operate at a higher level of maturity frequently establish a team specifically dedicated to reproducibility, which will help to ensure that reproducibility practices are implemented and maintained throughout the organization.

A reproducibility team is a group of individuals within an organization who are responsible for ensuring that algorithm design and development is conducted in a reproducible manner. The team's main role is to provide support and guidance to Big Data and data science teams in the organization to ensure that their research is conducted in an ethical and transparent manner, and that it can be replicated by other data scientists.

25.4 Reproducible research summary

The last critical capability in the design, development and maintenance is one that is frequently overlooked. Not only should algorithms perform the functions that they are supposed to be executing, it is also important that decision-makers trust these algorithms.

Reproducible research is the capability that safeguards this trust, by ensuring that the same algorithm can be recreated to create the same results. In order to achieve this, the Big Data teams need to ensure that the development and processes are properly documented.

In this section, we discussed some of the main components with which organizations can structure the reproducible research capability. By creating a reproducible policy for data scientists to follow, establishing the right data and document management systems, and the use of proper open-source tools, organizations can ensure that their work is reproducible, verifiable and auditable. Given the increased regulations and pressure on ethical algorithms (which will only become more significant), this is a critical capability for any organization to master.

Big Data Algorithms Maturity Assessment

Please respond to the following questions by indicating the relevant level of maturity for each activity in question and its importance to your organization.

The Capability Maturity Model levels are shown in Table 26.1.

Table 26.1   The Capability Maturity Model levels

Score	Description
0 – Non-existent	Describes a total lack of activity or lack of recognition that the activity exists.
1 – Initial	Describes evidence that the organization recognizes issues exist and need to be addressed.
2 – Managed	Describes activities designed so that similar procedures are followed by individuals. There is a high reliance on individual knowledge and skill level.
3 – Defined	Describes a standardized and documented level of activities which is being communicated through training, processes and tools.
4 – Controlled	Describes activities which are good practice and under constant improvement. Automation and tools are used to support the activities.
5 – Optimized	Describes activities that are considered leading and best practice and can be considered an example to other organizations.

Please note that responses to this survey should reflect how the organization performs the task today, not how you would like to see the organization perform the task in the future. Your choices should be based on your opinion of the organization, not just the way the task is performed in your own work group.

Table 26.2   Big Data Algorithms Maturity Assessment

#	Software Engineering	Score
12.1	Our organization creates and maintains standardized and coherent code across the organization.	
12.2	Our organization has established coding standards (or policy) for everyone that is working on creating, developing and maintaining the code for Big Data algorithms.	
12.3	Our organization has established procedures, systems and controls for adequate version control for all Big Data algorithms.	
12.4	Our organization has established professional and standardized testing procedures that ensures that algorithms work correctly and in line with data ethics and data privacy guidelines.	
12.5	Our Big Data and data science teams have implemented an Agile way of working, dividing work in iterative and incremental improvements.	
12.6	Our organization has established a formal training programme to educate teams about software engineering best practices, coding standards and testing approaches.	
	Data Cleaning and Data Wrangling	**Score**
13.1	Our organization has established clear goals that define what 'clean' is, and those goals are adequately cascaded into data cleaning and data wrangling processes and procedures.	
13.2	Our organization has adequate tools for automated data cleaning and data wrangling operations.	
13.3	Our organization has proper procedures for data acquisition and guidelines about the quality of what is stored in the data warehouse.	
13.4	Our organization actively adds semantics and metadata to incoming data, so it becomes easier to retrieve information at later stages.	
13.5	Our organization has procedures for data integration and data aggregation, and automatically combines disparate data sources into one uniform data format.	

(continued)

Table 26.2   (Continued)

13.6 Our organization actively monitors and reviews the quality of data on a periodic basis and undertakes additional cleaning or wrangling operations based on the reviews.

Descriptive Data Analysis	**Score**

14.1 Our organization has the knowledge and skills to aggregate and summarize internal data within a reasonable amount of time.

14.2 Our organization has the necessary technology and tools for dashboarding and visualizations.

14.3 Our organization has sufficient internal knowledge and skills to build dashboards and visualizations that support management decision-making.

14.4 Our organization periodically reviews which dashboards and visualizations are actively used and cleans up unused resources.

14.5 Our organization employs standards and best practices across the enterprise, so that data visualization and reports are displayed in a coherent, standardized look and feel.

14.6 The descriptive data analysis capability in our organization supports the day-to-day decisions of senior management.

Machine Learning	**Score**

15.1 Our organization uses machine learning models to make decisions.

15.2 Our organization has established a standardized process for the development of machine learning models.

15.3 Our organization has sufficient knowledge and skills to develop sound, unbiased and fair machine learning algorithms.

15.4 Our organization has developed quality criteria with regards to the quality and bias of machine learning algorithms.

15.5 Our organization actively monitors the performance of active machine learning algorithms, and improves algorithms based on performance.

15.6 Machine learning algorithms are tested against the organization's data ethics policies to prevent unfair or biased recommendations.

(continued)

Table 26.2   (Continued)

Reproducible Research	Score
16.1 The results of big data algorithms in our organizations are reproducible and would generate the same results if performed by different stakeholders.	
16.2 The way in which our organizations and teams develop algorithms is properly documented.	
16.3 Our organization has defined a reproducible research policy that establishes guidelines for documentation, commenting and testing.	
16.4 The reproducibility policy is adequately communicated to the organizations and teams are adequately trained and familiarized with this policy.	
16.5 Our organization utilizes best practice for data management and documentation, such as using unique identifiers for data and keeping detailed records of the data processing and analysis steps.	
16.6 Our organization uses open-source tools and platforms that support reproducibility, such as version control systems, data management systems and code sharing platforms.	

PART SIX
Big Data Processes

Big Data Processes 27

27.1 Introduction to Big Data processes

Executing Big Data projects that bring value to enterprises is difficult. Because of the volume, variety and velocity of available data sources, organizations can get lost and might not see the forest for the trees. Combined with management agendas, pressure to deliver results and complex algorithms, many organizations struggle to achieve the required return on investment from Big Data initiatives.

To avoid the potential pitfalls that Big Data brings, processes can help enterprises to focus their direction. Processes bring structure, measurable steps and can be effectively managed on a day-to-day basis. Additionally, processes embed Big Data expertise within the organization by following similar procedures and steps, embedding it as 'a practice' of the organization. Data analysis becomes less dependent on individuals and therefore greatly enhances the chances of capturing long-term value.

Setting up Big Data processes in the enterprise might be a time-consuming task at first but provides significant long-term benefits. In this macro-capability of the Enterprise Big Data framework, we will discuss how Big Data processes can provide structure for any enterprise.

Enterprise organizations need Big Data processes for a variety of reasons. Without proper processes in place, organizations will lose control over their data, bringing several data privacy and data security risks. This macro-capability is therefore crucial for any organization and provides the 'hygiene factor' for responsible and sustainable use of data.

Embedding and maturing Big Data processes will bring the following benefits to enterprise organizations:

- **Consistency and efficiency:** Big Data processes provide a standardized way of performing tasks and ensure that work is carried out in a consistent and efficient manner. By having a clear and defined Big Data process in place, employees know exactly what is expected of them and how to perform their work to the best of their abilities. This helps to eliminate inefficiencies and reduces the risk of data privacy and security errors.

- **Improved decision-making:** Big Data processes can provide a structured approach to decision-making, ensuring that all relevant information is considered and that decisions are made in a systematic and consistent manner. Well-defined Big Data processes help to eliminate bias and ensure that decisions are based on accurate and up-to-date information. This leads to better-informed decisions, which are more likely to be successful. The data governance and data management processes, in particular, which we will discuss in Chapters 28 and 29, will lead to improved decision-making.

- **Increased accountability:** Big Data processes help to clearly define roles, responsibilities and accountability, which reduces the risk of confusion and conflict and helps ensure that tasks are completed in a timely manner. When employees know what is expected of them and how their work fits into the bigger picture, they are more likely to take ownership of their tasks and to complete them to a high standard.

- **Cost savings:** Big Data processes can help enterprise organizations to identify areas where costs can be reduced and to implement more efficient working practices. By streamlining workflows and reducing the risk of errors, Big Data processes can lead to significant cost savings, especially in large and complex organizations.

- **Increased customer satisfaction:** Big Data processes can help organizations to better understand the needs and expectations of their customers and to improve the quality of their products and services. By having a clear understanding of customer requirements and by using data analytics processes to ensure that work is carried out in a consistent and efficient manner, organizations can improve customer satisfaction and build stronger, more successful relationships with their customers.

- **Competitive advantage:** Organizations that have well-designed and well-implemented Big Data processes are more likely to have a competitive advantage over those that do not. By having clear and efficient processes in place, organizations can respond more quickly to changing market conditions and customer needs, which can help them to maintain their competitive edge.

The benefits above outline some of the most important benefits of setting up and structuring Big Data processes in any organization. Paradoxically, the larger an enterprise becomes, the larger the need for mature Big Data processes. Organizations that are operating in multiple countries, with diverse rules and regulations, will see an increased need to have their Big Data processes operating at high levels of maturity.

27.2 Process definition and key characteristics

Big Data processes are not a new concept, but they have become increasingly important in recent years as organizations generate and collect increasing amounts of data. As data regulations have been growing, organizations have come under increased scrutiny to prove that they use data in a safe and responsible manner. As a result, organizations have had to develop new Big Data processes to handle these growing requirements.

Whilst there are many ways in which organizations set up and deal with processes, we will adhere to the following definition in the Enterprise Big Data Framework:

> A process is a set of steps or activities that are followed in a specific order to achieve a particular outcome.

In the context of Big Data, a process typically refers to a series of tasks or steps that are followed to protect, safeguard or control data assets, such as masking data (discussed in Part 4), data quality management and adhering to data privacy regulations. Big Data processes are designed to help organizations achieve their goals and objectives in a consistent, efficient and effective manner, and to ensure that work is completed in a controlled and predictable way.

Well-designed Big Data processes in the enterprise should be clear, concise and easy to follow, and should provide a framework for executing tasks and achieving results. A good process should also be flexible enough to accommodate changes and improvements as necessary, while still providing the structure and control needed to ensure consistent results.

For all of the Big Data processes that we will cover in this section, we will adhere to the following key characteristics that will define a process:

- **Measurable outcomes:** Processes should have specific, measurable outcomes, so that progress can be tracked and improvements can be made.

- **Clarity and consistency:** Processes should be well defined, clear and concise, so that everyone involved in the process understands their responsibilities and the steps that need to be taken.

- **Documented:** Processes should be well documented, so that they can be easily followed and understood by all stakeholders across the enterprise.

- **Continual improvement:** Processes should be regularly reviewed and improved to ensure they remain effective and efficient.

It is especially important for enterprises that processes are measurable. Measurable processes allow organizations to track their progress and monitor their performance. This can help to identify areas where improvements can be made and can provide valuable insights into the effectiveness of the process. As such, measurable processes provide a framework for continuous improvement. By regularly measuring and analysing process performance, organizations can identify areas for improvement and make changes to increase efficiency and effectiveness.

27.3 Enterprise Big Data processes

The Big Data processes that are set up in on organization should, over time, become the natural way of doing things within the enterprise. As a result, processes help to establish best practices by providing a structured and consistent approach to establishing a Big Data Centre of Excellence (discussed further in Part 7). By following a set of well-defined steps and procedures, organizations can ensure that work is completed in a consistent and controlled manner. This can help to ensure that best practices are consistently followed, and that work is completed to a high standard every time.

For example, a well-designed data governance process can help to ensure that data is properly classified and protected, and that it is only used for authorized purposes. This can help to protect sensitive information and reduce the risk of data breaches and other security incidents.

Processes should be regularly reviewed and improved to ensure that best practices are updated and kept current. By regularly examining the process and making changes where necessary, organizations can ensure that their processes are always aligned with the latest best practices and industry standards.

Figure 27.1 outlines the Big Data processes in the Enterprise Big Data Framework that we will discuss.

Figure 27.1   Overview of the Enterprise Big Data processes

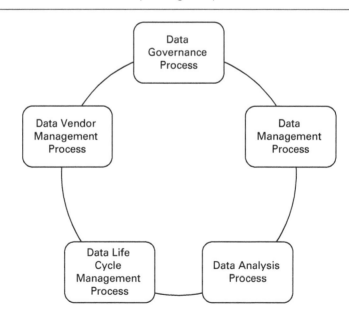

As might be expected, there is a significant overlap and dependency between these different processes. For example, it is impossible to set up a good data management process without properly documented roles and responsibilities (which is part of data governance). Similarly, the data analysis process depends on proper data life cycle management to ensure data is valid, current and trustworthy.

27.4 Process owners

Because processes are measurable, it is easy to appoint a person who will be responsible for managing and improving the process. This process custodian is also known as the process owner. A process owner is the individual responsible for the design, implementation and management of a specific Big Data process within the enterprise. The process owner is accountable for ensuring that the process meets the needs of the business, operates efficiently and complies with relevant policies, procedures and regulations.

The process owner is responsible for defining the process's objectives, identifying the inputs and outputs, and defining the steps required to achieve the desired outcome. They also oversee the implementation of the process and are responsible for monitoring and measuring its performance to ensure that it is delivering the desired results.

In addition, the process owner of every Big Data process is responsible for ensuring that the process is regularly reviewed and updated to reflect changes in the business environment and to ensure that it continues to meet the needs of the organization. They also play a key role in resolving issues and identifying opportunities for improvement, and they are responsible for communicating information about the process to other stakeholders, such as employees, customers and regulatory authorities.

The process owner is a critical role in every Big Data organization ensuring that business processes are designed and implemented effectively. In most organizations, the Big Data process owners will be an integral part of the Big Data Centre of Excellence (discussed further in Part 7).

The Data Governance Process

28

28.1 Introduction to the data governance process

Data governance is a set of policies, procedures and practices that define how an organization manages, uses and protects its data. The data governance process capability involves establishing standards and guidelines for the management of data, ensuring that data is accurate, complete and consistent, and defining the roles and responsibilities of individuals involved in data management.

The **data governance process** is a critical capability and input of effective data management (discussed further in Chapter 29), and it involves establishing a set of policies, procedures and practices for the management of data within an organization. A well-designed data governance process helps to ensure that data is accurate, complete and consistent, and that it is used in an ethical and responsible manner.

The concept of data governance has been around for several decades, but it has become increasingly important in recent years with the growth of digital data and the increasing need for organizations to effectively manage, use and protect their data assets.

Data governance has been a focus for organizations in industries such as healthcare and finance for many years, due to regulations such as the Health Insurance Portability and Accountability Act (HIPAA) and the Gramm-Leach-Bliley Act (GLBA), which require organizations to maintain the confidentiality and security of sensitive data.

In recent years, however, the data governance process has become a crucial priority for organizations across a range of industries, as they seek to maximize the value of their data assets and ensure that they are using data in a responsible and ethical manner. This has been driven by factors such as the increasing amount of digital data being generated, the growing importance of data analytics and data-driven decision-making, and concerns about data privacy and security.

In Chapter 8, we briefly introduced the purpose of data governance and introduced the Enterprise Big Data Framework Governance System. Figure 8.2 demonstrated how the data governance process and the data management process overlap with each other.

As Figure 8.2 illustrated, the leadership and governance capability is responsible for the strategic aspects of data governance, concerning themselves with strategy review, roles and responsibilities, legal and regulatory review and risk management. In the data governance capability, we will further build upon the Enterprise Big Data Framework Governance System, and structure processes for the development of **standards, policies and processes.**

One of the key benefits of the data governance process is the improvement of data quality and data management. By establishing policies and procedures for data collection, storage and maintenance, and by implementing data quality management practices, organizations can ensure that their data becomes more consistent. This helps to improve the accuracy and reliability of business decisions and to support the effective use of data in operations and analysis.

Another benefit of a well-structured data governance process is the improvement of data security and privacy. By establishing policies and procedures for data security and privacy, organizations can ensure that their data is protected from unauthorized access and use, and that they comply with relevant regulations and standards. This helps to reduce the risk of data breaches and to protect sensitive information, such as personal and financial data.

Finally, the data governance process can help organizations to better leverage their data assets for competitive advantage. By establishing standards and guidelines for data management and by improving the accuracy, security and privacy of data, organizations can improve their ability to use data to support business decisions and to drive innovation and growth.

An effective data governance process requires the involvement and collaboration of multiple stakeholders, including business leaders, data management and technology teams, legal and compliance teams, and data privacy and security teams. Data governance also requires a strong leadership commitment and a culture that values the management and use of data as a strategic asset.

28.2 Purpose and maturity levels of the data governance process

Purpose

The purpose of the data governance process is to ensure that an organization's data assets are managed, used and protected in a consistent, reliable and compliant manner. It provides consistency for making decisions about data management and for establishing standards, policies and procedures that can subsequently be used by data management processes.

The specific goals of the data governance process can vary from organization to organization, but some of the most common goals include:

1 **Data quality:** Ensuring that the data is accurate, complete and consistent, and that it meets the organization's standards for data quality.

2 **Data security:** Protecting the confidentiality, integrity and availability of the data, and ensuring that the data is protected from unauthorized access and theft.

3 **Data privacy:** Ensuring that the data is used in a responsible and ethical manner, and that the privacy of individuals and their personal data is protected.

4 **Data compliance:** Ensuring that the organization's data management practices comply with relevant regulations, such as those related to data privacy and security.

5 **Data integration:** Ensuring that the organization's data is integrated and consistent across all systems and applications, and that data from different sources can be easily combined and analysed.

The purpose of data governance is to provide a process framework for making decisions about control of data, and to ensure that an organization's data assets are managed in a consistent, reliable and compliant manner. This capability will help the organization to maximize the value of its data assets. The purpose of the data governance capability is outlined in Table 28.1.

Establishing sound data governance process capabilities is critical to any modern organization because it helps to ensure the effective and responsible management of the organization's data assets. By establishing these processes, organizations have a defined way to control their data assets. Additionally, processes make the results of specific actions verifiable and auditable. Because every process has measurable outcomes (as discussed in Chapter 27 section 27.2), the results of the data governance process can be easily verified.

Table 28.1 The purpose of the data governance capability

Capability	Purpose
Data governance process	Defines the ability of an organization to establish a process to govern the availability, usability, integrity and security of enterprise data, based on internal data standards and policies.

Maturity levels

The maturity of the data governance process is the level of development and implementation of data governance processes, policies and procedures within an organization. The maturity level of data governance can be evaluated based on various factors, such as the degree of standardization and automation, the level of data quality, the effectiveness of data security and privacy measures, and the overall level of data management capabilities.[1]

Examples of enterprise organizations with a high maturity in the data governance capabilities are typically financial institutions, such as banks or insurance companies. These organizations handle large amounts of sensitive and confidential information, such as customer data, financial transactions and personal information, and they must in almost all cases comply with strict regulations, such as the EU's General Data Protection Regulation (GDPR) and the Payment Card Industry Data Security Standard (PCI DSS).

In these organizations, the data governance process is critical to ensure the accuracy and reliability of the data, to protect sensitive information and to comply with regulations. They typically have a well-defined data governance system (see Figure 28.1), with clear roles and responsibilities, formalized processes and procedures, data cataloging and classification, and data quality management. They also have a data governance body in place (as discussed in Chapter 8), which oversees data governance activities and makes decisions about data-related issues.

Organizations with a high maturity level frequently have a strong focus on data security and privacy, with robust policies and processes in place to ensure that sensitive data is protected and used in a responsible manner. They have metrics and KPIs in place to monitor and evaluate the effectiveness of data governance, and they continuously review and improve their data governance processes.

To grow maturity in the data governance process, enterprise organizations can use the maturity levels as shown in Table 28.2.

By periodically measuring the data governance process maturity level, organizations can identify areas for improvement and make changes to enhance the quality and reliability of their data. They can also implement best practices and standardize processes to ensure consistent and effective data governance.

28.3 Structuring the data governance process

Structing data governance and its corresponding data governance process needs to be considered in the larger context of an organization's data governance system. More than with some other capabilities in the Enterprise Big Data Framework, there is a strong integration between the data governance process capability and the **leadership**

Table 28.2 Maturity levels of the data governance capability

Maturity Level	Description
Level 1 – Initial	The data governance process is informal, with little standardization or consistency in the management of data. There is no clear understanding of who is responsible for data governance or what processes and procedures are in place.
Level 2 – Managed	Data governance processes and procedures are starting to be defined and implemented, but they are still relatively rudimentary. There is a focus on data cataloging and classification, but data quality and security measures are still limited.
Level 3 – Defined	Data governance processes and procedures are more formalized, and there is a clearer understanding of who is responsible for data governance. There is a focus on improving data quality and security, and there are metrics in place to monitor and evaluate the effectiveness of data governance.
Level 4 – Controlled	Data governance processes and procedures are well-defined and mature, and there is a high level of standardization and automation in the management of data. Data quality and security measures are robust, and there is a focus on continuous improvement.
Level 5 – Optimized	Data governance processes and procedures are highly optimized, and there is a high degree of data management automation. There is a focus on using data as a strategic asset, and data governance is integrated into the overall business strategy.

and governance capability (discussed in Chapter 8) and the data management process capability (discussed in Chapter 29). The relation between these three capabilities is illustrated in Figure 8.2.

In this section, we will therefore limit the scope of data governance to the strategic and tactical activities that define data governance **standards, policies,** and **processes.** Standards, policies and processes are an effective way in which an organization can direct, monitor and control its enterprise data.[2] By setting these guidelines and periodically reviewing them (i.e. a process), every organization can establish a maturity data governance capability.

Data governance standards

Data governance standards are a set of guidelines, best practices and frameworks that organizations use to manage and protect their data assets. They provide a common language and methodology for data management, ensuring that data is collected, stored and used in a consistent, secure and compliant manner. Some of the key benefits of data governance standards include:

1 **Improved data quality:** Data governance standards help organizations ensure that data is accurate, complete, consistent and trustworthy. This is essential for making informed decisions and avoiding costly errors.

2 **Better data security:** Data governance standards provide guidelines for protecting sensitive and confidential information, such as personal data, financial information and trade secrets.

3 **Compliance with regulations:** Many industries have specific regulations, such as the European Union's General Data Protection Regulation (GDPR) or the Health Insurance Portability and Accountability Act (HIPAA) in the healthcare industry, which require organizations to manage data in a specific way. Data governance standards help organizations ensure compliance with these regulations.

4 **Improved data management:** Data governance standards provide a framework for managing data assets, including data classification, data quality, data security, data privacy, data retention and data access.

5 **Better data utilization:** Data governance standards help organizations leverage their data assets more effectively by ensuring that data is available, accessible and usable for decision-making and analysis.

Some examples of data governance standards include the Data Management Association's Data Governance Standard, the International Organization for Standardization's ISO/IEC 38500:2015 and the Federal Information Processing Standard (FIPS) 199. These standards provide organizations with a roadmap for establishing a data governance programme, and can be adapted to fit the specific needs of the organization. A brief overview of these standards is provided in Table 28.3.

Data governance standards are generic and evolve over time through versioning. For that reason, they cannot simply be copied and adopted by organizations. Instead,

Table 28.3   Data governance standards

Standard	Description
DAMA Governance Standard	The Data Management Association's (DAMA) Data Governance Standard is a set of best practices and guidelines for data governance. It provides organizations with a comprehensive framework for managing their data assets, including data quality, data security, data privacy, data retention and data access. The standard is designed to help organizations establish data governance programmes that are effective, efficient and aligned with the organization's strategic goals and objectives.[1]

(continued)

Table 28.3 (Continued)

Standard	Description
International Organization for Standardization's ISO/IEC 38500:2015	The International Organization for Standardization's (ISO) ISO/IEC 38500:2015 is an international standard for corporate governance of information technology (IT). It provides a set of best practices and guidelines for organizations to effectively manage their IT systems and ensure that they align with the organization's overall strategy and objectives. Whereas this standard is not specifically designed for data governance (but for IT governance), many organizations use this standard as an umbrella framework for data governance.[2]
The Federal Information Processing Standard (FIPS) 199	This standard provides guidelines for categorizing information systems based on the potential impact that a security breach could have on the organization. This categorization of information systems provides guidelines to the way in which data should be governed across different systems in the enterprise.[3]

1 B Quinto (2018) Big data governance and management, *Next-Generation Big Data: A Practical Guide to Apache Kudu, Impala, and Spark*, 495–506

2 S Bennett. What is information governance and how does it differ from data governance?, *Governance Directions*, 2017 69 (8), 462–67

3 S Radack (2004) Federal information processing standard (FIPS) 199, standards for security categorization of federal information and information systems (No. ITL Bulletin March 2004). National Institute of Standards and Technology.

Figure 28.1 Data governance process – standards

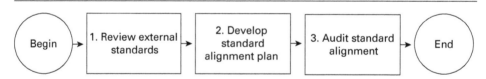

organizations need to review which standards are applicable and relevant, and how these standards can be adopted and adapted in the organization.

Organizations therefore need to set up a process to periodically review (minimum once per year) which data governance standards align to the corporate needs, and how they can be incorporated in the existing data governance structure. This activity can easily be converted into a process, as shown in Figure 28.1.

Setting up a comprehensive process for a data governance standards review consists of the steps outlined in Table 28.4.

The development of a data governance standards process is a critical component of a comprehensive data governance programme and can help organizations to ensure that their data governance practices are consistent, efficient and effective and that they align with the overall goals and objectives of the organization.

Table 28.4 Steps in the data governance standards process

Process	Description
1. Review external standards	A review of existing data governance standards is a systematic evaluation of the various standards, guidelines and best practices that exist for managing and governing data within an organization. The purpose of a review is to identify the most appropriate standards that can be adopted and integrated into the organization's data governance framework.
2. Develop standard alignment plan	The development of a standards alignment plan is a process that outlines the steps and strategies needed to align an organization's data governance practices with established data governance standards. The purpose of the plan is to ensure that the organization's data governance practices are consistent, efficient and effective and that they align with the overall goals and objectives of the organization.
3. Audit standard alignment	An audit of the data governance standards alignment is a process that evaluates the effectiveness and compliance of an organization's data governance practices with established data governance standards. The purpose of the audit is to identify areas where the organization's data governance practices may not be aligned with established standards and to make recommendations for improvement.

Data governance policies

Data governance policies are a set of rules and guidelines that govern how an organization manages its data assets. These policies define the roles, responsibilities and expectations of different stakeholders within the organization and provide a framework for making decisions about the creation, maintenance and use of data. Input to the development of data policies can come from data governance standards, as discussed in the previous section.

Data governance policies can cover a wide range of topics, including data security, data privacy, data quality, data retention, data access and use, data classification, data architecture, data management, data integration, data archiving and data disposal. They are designed to ensure that an organization's data assets are managed in a consistent, efficient and effective manner, and that they support the organization's business objectives and regulatory requirements.

The purpose of data governance policies is to:

- Ensure that data is managed in a consistent and controlled manner, so that it can be trusted and relied upon.

- Foster collaboration and communication between different stakeholders, so that they can work together to achieve common goals.

- Provide a framework for decision-making, so that decisions about data are made in a consistent and transparent manner.

- Support regulatory compliance, so that the organization can meet its obligations under relevant laws and regulations.

- Foster data quality and data security, so that data is protected against unauthorized access, loss or damage.

Data governance policies are an important component of a comprehensive data governance programme and play a critical role in ensuring that an organization's data assets are managed in a consistent, efficient and effective manner. They provide a foundation for building an effective data governance capability and for ensuring that the organization's data assets are aligned with its business objectives and regulatory requirements.

Every organization has unique needs and requirements when it comes to managing its data assets, but there are some common data governance policies that every organization should have in place. The following is a list of some of the most common data governance policies that organizations should consider:

1 **Data security policy:** outlines the measures an organization takes to protect its data assets from unauthorized access, loss or damage. It includes guidelines for data encryption, data backup and disaster recovery.

2 **Data privacy policy:** outlines the measures an organization takes to protect the privacy of its customers, employees and other stakeholders. It covers issues such as data collection, data storage and data sharing.

3 **Data quality policy:** outlines the measures an organization takes to ensure that its data assets are of high quality and free from errors, duplicates and inconsistencies. It covers issues such as data validation, data cleansing and data normalization.

4 **Data retention policy:** outlines the measures an organization takes to retain its data assets for a specified period of time and to dispose of them in a secure manner when they are no longer needed.

5 **Data access and use policy:** outlines the measures an organization takes to regulate who can access its data assets and how they can be used. It covers issues such as data access controls, data privacy and data sharing.

6 **Data classification policy:** outlines the measures an organization takes to classify its data assets based on their level of sensitivity and importance. It covers issues such as data security, data privacy and data retention.

7 **Data architecture policy:** outlines the measures an organization takes to design and maintain its data architecture. It covers issues such as data modelling, data integration and data warehousing.

8 **Data management policy:** outlines the measures an organization takes to manage its data assets throughout their life cycle. It covers issues such as data creation, data maintenance and data disposal.

These policies should be regularly reviewed and updated to ensure that they continue to meet the needs and requirements of the organization and to reflect any changes in laws, regulations or business objectives. Having well-defined and comprehensive data governance policies in place is critical for ensuring that an organization's data assets are managed in a consistent, efficient and effective manner and that they support the organization's business objectives and regulatory requirements.

The process for the development of data governance policies is listed in Figure 28.2.

Setting up a comprehensive process for data governance policy development and maintenance consists of the steps shown in Table 28.5.

Figure 28.2   Data governance policies – standards

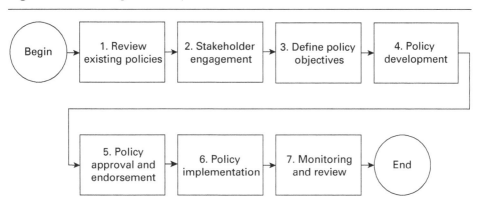

Table 28.5   Steps to set up a data governance policy development and maintenance process

Process	Description
1. Review existing policies	This step involves evaluating the current data governance polices processes and policies to identify areas for improvement.
2. Stakeholder engagement	In this step, it's important to engage with key stakeholders, including business leaders, IT, legal and data privacy teams to understand their perspectives and requirements.

(continued)

Table 28.5   (Continued)

Process	Description
3. Define policy objectives	Based on the findings of the review and stakeholder engagement, the organization should define clear data governance objectives and goals for each individual policy.
4. Policy development	In this step, policies are developed that align with the data governance objectives and goals. The policies should be clear, concise and actionable.
5. Policy approval and endorsement	The policies developed in the previous step should be reviewed, approved and endorsed by key stakeholders and relevant legal teams.
6. Policy implementation	After approval, the policies should be implemented across the organization, and relevant training and communication should be provided to ensure that all staff members understand the policies and how to comply with them.
7. Monitoring and review	The policies should be regularly monitored and reviewed to ensure that they remain relevant and effective, and to make any necessary updates or changes.

The process of establishing the various data governance policies may vary depending on the specific needs and requirements of the organization. However, the steps in Table 28.5 can easily be applied by any organization and showcase a defined (level 3) maturity level in this capability.

Data governance processes

Data governance processes are the set of activities, tasks and procedures that are put in place to manage and govern enterprise data. These processes ensure that data is collected, stored, processed and used in a consistent, secure and compliant manner. The aim of data governance processes is to support the organization in making effective and informed decisions based on the data available to it.

The specific data governance processes that an organization should have are dependent on the data governance policies that an organization has determined (as discussed in the previous paragraph). The data governance processes are subsequently the specific steps and procedures that organizations use to implement their data governance policies. They outline how data is to be collected, processed, stored and used, and provide a detailed description of how data is to be managed and governed throughout its life cycle.

These processes provide a systematic and repeatable way for organizations to ensure that their data governance policies are being effectively implemented, and to monitor and evaluate the effectiveness of their data governance efforts.

However, some common data governance processes include:

- **Data classification:** categorizing data based on its level of sensitivity, value and importance to the organization. This helps to ensure that the appropriate level of security, privacy and protection is applied to the data.

- **Data quality management:** checking the accuracy, completeness, consistency and validity of data, and ensuring that any issues are addressed and resolved.

- **Data privacy and security:** ensuring that the organization complies with relevant data privacy and security regulations and standards, and that appropriate measures are in place to protect sensitive and confidential data.

- **Data retention and archiving:** defining and managing the retention and archiving of data based on the organization's business and legal requirements.

- **Data access and usage:** defining and managing who has access to what data, and how it can be used. This is to ensure that the data is used in a compliant and ethical manner.

- **Data quality improvement:** continuous improvement of the data governance processes, including regular monitoring and review, to ensure that they remain effective and relevant.

For each of these processes, organizations should create process documentation, process flows, training and implementation in technology. Since these are operational steps that will vary greatly between different organizations, we will not provide detailed process steps for each individual process.

By having well-structured data governance processes in place, organizations can ensure that their data is managed effectively, efficiently and in compliance with relevant regulations and standards. This helps organizations to make informed decisions based on high-quality data, and reduces the risk of data breaches, data loss or data-related legal and regulatory issues.

28.4 Data governance process summary

In this section, we reviewed the first capability of the Big Data processes: the data governance process. The data governance process is responsible for ensuring that an organization can establish a process to govern the availability, usability, integrity and security of enterprise data, based on internal data standards and policies.

The data governance process capability should be considered in the larger context of an organization's data governance system (as outlined in Figure 28.1) and is strongly interwoven with the leadership and governance capability, as well as the data management process capability (which will be discussed in the next part).

The data governance capability consists of three main elements: standards, policies and individual processes. Standards provide internationally recognized best practices in data governance that organization can adapt and adopt. Data governance policies are the guidelines that organizations need to establish, and which subsequently need to be enforced by putting in place operational systems. Lastly, individual processes implement specific policy objectives by establishing documented processes, which contain detailed procedures and outline the way in which an organization will process data.

Notes

1   R Abraham, J Schneider and J Vom Brocke. Data governance: A conceptual framework, structured review, and research agenda, *International Journal of Information Management*, 2019 49, 424–38

2   T H Thabit, H S Ishhadat and O T Abdulrahman. Applying Data Governance Based on COBIT2019 Framework to Achieve Sustainable Development Goals, *Journal of Techniques*, 2020 2 (3), 9–18

The Data Management Process

29

29.1 Introduction to the data management process

The **data management process** is a process that involves the collection, storage, organization, processing and use of data. It is an essential aspect of any organization's operations, as it allows them to make informed decisions and gain insights from enterprise data sets.

Data management is a critical capability for several reasons. Firstly, it allows organizations to organize and store their data in a way that is easy to access and use. This makes it simpler to extract insights and information from data, which can lead to better decision-making. Second, a mature data management capability will help ensure data accuracy and integrity, which are essential for organizations to make informed decisions based on reliable information.

Data management also plays a critical role in compliance and regulatory requirements. Organizations must follow various regulations such as GDPR, HIPAA or SOX, which require them to protect and manage their data effectively. Failure to comply with these regulations can lead to severe consequences such as financial penalties and reputational damage.

As we saw in Chapter 28, data management is inherently related to data governance. Without a proper data governance structure, it will become impossible to set up a proper data management process. In addition, most find it difficult to set up structured data management processes for the following reasons:

1 **Lack of insight into data quality:** One of the significant challenges in data management is maintaining data quality. Data quality, as discussed in Chapter 2, is the accuracy, completeness and consistency of data. A lack of insights into the extent to which an organization has quality data makes it complex to set up proper data management processes.

2 **Increased data security and data privacy regulations:** In most countries around the world, data security and data privacy regulations are becoming increasingly strict. Setting up suitable data management processes (that comply to all these requirements) makes data management increasingly more complex.

The goal of setting up and structuring sound data management processes is to overcome these challenges and help define processes that are consistent and sound. As such, data management consists of many operational processes, which we will discuss in further detail in section 29.3.

Data management is a critical capability in any organization's operations. If structured properly, it will support every stage of the **data analysis process** (Chapter 30). Good data management processes help ensure data accuracy, integrity and security, which are crucial for organizations to make informed decisions based on reliable information. While data management has many operational challenges, mature data management processes can help overcome these challenges and achieve effective data management.

29.2 Purpose and maturity levels of the data management process

Purpose

The purpose of the data management process is to ensure that data is managed effectively and efficiently throughout its life cycle. The process involves several activities and subprocesses that need to safeguard the operational part of the Enterprise Big Data Governance System.

Effective data management processes are crucial for organizations to make informed decisions and gain insights from their data. It enables organizations to optimize their operations, improve customer service, and gain a competitive advantage.

The purpose of the data management process is outlined in Table 29.1.

Table 29.1 Purpose of the data management process capability

Capability	Purpose
Data Management Process	Defines the ability of an organization to establish a process to collect, process, validate and store enterprise data in line with corporate quality, security and privacy criteria.

Following the definition in Table 29.1, the data management process serves several purposes:

- **Improving data quality:** helps ensure that data is accurate, complete and consistent. This enables organizations to make informed decisions based on reliable information.

- **Ensuring data security:** helps protect data from unauthorized access, theft or misuse. This includes implementing security measures such as data encryption, access controls and intrusion detection systems.

- **Enhancing data privacy:** helps ensure that data privacy regulations are adhered to. This includes obtaining consent from individuals before collecting their data and providing transparency about its use.

- **Optimizing data storage and processing:** helps organizations optimize their data storage and processing methods. This includes using efficient storage and processing methods such as cloud storage and Big Data processing.

- **Enabling collaboration:** facilitates collaboration between different departments and stakeholders within an organization. This enables better decision-making and improved operations.

The purpose of the data management process is to ensure that data is managed effectively and efficiently throughout all stages of the data analysis life cycle (discussed in the next section). This enables organizations to make informed decisions, protect data from security threats and adhere to data privacy regulations.

Maturity levels

Maturity of the data management process is directly related to the maturity of the other two capabilities in of the Enterprise Big Data Governance System. The data management process is one of the most operational processes of the Enterprise Big Data Framework and executes the direction and policies that have been determined by data governance.

The maturity levels of the data management process describe the different stages of development and effectiveness of an organization's data management practices. These maturity levels are often used to assess an organization's current state of data management and identify areas for improvement. There are typically five maturity levels of the data management process, which are described in Table 29.2.

Similar to the other capabilities in the Enterprise Big Data Framework, the maturity levels of the data management process describe the different stages of development and effectiveness of an organization's data management practices. Since the data management practice includes many operational processes (as outlined in the next section), achieving a high maturity level requires a constant focus on process improvement.

Table 29.2 Maturity levels of the data management process

Maturity Level	Description
Level 1 – Initial	At this stage, the data management processes that an organization uses is inconsistent and reactive. There is no formal data management framework, and data is managed only when necessary. There may be a lack of awareness about the importance of data management, and data quality may be low.
Level 2 – Managed	The data management process is more consistent and formalized. The organization has established basic data management policies and procedures, and data quality is improving. However, there may still be silos of data and inconsistent data management practices across different departments.
Level 3 – Defined	The organization has a formal data management framework that is well-defined and documented. Data quality is high, and data management processes and practices are consistent across the organization. The organization has established data governance policies, and there is a clear understanding of the importance of data management.
Level 4 – Controlled	The organization has established metrics and measures for data management. Data is analysed to identify trends and patterns, and data quality is continuously monitored and improved. The organization has a well-defined data governance framework and a culture of continuous improvement.
Level 5 – Optimized	The organization has fully integrated data management into its operations. Data management processes and practices are optimized and automated, and there is a culture of data-driven decision-making. The organization continuously monitors and improves its data management practices, and data quality is consistently high.

Organizations that have a high maturity in data management typically have a well-established and fully integrated data management process that is used throughout the organization. They prioritize data quality, data governance and data security, and have invested in the necessary technology, processes and people to support their data management efforts. Some examples of organizations with a high maturity in data management include[1]:

- **Amazon:** has a well-established data management process that is used to support its e-commerce platform and cloud computing services. The company uses advanced analytics and machine learning algorithms to gain insights from its data and improve its operations.

- **Netflix:** uses a data-driven approach to develop and market its streaming service. The company collects and analyses data on user preferences and behaviour to personalize its recommendations and improve the user experience.

- **Procter & Gamble:** has a well-established data management process that is used to support its global operations. The company collects and analyses data on consumer behaviour to develop new products and marketing campaigns.

- **Coca-Cola:** uses a data-driven approach to develop and market its beverages. The company collects and analyses data on consumer preferences and behaviour to personalize its marketing and improve the user experience.

- **Google:** Google has a well-established data management process that is used to support its search engine, advertising platform and cloud computing services. The company uses advanced analytics and machine learning algorithms to gain insights from its data and improve its operations.

Organizations that have a high maturity in data management typically prioritize data quality, data governance and data security. They have invested in the necessary technology, processes and people to support their data management efforts and use a data-driven approach to improve their operations.

29.3 Structuring the data management process

Data management does not consist of one single process. Rather, with the data management process capability, we mean the **collection of data management processes** that together ensure that an organization has control over its enterprise data, and can safeguard its quality.

There are many different aspects that contribute to a mature data management process. To ensure consistency throughout this publication, we will consider (in this capability) the **operational data management processes** of the Enterprise Big Data Framework Governance System, as outlined in Figure 29.1. Each of these components can be implemented as a separate 'mini-process' with its own targets. KPIs and improvement objectives.

To structure the data management capability, it is imperative that organizations have a significant number (if not all) of these mini-processes in place.

Data accessibility

Data accessibility is the ability of authorized personnel within an organization to access and use data easily and efficiently.[2] Data accessibility is crucial for organizations to make informed decisions, gain insights, and improve their operations.

Figure 29.1 Components of the data management process

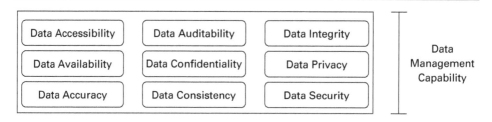

Figure 29.2 Activities to establish data accessibility

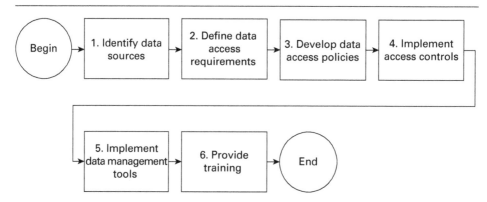

The process steps and activities for structuring data accessibility are outlined in Table 29.3.

Since enterprise data is a critical asset for any organization (as covered in Part 2), having access to accurate and timely data is essential for making informed decisions, improving operations and gaining a competitive advantage. Adequate data access processes ensure that authorized personnel can access and use data easily and efficiently, while maintaining data security and privacy.

To set up a proper process for data accessibility, an organization should identify data sources, define data access requirements, develop data access policies, implement access controls and data management tools, and provide training to authorized personnel.

Data auditability

Data auditability refers to the ability to track and monitor changes made to data over time. It is important for organizations to have a proper process in place to achieve data auditability to ensure data accuracy, maintain data integrity and comply

Table 29.3 Activity descriptions in data accessibility

Process	Description
1. Identify data sources	The first step in setting up a data accessibility process is to identify the data sources within the organization. This includes data that is generated internally as well as data that is obtained from external sources.
2. Define data access requirements	Once the data sources have been identified, the organization needs to define the access requirements for each type of data. This includes defining who needs access to the data, what level of access they require and the purpose for which the data will be used.
3. Develop data access policies	The organization should develop data access policies that outline the rules and guidelines for accessing data. This includes policies on data security, data sharing and data privacy.
4. Implement access controls	Access controls are measures used to restrict access to data to authorized personnel. The organization should implement access controls, such as user authentication, to ensure that only authorized personnel can access the data.
5. Implement data management tools	The organization should implement data management tools, such as data visualization and analytics tools, to make it easier for authorized personnel to access and use the data.
6. Provide training	The organization should provide training to authorized personnel on how to access and use the data effectively and efficiently. This includes training on data access policies, data governance and the use of data management tools.

with regulatory requirements. Maybe most importantly, data auditability safeguards compliance. Many industries and regulatory bodies require organizations to maintain a record of changes made to data. This includes regulations such as the Sarbanes-Oxley Act (SOX) and the General Data Protection Regulation (GDPR) which require organizations to track changes made to sensitive data to ensure that it is being used and protected appropriately.

Additionally, setting up data auditability improves every employee's accountability. By tracking changes made to data, organizations can hold individuals or departments accountable for any errors or inconsistencies in the data. This helps to improve accountability and transparency within the organization.

Lastly, a proper data auditability process reduces risk for the organization. Data auditability is therefore also a key component of risk management. Tracking changes made to data helps organizations identify and manage risks associated with the data. This includes identifying potential security breaches, unauthorized access to data or other data-related risks.

To achieve data auditability, enterprise organizations need to implement proper data management processes, as outlined in Figure 29.3.

This process has strong links with overarching data governance policies and procedures for data management, implementing proper data governance frameworks and ensuring that all employees are properly trained in data management best practices.

Enterprise organizations can use various tools to achieve data auditability, such as data management software, access control systems and data analytics tools. By implementing these tools and processes, organizations can track and monitor changes made to data over time, ensuring data accuracy, regulatory compliance and improved decision-making.

Data integrity

Data integrity is a container term that refers to the accuracy, consistency and reliability of data throughout its life cycle (discussed in more detail in Chapter 31). Data is considered to have integrity when it is complete, accurate and consistent, and when it can be relied upon to make important decisions or support critical business processes.

Data integrity is important for any enterprise organization for several reasons. The most important aspect is that data integrity is important for building and maintaining customer trust. If customers cannot trust the data an organization provides, they may lose faith in the organization and choose to do business elsewhere.

To achieve data integrity, organizations must implement proper data management processes specifically for data integrity as outlined in Figure 29.4.

The individual steps to establish data integrity are shown in Table 29.5.

By implementing these best practices, organizations can safeguard data integrity and ensure that data remains accurate, reliable and secure throughout its life cycle.

Figure 29.3 Activities to establish data auditability

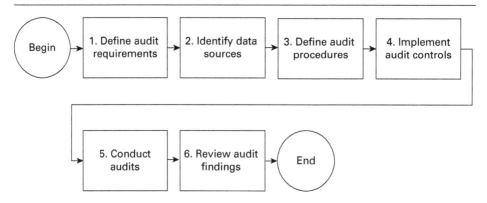

Table 29.4   Activity descriptions in data auditability

Process	Description
1. Define audit requirements	The first step is to define the audit requirements, including the types of data that need to be audited, the frequency of audits and the scope of the audit.
2. Identify data sources	The organization should identify the data sources that need to be audited, such as databases, spreadsheets and other data repositories.
3. Define audit procedures	The organization should define audit procedures, including the tools and techniques used to collect and analyse data. This may include using data analysis software or manual procedures to check data for accuracy and integrity.
4. Implement audit controls	Audit controls are measures used to ensure that changes to data are tracked and recorded. This includes implementing version control, access controls and change management processes.
5. Conduct audits	The organization should conduct regular audits to ensure that data is accurate, complete and consistent. This may involve checking data for errors, inconsistencies or discrepancies, and making necessary corrections.
6. Review audit findings	Finally, the organization should review the audit findings to identify any trends, patterns or issues that need to be addressed. This may involve making changes to data management policies, procedures or controls to improve data quality and integrity.

Figure 29.4   Activities to establish data integrity

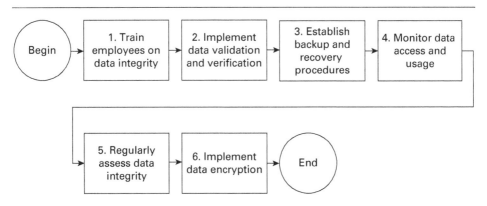

Data availability

Data availability is the ability of an organization to access and use its data when it is needed. This means that the organization must have systems and processes in place to ensure that data is always available, and that any disruptions or failures are minimized.

Table 29.5 Activity descriptions in data integrity

Process	Description
1. Train employees in data integrity	Employees should be properly trained on data management best practices, including data quality, data access and data security. This can include training on data entry and validation procedures, access control and encryption technologies.
2. Implement data validation and verification	Organizations should implement procedures to validate and verify data as it is entered into systems. This can include validation checks for data completeness, consistency and accuracy.
3. Establish backup and recovery procedures	Organizations should establish processes for backing up data and recovering data in the event of a data loss or system failure. This can include regular data backups, off-site data storage and disaster recovery planning.
4. Monitor data access and usage	Organizations should implement access controls to limit access to data to authorized personnel only. This can include user authentication, role-based access controls and encryption technologies.
5. Regularly assess data integrity	Organizations should regularly assess data quality and integrity to ensure that data remains accurate, complete and consistent. This can include data quality checks, data profiling and data auditing.
6. Implement data encryption	Organizations should implement data encryption and other security technologies to protect data from unauthorized access or data breaches. This can include encryption technologies, firewalls, intrusion detection systems and other security technologies.

For example, online retailers rely on data availability to ensure that their websites are up and running 24/7. If the website goes down, customers will not be able to access the site, make purchases or contact customer support. To ensure data availability, online retailers typically use redundant hardware, cloud-based data storage services and backup power supplies to minimize the risk of downtime.

To illustrate with another example, think about financial institutions. Financial institutions rely on data availability to ensure that their banking systems are up and always running. If the system goes down, customers may not be able to access their accounts, make transactions or contact customer support. To ensure data availability, financial institutions typically implement redundant hardware, backup systems and disaster recovery plans.

These examples showcase that data availability is critical to ensuring that critical business functions can continue uninterrupted. By implementing systems and processes that ensure data availability, organizations can minimize the risk of downtime, and help to ensure that their systems and data are available when they are needed.

The critical activities that are necessary to achieve data availability are outlined in Figure 29.5.

To ensure data availability, organizations must establish a process that includes the steps in Table 29.6.

By implementing these best practices outlined in these process steps, organizations can establish a process for data availability that ensures that data is available when it is needed, even in the event of a system failure or data loss. This helps to ensure that critical business functions can continue uninterrupted and helps to minimize the impact of system failures or disasters on the organization.

Figure 29.5 Activities to establish data availability

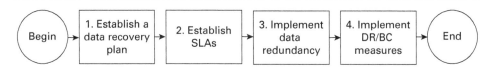

Table 29.6 Activity descriptions in data availability

Process	Description
1. Establish a data recovery plan	Organizations should establish a data recovery plan that outlines the steps that need to be taken to recover data in the event of a system failure or data loss. This can include procedures for restoring data from backups, verifying data integrity and testing the recovery process.
2. Establish SLAs	Organizations should establish service level agreements (SLAs) that define the expected level of data availability and the expected response times for data access and recovery. These SLAs should be regularly reviewed and updated to ensure that they are aligned with business needs.
3. Implement data redundancy	Organizations should implement data redundancy to ensure that data is available even in the event of a system failure. This can include implementing redundant hardware or using cloud-based data storage services that provide redundancy and failover capabilities.
4. Implement DR/ BC measures	Organizations should implement disaster recovery (DR) and business continuity planning (BCP) to ensure that critical business functions can continue in the event of a system failure or disaster. This can include establishing off-site work locations, implementing redundant communication channels and establishing backup power supplies.

Data confidentiality

Data confidentiality is the practice of ensuring that sensitive data is kept private and only accessed by authorized individuals or systems. This means that data is protected from unauthorized access, disclosure or modification. Confidential data can include personally identifiable information (PII), financial data, intellectual property, trade secrets and other sensitive information that could harm an individual or organization if accessed by unauthorized individuals.

Data confidentiality is critical for protecting sensitive data from unauthorized access and preventing potential harm to individuals or organizations. By implementing appropriate security controls and processes, organizations can minimize the risk of data breaches and protect their data throughout its lifecycle.

The need for data confidentiality can be seen in the healthcare industry. Healthcare organizations are responsible for protecting sensitive patient information, such as medical histories, test results and personal identifying information, from unauthorized access or disclosure. If this information is accessed by unauthorized individuals, it can result in significant harm to patients, including identity theft, insurance fraud and discrimination.

For instance, if a healthcare organization does not implement adequate security measures, such as access controls, encryption and monitoring, a cybercriminal could gain access to patient data and use it to commit fraud. They could use stolen patient information to open fraudulent credit accounts, apply for loans or benefits or even access medical treatments under a patient's identity. To prevent these risks, healthcare organizations must prioritize data confidentiality and implement appropriate security controls and processes to protect sensitive patient information.

To safeguard data confidentiality, organizations can structure a process that include the steps shown in Figure 29.6.

The detailed descriptions of these activities are outlined in Table 29.7.

By implementing these steps, organizations can establish a process that safeguards data confidentiality and protects sensitive data from unauthorized access or disclosure.

Data privacy

Data privacy is the protection of an individual's personal information, which may include their name, address, date of birth, Social Security number, financial information, medical history and other sensitive information. Data privacy is the right of an individual to keep their personal information private and to control how it is collected, used and shared.

Figure 29.6   Activities to establish data confidentiality

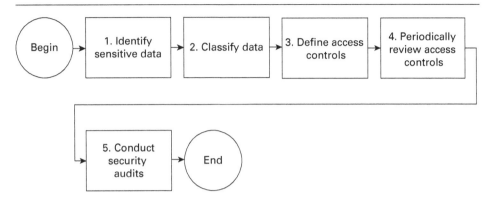

Table 29.7   Activity descriptions in data confidentiality

Process	Description
1. Identify sensitive data	Identify the types of data that require protection, such as personally identifiable information (PII), financial data, intellectual property and trade secrets. This includes data stored on servers, in databases and in physical files.
2. Classify data	Classify sensitive data according to its level of confidentiality, assigning each type of data a classification level (e.g. confidential, highly confidential, public). This will help to ensure that data is handled appropriately based on its sensitivity.
3. Define access controls	Define access controls to limit access to confidential data. This includes the use of user authentication, such as usernames and passwords, two-factor authentication or biometric authentication, as well as encryption, firewalls and intrusion detection systems. Please note that this activity needs to be aligned with the data accessibility process activities.
4. Periodically review access controls	Regularly review and update access controls and permissions to ensure that only authorized users have access to confidential data. This includes revoking access for employees who leave the organization or who no longer require access to confidential data.
5. Conduct security audits	Conduct regular security audits to identify potential security risks and vulnerabilities. This includes conducting penetration testing, vulnerability assessments and regular security scans to identify potential security threats.

Data privacy is essential in today's digital age, where individuals are constantly generating and sharing personal information online, through social media, online transactions and other activities. The increasing amount of personal data available online, combined with the growing sophistication of cybercriminals, makes it critical for individuals and organizations to protect personal data from unauthorized access, theft and misuse.

For enterprise organizations, data privacy is important because it ensures that the organization is compliant with data protection laws and regulations. Failure to protect personal data can result in legal and financial consequences, damage to reputation and loss of customer trust. For example, data privacy is protected by laws and regulations, such as the European Union's General Data Protection Regulation (GDPR) and the California Consumer Privacy Act (CCPA), which give individuals control over their personal data and require organizations to implement measures to protect personal data. In addition, data breaches can result in the loss of valuable intellectual property, trade secrets and other sensitive information that can have a significant impact on an organization's competitiveness.

Implementing effective data privacy measures can help organizations to build trust with their customers and stakeholders, which can lead to increased customer loyalty and long-term business success. Organizations can structure data privacy with a process that include the steps in Figure 29.7.

Since data privacy is such a critical part of the data management process, the activities to safeguard data privacy require the utmost priority in any organization.

By implementing data privacy processes and procedures, organizations can protect personal data, ensure compliance with data protection regulations and build trust with customers and stakeholders. It is important to regularly review and update these processes and procedures to ensure they remain effective in protecting personal data in the ever-changing landscape of data privacy.

Data accuracy

Data accuracy is a measure of how closely a particular piece of data reflects reality. It refers to the degree to which the data is free from errors, inconsistencies and mistakes. Accurate data is essential for making informed decisions, forecasting trends and developing strategies. Data accuracy is particularly important in industries such as healthcare, finance and research where inaccurate data can have serious consequences.

There are several factors that can impact the accuracy of data. These include:

- **Data entry errors:** When data is entered manually, there is a risk of errors such as typos or transpositions.
- **System errors:** Errors can occur in the system that stores or processes data, such as corrupt files or software glitches.

Figure 29.7   Activities to establish data privacy

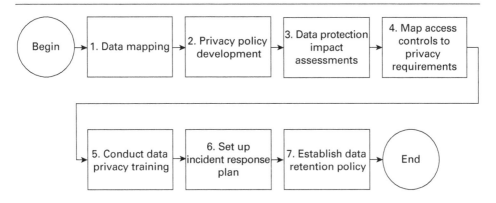

Table 29.8   Activity descriptions in data privacy

Process	Description
1. Data mapping	Conduct a thorough inventory of all personal data that the organization collects, processes and stores. This can help the organization to identify potential risks and vulnerabilities in the data handling process.
2. Privacy policy development	Develop and communicate a clear and comprehensive privacy policy that explains how personal data is collected, processed and stored, and how individuals can exercise their data rights.
3. Data protection impact assessments	Conduct regular assessments to identify and address potential risks to personal data, such as data breaches or unauthorized access.
4. Map access controls to privacy requirements	Implement access controls and other security measures to ensure that only authorized individuals have access to personal data. Data privacy requirements, rules and regulations must be mapped with the data accessibility activities discussed at the beginning of this section.
5. Conduct data privacy training	Provide regular training and awareness programmes to ensure that all employees understand the importance of data privacy and how to handle personal data appropriately.
6. Set up incident response plan	Develop and implement an incident response plan that outlines the steps to take in the event of a data breach or other privacy incident.
7. Establish data retention policy	Implement policies and procedures to ensure that personal data is retained for only as long as necessary and deleted in a secure and appropriate manner.

- **Incomplete data:** When data is missing key information, it can skew the accuracy of the analysis.
- **Data bias:** Biases can be introduced when collecting data, for example, if the sample size is too small or if the population is not representative.

To safeguard data accuracy, an organization can establish a process that includes the steps as shown in Figure 29.8.

This process can be subdivided into the steps outlined in Table 29.9.

By establishing a process that includes these steps, an organization can ensure that its critical data elements are accurate and reliable. This, in turn, can help the organization make better decisions, improve operational efficiency and reduce the risk of errors and inaccuracies in its business processes.

Data consistency

Data consistency is the degree to which data is uniform and in agreement across different systems, databases and applications. In other words, data consistency ensures that the same data elements have the same values in different parts of the organization.

To illustrate the importance of data consistency, suppose a large retail company operates multiple stores across different locations, and each store maintains its own database to track inventory levels. In this scenario, it is critical that the inventory data is consistent across all the stores to avoid stockouts or overstocking.

If the data is inconsistent, a store may assume that it has a certain quantity of a particular product but the stock level is much lower. This can lead to stockouts and lost sales, or overstocking, which ties up capital and leads to wasted resources.

To avoid these issues, the company can implement a data governance framework that ensures that the inventory data is consistent across all the stores. This could involve establishing data definitions and standards, implementing data integration processes and ensuring that the data is validated and cleansed regularly.

By ensuring data consistency, the company can avoid stockouts and overstocking, improve customer satisfaction and optimize its operations, leading to better business outcomes.

To safeguard data consistency, organizations can set up the process outlined in Figure 29.9.

This process can be subdivided into the steps outlined in Table 29.10.

By implementing these steps, organizations can safeguard data consistency, which is essential for making informed business decisions, optimizing operations and improving customer satisfaction.

Figure 29.8 Activities to establish data accuracy

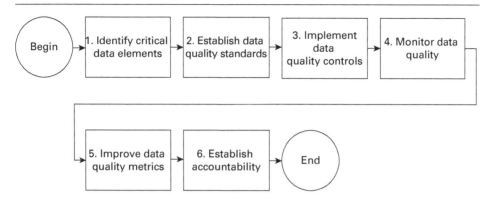

Figure 29.9 Activities to establish data consistency

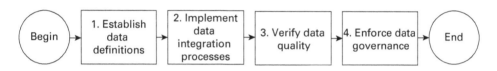

Table 29.9 Activity descriptions in data accuracy

Process	Description
1. Identify critical data elements	Identify the data elements that are critical to the organization's operations and decision-making processes.
2. Establish data quality standards	Develop data quality standards that specify the required level of accuracy for each critical data element. This can include rules for data entry, formatting and validation.
3. Implement data quality controls	Implement data quality controls to ensure that data is accurate and complete. This can include validation checks during data entry, automated data cleansing and manual data review.
4. Monitor data quality	Regularly monitor the quality of critical data elements to ensure they meet the established data quality standards. This can involve regular data profiling and analysis.
5. Improve data quality metrics	When data quality issues are identified, establish a process to address and resolve them. This may involve correcting data errors, revalidating data or implementing process improvements.
6. Establish accountability	Assign accountability for data accuracy to specific individuals or teams within the organization. This can include data stewards or data quality managers who are responsible for ensuring the accuracy of critical data elements.

Table 29.10   Activity descriptions in data consistency

Process	Description
1. Establish data definitions	It's important to define clear and consistent data definitions for key business concepts such as customer, product and sales, so that everyone in the organization understands the meaning of the data. This can include creating a data dictionary or metadata repository to store the definitions.
2. Implement data integration process	To ensure that data is consistent across different systems and databases, it's important to establish data integration processes that allow data to be shared and synchronized. This can include using ETL (Extract, Transform, Load) tools to move data from one system to another, or implementing APIs to allow systems to communicate with each other.
3. Verify data quality	To maintain data consistency, it's important to ensure that the data is accurate, complete and up to date. This can be achieved through data validation and cleansing processes that identify and correct errors and inconsistencies in the data.
4. Enforce data governance	To ensure that the data consistency is maintained over time, it's important to establish a data governance system that includes policies, procedures and controls for managing the data. This can include assigning data ownership and stewardship roles, establishing data quality metrics and monitoring data usage and access. The EBDFA data governance system was introduced in Part 8.

Data security

Data security is the protection of digital information from unauthorized access, theft, damage or corruption. It encompasses a range of practices and technologies designed to ensure the **confidentiality, integrity** and **availability** of data.

Data security is important for organizations for several reasons:

1 **Protecting sensitive information:** Many organizations collect and store sensitive information, such as customer data, financial records and intellectual property. Failure to protect this information can lead to data breaches, which can result in significant financial and reputational damage.

2 **Compliance with regulations:** Many industries are subject to regulations governing the protection of sensitive data. Failure to comply with these regulations can result in fines and legal action.

3 **Maintaining business continuity:** In the event of a data breach or cyberattack, organizations can suffer significant disruption to their operations. By implementing robust data security measures, organizations can minimize the risk of data loss or corruption and maintain business continuity.

4 **Building customer trust:** Data security is a key factor in building and maintaining customer trust. By demonstrating a commitment to protecting sensitive information, organizations can build a positive reputation and strengthen their relationships with customers.

Data security is a critical aspect of modern business operations, and organizations need to implement appropriate measures to protect their data from unauthorized access, theft and corruption.

It would easily be possible to complete another book on data security alone, and this topic requires special attention within the data management capability. Whereas all the other components of data management, as outlined throughout this section, can be accomplished by setting up adequate measures and processes, data security requires a deep understanding of cybersecurity technologies, attack patterns and vulnerabilities.

Safeguarding data security is a complex process that requires a combination of technical controls, policies and employee training. Figure 29.10 shows some steps an organization can take to establish a good process for safeguarding data security. The process therefore gives an overview of the most common activities in data security, although these steps alone will not provide a comprehensive data security process.

The detailed descriptions of these activities are outlined in Table 29.11.

A high-maturity and reliable process for safeguarding data security involves a combination of technical controls, policies, employee training, audits and incident response planning. By implementing these measures, organizations can protect sensitive data from cyber threats and maintain the trust of customers and stakeholders.

29.4 Data management process summary

As we have seen in this chapter, data management requires extensive effort, planning and a great number of activities. As one of the most operational capabilities in the Enterprise Big Data Framework, it will help safeguard the day-to-day trustworthiness, security and reliability of enterprise data.

Data management typically requires extensive effort and processes, especially in large organizations with complex data environments. Establishing a high-maturity data management process capability involves a wide range of tasks, activities, policies and procures, which at least include activities for the nine activities that we discussed throughout this chapter: data accessibility, data auditability, data integrity, data availability, data confidentiality, data privacy, data accuracy, data consistency and data security.

Figure 29.10   Activities to establish data security

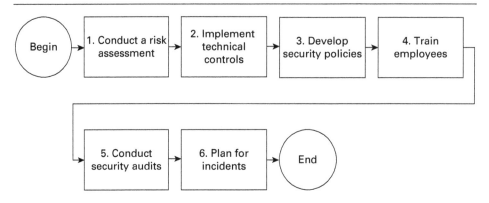

Table 29.11   Activity descriptions in data security

Process	Description
1. Conduct a risk assessment	A risk assessment helps an organization identify potential vulnerabilities and threats to its data security. This assessment can be used to prioritize security measures and develop a comprehensive security strategy.
2. Implement technical controls	Technical controls, such as firewalls, antivirus software and encryption, are essential for protecting data from unauthorized access and theft. Implementing a robust security infrastructure can help ensure that data is protected from cyberattacks and other security threats.
3. Develop security policies	Security policies outline the rules and procedures that employees must follow to ensure data security. These policies should cover areas such as data access, password management and the use of mobile devices. Policies should be reviewed regularly and updated as needed to reflect changes in technology and threats.
4. Train employees	Employees are often the weakest link in data security. Regular training on data security policies and procedures can help ensure that employees understand their role in protecting sensitive data.
5. Conduct security audits	Regular audits of security controls and policies can help identify gaps in the security infrastructure and ensure that policies are being followed. Audits should be conducted by an independent third party to ensure impartiality and thoroughness.
6. Plan for incidents	Even with robust security measures in place, data breaches can still occur. Organizations should have an incident response plan in place to minimize the impact of a breach and restore normal operations as quickly as possible.

To establish a robust data management process capability, organizations need to develop a data management programme that aligns with the goals and objectives that have been defined in data governance. These goals and objectives should define the scope of the data management programme, including the data types, sources and systems that are covered. It should also identify the data management processes and tools required to support the programme.

Notes

1 S Sakr, A Liu, D M Batista and M Alomari. A survey of large scale data management approaches in cloud environments, *IEEE Communications Surveys & Tutorials*, 2011 13 (3), 311–36

2 L Cheng, F Liu and D Yao. Enterprise data breach: causes, challenges, prevention, and future directions, *Wiley Interdisciplinary Reviews: Data Mining and Knowledge Discovery*, 2017 7 (5), e1211

The Data Analysis 30
Process

30.1 Introduction to the data analysis process

To find an answer to any Big Data or data science question, data scientists need to follow a methodical process that will lead towards a specific result. This process is known as the data analysis process, and this process is a cornerstone of a processional Big Data organization.

The domain of data analysis is more popular now than it has been at any time before. Yet most of its essential characteristics have been around for decades, captured in what is known as the academic field of statistics. Already more than 50 years ago, the famous American mathematician John Tukey predicted that something like today's data science movement would be coming.[1] In 'The Future of Data Analysis', John Tukey shocked his readers (academic statisticians) with the following introductory paragraphs:

> For a long time I have thought I was a statistician, interested in inferences from the particular to the general. But as I have watched mathematical statistics evolve, I have had cause to wonder and to doubt.... All in all, I have come to feel that my central interest is in data analysis, which I take to include, among other things: procedures for analysing data, techniques for interpreting the results of such procedures, ways of planning the gathering of data to make its analysis easier, more precise or more accurate, and all the machinery and results of (mathematical) statistics which apply to analysing data.[2]

This paper was published in 1962 in *The Annals of Mathematical Statistics*, the leading journal of statistical research at the time. It is an important article because, for the first time, it introduces the term 'data analysis' and it positions data analysis as a separate work field, a summary for the work that applied statisticians do. Secondly, the article also makes it clear how data analysis differentiates from statistics. Data analysis includes procedures, techniques, tools and planning activities that extract value from the data. It focuses not just on the understanding and development of mathematical formulas, but on the structured process of deducting valuable information from data sets. These words were as true in 1962 as they are today. Although the volume and variety of 'big' data sets have increased tremendously over the years, data analysis is still very much focused on 'the process' of obtaining valuable results. Mastering this process is therefore a critical capability.

The analysis of large data sets requires a structured and process-oriented approach. A **data analysis process** contains the sequential steps that an organization takes in order to process Big Data, and obtain actionable insights. Ideally, the same process is used for every Big Data project to ensure consistency between projects and improve performance and efficiency across the enterprise. As with any process, the data analysis process is sequential and has a clearly identified start (the trigger) and end result (the outcome). By managing the stages in the data analysis process, enterprises can better control the outcomes and results of their Big Data projects.

Although the data analysis process seems simple and straightforward, the adequately design of this process and capability is quite complex. The data ingestion, data preparation and data analysis steps require constant updates, trial-and-error experiments and sometimes even complete revision. In section 30.4, we will expand upon this data analysis process in further details.

30.2 Purpose and maturity levels of the data analysis process

Purpose

The data analysis process is the structured approach that organizations follow to interpret, clean, transform and model data with the objective of discovering useful information, making conclusions and supporting decision-making. It is an essential step in every business domain that relies on data to extract insights, detect patterns and solve problems.

The primary purpose of the data analysis process is to extract meaningful and actionable insights from data. By analysing data in a structured manner, organizations can identify trends, patterns and relationships that are not immediately apparent and make informed decisions based on them. The data analysis process can help organizations identify opportunities for growth, assess risks and optimize their operations.

The purpose of the data analysis process is outlined in Table 30.1.

The data analysis process can help organizations communicate insights and results to stakeholders effectively. By presenting data in a clear and understandable way, organizations can ensure that decision-makers have the information they need to make informed decisions. By structuring the data analysis process effectively, Big Data teams can help transform complex data into actionable insights that can be communicated effectively to non-experts. For instance, data visualization techniques

Table 30.1   Purpose of the data analysis process capability

Capability	Purpose
Data analysis process	Defines the ability of an organization to set up a structural process for the day-to-day execution of data analysis activities in the enterprise.

Table 30.2   Maturity levels of the data analysis process capability

Maturity Level	Description
Level 1 – Initial	The organization lacks a structured approach to data analysis. Data analysis is undertaken based on best effort and performed by individuals or small groups within the organization. There are no established processes, tools or methods for data analysis.
Level 2 – Managed	The organization has begun to recognize the importance of data analysis but has not yet implemented a cohesive strategy. Different departments or business units within the organization may have their own data analysis processes, but there is no centralized approach.
Level 3 – Defined	The organization has developed a centralized approach to data analysis. There is a defined process for data collection, analysis and reporting that is integrated across departments and business units. The organization has invested in tools and technology to support data analysis and has established data quality standards.
Level 4 – Controlled	The organization has developed advanced capabilities for data analysis. They have established a culture of data-driven decision-making and use sophisticated tools and techniques to support data analysis, such as machine learning and predictive modelling.
Level 5 – Optimized	The organization has achieved full optimization of the data analysis process. They have a comprehensive understanding of their data and have implemented best practices for data governance, security and privacy. They use data analysis to drive innovation and continuous improvement across all areas of the organization.

(the last stage of the process) such as charts and graphs can help present complex data in a simple and intuitive way.

Maturity levels

The maturity levels of the data analysis process determine the stages of development an organization goes through in their ability to effectively analyse data. Establishing a mature practice typically requires a process that is well established, well communicated and embedded in the day-to-day work of the Big Data teams. The five maturity levels of data analysis that organizations can achieve are outlined in Table 30.2.

Establishing high maturity in this capability will help organizations work more effectively, and bring structure to the way they operate. Organizations frequently use the five levels of the data analysis process as a benchmark for evaluating their current data analysis practices and developing a roadmap for improving their capabilities.

30.3 Structuring the data analysis process

Structuring a data analysis process is critical to ensure that the analysis is thorough, accurate and actionable. As we saw in section 30.1, there are five generic steps that structure a data analysis process. In this section, we will build upon these steps and discuss the core activities that should be part of every data analysis.

The data analysis process can be seen as a project, where every new data analysis request can be regarded as the trigger to kick-start the process. Over time, as organizations become mature in the execution of this process, the data analysis process becomes the 'way of work' and starts to establish an operating model for the Big Data and data science teams.

As can be seen in Figure 30.1, the data analysis process is highly operational. Instead of outlining an organizational procedure, these steps represent the sequential tasks that every data analyst or scientist would be performing daily. The value and maturity in this process can therefore easily be observed by watching the activities that Big Data and data science teams perform.

Figure 30.1 Activity steps in the data analysis process

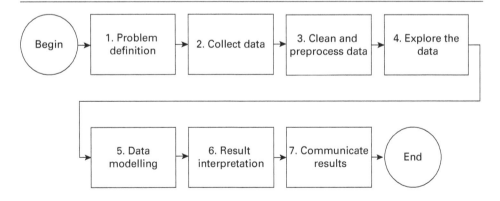

Problem definition

The first step of the data analysis process involves defining the problem that needs to be solved through data analysis. It is a crucial step in the data analysis process as it sets the foundation for the rest of the analysis. To identify the problem that needs to be solved requires a sound understanding of the business and organizational context in which the problem occurs, the objectives of the analysis and the questions that need to be answered through the analysis. To formulate a correct problem definition, it is important to identify the stakeholders who will be affected by the problem and the analysis, as well as their interests and concerns.

Once the problem is identified, the next step is to define the scope of the analysis. This involves defining the data sources that will be used, the time that will be analysed and the variables that will be included in the analysis. It is important to define the scope clearly to ensure that the analysis is focused and relevant to the problem being solved.

Once the problem is defined, and the scope is established, the next step is to develop a data collection plan. This involves identifying the data sources that will be used, the data collection methods that will be employed and the data collection tools that will be utilized.

Lastly, you should also already think about the result during the problem definition stage. Performance metrics are the criteria that will be used to measure the success of the analysis. These metrics should be aligned with the objectives of the analysis and should be specific, measurable, achievable, relevant and time-bound (SMART). Setting performance metrics during the first step already helps to evaluate the effectiveness of the analysis at the end.

Collect the data

The second step in the data analysis process involves collecting the data that will be used for analysis. This step is crucial as the accuracy and completeness of the data will have a significant impact on the results of the analysis. In this second step, the main question we want to ask ourselves is, Where does the data come from?

To answer this question, we need to identify data sources. Data can be collected from a variety of sources such as databases, spreadsheets, text files or APIs. Before data is ingested, you need to ensure that the data sources are reliable, relevant and appropriate for the analysis. Analysis that is done on faulty or incorrect data sources will result in wrong predictions. This is known as the garbage in, garbage out (GIGO) principle.

Clean and preprocess the data

After we have collected and ingested the data, the next steps in the data analysis process is to clean and preprocess the data. This step will ensure that the data is accurate, complete and consistent before it can be analysed. We covered data cleaning and data wrangling operations in detail in Chapter 22.

Explore the data

Next, we want to get a better understanding of our data set. The inspection of data is known as data exploration or data inspection. For this stage, organizations typically have defined a number of best practices to quickly get insights into the data sets of interest.

A good place to start would be the identification of variables, and determining which variables are relevant to the problem being solved. This involves identifying the dependent variable, which is the variable being predicted, and the independent variables, which are the variables that are thought to influence the dependent variable.

Additionally, one of the main practices into exploring the data is to determine the summary statistics of the data sets. The summary statistics, like the mean, median and standard, will give you a quick insight in the way your data set is organized. These statistics provide insights into the central tendency, spread and distribution of the data. To display summary statistics, it might also by useful to create some initial visualizations, which might provide you with an initial idea about correlations and data distributions.

Data modelling

The data modelling stage of the data analysis process typically adds the most value. In this stage, critical decisions need to be made about the model or algorithm that will process the data. The model can be very simple, like providing an summary, or can be very complex, like establishing a machine learning or artificial intelligence model.

In most cases, there are various modelling techniques that can be used depending on the problem being solved and the type of data available. Some of the common modelling techniques include regression analysis, machine learning algorithms, clustering and time series analysis. (which were discussed in Part 5). The appropriate modelling techniques need to be selected based on the problem being solved and the available data.

Once the appropriate modelling technique has been selected, the models need to be built. This involves selecting the variables to be included in the model, defining the model specifications and running the model. Depending on the complexity of the problem, multiple models may need to be built to test different hypotheses or to evaluate the performance of different models.

The final step in data modelling is to determine whether the model is valid and accurate. This involves evaluating the model's performance on a test dataset that was not used during model development. Various performance metrics can be used to evaluate the models, such as accuracy, precision, recall and F1 score.

Result interpretation

Once the data has been collected, cleaned, explored and modelled, it's time to make sense of the findings and draw conclusions. This step involves summarizing the findings and identifying the implications for the problem being solved.

Based on the findings and implications, conclusions can be drawn about the problem being solved. This involves making recommendations and decisions based on the insights and trends identified in the data. The conclusions should be based on sound reasoning and should be supported by the data.

Communicate the results

The final step in the data analysis process is the communication of the results. The results of any data analysis exercise should be communicated to stakeholders in a clear and concise manner. Effective communication of the results is crucial to ensure that decision-makers can understand the findings and make informed decisions.

In the communication of the results, it is best practice to use visualization, graphs and data stories. Data visualization techniques such as charts, graphs and tables can help present complex data in a clear and concise manner. These techniques can help stakeholders understand the data and identify the key insights quickly.

Lastly, it is important to provide context when communicating the results. This involves explaining the methodology used, the data sources and the limitations of the analysis. The reproducible research capability (discussed in Chapter 25) can provide guidelines to clearly establish the context. Providing context helps stakeholders understand the data's credibility and limitations and can help them make informed decisions.

30.4 Data analysis process summary

The data analysis process is one of the most operational capabilities of the Enterprise Big Data Framework. This capability outlines the steps that every Big

Data or data science project should take to move from the initial question, towards a reliable result.

In this section, we have seen the steps that are part of the data analysis process. Data analysis starts with the asking the right questions, and formulating an adequate problem definition. After the problem has been defined, we need to collect, clean and explore the data that we have, to determine whether we can solve the business objective with the available data sets.

Then the fundamental process of model building begins. Model building can be very simple, like summarizing or aggregating data, or very complex, like building machine learning or artificial intelligence algorithms. Model building is typically the task of data analysts and data scientists.

With the right model, and the right data sets, we can generate the results that we are looking for. These results should provide an answer to the problem definition. As a final step, we therefore need to interpret the result, and communicate that to the relevant stakeholders. Techniques from storytelling with data, as well as visualization techniques, can significantly help to communicate the result in an efficient and engaging way.

Notes

1 J W Tukey. The future of data analysis. *The Annals of Mathematical Statistics*, 1962 33 (1), 1–67
2 J W Tukey (1977) *Exploratory Data Analysis*, vol. 2, 131–60

The Data Life Cycle Management Process

31.1 Introduction to the data life cycle management process

Data life cycle management is the process of managing data from its initial creation or acquisition, through its usage, storage and eventual disposal. It involves a set of policies, procedures and practices for managing the data throughout its entire life cycle, to ensure its availability, accuracy, security and regulatory compliance.

The data life cycle typically includes the following stages:

1 **Data creation or acquisition:** the initial stage where data is created or acquired from various sources, such as customer interactions, sensor readings, social media or other data feeds.

2 **Data processing and analysis:** transforming and analysing the data to extract valuable insights and information, using tools such as data mining, machine learning or other analytical techniques.

3 **Data storage and retention:** storing the data in various types of storage systems, such as databases, data warehouses or data lakes, and retaining it for a certain period of time based on business and regulatory requirements.

4 **Data sharing and dissemination:** sharing the data with authorized users or stakeholders, either within the organization or outside, through various channels such as APIs, dashboards or reports.

5 **Data archiving and disposal:** archiving the data that is no longer actively used but still has long-term value, and disposing of the data that is no longer needed or has reached the end of its useful life, based on legal and ethical guidelines.

The data life cycle management capability is frequently one that is overlooked, yet it is a critical process for any organization that aims to keep their data current and relevant. Effective data life cycle management helps organizations to optimize their data assets, minimize risks and comply with data protection laws and regulations.

Note that the data management and data life cycle management are different capabilities. As we saw in Chapter 29, the data management capability defines the ability of an organization to establish **operational processes** to collect, process, validate and store enterprise data in line with corporate quality, security and privacy criteria. Data management's primary focus is quality.

Data life cycle management, on the other hand, focuses on the ability of an organization to set up a process to understand, map and controls its enterprise data flows throughout the data life cycle from creation or acquisition to retirement. With data life cycle management, there is always **an element of time** involved. The primary focus of data life cycle management is therefore efficiency.

31.2 Purpose and maturity levels of data life cycle management

Purpose

The purpose of data life cycle management is to ensure that data is effectively managed throughout its entire life cycle, from creation to disposal. This includes ensuring that data is available, secure, accurate and compliant with regulatory requirements.

Data life cycle management is important for the following reasons:

- **Optimizing data usage:** By effectively managing data throughout its life cycle, organizations can optimize its usage by ensuring that it is available, accurate and relevant to the business needs. This can help in improving decision-making, identifying opportunities for growth and enhancing customer experience.

- **Minimizing risks:** Data can be vulnerable to various risks, such as data breaches, cyberattacks or data loss. By implementing effective data life cycle management practices, organizations can minimize these risks by ensuring that data is secure, backed up and easily recoverable in case of an incident.

- **Complying with regulations:** It is important for organizations to comply with various regulations and laws related to data privacy, security and retention. Failure to comply with these regulations can result in legal and financial consequences.

- **Enhancing data governance:** It is an essential component of data governance, which involves managing the availability, usability, integrity and security of data. Effective data governance processes (as discussed in Chapter 28) can help in improving the quality of data, reducing data silos and ensuring that data is aligned with business objectives.

The purpose of the data life cycle management process is outlined in Table 31.1.

Table 31.1   Purpose of the data life cycle management process capability

Capability	Purpose
Data life cycle management process	Defines the ability of an organization to set up a process to understand, map and control its enterprise data flows throughout the data life cycle from creation or acquisition to retirement.

The data life cycle management capability is critical for the process of managing data assets and ensuring that data assets remain controlled throughout its life cycle.

Maturity levels

Establishing a mature data life cycle management process requires that an organization is in control of its data assets at all times. This means that data needs to be stored properly, and that an historic audit trail needs to be present. At all moments, an organization needs to be able to explain when data entered the organization, who generated it, how it was classified or labelled and, maybe most importantly, how it has been used. This last step in particular is something that most organizations don't control, and they are unable to prove or disprove which users in the enterprise have used specific data sets.

We can establish maturity levels of the data life cycle management process capability by the levels specified in Table 31.2.

As can be deduced from the maturity levels outlined in Table 31.2, reaching high levels of maturity requires an organization to be in control of its data at all times, and have suitable tracking and tracing systems. These objectives cannot be achieved without suitable technologies and practices, as we will discuss in further detail in the next section.

31.3 Structuring the data life cycle management

The data life cycle management process encompasses the entire life cycle of an organization's data, from creation to archiving or deletion. For high levels of maturity, it requires that an organization manages its data in a structured and controlled manner to ensure its accuracy, reliability and security.

A well-designed data life cycle management process can help organizations to comply with regulatory requirements, optimize storage utilization, improve data quality and enable effective decision-making. In this section, we will discuss several best practices that will contribute to this goal.

Table 31.2 Data life cycle management maturity levels

Maturity Level	Description
Level 1 – Initial	The organization has inconsistent practices for managing data throughout its life cycle. There is little or no awareness of the importance of data life cycle management, and no formal policies or procedures in place.
Level 2 – Managed	The organization has established basic policies and procedures for managing data throughout its life cycle. However, these practices are not consistently followed across the organization, and there is limited awareness of the benefits of data life cycle management.
Level 3 – Defined	The organization has well-defined and documented policies and procedures for managing data throughout its life cycle. These practices are consistently followed across the organization, and there is a growing awareness of the importance of data life cycle management.
Level 4 – Controlled	The organization has established metrics and measurement systems for monitoring and improving data life cycle management practices. There is a focus on continuous improvement, and data life cycle management is seen as a critical component of the organization's overall performance.
Level 5 – Optimized	The organization has a culture of continuous improvement and innovation in data life cycle management. There is a focus on maximizing the value of data assets, and data life cycle management practices are integrated into all aspects of the organization's operations.

Define data life cycle stages

The first step in implementing a data life cycle management process is to define the stages in the data life cycle. The stages represent the various phases through which data passes from creation to disposal. Common data life cycle stages include:

- **Creation:** This is the first stage of the data life cycle, where data is created, captured or entered into an organization's systems or applications. This stage includes data input and creation, as well as data acquisition from external sources.

- **Storage:** After data is created, it is stored in an organization's systems or applications. The storage stage includes the management of data storage, such as backup, recovery, replication, archiving and compression.

- **Usage:** During this stage, data is accessed and used by authorized personnel for specific purposes, such as analytics, reporting, decision-making or customer service.

- **Maintenance:** This stage involves the ongoing maintenance of data, such as data cleansing, normalization and de-duplication. The maintenance stage also includes data quality checks and data governance activities, such as data lineage, metadata management and data profiling.

- **Archival:** After data has served its primary purpose, it may be moved to a lower tier of storage or archived for long-term retention. This stage includes the management of archived data, such as retrieval, indexing and storage optimization.

- **Deletion:** This is the final stage of the data life cycle, where data is securely deleted or destroyed in compliance with regulatory requirements and organizational policies. Data may be deleted due to end-of-life, redundancy or other reasons.

To define data life cycle stages, an organization should analyse its data flow, systems and applications to identify the points at which data is created, stored, accessed and deleted. The organization should also consider its business requirements and regulatory compliance obligations to determine the appropriate retention and deletion policies for different types of data.

Establish and configure data life cycle management tools

Establishing a proper data life cycle management process is heavily dependent on configuring the right tools and technologies. With these tools, organizations can gain control over the different stages in the data life cycle.

Figure 31.1   Stages of the data life cycle

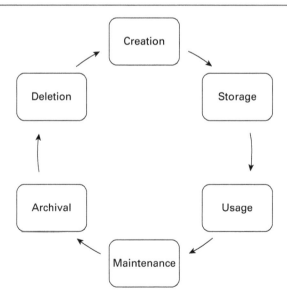

A high maturity data life cycle management process requires the use of various IT tools to manage data across the entire data life cycle, from creation to deletion. In order to manage the different stages of the data management life cycle, organizations need to source and configure the following tool sets:

1 **Data integration tools:** extract, transform and load data from various sources into a centralized data warehouse or data lake. These tools help to ensure that data is accurate, complete and consistent across different systems and applications.

2 **Data quality tools:** monitor and improve the quality of data throughout its life cycle. These tools help to identify and fix errors, inconsistencies and redundancies in the data.

3 **Data governance tools:** manage the policies, procedures and standards for data management within an organization. These tools help to ensure that data is managed in compliance with regulatory requirements and organizational policies.

4 **Backup and recovery tools:** create backups of data at regular intervals and to recover data in the event of a system failure or data loss. These tools help to ensure that data is always available when needed.

5 **Archiving tools:** move data that is no longer actively used to a lower tier of storage for long-term retention. These tools help to optimize storage utilization and reduce costs.

6 **Access control tools:** manage user access to data, applications and systems. These tools help to ensure that data is only accessed by authorized personnel.

7 **Security tools:** protect data from unauthorized access, modification or disclosure. These tools include firewalls, intrusion detection systems, encryption and other security measures.

8 **Analytics tools:** analyse and interpret data for insights and decision-making. These tools help to identify trends, patterns and anomalies in the data.

The need for proper tools is critical for the effective management of the different stages in data life cycle management. It's also important to integrate these tools and systems to ensure that data is managed in a consistent and efficient manner.

Data archiving and data deletion

A special consideration in the data life cycle management process goes to data archiving and data deletion, the two final stages of the data life cycle. These stages are especially important, because they are frequently overlooked.

Because data archiving and data deletion is, in most countries, driven by laws and regulations, organizations should consult with legal and compliance experts to ensure that their data archiving and deletion practices comply with all applicable laws and regulations. Additionally, organizations should regularly review and update their retention and deletion policies to ensure that they remain effective and up to date with changing business needs and regulatory requirements.

To structure data archiving and data deletion, organizations should consider the guidance from organizations with high maturity in the data life cycle management process, as shown in Table 31.3.

Table 31.3   Data retention and data deletion best practices

Data Retention	Best Practice
Define data retention policies	Organizations should establish retention policies for different types of data to determine when data should be archived. These policies should be based on legal and regulatory requirements, business needs and the data's value to the organization. We discussed data retention policy in Chapter 28.
Categorize data	Data should be categorized based on its importance, sensitivity and relevance to the organization's goals. This categorization should inform the retention policies and the type of storage used for the archived data.
Choose appropriate storage	Data should be stored in an appropriate storage medium that balances the cost, accessibility and durability of the data. Organizations should consider using cloud-based storage or tape-based storage for archival purposes.
Test data retrieval	Organizations should periodically test the retrieval of archived data to ensure that it is easily accessible and can be restored in a timely manner if needed.
Data Deletion	
Define data deletion policies	Organizations should establish deletion policies for different types of data to determine when data should be deleted. These policies should be based on legal and regulatory requirements, business needs and the data's value to the organization.
Use secure deletion methods	Data should be securely deleted using appropriate deletion methods, such as overwriting or shredding. This helps to ensure that data cannot be recovered by unauthorized individuals.
Monitor deletion process	Organizations should monitor deletion processes to ensure that data is deleted in compliance with the deletion policies and that the deletion is complete.
Documents deletion	Organizations should document the deletion process, including the reason for the deletion, the date of the deletion and who authorized the deletion. This helps to demonstrate compliance with regulatory requirements and organizational policies.

31.4 Data life cycle management process summary

The data life cycle management process capability manages the different stages of data in the organization, from the moment that data enters the organization until it is archived and discarded. Although there is some overlap with data management, which mainly focuses on data quality, the data management life cycle focuses on the controlling of data throughout all the different phase of the life cycle.

In order to establish a high-maturity data life cycle management process, organizations need to consider a number of factors. First, they need to define a data life cycle management process for their organization, and define the different stages that need to be managed. Second, they need to consider which IT tools and technologies can support each of these stages. Having control of all stages in the data life cycle is impossible without properly configured technology. Finally, organizations need to consider how they will deal with the final stages of the data life cycle, and establish sound procedures for data archiving and data deletion.

The Data Vendor Management Process 32

32.1 Introduction to the data vendor management process

Data vendor management is the process of selecting, evaluating and managing third-party data vendors who provide data products and services to an organization. The process involves ensuring that the data vendor is reliable, trustworthy and can provide high-quality data that meets the organization's requirements.

Depending on the nature of their business, organizations may need to use third-party data vendors to acquire data that is not available internally or to supplement their internal data with external data. Some common types of third-party data vendors that organization might need to deal with include:

- **Data brokers:** collect, aggregate and sell data from various sources, such as social media, public records and consumer surveys. They provide organizations with access to large datasets for marketing, research and analysis purposes.

- **Marketing data providers:** specialize in collecting and selling data related to consumer behaviour, preferences and demographics. They provide organizations with insights into customer segments, market trends and competitor analysis.

- **Financial data providers:** collect and sell financial data, such as stock prices, trading volumes and financial statements. They provide organizations with insights into market trends, investment opportunities and risk management.

- **Geospatial data providers:** specialize in collecting and selling location-based data, such as maps, satellite imagery and geocoded data. They provide organizations with insights into customer location, site selection and supply chain management.

- **Healthcare data providers:** collect and sell data related to medical conditions, patient outcomes and healthcare spending. They provide organizations with insights into disease management, population health and healthcare analytics.

- **Social media data providers:** specialize in collecting and selling data related to social media activity, such as posts, comments and shares. They provide organizations with insights into customer sentiment, brand reputation and social media engagement.

As the importance and value of data is increasing, the number of third-party data providers that organizations may need is growing equally as well. Many organizations rely on third-party data providers for critical business decisions. For that reason, it's important for organizations to evaluate the reliability, quality and privacy of third-party data vendors before acquiring data from them. Organizations should also ensure that they have the legal right to use the data and that they comply with all applicable laws and regulations regarding data privacy and security.

32.2 Purpose and maturity levels of data vendor management

Purpose

The purpose of the data vendor management process is to ensure that organizations are obtaining high-quality, secure and compliant data from reputable sources. Data vendor management involves the selection, contracting and ongoing management of third-party data vendors who provide the data that the organization requires for its operations, decision-making and analysis.

The purpose of the data vendor management capability is stated in Table 32.1.

Establishing an effective data vendor management capability is critical for several reasons. First, it ensures that organizations obtain high-quality data that is accurate, reliable and relevant to their business needs. Low-quality data can lead to erroneous conclusions and poor decision-making, which can negatively impact the organization's performance.

Second, data vendor management helps to ensure that the data obtained from third-party vendors is secure and protected from unauthorized access or disclosure. This is particularly important for sensitive or confidential data, such as customer information or financial data, which can be a target for cybercriminals.

Table 32.1 Purpose of the data vendor management process capability

Capability	Purpose
Data Vendor Management Process	Defines the ability to manage interactions between the Big Data function and suppliers of critical Big Data technology or data.

Third, data vendor management helps to optimize costs by negotiating favourable pricing and contract terms with data vendors. This can help organizations to reduce data acquisition costs and improve their bottom line.

Lastly, the data vendor management capability helps to ensure that the organization is compliant with all applicable laws and regulations regarding data privacy, security and usage. Compliance is particularly important in industries such as healthcare and finance, where strict regulations govern the collection, use and storage of sensitive data.

Maturity levels

Since the dependence on (and existence of) third-party data vendors is relatively new, most data management vendor activities at organizations are managed by a centralized procurement department. Although there is merit, from an efficiency point of view, high-maturity organizations typically establish data vendor management as a separate or dedicated function. Particularly for organizations who rely on third-party data for critical high-cost decision (for example, where to place a pipeline), the management of third party data vendors is a strategic activity.

The maturity levels for the data vendor management process are outlined in Table 32.2.

The maturity of data vendor management processes varies significantly across organizations. While some organizations have highly mature data vendor management processes, others may have only basic or unstructured approaches to vendor management.

In recent years, there has been growing recognition of the importance of effective data vendor management, particularly as organizations increasingly rely on external data sources for decision-making and analysis. As a result, many organizations are investing in the development and improvement of their data vendor management processes.

32.3 Structuring the data vendor management process

As dependency on third-party data providers increases, organizations should start to establish a data vendor management process. With a data vendor management process, organization can establish better controls, increase compliance and, in most cases, realize cost savings. Most third-party data providers are commercial organizations, with whom there is typically room for negotiation.

Table 32.2 Data vendor management maturity levels

Maturity Level	Description
Level 1 – Initial	The organization has not yet established a formal data vendor management process. There may be basic approaches to vendor selection and management, with little or no documentation or tracking of vendor performance.
Level 2 – Managed	The organization has established a formal data vendor management process, with documented policies and procedures for vendor selection, contract negotiation, and ongoing vendor management. Vendor performance is tracked and evaluated on a regular basis, and there may be some efforts to optimize vendor costs.
Level 3 – Defined	The data vendor management process is fully defined and standardized across the organization. There are clear roles and responsibilities for vendor selection and management, and all vendors are evaluated using the same criteria. The organization has established relationships with preferred vendors, and there may be ongoing efforts to negotiate better pricing and terms.
Level 4 – Controlled	The organization has established metrics and performance indicators to measure the effectiveness of the data vendor management process. There is a focus on continuous improvement, with data-driven decision-making and ongoing process refinement.
Level 5 – Optimized	The data vendor management process is fully optimized and integrated with the overall data management strategy. The organization has a deep understanding of its data needs and the capabilities of its vendors, and there is ongoing collaboration and innovation with vendors to drive business value. The data vendor management process is viewed as a strategic asset that helps the organization achieve its goals and objectives.

The data vendor management process can consist of the following steps to build a mature capability.

Identify data needs

The first activity in the data vendor management process is to identify data need. Here, it could be useful to begin by identifying the types of data your organization needs to support its business goals and objectives. This may involve working with key stakeholders across the organization to understand their data requirements.

To identify data needs, it is important to have a thorough understanding of the business. It is useful to start by defining the business objectives that your organization

Figure 32.1   Activities in the data vendor management process

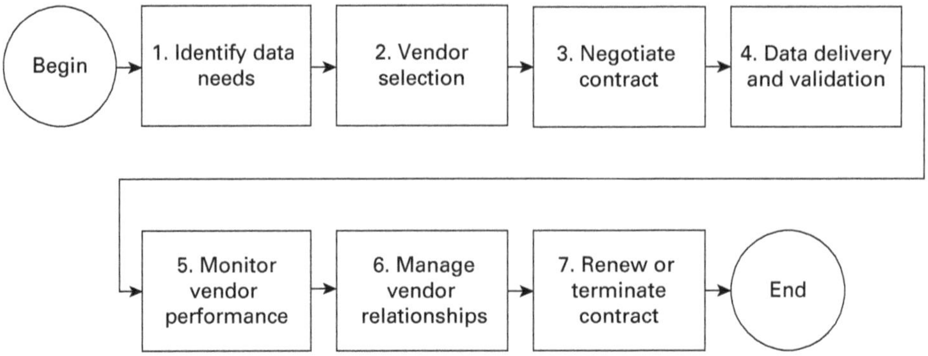

is trying to achieve. This will help you understand the types of data that you need to support your business goals. Once you have defined your business objectives, you can identify the data gaps that exist within your organization. This may involve reviewing existing data sources and identifying areas where additional data is needed.

To ensure that your data needs are aligned with the needs of the business, it's important to involve key stakeholders from across the organization. This may include business leaders, data analysts and subject matter experts.

Once you have identified your data needs and prioritized them, you can begin to define your data requirements. This may involve specifying the types of data you need, the quality standards that data must meet, and any compliance requirements that data must adhere to. These data requirements can then be shared with potential vendors in step 2.

Vendor selection

There are hundreds, if not thousands, of data vendors available. And this number keeps on growing. To select suitable data vendors, you can utilize some of the following best practices:

- **Define vendor criteria:** Begin by defining the criteria that you will use to evaluate potential data vendors. This may include factors such as data quality, data security, data compliance, pricing and customer service.

- **Conduct market research:** Conduct research to identify data vendors that meet your criteria. This may involve searching online directories, attending industry conferences and leveraging industry contacts.

- **Evaluate vendor directories and databases:** Many organizations maintain directories or databases of data vendors that may be of interest. Consider reviewing these directories to identify potential vendors that meet your criteria.

- **Seek referrals:** Ask industry contacts for referrals to data vendors that they have worked with and can recommend.

- **Leverage RFPs:** If you have a specific data need or project, consider issuing a request for proposal (RFP) to potential vendors. This can help you identify vendors that are capable of meeting your specific data requirements.

- **Consider specialized vendors:** Depending on your data needs, you may need to work with specialized vendors that focus on specific types of data or industries. Consider researching and identifying vendors that specialize in your area of interest.

- **Evaluate vendor reputation:** Once you have identified potential vendors, research their reputation by reviewing customer reviews, testimonials and case studies. This can help you evaluate whether a vendor is a good fit for your organization.

By following these best practices, you can identify potential data vendors that meet your criteria and are capable of delivering the data you need. It is important to take the time to thoroughly evaluate potential vendors to ensure that they are a good fit for your organization and can deliver data that meets your needs.

Negotiate contract

The next step in the data vendor management process is the negotiation of the contract. This activity will not differ greatly from other procurement negotiation processes, so it might be useful to get input from the procurement department for this step, or to let a trained negotiator handle the negotiation meetings.

Once you have identified and evaluated potential vendors, you can begin negotiating vendor contracts that define the terms of your relationship with the vendor. This may involve defining data quality metrics, establishing service level agreements (SLAs) and setting pricing and payment terms.

Data delivery and validation

The next activity, after the contract has been signed, is the delivery and validation of the data sets. In this step, you will need with the data vendor to determine the best method for delivering the data to your organization. This may include options such as email, FTP, API or web-based platforms.

Once you have determined the data delivery method, work with the data vendor to establish data transfer protocols that ensure data security and compliance. This may include encrypting data during transfer, requiring multi-factor authentication or establishing data access controls.

Lastly, once the data has been delivered, it is appropriate to conduct an initial validation to ensure that it meets your defined criteria. This may involve using automated tools, manual processes or a combination of both. If any data quality issues are identified during the initial validation, work with the data vendor to address those issues. This may involve reformatting data, correcting errors or providing additional data.

Monitor vendor performance

The organization should regularly monitor the vendor's performance to ensure that the vendor is meeting the agreed-upon terms and conditions, including the quality of the data, the delivery schedule and the customer support. Some key activities that need to be performed on a period basis are:

- **Define performance metrics:** Define the key performance metrics that you will use to evaluate vendor performance. These metrics may include data quality, data security, data compliance, customer service and timeliness of data delivery.

- **Establish SLAs:** Establish SLAs with vendors that define expectations around key performance metrics. SLAs should be specific, measurable and time-bound.

- **Monitor vendor performance regularly:** Regularly monitor vendor performance against established SLAs and other performance metrics. This may involve conducting periodic audits, reviewing vendor reports and tracking performance metrics over time.

- **Address issues promptly:** If issues arise with vendor performance, address them promptly to ensure that performance issues are resolved quickly. This may involve engaging with vendors directly to resolve issues or escalating issues to senior management if necessary.

- **Conduct periodic vendor reviews:** Conduct periodic reviews of vendor performance to assess overall performance and identify areas for improvement. These reviews should be conducted on a regular basis and may involve gathering feedback from internal stakeholders who work directly with the vendor.

Regular monitoring and communication with vendors can help organizations identify issues early and address them before they become major problems. This can help to ensure that vendor relationships remain productive and contribute to the overall success of the organization.

Manage vendor relationships

Managing vendor relationships is a critical step in the data vendor management process. To make sure that the relationship will be long term, it is critical to establish clear communication channels with your data vendors to ensure that you are able to effectively communicate with them on an ongoing basis. This may involve setting up regular check-ins, scheduling periodic reviews and establishing a point of contact for vendor-related inquiries.

If issues or concerns arise with vendors, it is important to address them promptly to ensure that they do not impact your organization's ability to access and use data. This may involve working with vendors to resolve issues or escalating issues to senior management as needed.

By managing vendor relationships effectively, you can ensure that your organization is able to access and use data that meets its needs. This involves establishing clear communication channels with vendors, monitoring vendor performance, addressing issues and concerns promptly, conducting periodic reviews, evaluating vendor contracts and developing a vendor risk management plan. By taking a proactive approach to vendor management, you can mitigate risks and ensure that your organization is able to leverage data effectively to support its business goals and objectives.

Renew or terminate contract

The last step is the decision to renew or terminate the contract. This decision should be based on periodic reviews of the contract. By performing formal review on an ongoing basis, you can ensure that vendors continue to meet your organization's needs. This may involve renegotiating contract terms, terminating contracts for cause or selecting new vendors to replace underperforming vendors.

32.4 Data vendor management process summary

Because organizations have become more and more reliant on data from external sources for critical business decisions, it is important to set up a data vendor management process. The data vendor management process is a structured approach that organizations use to identify, evaluate, select and manage third-party vendors that provide data services or products. The goal of a data vendor management process is to ensure that an organization can access high-quality data that meets its needs while minimizing risks associated with using third-party vendors.

In this section, we considered steps and activities to establish a mature data vendor management process. Establishing a suitable process is a critical capability to ensure that the data that you receive from external third parties meets the organization's requirements, is obtained in safe and legal ways and ultimately that your organization can trust third-party datasets to make critical business decisions.

Big Data Processes 33
Maturity
Assessment

Please respond to the following questions by indicating the relevant level of maturity for each activity in question and its importance to your organization.

The Capability Maturity Model levels are shown in Table 33.1.

Table 33.1 Capability Maturity Model levels

Score	Description
0 – Non-existent	Describes a total lack of activity or lack of recognition that the activity exists.
1 – Initial	Describes evidence that the organization recognizes issues exist and need to be addressed.
2 – Managed	Describes activities designed so that similar procedures are followed by individuals. There is a high reliance on individual knowledge and skill level.
3 – Defined	Describes a standardized and documented level of activities which is being communicated through training, processes and tools.
4 – Controlled	Describes activities which are good practice and under constant improvement. Automation and tools are used to support the activities.
5 – Optimized	Describes activities that are considered leading and best practice and can be considered an example to other organizations.

Please note that responses to this survey should reflect how the organization performs the task today, not how you would like to see the organization perform the task in the future. Your choices should be based on your opinion of the organization, not just the way the task is performed in your own workgroup.

Table 33.2   Big Data Processes Maturity Assessment

#	Data Governance Process	Score
17.1	Our organization has established a data governance framework that is based on international standards and best practices.	
17.2	Our organization has defined data governance policies that are clearly communicated and understood in the rest of the organization.	
17.3	Our organization has set up data governance processes and procedures for data classification, data privacy, data security, data retention and archiving.	
17.4	Roles and responsibilities have been assigned for the management and improvement of the data governance framework, policies and processes.	
17.5	The data governance policies and processes have been properly integrated with the data management process capability.	
17.6	Our organization's data governance framework, policies and practices are being regularly monitored, assessed and improved.	
	Data Management Process	**Score**
18.1	Our organization has suitable data management processes in place to safeguard the accuracy and quality of our enterprise data.	
18.2	Our organization has suitable processes in place to ensure that data is collected and stored in accordance with laws and regulations.	
18.3	Our organization has suitable technology and processes in place to ensure that data usage can be tracked and traced throughout the organization.	
18.4	Our organization has a suitable team that is responsible for data management processes and that has sufficient resources.	
18.5	Our organization has set up a suitable data classification system, and access to data is provided to employees, vendors and other stakeholders based on the classification system.	
18.6	The quality of our data is automatically and continuously monitored and reviewed, and data improvement initiatives are started based on these reviews.	

(continued)

Table 33.2 (Continued)

	Data Analysis Process	Score
19.1	Our organization has a defined process with clear steps for the execution of any data analysis.	
19.2	Different teams across the organization or across different geographical regions are using the same data analysis process.	
19.3	Data security and data privacy considerations have been embedded in the data analysis process.	
19.4	The Big Data and data science teams have adequate tools, subdivided into the different steps of the data analysis process, which support the process.	
19.5	Adequate reviews, approvals and sign-offs are in place between the different stages of the data analysis life cycle.	
19.6	Our organization provides periodic training or workshops about the data analysis process and the way the Big Data teams operate.	
	Data Life Cycle Management Process	**Score**
20.1	Our organization has defined a data life cycle management process, and has defined different stages as part of the data life cycle.	
20.2	Our organization manages data based on the defined stages in the data life cycle management process.	
20.3	Our organization retains and stores data in line with the requirements as defined in our data retention policy.	
20.4	Our organization actively discards and deletes data in compliance with national regulations and the data deletion policy.	
20.5	Our organization has adequate data life cycle technology tools and has configured these tools according to the data life cycle management process.	
20.6	An individual or team has been assigned that is accountable for the data life cycle management process.	

(continued)

Table 33.2   (Continued)

	Data Vendor Management Process	Score
21.1	Our organization has defined a data vendor management process and the organization operates in line with this process.	
21.2	Our organization has a consistent policy with regards to sourcing data from third-party vendors.	
21.3	Our organization has defined quality criteria for third-party data vendors, and these quality criteria are used during the sourcing process.	
21.4	Our organization has a process in place to validate the quality of data received from third-party data vendors.	
21.5	Our organization actively monitors performance of data vendors, and actively manages data vendors based on their performance scores.	
21.6	The quality criteria for third-party data vendors are documented and shared with (prospective) data vendors.	

PART SEVEN
Big Data Functions

Big Data Functions

34

34.1 Introduction to Big Data functions

When people think about Big Data, they initially think about its technology and technical components. It is easy to describe large quantities of data by focusing on databases, storage mechanisms and data processing techniques. Yet, the most important capability to make Big Data successful in any organization is the human aspect. The data analysts, scientists and engineers bring together technical solutions, are the people that spend hours cleaning and updating data sets and have the skills to interpret, predict and communicate results.

In this section, we will therefore focus on the human side of Big Data. We have called this section Big Data functions because organizations have a functional approach to organizing their departments. Additionally, it is important to highlight the group or team element. Success in Big Data requires dedicated and committed teams. As we have seen in the previous chapters, building capabilities in Big Data requires different skill sets, from different people.

So that brings us to the question, how best to organize Big Data teams? And how to best structure the Big Data function? Organizations need to create an environment where Big Data teams can be successful, focus on solving the problems at hand and where they have the tools to deep-dive into their work. Data scientists need to have the opportunity to deep-dive into data structures and algorithm design, in an environment that supports this.

Since dependency on data becomes larger and larger in every enterprise, time pressure in Big Data organizations is significant. Teams are often expected to solve complex problems within short periods of time, because management requires these insights to make strategic decisions. As a result, most Big Data functions have high workloads, and are under constant pressure to deliver. If the Big Data function is not managed properly, it can lead to burnt-out teams, and a decline in innovative solutions. Unfortunately, this situation is common in many organizations.

In this chapter, we will focus on the critical capabilities that address these challenges. We will outline several best practices that showcase how organizations can structure and strengthen their Big Data function. Just like setting up a Big Data architecture takes time and careful planning, structuring the human aspect of Big Data takes time and careful consideration.

34.2 Common challenges in Big Data functions

Before we start diving into solutions that enable people to work in Big Data functions effectively, let's first discuss some of the main organizational challenges that are common in most Big Data organizations. Some of the common challenges that most Big Data organizations struggle with include the following.

Time pressure

As most organizations are transforming into data-driven enterprises, the dependency on data become more significant. And that means that the pressure to deliver results quickly is ever increasing. Many Big Data teams are therefore under significant time pressure to provide analysis or predictions quickly, without ample time for adequate quality control or peer-review. Since many leaders see the benefits of data-driven decision-making, the demand for analytics and their associated predictive solutions is not expected to stop any time soon, and therefore the pressure to keep delivering results will keep increasing.

Complexity

Organizations want to have quick predictions, but in many cases fail to realize the complexity of Big Data projects. Building, testing and validating predictive algorithms to solve business problems is inherently complex. Data is frequently distributed across the enterprise, and it requires time to understand and comprehend these data sets in full. Building a subsequent predictive model, even with predefined libraries or standard functions, requires time and a deep understanding of how algorithms process data. Understanding this complexity takes years of training and experience. Even with the best tools and people in the world, Big Data problems (and finding their solutions) remains complex work.

Lack of business data literacy

Since analytics and Big Data are relatively new domains, many businesses leaders and executives have trouble understanding how data and algorithms lead to certain predictions. For many senior leaders, the Big Data function is a black box, where data is going in and reports or presentations are coming out. The way that algorithms work, or how these reports are generated, eludes most business leaders.

It is of course not necessary that every business leader becomes a data specialist, but the lack of business data literacy in most organizations typically leads to several problems. First, because of a lack of understanding, most business leaders find it difficult to articulate their exact requirements for their business problems. As we saw in Part 5, there are hundreds of different algorithms that can be used, and minor design choices can have significant impact on the end results. Better requirements, and a better scope definition by the business, helps the Big Data function significantly in their design.

Second, because of this lack in business data literacy, business expectations are frequently over-ambitious or unrealistic. Many people think that data analysts and data scientists just need to push a few buttons to create a report. They forget the significant amount of work involved with data collection, cleaning, preprocessing and testing – all of which leads to longer lead times (if done properly).

Significant open vacancies

Due to the high demand for people with Big Data analytical skills, many organizations are struggling to fill their open positions. They want to invest in extra capacity and capability but find it difficult to fill the positions. Experienced data engineers and data scientists are hard to find, and many enterprise organizations need to compete against the big tech conglomerates, which have equal demand for these positions. As a result, many organizations have open Big Data vacancies that take a long time to fill, once again increasing the time pressure and workload on the rest of the Big Data function.

Lack of training and development

Commensurate with time pressure, complexity of projects and lack of resources, most Big Data functions lack adequate and consistent training programmes. Big Data techniques are evolving fast, and to stay current and up to date with industry trends continuous upskilling and training is a fundamental pre-requisite to success. Some studies suggest that – to keep developing – Big Data roles should spend one day per month in training to enhance their skill sets.

The reality in most Big Data functions is that this is not properly organized. Most teams depend on 'self-learning' or 'on-the-job' learning, without more structured career planning and development opportunities. Even though a motivated Big Data professional will always find time for self-study (it is an integral part of their jobs), organizations can benefit significantly from setting up in-house formal training programmes.

34.3 The Big Data Centre of Excellence

As established already a number of times throughout this book, Big Data is primarily a knowledge domain. Technology is indispensable, but to obtain long-term value from massive data sets, it is first and foremost about knowledge. An organization that wants to achieve long-term success will therefore first need to consolidate and organize its Big Data knowledge in the enterprise. It needs to establish a Big Data Centre of Excellence (BDCoE).

A BDCoE is a centralized function in an organization that takes responsibility for realizing value with Big Data. The Centre of Excellence can be organized as a department or division, which is the most common approach. Alternatively, it can be organized as a cross-functional group, with data enthusiasts sharing knowledge across different functional departments. Although the cross-functional option could be a great place to start, a BDCoE that is institutionalized – with appropriate budgets and management structures – is the more sustainable option.

A BDCoE functions as the one-stop shop that the rest of the organization can contact for insights and foresights. A marketing department that wants to create the best customer personas can contact the Centre of Excellence. If the Supply Chain Director wants to have a predictive analysis about supply chain bottlenecks, he or she can contact the Centre of Excellence. By setting up this centralized function, it becomes clear for everyone in the organization where they can (or need to) go with their Big Data business problems and challenges.

There are many benefits in setting up a BDCoE, the most notable of which is that it provides an opportunity for the enterprise to build up knowledge in a coordinated way. In the BDCoE, teams can discuss how to tackle problems, share experiences and deep-dive into complicated assignment or business challenges. The knowledge that a BDCoE builds is not to be underestimated, and one of the key reasons some organizations operate at a higher level of maturity is that they have formally established such a centre.

However, setting up a BDCoE is far from an easy task. Many organizations have struggled for years to find the right balance between running the data and analytics department as a cost centre (i.e. as an operational function) and building up knowledge to support future decision making (i.e. the centre of excellence function). In this chapter, we will look at some of the necessary capabilities to set up and structure a robust BDCoE.

To build a well-functioning BDCoE, many capabilities are required, which we will cover extensively in the next few sections. For a start, a well-structured Big Data function works as a **knowledge centre** and has processes and practices in place to store knowledge and exchange ideas. Secondly, it functions as a **uniform entry point** for the rest of the organization and enables engagement between the Big Data and analytics function and other parts of the organization. Finally, the BDCoE functions as a **career development centre**, enabling workforce planning, talent management and training best practices. These three functions of the BDCoE will be covered in the five capabilities that we will consider in the following sections, and which are outlined in Figure 34.1.

34.4 Roles and responsibilities in the Big Data function

One of the first questions to answer in structuring a BDCoE is which roles and responsibilities are required. What kind of skills does an organization need, and what are the types of job roles with which the centre can be structured?

Since every organization is different, there is not a uniform answer to this question. We have, however, outlined an attempt to structure **the most common job roles** that are observed in Big Data Centres of Excellences around the world, based on the competency model of the Skills Framework for the Information Age (SFIA), the European e-Competence Framework (e-CF) and the US-based Digital Skill for a Digital Age (DSDA) model. These common job roles aim to separate technical skills, and soft-skills, and can be applied to any type of organization. The course curriculum of the Enterprise Big Data Framework has been structured around these roles and responsibility profiles.

The five competency levels are matched to the following five levels of the European e-Competence Framework.[1]

Figure 34.1 Capabilities of the Big Data function

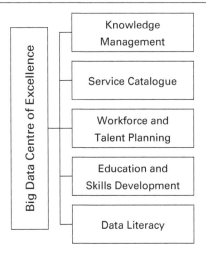

Table 34.1 Five competency levels of Big Data job profiles

Level	Complexity	Behaviour	Autonomy
Level 1	Stable	Plain problem solving	Responsible for own actions
Level 2	Unstable – predictable	Complex problem solving	Independence within supervised boundaries
Level 3	Unpredictable	Innovation	Works independently
Level 4	Complex – Unpredictable	Strategic development	Fully responsible
Level 5	Unpredictable	Shaping the future	Accountable

Enterprise Big Data professional

The enterprise Big Data professional is an entry-level job role, suitable for everyone in the organization that aims to have 'beyond-average' data analysis and analytics skills. Enterprise Big Data professionals are frequently business users, who reside in business functions outside the BDCoE, but who are inclined to use data-driven decisions in their everyday use. Examples include marketing managers that steer marketing expenses based on factual data, or finance professionals that use predicted models to back financial decisions (for example portfolio balancing).

The enterprise Big Data professional is therefore an all-purpose term that summarizes a group of professionals that either want to make a career in Big Data, or who can become business partners for the BDCoE. Enterprise Big Data professionals are characterized by the fact that they understand how data analysis works, what the key benefits are and how data-driven decisions can help the organization get a competitive advantage for the future.

The competency profile for an enterprise Big Data professional is outlined in Table 34.2, which is subdivided into technical and soft skills.

Enterprise Big Data analyst

An enterprise Big Data analyst is an intermediate-level job role that focuses primarily on retrieving value from large data sets. To accomplish this objective, the enterprise Big Data analyst needs to have an in-depth understanding about data structures and algorithms. More than anything, this role needs to understand how to solve business problems and be able to select and configure the best possible algorithm to solve the problem.

Table 34.2 Competency profile of the enterprise Big Data professional

Domain	Skill	L1	L2	L3	L4	L5
Technical Skills	Data modelling and design	●	●	●		
	Information management		●	●		
	Algorithm design/development	●	●			
	Data life cycle management		●	●		
	Data engineering	●				
	Programming languages	●				
	Data visualization		●	●		
Soft Skills	Leadership skills	●	●			
	Analytical skills		●	●		
	Statistical skills	●	●			
	Communication skills		●	●		
	Ethical hacking skills	●	●	●		

As we have seen in Part 5 (Big Data Algorithms), there are dozens of different ways to solve a business problem, and hundreds of potential algorithms that can be utilized, altered or adjusted. An enterprise Big Data analyst should therefore first and foremost study different classes and types of algorithms to understand their structure, process and mathematical foundation. The role requires a deep understanding of the different **exploratory data analysis, classification, clustering, outlier detection and cognitive algorithms** that exists, and how these algorithms operate and function. And, maybe more importantly, a Big Data analyst needs to be able to argue why a particular algorithm works best to solve a business problem. Being able to explain to the business why certain choices have been made is crucial for the acceptance of the result, and the validity of the predictions.

The more algorithms an enterprise Big Data analyst understands and can utilize, the better he or she is equipped to fulfil their role. Algorithms can be considered the data analyst's **toolbox** and equip any seasoned practitioner to make the right decision in the right situation. In most cases, data analysts have a background in (or fondness for) mathematics, statistics or computer science, and love solving complex problems and puzzles.

In the BDCoE, the team of data analysts typically form the bridge with the business. Business functions explain their needs and data requirements to the team, and the team of data analysts subsequently translates these requirements into machine learning models and understandable visualizations. Because of this 'bridging function', it is important that enterprise Big Data analysts are strong communicators, so that they ask the right questions to build their solutions. A sound understanding of underlying business processes typically also helps to understand the best way to build a model.

The competency profile for an enterprise Big Data analyst is outlined in Table 34.3, which is subdivided into technical and soft skills.

Note that some technical skills vary across the five different profiles of the five different roles in this section, but that the identified soft skills remain consistent across the roles. As a result, Big Data Centres of Excellences can create and set up dedicated soft-skill development programmes for entire teams.

Table 34.3 Competency profile of the enterprise Big Data analyst

Domain	Skill	L1	L2	L3	L4	L5
Technical Skills	Data modelling and design			●	●	
	Data structures		●	●		
	Algorithm design/development	●	●	●		
	Data life cycle management			●	●	
	Application development	●	●			
	Programming languages	●	●	●		
	Data visualization				●	●
Soft Skills	Leadership skills			●	●	
	Analytical skills			●	●	
	Statistical skills				●	●
	Communication skills			●	●	
	Ethical hacking skills		●	●		

Enterprise Big Data scientist

The most famous – or infamous depending on your point of view – role in the Big Data and Analytics domain is the enterprise Big Data scientist. Famously coined 'the sexiest job of the 21st century' by *Harvard Business Review* in 2012, the demand and interest in data scientists has skyrocketed ever since.[2] The article is simultaneously perhaps the biggest virtue as well as the biggest vice of the Big Data domain. On the one hand, it has generated an interest in Big Data and data science that is unprecedented. Whereas the domain of data was previously attributed to nerds and dusty statisticians, working in data is now 'cool' and respected. Most reputable universities in the world now offer Big Data degrees, and interest in these programs is vast amongst young students.[3] As a result, companies that previously struggled to find suitably skilled mathematicians can now choose from freshly graduated and skilled data scientists.

However, on the other hand, the interest and attention it has gained has arguably been the biggest problem or vice of the Big Data industry. The term 'data scientist' is an unprotected title, and many people, not hindered by any skills or experience, label themselves a data scientist after having participated in a two-week part-time online course. It is safe to say that this job title has been inflated over the last decade, which makes is difficult to determine whether any proper scientific basis exists. It is important to keep in mind that anyone that aspires to be an enterprise Big Data scientist needs to have a proper scientific basis. Core competencies such as programming, mathematics and computers science are a pre-requisite, but the most critical scientific capability (as any engineer will tell you) is that of proper and sound design. An enterprise Big Data scientist role should primarily be involved in the **design of Big Data solutions** and the **design of its corresponding algorithms**.

The roles of the enterprise Big Data analyst and the enterprise Big Data scientist are frequently confused or are intertwined, yet the difference is quite straightforward. Any role that uses **existing algorithms** (or fills in parameters) to extract value from massive datasets is an enterprise Big Data analyst. Alternatively, any role that is involved in the design and creation of **new algorithms** to predict unique value or insights from massive data sets is an enterprise Big Data scientist. To illustrate this with an example, consider the following difference: financial investment firms that analyse stock markets (based on past performance) require skilled Big Data analysts to predict which stocks have profitability success ratios (a predictive classification exercise); if the same financial investment firm wants to build an algorithm that analyses different news sources, to predict which stock will rise, they require the knowledge of an enterprise Big Data scientist.

An enterprise Big Data scientist is therefore a senior-level job role, which requires an expert understanding in data structures, algorithms and software engineering design principles. An enterprise Big Data scientist does not only need to understand how existing algorithms work, he or she also needs to be able to create them. Besides the obvious technical expertise that is required for this role, the most important challenge for enterprise Big Data scientists is to come up with the best design. This design ensures that algorithms can be maintained, updated and perform well (in terms of speed) when tasked with processing massive quantities of data.

The competency profile for an enterprise Big Data scientist is outlined in Table 34.4, which is subdivided into technical and soft skills.

Given the in-depth knowledge required, and the value that enterprise Big Data scientists bring to an organization, this role is frequently the most senior within any BDCoE. Given the significance and value of the role, the United States even appointed its first national chief data scientist in 2015.[4]

Enterprise Big Data engineer

The fourth major job role in the BDCoE is that of the enterprise Big Data engineer. Enterprise Big Data engineers prepare Big Data for analytical or operational use.

Table 34.4 Competency profile of the enterprise Big Data scientist

Domain	Skill	L1	L2	L3	L4	L5
Technical Skills	Data modelling and design				●	●
	Data structures			●	●	
	Algorithm design/development				●	●
	Data lifecycle management			●	●	
	Application development				●	●
	Programming languages				●	●
	Data visualization			●	●	
Soft Skills	Leadership skills				●	●
	Analytical skills				●	●
	Statistical skills				●	●
	Communication skills			●	●	
	Ethical hacking skills			●	●	

Their knowledge concentrates on the first few stages of the data analysis process (see Part 6), ensuring that data in the organization is properly formatted and stored in enterprise data storage solutions and data catalogues.

Compared with enterprise Big Data analysts, the role of the enterprise Big Data engineer is more technical in nature. They require a deep understanding of data structures and data storage techniques. In most organizations, they are responsible for building data pipelines that bring together data from different source systems. Additionally, they maintain the enterprise data in a searchable, easy-to-process format, frequently in the form of a data lake.

Besides the generic technical expertise required for any Big Data role, enterprise Big Data engineers specialize in data storage solutions and data processing languages. Programming skills in Structured Query Language (SQL) and non-tabular data formats (e.g. documents, images, audio, etc.) are required. For that reason, most enterprise Big Data engineers have a computer science background.

The competency profile for an enterprise Big Data engineer is outlined in Table 34.5, which is subdivided into technical and soft skills.

Table 34.5 Competency profile of the enterprise Big Data engineer

Domain	Skill	L1	L2	L3	L4	L5
Technical Skills	Data modelling and design		●	●		
	Database technology			●	●	
	Algorithm design/development		●	●		
	Data lifecycle management		●	●		
	Data engineering			●	●	
	Programming languages		●	●		
	Network technology		●	●		
Soft Skills	Leadership skills		●	●		
	Analytical skills		●	●		
	Statistical skills	●	●			
	Communication skills		●	●		
	Ethical hacking skills		●	●		

Enterprise Big Data architect

The final common job role that organizations require to structure their BDCoE is that of the enterprise Big Data architect. As the job title suggest, an enterprise Big Data architect focuses on design. Not the design of algorithms (which is the job of data scientists), but the design of the technical infrastructure that enables the organization to ingest, process and store massive quantities of data.

As we have discussed in detail in Part 4 (Designing a Big Data Architecture), Big Data environments require distinct distributed processing and storage technologies. The enterprise Big Data architect is responsible for the design and implementation of all technical components that enable the organization to adequately process large data sets with reliable partners and reasonable costs.

A Big Data architecture is part of the wider enterprise IT landscape, and because of that reason, Big Data architects need to understand the broader perspective of services and infrastructure that supports the organization. A Big Data architect is therefore primarily involved with making a proper design that integrates all technical components together, providing a transparent and cost-effective approach to the organization. The decisions that the enterprise Big Data architect makes have significant consequences for the cost structure (and therefore the ROI) of the BDCoE. A significant amount of the ongoing operational costs of Big Data environments is determined by the license fees of vendors, and the different building blocks that the architect selects.

Just like structural architects work with blueprints to design an optimal building structure, enterprise Big Data architects design **Big Data infrastructure blueprints** that provide an optimal way in which the different services, networks and infrastructure components are connected. The NIST Big Data Reference Architecture (discussed in Part 4) can provide a suitable vendor-neutral background upon which any Big Data architect can base its design decisions.

The competency profile for an enterprise Big Data architect is outlined in Table 34.6, which is subdivided into technical and soft skills.

Other roles in the Big Data Centre of Excellence

In the previous sub-sections, we have provided five of the most common job roles in the BDCoE. One generic entry-level job role (Big Data professionals), two intermediate-level job roles (Big Data analysts and Big Data engineers) and two expert-level job roles (Big Data scientists and Big Data architects). The goal of this classification is to provide a generic structure (and competency profiles) that can be used by any organization and that, together, cover the breadth and scope of Big Data organizations.

Obviously, many other job roles exist in the industry. Data stewards, machine learning engineers, data modellers, database specialists, AI developers, etc. are all

Table 34.6 Competency profile of the enterprise Big Data architect

Domain	Skill	L1	L2	L3	L4	L5
Technical Skills	Data modelling and design		•	•		
	Database technology			•	•	
	Algorithm design/development		•	•		
	Data lifecycle management		•	•		
	Data engineering			•	•	
	Programming languages		•	•		
	Network technology		•	•		
Soft Skills	Leadership skills		•	•		
	Analytical skills		•	•		
	Statistical skills	•	•			
	Communication skills		•	•		
	Ethical hacking skills		•	•		

common job roles coming back in professional organizations. With the five roles described above, we do, however, think any organization is able to cover the most important technical and soft skills that are necessary for structurally building Big Data capabilities.

Notes

1 V Kirinić and M Kozina (2018). Analysis of quality-related competencies within the European e-Competence Framework (e-CF). In 2018 4th International Conference on Information Management (ICIM), May, 170–74. IEEE

2 T H Davenport and D J Patil. Data scientist, *Harvard Business Review*, 2012 90 (5), 70–76

3 R D De Veaux, M Agarwal, M Averett, B S Baumer, A Bray, T C Bressoud, L Bryant, L Z Cheng, A Francis, R Gould and A Y Kim. Curriculum guidelines for undergraduate programs in data science, *Annual Review of Statistics and its Application*, 2017 4, 15–30

4 M Loukides, H Mason and D J Patil (2018) *Ethics and Data Science*. O'Reilly Media

Knowledge Management   35

35.1 Introduction to knowledge management

The Enterprise Big Data Centre of Excellence (BDCoE) is first and foremost a centralized place in an organization where knowledge about Big Data (and related data practices) is exchanged. The primary reason organizations set up a BDCoE is to build knowledge and best practices in a structured manner. With all the technologies and solutions that exist in Big Data organizations, it becomes easy to forget that the primary source of knowledge is frequently in the minds and memory of the employees. In most companies, it is not embedded or written down anywhere, meaning that if an individual leaves the organization to pursue a different career opportunity, the knowledge leaves the organization as well.

To benefit long term from a BDCoE (and the Big Data Function in general), organizations should actively set up **knowledge management**. Knowledge management in a BDCoE is the collection of methods relating to creating, sharing, using and managing the Big Data knowledge and information of an organization.[1] And even though this sounds like a straightforward and easy capability to build, very few organizations have structured methods in place to actively manage the Big Data knowledge of the organization.

35.2 Purpose and maturity levels of knowledge management

Purpose

Knowledge management is a generic capability, which is equally important in other corporate functions, such as HR, Finance or Operations. However, given the technical complexity of Big Data organizations, it can be argued that it is even more important to capture knowledge in an BDCoE than in other functional departments. As a result, it is important to start building a knowledge management capability so that the organization can capture critical skills, methods and ideas in a structured manner.

Table 35.1   The purpose of the knowledge management capability

Capability	Purpose
Knowledge management	Defines the ability of an organization to create, share, use and manage internal knowledge about Big Data best practices in the organization.

The purpose of the knowledge management capability can be defined as outlined in Table 35.1.

The purposes and motivation for active knowledge management in any organization are simple. It has long been proven that effective knowledge management is a crucial component for innovation.[2] Organizations that have effective knowledge management procedures and systems in place create more innovative products and solutions, and hence have a competitive advantage. Additionally, organizations that have a mature knowledge management capability have a better knowledge-sharing culture, which is generally considered more inclusive.[3] These two factors – innovation and culture – alone are compelling enough to actively start building this capability.

Maturity levels

The knowledge management capability is easy to explain, but hard to build. What makes an organization effective in knowledge management? And what would be a suitable method to measure this? Since the concept of knowledge itself is abstract, defining knowledge management capability levels is even more abstract. To establish measurable levels the defined maturity will be outcome based.

Despite the importance of the knowledge management capability, many organizations fail to establish a mature practice.[4] Many factors contribute to its complexity, which is the reason why it is so difficult to build this capability structurally. As we will discuss further over the next sections, building an effective knowledge management practice requires the appropriate tools, a change in organizational culture and active management on knowledge items. Maybe the most important challenge lies in changing people's behaviours and habits and establishing a culture in which people actively write down and distribute knowledge to others.

By establishing a mature knowledge management capability, an organization can ensure that knowledge that frequently resides in the minds of just a few individuals can be used more effectively. It helps organization to reduce the need to search for answers and improves efficiency. Maybe most importantly, it establishes a knowledge-sharing culture in which people are proud to share their thoughts with others.

Table 35.2   Maturity levels of the knowledge management capability

Maturity Level	Description
Level 1 – Initial	Knowledge management is ad hoc. Knowledge about Big Data projects is not shared across colleagues or maintained after a Big Data project is completed.
Level 2 – Managed	Some knowledge management practices are in place at the BDCoE. Colleagues actively share knowledge with each other, and there is some tool in which knowledge is captured and shared.
Level 3 – Defined	Standardized knowledge management activities are planned and executed on a periodic basis. A programme has been established that motivates BDCoE members to actively share knowledge, and the knowledge management tool is actively used by the BDCoE team.
Level 4 – Controlled	Knowledge management is part of the organization's culture. Comprehensive and effective processes and procedures exist to continually improve knowledge within and outside the organization,
Level 5 – Optimized	The knowledge management practice is itself subject to continual improvement and function and is frequently consulted by different parts of the organization. A knowledge manager is appointed who actively increases the maturity of the knowledge management capability.

35.3 Structuring knowledge management

Building a knowledge management capability requires an integrated approach that involves people, process and technology. In this section, we will consider some of the most important components that can help any BDCoE to take the steps to grow this capability.

To consider the components of effective knowledge management, we can first consider what an ideal situation would look like. In the ideal BDCoE, a new data analyst who just joined the organization is first formally onboarded, with proper instructions as to where key information can be found. The data analyst gets access to an extensive knowledge base, where there are hundreds of questions with their respective answers. Additionally, the new data analyst is assigned a mentor, who helps with questions that are not in the knowledge base. The mentor periodically sits down with the new hire to help get answers to questions and has the time to follow up on outstanding questions.

On the first project the data analyst is involved in, the analyst needs to combine different data sources to make a prediction for a client, based on an established machine learning model. The assignment is properly described, as established in the service catalogue, and a budget has been agreed. To accomplish this project, the data analyst logs into the organization's data catalogue, where all company data is neatly ordered and sorted. There are proper descriptions about each data sets, and indications about the quality and source of the data. Based on this input data, the data analyst starts building their machine learning model. In the knowledge base, he or she finds a similar project that was conducted six months ago by a different analyst. In this knowledge article, the analyst retrieves the script and codebook. Because the script is properly commented, and there are clear descriptions of all the variables used, the analyst can reuse a significant part of the earlier developed script, which speeds up the delivery time drastically. It even means that there is plenty of time available for the analyst to contribute their own knowledge article, and a detailed description as to how he or she tackled their first project for the organization, using all the steps above.

Does the scenario above sound like a utopia? For most people who are working in Big Data the answer is probably yes. But that does not mean that it should be this way. By building the knowledge management capability, every organization can get (at least a few steps) closer to the scenario listed above. This scenario additionally (and deliberately) gives some practical pointers that explain how knowledge management can be structured.

Onboarding programme

The first crucial step in enabling any new team member to get up to speed quickly is to establish a formal onboarding programme for new joiners. There are many benefits of setting up a structured onboarding programme, many of which go beyond just the scope of knowledge management. A formalized onboarding programme enables new team members of the BDCoE to get up to speed quickly on the ways in which an organization works, it processes and procedures.

Creating an onboarding programme additionally forces any organization to think about the knowledge they would like to transfer during the onboarding programme. Knowledge deemed important therefore needs to be captured and documented. In this way, the onboarding programme will also drive the documentation of established work procedures. It requires a documented approach (i.e. knowledge) where certain information can be found, and where any employee can find the answers to questions. Because most onboarding programmes are typically done in batches or cohorts, it also provides an opportunity for new joiners to immediately create a small network of peers, that can be used for any follow-up programmes.

Knowledge management system

To make it possible to store and share knowledge effectively and efficiently, every BDCoE needs to have a **knowledge management system (KMS)**, in most organizations better known as a knowledge base. A KMS is a software tool that enables anyone in the organization to create and store knowledge, and to efficiently search and find information.

A good KMS is a software tool that is easy to use, graphically intuitive, logically structured and provides answers to its users quickly. It has functionality where people can comment on knowledge articles, ask questions and where other users can 'upvote' the most useful information. Many good tools exist, but only very few BDCoEs are using these tools. If a KMS is even in place, it is often clunky, limited in features and functionality, and not well supported.

Most Big Data professionals, regardless of their role, rely extensively on KMSs for their day-to-day job. Yet instead of internal knowledge management systems, they rely on external platforms such as YouTube and Stack Overflow. Although these are great platforms by themselves, and provide the answers to many questions, from an enterprise perspective there are two problems. First, the use of external platforms will not **embed** knowledge in the organization. There is no long-term enterprise value if individuals contribute knowledge to external platforms. Secondly, these public platforms are unsuitable to discuss proprietary or confidential information. If, for example, an organization is building algorithms that provide a competitive advantage, it would be unwise to publish information about these algorithms in the public domain.

A common and frequently heard argument against starting to use an enterprise Knowledge Management System is that internal BDCoEs are small, and therefore the value of an internal KMS is limited (compared to public platforms). Although this argument is initially true, a knowledge base does need to start somewhere. Additionally, the creation of every new article will add value to the knowledge base, even after the people who wrote them have long left the organization. The establishment of an internal KMS should therefore be considered a long-term strategic initiative, one in which the organization will only reap the rewards sometime later.

Mentor-mentee programmes

Since Big Data is a technical complex domain, a lot can be learned from experience. Data analysts or data scientists who have been working in an organization for longer periods of times have frequently seen more bugs, problems and errors, and generally know how to solve common issues. From a knowledge management perspective, it is therefore tremendously valuable if more experienced team members share their knowledge with more junior team members.

Although this will already happen informally in many organizations, the establishment of a formal mentor-mentee programme creates a structural way of knowledge transfer. In a mentor-mentee programme, a more senior leader is coupled with a less experienced employee, so that he or she can help the other get up to speed more quickly. For the more junior role, it also provides a first stop for any questions.

Knowledge-sharing culture

So far, we have discussed several very practical aspects for growing the knowledge management capability in the Big Data Center of Excellence. Onboarding programmes, a knowledge management system and mentor-mentee programmes are all components that can be achieved through projects. With a certain budget and a responsible project manager, these activities can all be executed within a reasonable amount of time.

The last aspect is, however, slightly more difficult. To get the knowledge management capability to higher levels of maturity, a knowledge-sharing culture is required. By knowledge-sharing culture, we mean an organization where the sharing of knowledge and information comes naturally to its employees, and where knowledge sharing activities are happening on an ongoing basis.

In a BDCoE with a knowledge sharing culture, it is natural for people to exchange ideas and share knowledge. People create knowledge articles because they like to share their work, instead of being told that they need to create work. They actively look for new developments and technologies, and brief the organization accordingly, and they actively organize knowledge-sharing sessions.

The question of course is how to establish such a knowledge-sharing culture. And unfortunately, there is no one uniform answer to this. Case studies from successful knowledge-sharing cultures suggest that ongoing communication (about the importance of knowledge sharing) and management examples are crucial factors, but also that knowledge sharing is driven by personal preferences and habits.[5] It requires a continual effort to recognize knowledge-sharing efforts, measurement of contributions and ongoing effort to 'sell' the benefits.[6] The combination of all these efforts will gradually result in an organizational culture where knowledge sharing becomes second nature, and where the utopian scenario that was discussed at the beginning of this section might become a reality.

35.4 Knowledge management summary

The first critical capability that we discussed as part of the enterprise Big Data function is knowledge management. To build an effective and efficient Big Data organization, it is crucial that knowledge is shared across the BDCoE. Although much focus in Big Data is aimed at technology, the knowledge that is necessary to deduct value from massive data is primarily in people's heads.

The knowledge management capability's objective is to capture the information in those beautiful minds and translate this knowledge into something that is shareable across the organization. This way, lasting value will be created, even if some people move on in later stages to retire or pursue other career opportunities.

Setting and growing a knowledge management capability is difficult, and few organizations manage to move past the basic levels of maturity. The most difficult objective is to create a culture in which there is continual focus on the creation, distribution and sharing of knowledge. In this chapter, we have provided some best practices and guidance on steps that organizations can take to start building their knowledge management capability.

Notes

1 S Erickson and H Rothberg. Big data and knowledge management: establishing a conceptual foundation, *Leading Issues in Knowledge Management*, 2015 2, 204

2 A Brand. Knowledge management and innovation at 3M, *Journal of Knowledge Management*, 1998

3 J Liebowitz. 'Think of others' in knowledge management: making culture work for you, *Knowledge Management Research & Practice*, 2008 6 (1), 47–51

4 A Perrin, P Vidal and C Jennifer McGill (2004) Valuing knowledge management in organizations, from theory to practice: the case of Lafarge group, https://scholar.google. com/scholar?hl=en&as_sdt=0%2C5&q=A+Perrin%2C+P+Vidal+and+C+Jennifer+McGill+%282004%29+Valuing+knowledge+management+in+organizations%2C+from+theory+to+practice%3A+the+case+of+Lafarge+group&btnG= (archived at https://perma.cc/TL69-5UG8)

5 D Gurteen. Creating a knowledge sharing culture, *Knowledge Management Magazine*, 1999 2 (5), 1–4

6 H A Smith and J D McKeen. Instilling a knowledge-sharing culture, *Queen's Centre for Knowledge-Based Enterprises*, 2003 20 (1), 1–17

Big Data Catalogue 36
of Services

36.1 Introduction to a Big Data catalogue of services

The Big Data Centre of Excellence (BDCoE) provides a uniform entry point for the rest of the organization to request data insights and services. It is typically structured as an independent function or unit, mostly as a part of the IT department. Because it is a uniform entry point for the business to request Big Data services, it should be clear to the rest of the organization which services the BDCoE provides. For that reason, a BDCoE should have a comprehensive service catalogue that outlines which services the BDCoE provides, including the expected service levels and (if appliable) costs involved.

Whereas most commercial, externally facing Big Data organizations have a clearly defined service catalogue – this is, after all, what they sell to their customers – most internal BDCoEs have not defined which services they specifically offer. As a result, usually other business functions find it difficult to explain what the BDCoE offers.

Establishing a well-defined BDCoE catalogue of services has many advantages. First of all, it forces the BDCoE leadership to consider which services they will provide to the business as 'standardized services', and which services they consider out of scope or on request only. For standardized services (for instance algorithm design or data catalogue management), the team can define target service levels (to measure performance) and costs (to cross-charge different departments). As with any business function, the BDCoE needs to make choices on what services they provide, with which technology and with which scope. The exercise of creating a service catalogue will help with that decision-making process.

The second main benefit is that the service catalogue provides clarity to the business. A marketing executive, for example, who wants to engage the internal BDCoE to predict the best marketing spend, can browse through the service catalogue to easily determine if the internal BDCoE team delivers these services, at what costs and with which service levels. Based on the information in the service catalogue, the marketing executive can then determine whether the offering meets his or her requirements. In this second goal, the service catalogue functions as the proverbial 'menu' in a restaurant. It makes it clear what you can order, and at which pricing.

You can always ask the kitchen to prepare something that is not on the menu, but there might be additional costs involved.

The third and final benefit is that the service catalogue provides clarity to internal staff within the BDCoE. Different team members can be assigned to different services (as defined in the catalogue) and product or service improvement can be focused on some specific services. Newly developed services can be added to the service catalogue, and services that are no longer required (i.e. retired) can be taken down. In this capacity, the service catalogue outlines to the rest of the team which services are active, who is responsible for each service (i.e. the service owner) and which teams are providing support for different services.

The three reasons above are compelling for any BDCoE to start defining or professionalizing their service catalogue. In the next few sections, we will determine the scope, maturity levels and best practices through which to structure this capability.

36.2 Purpose and maturity levels of a Big Data catalogue of services

Purpose

The concept of a service catalogue is nothing new. It is in fact a practice that many IT organizations use to describe their support service and to describe their service levels. The service catalogue has its roots in IT service management, where IT departments needed to find a way to manage their ever-growing and complex IT offering to the business.[1] Many valuable lessons and approaches from this domain serve the BDCoE well and can be adapted to provide clarity in the services that the BDCoE provides.

In line with the three main benefits of the service catalogue discussed in the previous section, the Big Data service catalogue should be written with three common audiences in mind:

1 **Customer view:** the service catalogue as 'a menu', which outlines which service the BDCoE provides and against which services.

2 **Internal view:** the service catalogue as an internal document that outlines which services the BDCoE needs to deliver, and which expertise and resources are required to deliver these services.

3 **Management view:** the service catalogue as a management tool that enables management to assign resources to individual services, measure performance of individual services and formulate improvement initiatives.

Table 36.1   The purpose of the service catalogue capability

Capability	Purpose
Service catalogue	Defines the ability of an organization to define which Big Data and data science services they provide to internal and external customers, including offered service levels and costs.

A well-defined service catalogue captures all three different perspectives, and (depending on the audience) showcases information. The purpose of a BDCoE catalogue of services can be captured as shown in Table 36.1.

A quick glance at this definition of a service catalogue outlines three distinct elements that need to be considered in establishing a well-defined catalogue of services. The individual services need to be defined, the terms and conditions against which these services are offered (i.e. the service levels) and lastly the costs at which those services are offered.

To illustrate this with an example, consider the finance department of an insurance provider that wants to engage the BDCoE to develop an algorithm to predict a risk score for new insurance applicants. In their service catalogue, the BDCoE has an algorithm development and support service, which outlines that the development of an algorithm requires two weeks and will be delivered in the form of a web application (for entering customer data and receiving a risk score) with a 99 per cent uptime. The one-time algorithm development fee for internal cross-charging will be $40,000 and the annual maintenance fees (for keeping the application up and running) will be $35,000 per year. This information immediately makes it clear to all parties involved what the expectation back and forth will be, even if the parties are working for the same organization. Note that the fees in the example above are just random examples.

Maturity levels

The creation, application and scope of the use of an BDCoE service catalogue is, from a maturity perspective, easy to measure. A service catalogue is either established or not, and it is either actively used or not in operation. The five different levels can be defined as listed in the Table 36.2.

The five different levels provide additional depth and increased maturity over time. From level 3 onwards, it is recommended to appoint a service catalogue manager role, a person who is responsible for maintaining the accuracy and information in the BDCoE service catalogue, and who drives improvement initiatives.[2]

Table 36.2   Maturity levels of the knowledge management capability

Maturity Level	Description
Level 1 – Initial	A basic and documented service catalogue is in place that describes the Big Data services that the BDCoE provides. The service catalogue is a standalone document and is not further integrated in any business practices.
Level 2 – Managed	A comprehensive service catalogue exists, which describes the service the BDCoE provides, and which is coupled to service levels. Agreements with internal and external customers are based on the documented services in the service catalogue.
Level 3 – Defined	The service catalogue functions as the primary entry point for internal and external customers. It is easily accessible and describes services, service levels and costs. The service catalogue is integrated in a system or tools, so it can be easily accessed by the rest of the organization.
Level 4 – Controlled	There are processes in place to actively maintain the items and services in the service catalogue. There is a structured process for adding new Big Data service to the service catalogue, and there is a process to periodically remove retired services.
Level 5 – Optimized	The service catalogue is continuously monitored and updated. There are metrics and KPIs in place that measure the quality of information in the service catalogue. Based on these measurements, the quality of the service catalogue is continually improved.

36.3 Structuring a Big Data catalogue of services

Building a service catalogue from scratch that outlines the Big Data services that the BDCoE provides is a time-consuming but rewarding exercise. It forces management to rethink its service offering, and frequently provides opportunity for improvements, like the rationalization of the portfolio. It helps find answers to questions like, why are we delivering these services in the first place? Do the insights the BDCoE provides provide business value? And are there combinations of services that can be offered that complement or enhance each other?

Since Big Data and Big Data functions are relatively new, very few organizations have already taken the steps to define a service catalogue for Big Data services. In this chapter, we will therefore provide some guidance on how to establish a Big Data service catalogue from scratch and explain the recommended steps to get results quickly based on established best practices. We will also consider some examples of well-established service catalogues and define some KPIs that can be useful to determine the success of the service catalogue.

Steps to defining a Big Data catalogue of services

There are many ways to define a service catalogue for Big Data services. As a general first step, it is important to recognize that building a service catalogue is a team exercise within the BDCoE. It requires teams to think about the way they currently deliver services, and to document that into a comprehensive service offering. Developing a service catalogue is therefore an iterative process, requiring the input of multiple stakeholders over a series of rounds. Determining the service itself is usually not the most difficult part; it is generally the definition of service levels (i.e. the terms against which services are delivered) and the identification of the proper cost model that are the most time-consuming.

Creating a service catalogue can be done in several steps, which cover the initial planning activities, documentation, communication and evaluation, as depicted in Figure 36.1.[3]

Figure 36.1   Defining a Big Data service catalogue

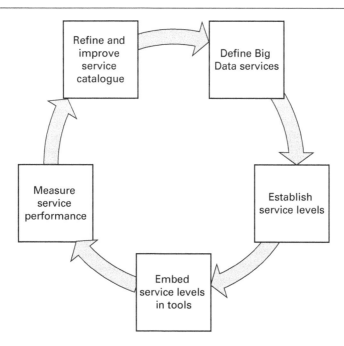

The five steps can be summarized as follows:

1. Define Big Data services

The first and obvious step in the creation of a BDCoE catalogue of services is to define the services themselves. Although it might seem a simple exercise (it is after all, defining the work that is actually done), there are a number of important elements to take into consideration. A well-defined BDCoE service catalogue offers a comprehensive number of services. The services need to be defined in enough detail so it is clear for all stakeholders (internal view, external view and management) what the services are that can be delivered. However, on the other hand, a service catalogue that contains hundreds of services is not useful, because it will confuse stakeholders over which services are delivered.

So, what is a good number of services to offer? Depending on the size of the organization, and the maturity of their BDCoE, a comprehensive overview typically has five–seven categories, with about three–five different services per category. This means that on average, a BDCoE service catalogue has around 15–35 different services defined. Enough to provide sufficient detail, and comprehensive enough to make it explainable to the internal and external stakeholders.

Common categories that are used in the BDCoE are (in no particular order of importance):

- **Algorithm design:** Services for the design of specific algorithms.
- **Analytics and insights:** Services that provide periodic or real-time management information and reports that support executive decision-making. In most cases, this includes comprehensive data visualization services.
- **Data catalogue services:** Services that focus on the structuring and maintenance of an up-to-date service catalogue.
- **Data engineering:** Services that involve the building and creation of data pipelines that support batch and real-time data.
- **Data literacy:** Services that enhance knowledge sharing and education across the enterprise.
- **Support services:** Supporting the rest of the organization with ad hoc requests, immediate management information or support in case of knowledge requests, errors or other problems.

Data catalogues are discussed in more detail in Chapter 16. The topic of data literacy – because it is such a crucial function in the BDCoE – is discussed in further detail in Chapter 39.

2. Establish service levels

After the individual services have been defined (for example a data ingestion service), the next step is to define the appropriate service levels of each individual service. Service levels are based on the enterprise size, strategic dependency on the BDCoE and budgetary constraints. For example, for the same data ingestion service, the defined service level will be that the service is executed within 48 hours, support is provided from 08:00–18:00 during office hours and that the imported data is accessible 24/7 through the data catalogue.

Most organizations start with defining a reference service level per service and, as maturity grows, gradually introduce more complex forms of service levels. A common approach is to indicate certain packages (gold, silver, bronze) that provide different levels of services. The gold package could, for example, include higher availability or speed, compared to a silver package.

Another common approach, although slightly more complex to manage, is to provide different service levels per customer. For example, this might mean that the trading division of a bank receives a higher level of service that the marketing department. Because the trading division is more strategic and requires real-time insights in the market, it receives a higher service level. Obviously, this also results in higher levels of cross-charges, in line with the higher level of services.

Defining service levels enables the management team to think about the way they deliver services, and against which terms. The result of this exercise is to have documented service levels, which are typically put into agreements with customers as service level agreements (or SLAs).[4] These SLAs then provide the agreement between the BDCoE and their internal or external customer. By using SLAs, it becomes clear for all parties involved what the expectations are and which targets and KPIs can be measured to determine whether the 'right' service level are being achieved (see step 4).

3. Embed service levels in tools

A BDCoE that has defined its services and service levels will need to make its catalogue available to its internal or external customers. This means that the service catalogue must be clear, comprehensible and preferably nicely formatted.

Since a service catalogue contains quite some information and needs to be updated periodically, the most comprehensive solution is to use some automated tool to distribute its contents to customers. Many good and reliable service catalogue tools exist, with varying forms of functionalities and cost structures.[5] What most tools have in common is that they provide graphical webpage interfaces, where customers can browse and select services. These tools make it easy to always provide stakeholders with the right amount of information.

Besides adequate service descriptions and accompanying service levels, it is also recommended to put some effort into the graphic design and look and feel of the digital service catalogue, a point which is neglected in many organizations. A service catalogue that looks nice immediately leaves a professional impression to prospective customers as well as (prospective) BDCoE employees. Consider that the service catalogue is frequently the first interface that other business units or clients have with the BDCoE. And as the famous poet Oscar Wilde said, you never get a second chance to leave a first impression.[6]

4. Measure service performance

One of the main benefits of defining service levels (see step 2) is that it provides measurable targets. This is primarily beneficial for management because it provides an unbiased and objective approach to measure the quality of different services. With service levels, it is immediately possible to determine which services are performing well and which services might need quality improvement. For larger organizations, which typically have different teams on different services, it also provides input on which teams are performing well.

To measure the agreed service levels for different customers, some form of performance management needs to be installed. The identified metrics as KPIs in themselves are useless if they are not actively monitored. Performance of service therefore needs to measured daily, and preferably in an automated manner. As you might expect, most service catalogue tools (discussed in step 3) have modules available for performance management. Besides defining services, these tools can be used for service monitoring and reporting. When selecting a toolset, it is therefore recommended to consider the measurement of service performance levels and service level agreements as well.

5. Refine and improve service catalogue

The final step of defining a service catalogue brings us back to the beginning, making it a life cycle approach. It is clear that defining and maintaining an adequate service catalogue is a process that is never finished. There is always opportunity for improvement, and there is always an opportunity for further enhancement.

Based on the measurements from step 4, an organization obtains valuable information about which services are performing well and which ones might need to be improved. This data (although not Big Data) can drive further optimization, quality improvement and ultimately increase performance to customers. This continual focus on improvement can help make the service catalogue one of the strongest backbones of the BDCoE.

Components of a BDCoE service catalogue

In the previous section, we discussed the main steps that organizations can take to define and establish a BDCoE catalogue of services. To make it more comprehensive, the following box showcases an example of a Big Data service, complete with corresponding service levels and cost structure.

Big Data catalogue item for Big Data pipeline service

Service: Big Data pipeline

Description: A Big Data pipeline service provides a fully managed pipeline for ingesting, processing and storing large amounts of structured and unstructured data, leveraging the latest Big Data technologies such as Apache Hadoop, Apache Spark and Apache Kafka.

Service level agreement (SLA):

- Availability: 99.9% uptime guarantee
- Data processing throughput: minimum of 10,000 records per second
- Data storage: minimum of 10 terabytes of storage capacity
- Support: 24/7 technical support

Cost example:

- Set-up fee: $10,000 (one-time fee)
- Monthly fee: $25,000 (for up to 10 terabytes of storage and 10,000 records per second)
- Additional storage: $1,000 per terabyte per month
- Additional data processing throughput: $5,000 per 10,000 records per second per month
- Additional technical support: $500 per hour

Important note: these SLAs and cost examples are for illustrative purposes only and may vary depending on the vendor and specific requirements of the organization.

36.4 Big Data catalogue of services summary

In order to formulate which Big Data services an organization is providing to internal and external customers, a defined and well-managed Big Data catalogue of services is indispensable. The Big Data catalogue of services capability enables an organization to define which Big Data and data science services they provide to internal and external customers, including offered service levels and costs.

By defining a Big Data catalogue of services, organizations can standardize their approach to Big Data, making it easier for different teams and stakeholders to understand what services are available, how they work, and what their benefits and limitations are.

Additionally, as we have seen throughout this chapter, a Big Data catalogue of services can help organizations optimize their Big Data operations by identifying the most effective and efficient tools and technologies for specific use cases. This can reduce duplication of effort and enable organizations to focus their resources on the areas that will provide the greatest impact.

Notes

1   V Mazvimavi and R V Benyon (2009) A Theoretical Model for Developing an IT Service Catalogue. In CONF-IRM 2009 Proceedings
2   C Mendes and M M da Silva (2010) Implementing the service catalogue management. In 2010 Seventh International Conference on the Quality of Information and Communications Technology, September, 159–64. IEEE
3   V Mazvimavi and R V Benyon (2009) A Theoretical Model for Developing an IT Service Catalogue. In CONF-IRM 2009 Proceedings
4   A Wegmann, G Regev, G A Garret and F Maréchal (2008) Specifying services for ITIL service management. In 2008 International Workshop on Service-Oriented Computing: Consequences for Engineering Requirements, September, 8–14. IEEE
5   M O'Loughlin (2010) *The Service Catalog*. Van Haren.
6   M J Harris and C P Garris (2008) *You Never Get a Second Chance to Make a First Impression: Behavioral consequences of first impressions*. Guilford Publications

Workforce and Talent Planning 37

37.1 Introduction to workforce and talent planning

The workforce and talent planning capability in the Big Data Centre of Excellence (BDCoE) is the process of identifying, attracting, developing, and retaining the right people with the right skills to effectively leverage Big Data to achieve business objectives.

In a BDCoE, workforce planning involves analysing the company's strategic goals, identifying the critical skills and competencies needed to achieve those goals and assessing the current workforce to identify gaps in skills and capabilities. This analysis helps the organization identify the roles and responsibilities needed to support its Big Data initiatives, and then develop a plan for recruiting, training and developing the necessary talent.

Talent planning, on the other hand, focuses on identifying and developing individuals with the potential to meet the organization's future needs. This involves identifying high-potential employees, assessing their strengths and areas for development, and providing opportunities for training and development to ensure that they have the skills and experience needed to support the company's Big Data initiatives.

The workforce and talent planning capability is essential for Big Data organizations for several reasons:

- **Big Data requires specialized skills:** Leveraging Big Data requires specialized skills such as data analysis, data science, machine learning and programming. These skills are in high demand, and the competition for top talent is fierce. Therefore, it is critical for Big Data organizations to have a well-planned workforce and talent strategy to attract and retain the necessary skilled professionals.

- **Talent scarcity:** As mentioned earlier, the demand for skilled Big Data professionals far exceeds the supply, making it difficult for organizations to find and retain top talent. Workforce and talent planning can help Big Data organizations identify critical skills gaps and develop strategies to address them proactively.

- **Changing technologies and business needs:** The field of Big Data is constantly evolving, with new technologies and tools emerging regularly. Workforce and talent planning helps Big Data organizations stay ahead of the curve by identifying emerging trends and technologies and ensuring that they have the necessary skills and talent to take advantage of them.

- **Success of Big Data initiatives:** Big Data initiatives can be costly and time-consuming, and their success depends heavily on the skills and experience of the people involved. Workforce and talent planning can help Big Data organizations ensure that they have the right people in the right roles to deliver successful outcomes.

The workforce and talent planning capability is essential for any BDCoE to attract, retain and develop the necessary talent to effectively leverage data and achieve business objectives.

37.2 Purpose and maturity levels of workforce and talent planning

Purpose

Because the demand for Big Data knowledge and expertise is ever growing, the need to structure a mature workforce and talent capability is equally increasing. The purpose of a workforce and talent planning capability is to ensure that an organization has the right people with the right skills in the right roles to achieve its strategic goals.

A well-designed workforce and talent planning capability can help organizations proactively address current and future skills gaps, anticipate and respond to changes in business needs, and foster a culture of continuous learning and development.

The purpose of the workforce and talent planning capability is outlined in Table 37.1.

Table 37.1   The purpose of the workforce and talent planning capability

Capability	Purpose
Workforce and talent planning	Defines the ability of an organization to manage the Big Data workforce to ensure adequate availability of competent employees.

Maturity levels

An organization with a high maturity level in workforce and talent planning would have a well-developed and integrated talent management strategy that aligns with the organization's overall business objectives. Such an organization would have a deep understanding of its workforce, including the skills and capabilities of its employees, as well as the talent market trends and supply and demand of specific skills in the industry.

Any BDCoE that has a high maturity level in this capability can be identified by the following three characteristics:

- **Strategic alignment:** The organization's workforce and talent planning initiatives are aligned with its strategic goals and objectives. The talent management strategy is a core part of the organization's overall business strategy, and there is a clear understanding of how talent management can contribute to achieving those goals.

- **Continuous evaluation:** The organization continuously evaluates its workforce and talent planning strategies to ensure they remain relevant and effective. The organization tracks key metrics such as turnover rates, time-to-fill vacancies and employee engagement, and uses data-driven insights to adjust its strategies accordingly.

- **Comprehensive talent management practices:** The organization has comprehensive talent management practices that cover the entire employee life cycle, including attracting, developing, engaging and retaining employees. These practices are aligned with the organization's values, culture and business strategy, and are consistently applied across the organization. A comprehensive overview of these practices will be discussed in section 37.3.

Organizations can assess their workforce and talent planning capability by the five levels of maturity shown in Table 37.2.

Table 37.2   Maturity levels of the workforce and talent planning capability

Maturity Level	Description
Level 1 – Initial	The organization does not have a formal workforce and talent planning process in place. There is limited coordination between HR and business leaders, and little focus on workforce analytics or skills assessment.
Level 2 – Managed	The organization is beginning to develop a more formal workforce and talent planning capability. There is a focus on skills assessment, and HR and business leaders are starting to collaborate more closely to identify critical skills and competencies.

(*continued*)

Table 37.2 (Continued)

Maturity Level	Description
Level 3 – Defined	The organization has a well-defined workforce and talent planning process in place. There is a clear understanding of the skills and competencies needed to achieve business goals, and HR and business leaders work together to develop and execute talent strategies.
Level 4 – Controlled	The organization has a comprehensive workforce and talent planning capability that is fully integrated into its overall business strategy. There is a strong focus on data analytics and metrics to measure the effectiveness of talent strategies, and there is ongoing monitoring and adjustment of talent plans as business needs evolve.
Level 5 – Optimized	The organization has achieved a high level of maturity in its workforce and talent planning capability. The organization is continuously innovating and improving its talent strategies, leveraging advanced analytics and predictive modelling. People, talent and skills are considered a strategic asset in the BDCoE.

It is crucial for a BDCoE to have a mature workforce and talent planning capability. A mature workforce and talent planning capability helps a BDCoE ensure that it has the right people with the right skills and competencies to deliver high-quality solutions that meet the needs of the business.

37.3 Structuring workforce and talent planning

To structure the workforce and talent planning capability in an effective way, organizations need the HR department and BDCoE to join forces. HR and the BDCoE need to collaborate closely to structure workforce and talent planning successfully. HR brings expertise in talent management, recruitment, employee development, and compensation and benefits, while the BDCoE brings expertise in Big Data and analytics.

Collaboration between HR and the BDCoE can help ensure that the talent strategy aligns with the organization's business strategy and that it addresses the specific needs of the BDCoE. HR can help the BDCoE identify critical skills, assess the current workforce's capabilities, and develop targeted recruitment and employee development programmes. The BDCoE can help HR understand the specific technical skills and competencies needed to deliver Big Data solutions and identify opportunities for employee development and upskilling. Both departments need to work together to establish a number of activities, as outlined in the rest of this chapter.

Identification of critical skills

A workforce and talent planning capability helps organizations identify the critical skills and competencies needed to achieve their strategic objectives. This involves analysing current and future business needs, assessing the workforce's capabilities and identifying gaps in skills and experience.

Identifying critical skills for a BDCoE requires a thorough understanding of the organization's business strategy, goals and objectives. Here are some activities an organization can take to identify critical skills and increase their maturity levels:

- **Understand the business strategy:** The BDCoE's critical skills must align with the organization's business strategy. Therefore, it's crucial to understand the organization's business strategy, goals and objectives to identify the critical skills needed to achieve them.

- **Conduct a skills gap analysis:** The organization should conduct a skills gap analysis to identify the current skills and competencies of the BDCoE's workforce and compare them to the skills and competencies required to achieve the business strategy. This analysis can be done through surveys, interviews and assessments.

- **Identify emerging technologies and trends:** The BDCoE should keep track of emerging technologies and trends that may impact the organization's business strategy. This includes understanding the latest developments in artificial intelligence, machine learning and data science. For example, new developments like generative AI might require new knowledge and skills.

- **Consult with subject matter experts:** The BDCoE should consult with subject matter experts, both internal and external, to identify critical skills. This includes speaking with data scientists, analytics experts and other Big Data professionals to understand the skills and competencies needed to deliver high-quality Big Data solutions.

- **Look at successful BDCoEs:** The organization can also look at successful BDCoEs within its industry or other industries to identify critical skills. This can be done through research or by speaking with other organizations' BDCoE leaders to understand the skills and competencies needed to achieve success.

A thorough identification of critical skills can help ensure that the BDCoE has the necessary skills and competencies to deliver high-quality Big Data solutions that meet the organization's business objectives.

Attracting and retaining top talent

A mature workforce and talent planning capability helps organizations attract and retain top talent by developing targeted recruitment strategies and offering competitive compensation and benefits packages. It also helps organizations identify and address factors that may contribute to employee turnover, such as inadequate training and development opportunities.

Attracting and retaining top talent is not easy, especially in today's global competitive market. However, it is critical for the success of a BDCoE. The first thing to think about is that the BDCoE of any organization should offer competitive salaries and benefits to attract and retain top talent. This includes providing generous bonuses, stock options and other incentives that reward top performers.

Additionally, a positive work environment is essential for attracting and retaining top talent. The BDCoE should create a culture that fosters creativity, collaboration and innovation. This includes providing a flexible work schedule, opportunities for professional development and a supportive leadership team.

Lastly, and maybe most importantly, every BDCoE should provide challenging work. Top talent wants to work on challenging and meaningful projects. The BDCoE should provide opportunities for employees to work on projects that have a real impact on the organization's business objectives. This includes providing opportunities to work with emerging technologies and cutting-edge tools.

Developing employees

A workforce and talent planning capability helps organizations develop their employees by providing opportunities for training, mentoring and career development. This can include creating career paths and development plans for employees and offering targeted training programmes to address skills gaps.

Developing employees and addressing skills gaps are critical for the success of a BDCoE. Some of the main learnings, taken from HR best practices, include:

- **Provide training and development opportunities:** The BDCoE should provide training and development opportunities to help employees acquire new skills and knowledge. This includes offering formal training programmes, workshops and on-the-job training opportunities. The BDCoE should also provide opportunities for employees to attend conferences and participate in industry events.

- **Provide mentorship and coaching:** Mentorship and coaching are essential for employee development. The BDCoE should provide employees with access to mentors and coaches who can guide them in their career development.

- **Encourage cross-functional collaboration:** Encouraging cross-functional collaboration can help employees develop new skills and learn from their colleagues.

The BDCoE should encourage employees to work with colleagues from different departments and disciplines.

- **Provide access to emerging technologies and tools:** The BDCoE should provide employees with access to emerging technologies and tools. This includes providing access to cutting-edge tools and technologies like artificial intelligence, machine learning and data science.

- **Create a culture of continuous learning:** The BDCoE should create a culture of continuous learning, where employees are encouraged to learn and grow throughout their careers. This includes providing opportunities for employees to give and receive feedback, and creating a culture of experimentation and innovation.

By implementing these strategies, a BDCoE can ensure that its employees have the skills and competencies needed to deliver high-quality Big Data solutions that meet the organization's business objectives. More details about employee development will be discussed in Chapter 38, which will cover the education and skills development capability.

Responding to changing business needs

A workforce and talent planning capability helps organizations anticipate and respond to changes in business needs by proactively developing the skills and capabilities required to meet those needs. This involves monitoring trends and changes in the industry, analysing the workforce's current skills and capabilities, and identifying areas where additional training or development may be needed.

By structuring this capability to a mature level, workforce and talent planning can facilitate **agile workforce planning**. This involves creating a flexible workforce that can adapt quickly to changing business needs. By having a talent strategy in place, organizations can quickly identify the skills and competencies required to meet changing business needs and take steps to acquire or develop those skills.

This strategy additionally plays a significant role in proper succession planning. **Succession planning** involves identifying and developing talent within the organization to ensure a smooth transition of leadership and management roles. By identifying talent with the potential to fill key roles within the organization, workforce and talent planning can ensure that the organization is well-prepared for changes in leadership.

37.4 Workforce and talent planning summary

People are the most important asset of any Big Data Centre of Excellence and any Big Data function. The workforce and talent planning capability helps organizations to proactively manage the workforce and provides the activities to attract and retain talent with the necessary skills to operate the BDCoE.

Workforce and talent planning is a mix in which the HR department needs to work very closely with the BDCoE. This collaboration, if properly structured, can ensure that the organization provides a function where people like to work. Throughout this chapter, we have covered some of the most important aspects of workforce and talent planning, including the need to identify critical skills, the ways in which an organization can attract and retain top talent and the programmes necessary to develop the workforce.

By structuring the workforce and talent planning capability in an organized way, organizations can appropriately respond to changing business needs. With rapidly evolving technology in Big Data, it is imperative that the BDCoE remains agile to respond to different business needs.

Education and Skills Development

38

38.1 Introduction to education and skills development

The education and skills development capability builds on, and is integrated with, two other capabilities that we have discussed in this book before. In the innovation management capability (discussed in Chapter 7), we looked at how innovation is continuously pushing the world of Big Data forwards.

To establish innovation, organizations need to ensure employees remain up to date with the latest technology, and continuously trained for new skills. Additionally, in Chapter 37, we discussed the workforce and talent planning capability. To attract and retain a professional Big Data workforce, a suitable education and skills development programme needs to be established.

Education and skills development is an organization's capability of acquiring new knowledge, skills and abilities that enable individuals to perform better in their current roles or to prepare for future roles.[1] Education can involve formal academic programmes, while skill development can be achieved through various methods, such as training, coaching, mentoring or on-the-job learning.

Education and skills development are essential for individuals to adapt to the changing demands of the job market and for organizations to stay competitive. With the rapid advancements in technology and the increasing complexity of business operations, education and skills development have become crucial for employees to acquire new skills and stay up to date with industry trends.

Education and skills development in a Big Data Center of Excellence can take place at different levels, such as technical, behavioural, or managerial. Technical education and skills development focuses on job-specific competencies, such as programming, data analysis, or algorithm design.[2] Behavioural education and skills development focuses on soft skills, such as communication, teamwork, or problem-solving. Managerial education and skills development focuses on leadership, strategy, and decision-making.

The education and skills development capability is especially important in a Big Data Centre of Excellence (BDCoE) for several reasons:

- **Rapidly evolving technology:** The field of Big Data is rapidly evolving, with new technologies, tools and techniques being developed all the time. To stay current and effective in their roles, employees in a BDCoE need to constantly update their skills and knowledge.

- **Diverse skill sets:** A BDCoE typically requires a range of skills, from data engineering and analysis to data visualization and storytelling. Education and skills development can help employees develop the specific skills they need to contribute to the BDCoE's goals and objectives.

- **Cross-functional collaboration:** A BDCoE typically involves collaboration between different departments and functions, such as IT, marketing and finance. Education and skills development can help employees develop the communication, teamwork and problem-solving skills needed to work effectively in cross-functional teams.

- **Innovation:** As discussed in Chapter 34, a BDCoE is often responsible for driving innovation and identifying new opportunities for the organization. Education and skills development can help employees develop the critical thinking, creativity and adaptability needed to drive innovation and stay ahead of the competition.

- **Attracting and retaining top talent:** As discussed in Chapter 37, employees in a BDCoE are in high demand, and education and skills development opportunities can be a key factor in attracting and retaining top talent. By investing in the development of their employees, organizations can create a culture of continuous learning and growth, which can help to attract and retain the best and brightest talent in the field.

The education and skills development capability is essential in a BDCoE to stay current and effective in a rapidly evolving field, develop the necessary cross-functional collaboration and innovation skills, and attract and retain top talent.

38.2 Purpose and maturity levels of education and skills development

Purpose

The purpose of an educational and skills development capability in a BDCoE is to ensure that employees have the necessary knowledge and skills to effectively contribute to the BDCoE's goals and objectives.

The specific purposes of the educational and skills development capability are shown in Table 38.1.

Table 38.1   The purpose of the education and skills development capability

Capability	Purpose
Education and skills development	Defines the ability of an organization to set up educational programmes to increase knowledge about Big Data.

Education and skills development in a BDCoE should be a shared responsibility between various stakeholders, including the BDCoE itself, HR and the employees themselves.

The BDCoE should drive education and skills development by identifying the specific skills and knowledge areas that are needed to achieve the BDCoE's goals and objectives, and by creating training programmes, workshops and on-the-job learning opportunities that are tailored to the needs of the organization. The BDCoE can also partner with external training providers or academic institutions to ensure that employees have access to the latest knowledge and skills in the field.

HR should play a role in supporting education and skills development by providing resources and guidance for employees to access training and development opportunities. HR can also work with the BDCoE to identify skills gaps and develop training programmes that address these gaps.

Finally, employees themselves should take responsibility for their own education and skills development by seeking out learning opportunities and taking advantage of training programmes and workshops offered by the BDCoE and other sources. Employees can also work with their managers and HR to develop individualized learning and development plans that align with their career goals and the needs of the BDCoE.

Maturity levels

An organization that has a high maturity level in education and skills development will need to establish a culture of continuous learning. These organizations would have a culture that values continuous learning and development, with employees regularly participating in training and development programmes to keep their skills up to date and stay on top of industry trends.

In addition, an organization with a high maturity level in the education and skills development capability in a BDCoE would demonstrate a strong commitment to employee development and would have established a comprehensive range of training and development programmes to support the achievement of business objectives.

The five levels of maturity of the education and skills development capability are listed in Table 38.2.

Table 38.2   Maturity levels of the education and skills development capability

Maturity Level	Description
Level 1 – Initial	The organization has a simplistic approach to education and skills development, with no formal processes or practices in place. Training and development are generally reactive, based on employee requests, with little consideration given to the needs of the organization or individual employees.
Level 2 – Managed	The organization has established some basic processes and practices for education and skill development. There may be some formal training programmes in place, but these are generally not well-defined or aligned with the needs of the organization. Training and development are still largely reactive, with little emphasis on proactive planning.
Level 3 – Defined	The organization has established a formal education and skill development programme, with defined processes and practices in place. There is a focus on aligning training and development with the needs of the organization, and training is planned proactively to address skills gaps or support business objectives.
Level 4 – Controlled	The organization has established a data-driven approach to education and skills development. Training and development programmes are evaluated using metrics, and data is used to continuously improve the effectiveness of training and development efforts.
Level 5 – Optimized	The organization has achieved a high degree of maturity in education and skills development. The organization has a culture of continuous learning, with training and development programmes that are designed to support ongoing growth and development of employees. The organization is also actively seeking out new opportunities to improve its education and skills development programmes, and is constantly evolving its approach to stay ahead of industry trends and best practices.

Achieving a high maturity level in the education and skills development capability can be challenging, as it requires a significant investment of time, resources and effort. The level of difficulty in achieving a high maturity level can depend on several factors, including the size and complexity of the organization, the existing culture around education and skills development and the availability of resources to support these efforts.

Some of the challenges that organizations may face when working to achieve a high maturity level in this capability include:

- **Resistance to change:** Employees and leaders may be resistant to new approaches to education and skills development, particularly if these approaches require significant changes to existing processes and practices.

- **Limited resources:** Developing and delivering high-quality training programmes can be costly, and organizations may not have the necessary resources to invest in these efforts.

- **Lack of alignment:** It can be challenging to ensure that education and skills development programmes are aligned with the needs of the organization and that they are addressing the right skills and competencies.

- **Difficulty in measuring impact:** It can be difficult to measure the impact of education and skills development programmes on the organization, particularly if these efforts are not closely aligned with specific business objectives.

Despite these challenges, achieving a high maturity level in the education and skills development capability is achievable with the right approach and commitment. We will discuss ways in which to structure the education and skills development capability in the next section.

38.3 Structuring education and skills development

Establishing a structured education and skills development capability will bring significant, long-term benefits for an organization. An example of an organization with a high maturity in education and skills development is, for instance, IBM.[3] IBM has a strong culture of learning and development, with a focus on building skills and competencies that align with their business strategy. IBM offers a range of training and development programmes for employees, including formal courses, on-the-job training, mentoring and coaching.

One of the key elements of IBM's education and skills development programme is their online learning platform, IBM Skills Gateway. This platform provides employees with access to thousands of courses and learning resources that cover a range of topics, from technical skills to leadership and management development.

IBM also has a programme called 'SkillsBuild', which provides free online training and personalized coaching to help people develop in-demand skills for the digital economy. This programme is available to both IBM employees and external learners.

If we break down how IBM has built their education and skills development capability, we can extract a number of important practices. The practices involve developing a clear vision and strategy for education and skills development, establishing processes and practices to support these efforts, investing in high-quality training programmes and resources and regularly evaluating and measuring the impact of these programmes on the organization.

Education and skills development vision

Establishing a vision is an important first step in achieving a high maturity level in education and skills development. A clear vision statement helps to define the purpose and goals of the education and skills development programme, as well as communicating it to employees and stakeholders.

The vision statement should be aligned with the organization's overall strategic goals and objectives, and should consider factors such as the current state of the workforce, anticipated changes in the industry or market and the organization's culture and values.

An example of such a vision statement could be as follows:

> Our vision is to cultivate a workforce of highly skilled and innovative professionals who are equipped with the knowledge and expertise needed to drive the organization's success in a rapidly changing digital landscape. We aim to provide comprehensive and engaging learning opportunities that foster creativity, collaboration and continuous improvement, and to empower employees to take ownership of their own professional development. By investing in our employees' education and skills development, we will build a culture of learning that drives innovation, enhances organizational effectiveness and positions us as a leader in the industry.

Once a vision statement is established, the organization can then develop a plan for implementing the education and skills development programme, including identifying key stakeholders, defining specific goals and objectives, allocating resources and establishing metrics for measuring success.

Practices and processes to support learning

After the creation of a vision statement, developing processes and practices is essential to achieving a high maturity level in education and skills development. This includes establishing clear guidelines and procedures for identifying learning needs, selecting and delivering training programmes, evaluating their effectiveness and tracking employee progress and performance.

Some key processes and practices that organizations can develop to support the education and skills development capability in a BDCoE include:

- **Needs assessment:** Conducting regular assessments to identify the knowledge and skills gaps within the workforce and aligning learning initiatives with business needs.

- **Curriculum development:** Creating comprehensive and relevant training programmes that are tailored to the organization's specific needs and goals.

- **Delivery methods:** Providing a range of learning options, including instructor-led training, e-learning modules, on-the-job training, and coaching and mentoring programmes.

- **Evaluation and feedback:** Collecting data and feedback to measure the effectiveness of the learning initiatives and to continuously improve the quality of the education and skills development programmes.

- **Recognition and rewards:** Recognizing and rewarding employees who demonstrate strong performance and commitment to ongoing education and skills development.

By developing and implementing these processes and practices, organizations can create a culture of learning and skills development, and empower their employees to continuously improve and innovate in the field of Big Data.

Investing in high-quality training programmes

It will not be a big surprise that establishing a mature education and skills development capability requires investments in terms of time and money. Investing in high-quality training programmes is essential to achieving a high maturity level in education and skills development. By providing employees with access to high-quality training programmes, organizations can help them develop the skills and knowledge needed to excel in their roles and contribute to the success of the BDCoE.

High-quality training programmes should be designed to meet the specific needs and goals of the organization and should be delivered by experienced instructors or subject matter experts. They should also be delivered using a variety of methods, such as classroom training, e-learning, on-the-job training, and coaching and mentoring programmes to ensure that employees have access to the learning opportunities that best suit their individual learning styles and preferences.

Evaluating and measuring

Finally, organizations should regularly evaluate the effectiveness of their training programmes to ensure that they are meeting the needs of employees and the BDCoE, and to identify areas for improvement. By continuously improving the quality of their training programmes, organizations can create a culture of learning and skills development, and ensure that their employees are well-equipped to tackle the challenges of working in a rapidly changing field like Big Data.

Organizations can measure and evaluate the effectiveness of the education and skills development capability using a variety of methods, such as:

- **Employee feedback:** Organizations can gather feedback from employees who have completed training programmes or participated in skills-development initiatives. This can be done through surveys, focus groups or one-on-one meetings. This feedback can help organizations identify what is working well and what needs improvement.

- **Skill assessments:** Organizations can conduct skill assessments before and after training programmes to measure the impact of the training on employees' skills and knowledge. This can help organizations identify areas where employees have improved and areas where further development is needed.

- **Performance metrics:** Organizations can use performance metrics, such as productivity, quality and customer satisfaction, to evaluate the impact of education and skills development on business outcomes. If employees who have completed training programmes are performing better than those who have not, it is a good indication that the training is effective.

- **Return on investment (ROI):** Organizations can calculate the ROI of education and skills development initiatives by comparing the cost of the initiative to the value it has generated for the organization. This can include increased productivity, reduced errors and improved customer satisfaction. If the ROI is positive, it is a good indication that the initiative is effective.

- **Benchmarking:** Organizations can benchmark their education and skills development initiatives against industry best practices or competitors to identify areas where they can improve. This can help organizations stay competitive and ensure they are providing employees with the skills and knowledge needed to succeed in the industry.

By using these methods, organizations can continuously evaluate the effectiveness of their education and skills development initiatives, make improvements where necessary and ensure that they are providing employees with the resources they need to succeed.

38.4 Education and skills development summary

In the rapidly evolving field of Big Data, education and skills development is crucial for organizations to remain competitive and meet changing business needs. A high maturity level in this capability allows organizations to attract and retain top talent, address skills gaps and develop their employees to reach their full potential.

By establishing a clear vision, developing processes and practices and investing in high-quality training programmes, organizations can ensure that their employees have the necessary skills and knowledge to drive business outcomes. Effective education and skills development initiatives can be measured and evaluated using methods such as employee feedback, skill assessments, performance metrics, ROI and benchmarking, helping organizations to continuously improve and stay ahead in the industry.

Notes

1 H Chen, R H Chiang and V C Storey. Business intelligence and analytics: From big data to big impact, *MIS Quarterly*, 2012 36 (4), 1165–88

2 M Janssen and G Kuk. Reshaping the big data landscape: How structuredness and usage matter, *Journal of Business Research*, 2016 69 (5), 1665–73

3 F Qin and T Kochan (2020) *The Learning System at IBM: A Case Study*, https://workofthefuture.mit.edu/wp-content/uploads/2020/12/2020-Working-Paper-Qin-Kochan2.pdf (archived at https://perma.cc/P75P-73B4)

Data Literacy 39

39.1 Introduction to data literacy

Data literacy is to the ability to read, analyse, understand and communicate with data. It is becoming increasingly important in today's data-driven world, as more and more decisions are made based on data insights. At its core, data literacy involves a combination of technical and critical thinking skills. Technical skills include understanding data structures, analysing data using software tools and being able to use statistical methods to derive insights. Critical thinking skills include the ability to question data, evaluate its accuracy and relevance and interpret findings in context.

Having a strong data literacy culture and capability within an organization can help employees at all levels make informed decisions, solve complex problems and drive business outcomes. Note that with the data literacy capability, we don't so much mean the literacy within the Big Data Centre of Excellence (BDCoE) (which is required for the profession in the first place), but data knowledge and skills that the rest of the employees in the organization have, such as in the finance or marketing departments.

It is important for a BDCoE that the rest of the organization is data literate because data is no longer confined to the domain of data professionals, data scientists or analysts. Data is a strategic resource that is now available to all employees and teams, regardless of their level or function. To fully leverage the potential of data-driven decision-making, it is essential that all employees across the organization have a basic understanding of data literacy.

When employees are data literate, they can effectively analyse, interpret and communicate data in order to make informed decisions. This means that decision-makers at all levels of the organization can use data to drive strategic initiatives, develop new products and services and identify new opportunities for growth.

Additionally, data literacy promotes a culture of transparency, trust and collaboration across the organization. When everyone has access to data and understands how to use it, there is less room for misinterpretation or misunderstanding. This leads to more effective communication, more informed decision-making and better outcomes for the organization.

Lastly, establishing a data literacy capability can help to bridge the gap between IT and business teams. Often, there is a disconnect between the technical skills of IT teams and the business acumen of non-technical teams. Data literacy can help to bridge this gap by enabling non-technical employees to better understand the technical aspects of data and analytics. This can improve collaboration and communication between teams, leading to more successful data-driven initiatives.

39.2 Purpose and maturity levels of data literacy

Purpose

The purpose of the data literacy capability is to enable individuals to understand, analyse and communicate data effectively. The BDCoE plays a central role in advocating data literacy within an organization. As a centre of expertise for Big Data, the BDCoE can help to define what data literacy means for the organization and communicate its importance to key stakeholders across the company.

The BDCoE can also develop and deliver training programmes and resources to help employees improve their data literacy skills. This could include training on how to collect, analyse and interpret data, as well as best practices for using data to make informed decisions.

In addition, the BDCoE should work with other departments to embed data literacy into their workflows and processes. This could involve identifying areas where data can be used to improve efficiencies or drive innovation, and working with relevant stakeholders to integrate data-driven decision-making into their day-to-day activities.

The purpose of the data literacy capability is outlined in Table 39.1.

Data literacy is a crucial factor in enabling data-driven decision-making. It ensures that decision-makers across an organization can understand and use data effectively to make informed decisions that align with their goals and objectives.

With data literacy, employees can access, interpret and analyse data, as well as communicate insights effectively. This allows them to use data as evidence to support their decisions and provide data-driven recommendations to others. Data literacy also empowers employees to identify patterns, trends and insights within data that may not have been initially apparent, which can lead to more effective and efficient decision-making.

Table 39.1 The purpose of the data literacy capability

Capability	Purpose
Data literacy	Defines the ability of an organization to establish a culture of data-driven decision-making by data literate employees.

Maybe even more importantly, data literacy can improve the quality of decisions by reducing the likelihood of biases and errors. When employees are data literate, they are less likely to make decisions based on assumptions or incomplete data, and more likely to rely on empirical evidence to support their decisions.

Maturity levels

It is important for an organization to build mature data literacy capabilities. This is because data is becoming an increasingly important strategic asset for organizations, and having a workforce that is data literate enables them to make informed decisions based on data. In addition, having a data literate workforce can lead to improved efficiencies, cost savings and increased innovation.

Organizations that have mature data literacy capabilities are also better equipped to respond to the challenges of a rapidly changing business environment. They are able to adapt to new technologies and processes, and are more agile in responding to market demands. Furthermore, organizations with a data literate workforce are better positioned to attract and retain top talent, as employees are increasingly looking for opportunities to develop their skills in this area.

To build a mature data literacy capability, organizations can use the five levels as outlined in Table 39.2.

Table 39.2   Maturity levels of the data literacy capability

Maturity Level	Description
Level 1 – Initial	There are no formal training programmes or initiatives for data literacy. Some employees may have developed data skills on their own or through personal individual training, but there is no systematic approach to building data literacy across the organization.
Level 2 – Managed	The organization has recognized the need for data literacy and has defined the basic competencies and skills required. There are some training programmes available, but they are not widely adopted or integrated into the workflow of employees.
Level 3 – Defined	The organization has a formal data literacy programme in place that is fully integrated into daily operations. Employees have access to training and resources to improve their data skills and knowledge.

(continued)

Table 39.2   (Continued)

Maturity Level	Description
Level 4 – Controlled	The organization has established metrics and processes for measuring the effectiveness of the data literacy programme. Employees at all levels have a solid understanding of data concepts and tools, and can apply them to their work.
Level 5 – Optimized	The organization is continuously improving its data literacy programme based on feedback from employees and data-driven insights. The programme is integrated into all aspects of the organization, and employees are empowered to make data-driven decisions at every level.

Whereas most capabilities that are discussed throughout this book focus specifically on the BDCoE, it is important to note that the data literacy capability will have an impact on the entire organization.

Driving data literacy in an organization is a collective responsibility that involves various stakeholders. The BDCoE, data and analytics leaders and HR can all play a significant role in promoting and facilitating data literacy. However, it is also essential to involve business leaders and frontline employees who work with data regularly in the data literacy programme. This can help ensure that data literacy is integrated into the organization's culture and becomes a part of how business is conducted. Ultimately, a successful data literacy programme requires a collaborative effort from all stakeholders involved.

39.3 Structuring data literacy

Structuring data literacy in an organization involves a combination of various factors that address the needs of the organization and its employees. The steps outlined in Figure 39.1 can help to establish a data literacy structure.

Establishing a data literacy capability is an ongoing activity that requires continuous efforts and improvements. As data technologies and tools evolve, new data sources become available and business needs change, so organizations must keep their workforce up to date with the latest knowledge and skills. Therefore, data literacy programmes need to be designed with the understanding that they are ongoing initiatives and must be continuously assessed and updated to stay relevant.

To ensure ongoing success, data literacy programmes need to be supported by a culture of continuous learning, where employees are encouraged to continuously

Figure 39.1   Activities to structure data literacy

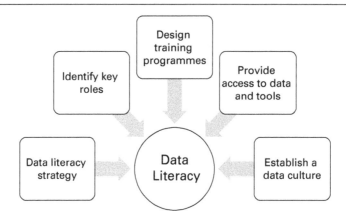

improve their data skills and knowledge. This requires buy-in from leadership and a commitment to providing ongoing training and development opportunities.

Develop a data literacy strategy

The organization needs to define its objectives and goals for data literacy, and how it aligns with its overall business strategy.[1] The strategy should also consider the organization's culture, structure and resources.

The following are some best practices and activities for developing a data literacy strategy:

- **Identify the organization's data goals:** It is essential to determine the goals of the data literacy programme to ensure that it aligns with the organization's overall business objectives. Most importantly, the data literacy programme should align with the formulated Big Data strategy, which we discussed in Chapter 6. For example, the goals of the data literacy programme may include improving decision-making or increasing productivity.

- **Determine the target audience:** It is necessary to identify the target audience for the data literacy programme, such as business leaders, managers and employees, to create tailored training programmes that address their specific needs. Most enterprise organizations have significant numbers of employees, and it is important to tailor the programme towards different target audiences.

- **Assess the current state of data literacy:** An organization needs to understand the current state of data literacy within the organization to identify gaps and prioritize areas for improvement. This can be done by conducting surveys, interviews or assessments.

Note that the data literacy strategy should guide subsequent investment, learning programmes and training methodologies. As such, the data literacy strategy is an important document that requires executive-level support.

Identify key roles

Organizations need to identify key roles that require a high level of data literacy. These roles should be prioritized and given specific training and resources to develop their skills. Identifying roles that require a high level of data literacy is important for several reasons. First, it allows an organization to focus its data literacy efforts on the roles that have the most impact on data-driven decision-making. Second, it ensures that individuals in those roles have the necessary skills and knowledge to effectively work with data and make informed decisions. Third, it enables the organization to tailor its data literacy programmes to the specific needs and challenges of those roles.

By identifying roles that require a high level of data literacy, an organization can also gain a better understanding of the types of data and analytics tools that are most important to its operations. This can help inform decisions about investments in technology, training and other resources that support data literacy.

In addition, identifying roles that require a high level of data literacy can help an organization to address any gaps in its current workforce. For example, if the organization identifies that certain roles lack the necessary data literacy skills, it can develop targeted training programmes to address those gaps.

Design training programmes

Training programmes should be designed to address the identified gaps in skills and knowledge. Training can be delivered through a variety of formats, such as classroom training, online courses or self-paced learning modules. It's important to ensure that the training is accessible, engaging and relevant to the roles and responsibilities of employees.

Organizations should subsequently deliver data literacy training programmes to ensure that their employees have the necessary knowledge and skills to effectively work with data. By doing so, employees will be able to use data to inform decision-making, identify opportunities for growth and optimize business operations. A data literate workforce also enables an organization to more effectively leverage advanced analytics, artificial intelligence and other emerging technologies that rely heavily on data. Additionally, providing data literacy training can help to foster a culture of data-driven decision-making and innovation within the organization.

An overview of suitable data literacy training programme topics is listed in Table 39.3.

Table 39.3 Example data literacy course outline

Outline Data Literacy Course
Introduction to Data Literacy
• **Overview of data literacy and its importance in today's business world**
• Understanding data concepts and terminology
• Data literacy levels
Fundamental Data Concepts
• Understanding data types
• Structured and unstructured data
• Metadata
• Data storage
• Data security and data privacy
Understanding Datasets
• Exploratory data analysis
• Descriptive statistics
• Frequency distributions
• Data cleaning
• Data wrangling
Data Visualization
• Bar charts and histograms
• Line graphs and scatter plots
• Boxplots
• Heat maps and maps
Storytelling with Data
• Key elements of data storytelling
• Collecting and organizing data
• Data storytelling techniques
Data Ethics
• Data ethics
• Data ethics and privacy
• Data ethics policies and procedures

Not everyone in the organization will have the same level of data literacy or use the same tools. Therefore, it is important to tailor the training to the specific audience and their roles, so they can learn the skills they need for their work.

Provide access to data and tools

Employees need access to data and tools to practice and apply their newly acquired skills. This includes access to data platforms, visualization tools and other technologies that support data-driven decision-making.

Providing access to data and tools is crucial for enabling data literacy within an organization. The data catalogue, which we discussed in Chapter 16. can play a central role in distributing enterprise data sets to the rest of the organization. When employees have access to relevant data and the necessary tools to analyse and interpret it, they can develop their skills and confidence in working with data. This leads to more informed decision-making, better problem-solving and the ability to identify new opportunities for the business.

Access to data and tools also fosters a culture of data-driven decision-making, where employees are encouraged to seek out and use data to support their ideas and proposals. This can lead to more collaboration across teams and functions, as well as a more innovative and agile organization.

In addition, providing access to data and tools can improve employee engagement and retention. When employees feel that their organization values their development and provides them with the resources they need to succeed, they are more likely to be satisfied with their work and stay with the company for the long term.

Establish a data culture

To build a long-term, high maturity data literacy capability, a data culture should be promoted within the organization. This involves creating an environment where employees are encouraged to use data to inform decision-making. Data should be viewed as a strategic asset that can be leveraged to gain a competitive advantage.

Building trust and collaboration among employees is essential to creating a data culture. This involves encouraging open communication and sharing of information and ensuring that data is used in a transparent and ethical manner. Encouraging experimentation and innovation with data can help organizations identify new insights and opportunities. This involves creating an environment where individuals are encouraged to try new approaches and take calculated risks with data.

39.4 Data literacy summary

The final capability that we discussed in the Big Data function macro-capability is the data literacy capability. An organization's data literacy capability is its ability to establish a workforce that understands and uses data effectively in their work. This includes skills in data analysis, visualization and interpretation. A high level of data literacy is crucial for organizations to make informed decisions based on data, drive innovation and remain competitive in today's data-driven business environment. Particularly in an organization that has established a BDCoE, it is important that others in the organization understand and have the capability to understand data, visualization and to correctly use data in decision-making.

Establishing a strong data literacy capability requires a strategic approach that involves identifying roles that require high levels of data literacy, providing access to data and tools, delivering effective training programmes and promoting a data-driven culture. The BDCoE plays a central role in advocating for data literacy and developing the necessary processes and practices to support it.

To structure data literacy in an organization, it is important to establish a vision and set clear goals for the data literacy capability. This involves identifying the specific skills and competencies that employees need to develop, as well as the data and tools that they require to do so. Best practices for developing a data literacy strategy include engaging stakeholders across the organization, providing ongoing training and support, and leveraging data champions to promote the use of data in decision-making. In summary, establishing a mature data literacy capability can provide significant benefits for organizations, including improved decision-making, innovation and competitive advantage.

Note

1 J-W Middelburg (2023) *Data Literacy Fundamentals*, eBook

Big Data Functions Maturity Assessment

## 40

Please respond to the following questions by indicating the relevant level of maturity for each activity in question and its importance to your organization.

The Capability Maturity Model levels are shown in Table 40.1.

Table 40.1 The Capability Maturity Model levels

Score	Description
0 – Non-existent	Describes a total lack of activity or lack of recognition that the activity exists.
1 – Initial	Describes evidence that the organization recognizes issues exist and need to be addressed.
2 – Managed	Describes activities designed so that similar procedures are followed by individuals. There is a high reliance on individual knowledge and skill level.
3 – Defined	Describes a standardized and documented level of activities which is being communicated through training, processes and tools.
4 – Controlled	Describes activities that are good practice and under constant improvement. Automation and tools are used to support the activities.
5 – Optimized	Describes activities that are considered leading and best practice and can be considered an example to other organizations.

Please note that responses to this survey should reflect how the organization performs the task today, not how you would like to see the organization perform the task in the future. Your choices should be based on your opinion of the organization, not just the way the task is performed in your own workgroup.

Table 40.2 Big Data Functions Maturity Assessment

#	Knowledge Management	Score
22.1	Our organization actively manages knowledge in the organization and knowledge management practices have been established.	
22.2	Our organization has established formal onboarding programmes to transfer knowledge to new hires effectively.	
22.3	Our organization has implemented a knowledge management system or tool, where employees can look for knowledge.	
22.4	Our organization proactively manages the content in the knowledge management systems to ensure information is current and up to date.	
22.5	Our organization has established mentor-mentee programmes to exchange knowledge between senior and junior employees.	
22.6	Our organization's knowledge management processes, procedures and systems support employees in finding information quickly.	
	Service Catalogue	**Score**
23.1	Our organization has established and documented a service catalogue of services the Big Data Centre of Excellence (BDCoE) provides.	
23.2	The service catalogue is available to internal stakeholders and other departments can view which services the BDCoE provides.	
23.3	Service levels and service level agreements (SLAs) are standardized and in line with the items in the service catalogue.	

(*continued*)

Table 40.2 (Continued)

23.4 Our organization supports different views (internal, customer, external) to support different stakeholders.

23.5 Service levels and corresponding metrics are adequately embedded in technology tools, so that performance can be tracked.

23.6 Our organization periodically reviews whether the service catalogue is still current and makes updates accordingly.

Workforce and Talent Planning	Score

24.1 Our organization proactively manages the Big Data workforce to ensure adequate availability of competent employees.

24.2 Our organization's has defined and documented critical skills for the Big Data Centre of Excellence (BDCoE).

24.3 Our organization periodically conduct a skills gap analysis to identify the current skills and competencies of the BDCoE's workforce to compare them to the skills and competencies required to achieve the business strategy.

24.4 The BDCoE keeps track of emerging technologies and trends that may impact the required skills and talent the organization needs.

24.5 Our organization is actively establishing programmes to attract and retain top talents in the Big Data industry.

24.6 Our organization's workforce and talent planning effectively contributes to agile teams and succession planning.

Education and Skills Development	Score

25.1 Our organization's skills and development programmes are based on the overall strategic needs of our organization.

25.2 We have developed an education and skills vision statement that outlines the purpose of education and skills development in the Big Data Centre of Excellence (BDCoE).

25.3 Our organization has practices and processes in place that support education and learning.

(*continued*)

Table 40.2 (Continued)

25.4	Our organization proactively identifies learning needs and establishes training programmes accordingly.
25.5	Our BDCoE has sufficient resources (people and budget) available for planning and delivering education and skills development programmes.
25.6	Our organization regularly evaluates the effectiveness of training programmes to ensure that they are meeting the needs of employees and the BDCoE.

Data Literacy	**Score**
26.1 Our organization has established a formal data literacy programme that is endorsed by senior management.	
26.2 Our organization has identified required data literacy knowledge and skill for critical stakeholders and has developed data literacy programmes in line with these needs.	
26.3 Our organization has established and formalized data literacy training programmes across the enterprise, and all employees take part in becoming more data literate.	
26.4 Our organization provides access to enterprise data and tools, so all employees can practice with the knowledge they obtained.	
26.5 The effectiveness and results of the data literacy programmes are periodically reviewed, and the programme is adjusted based on these results.	
26.6 Our organization has a data culture, where the majority of decisions are based on or informed by data.	

PART EIGHT
AI and Big Data

Artificial Intelligence

41

41.1 Introduction to artificial intelligence

Artificial intelligence (AI) is the domain that focuses itself on mimicking the way that people make decisions. Whereas people use their **natural intelligence**, the scientific domain of **artificial intelligence** is trying to establish computers that make decisions in the same way that people do. Artificial intelligence is slowly but surely impacting the way we live, behave, consume and learn, from the support that receive from virtual assistants (Siri and Alexa) to the way autonomous cars (and soon planes) drive us, quite literally, through life.

Anyone who reads this book will have heard about AI in one way or another. The last decade has seen an unprecedented growth in the attention given to, investment in and popularity of the artificial intelligence knowledge domain.[1] Where AI was previously confined to the world of computer science, it is now at the forefront of technology companies, who market their AI solutions and capabilities.

The domain of artificial intelligence is complex, highly scientific and would provide enough content to easily complete another publication of the same size as this one. So why is it included on the Enterprise Big Data Framework? And why is it displayed as an external concentric ring in the image of the Enterprise Big Data Framework (as discussed in Part 2)? There are two important reasons why AI has been included in the Enterprise Big Data Framework, and why this represents the final capability that we will discuss in this book.

First, AI is not a standalone domain. It builds on all the five capabilities that have been discussed in the previous parts. AI requires knowledge about computer science, processes, data architecture and algorithms – the exact same capabilities that are covered in the Enterprise Big Data Framework. To build useful AI capabilities, organizations need to utilize the exact same structure and capabilities. Consider a self-driving car, for example: for a self-driving car to function properly it needs to collect input data (speed, surrounding cars, traffic lights) at record speeds. It subsequently needs to process this data, and predict the most optimal decision, by comparing databases with driver history and traffic regulations. All of this in split seconds, because the car needs to react instantly to changing conditions. Additionally, since the self-driving car could make potential life-or-death decisions, topics such as data security, data management and data governance are of paramount importance.

The example above illustrates that AI and Big Data are strongly interwoven, and as data volumes grow, this dependency will only become larger. In the same example, a self-driving car that can pull information from millions of previous traffic situations will have the ability to make better decisions than the same car that has just a few thousand traffic situations stored into its databases.

The second reason we discuss AI as the last capability in the Enterprise Big Data Framework is because artificial intelligence – especially in an enterprise environment – can benefit from a framework approach, rooted in the systematic creation of capabilities. Most organizations will need to find a practical, tangible approach to AI. These organizations are unlikely to hire separate AI researchers to develop scientific AI models. Rather, these organizations aim to follow a pragmatic approach, where AI is primarily used to achieve a return on investment.

As the last capability of the Enterprise Big Data Framework, we will therefore only look at **pragmatic corporate artificial intelligence (PCAI)**. By PCAI, we mean a functional use of AI techniques and solutions that have utilitarian use in an organization. To be clear, this means we will not consider the latest scientific breakthroughs in natural language processing (NLP), Automated Reasoning or generative AI, but will focus on existing functional use of proven methodologies. For example, we will cover how AI algorithms can be used to improve customer experience.

To denominate the domain of PCAI in this section, we will primarily look at AI as an extension of analytics, which we have already covered in Part 4, and summarize PCAI as a separate class of '**cognitive analytics**'. With cognitive analytics, we mean the set of techniques and algorithms that can be used for practical enterprise use cases.

Looking at AI from a functional pragmatic perspective also explains why AI is depicted as the outer ring in the Enterprise Big Data Framework. AI as a capability forms a logical extension to other framework capabilities. For an organization that aspires to use AI solutions in their offering, it also means that they do not need to start from scratch. If organizations have already invested in their Big Data environments, AI can simply be seen as a logical next step that builds on the capabilities that are already in place.

Figure 41.1   Cognitive analytics

41.2 A brief background on artificial intelligence

The fascination with the mind is nothing new. Already in the ancient Greek and Roman civilizations, now-famous philosophers tried to find explanations about the extraordinary way in which the mind works. The Greek philosopher Plato (428/427 or 424/423–348/347 BC) asked the famous question, 'What is it that, when present in a body, makes it living? – A soul.'[2] The way in which the mind works, how it processes information, reasons and ultimately makes decisions is a process that, even until this day, is something of a mystery. And man's quest to find the ultimate way in which the brain works (and whether or not that is desirable) is something that we leave to modern science and philosophy.

The quest to mimic the human decision-making process with the use of artificial technology is from more recent times, although AI as a domain of computer science is quite old already. The term 'artificial intelligence' was introduced in 1956 during an event which is now known as the Dartmouth Workshop. During this workshop two of the attendees, Herbert Simon and Allen Newell, proposed that human minds and modern digital computers were 'species of the same genus', namely symbolic information processing systems; both take symbolic information as input, manipulate it according to a set of formal rules, and in so doing can solve problems, formulate judgments and make decisions.[3]

Even though the term artificial intelligence was introduced during the Dartmouth Workshop in 1956, much of the mathematical groundwork on artificial intelligence should be credited to the computer scientist Alan Turing. In 1950, Alan Turing published a paper titled 'Computing Machinery and Intelligence', in which the famous first phrase read: 'Can machines think?'[4] This question puts the most fundamental problem of artificial intelligence forward: is it possible to build a computer that can think, and which people would credit with the possession of intelligence?

Turing lacked the technical resources to answer this question, but he did devise a hypothetical thinking experiment (an 'imitation game') that tried to find an answer to this question (displayed in Figure 41.2). Suppose there is a human interrogator that asks questions to two responders, one a human, the other a computer. The interrogator starts asking questions to the two responders with the objective of identifying which one is the actual person. If the computer would be able to convince the interrogator that it was the actual person, could we attribute 'intelligence' to the machine?

The hypothetical thought experiment described above, now known as the Turing Test, is still subject to much debate. Some scholars argue that this definition of intelligence is too narrow, where others argue that intelligence is also possible without passing the Turing Test. For the purpose of PCAI, we will however consider the Turing Test 'sufficient' to claim intelligence in computer systems. Most enterprises

Figure 41.2   The Turing Test

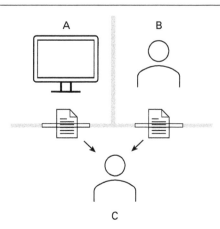

will never reach this threshold of intelligence, nor do they need to utilize AI solutions to gain a competitive advantage or suitable return on investment.

Since the days of Alan Turing, the knowledge about AI systems, technologies and applications has taken a massive flight. One of the domains where early AI break-throughs were discovered was the game of chess. Like the fascination with the brain, the game of chess has always been intriguing, since winning at chess is a clear man-made show of intelligence. Many AI researchers since the 1950s have taken great efforts to come up with algorithms that were intelligent enough to beat man at its own game. The IBM-built Deep Blue machine ultimately proved that this was possible by beating the world champion Garry Kasparov in 1997 in the well-known match between humans and machines.

In the recent decades (from the early 2000s to the present), artificial intelligence solutions have become more standardized and more affordable, and are now frequently embedded in all types of applications. Digital assistants (Siri, Cortana and Alexa) are built into almost every phone, and smart language processors give us the ability to translate written or spoken languages almost seamlessly to any language of choice. Research keeps on developing and applications and use cases (discussed in Chapter 1 section 1.5) will keep on growing.

It is safe to say that new AI comes to the market every day.[5] In order to understand how to build meaningful (business) applications with the use of Big Data and AI, it is first of all important to understand how AI is structured, and what capabilities are necessary to say that a system is intelligent. And even then, the question remains whether these solutions can truly be considered intelligent, or just a smart application of cognitive analytical algorithms. For PCAI, we will see many useful applications and capabilities in the upcoming chapters. But, as Plato already referenced more than two centuries ago, the question of 'soul' remains...

41.3 Capabilities in artificial intelligence

To set up PCAI, organizations would need to establish capabilities that enable them to develop, maintain and improve cognitive analytics. The ability to mimic human decision-making will bring some additional challenges that are unique to the domain of AI. Mimicking the human brain will require knowledge about the thought process in which people store and retrieve information. People store information about previous experiences as 'memories' in dedicated parts of the brain, typically with the ability to retrieve memories from years ago within split seconds. A corporate solution that aims to imitate this therefore also needs the ability to store massive quantities of data within split seconds.

A second challenge is introduced by the fact that different people process information in different ways, with vastly different results and vastly different decisions. An obvious example is in the education system, where students who have gone to the same school, with the same teachers and the same study materials, will perform quite differently on standardized tests. This complexity (and the resulting personalization) is difficult to mimic for computers. Although some customization can be achieved based on individual profiles, almost every computer reasons functionally in terms of statements. Given the same input data and the same algorithm, computers will always come up with the same recommendations and results. For people this is not necessarily the case. To build capability in AI, it is therefore necessary to mimic different reasoning processes in machines, which is incredibly complex.

Lastly, and maybe even most challenging, is that AI immediately brings the field of ethics into consideration. Where most computer algorithms (as discussed in Part 5) function in a straightforward way, in AI solutions, ethical considerations immediately come into play. Just as there are people who make flawed, biased or unethical decisions, AI solutions are confronted with the same ethical and moral dilemmas. To illustrate this, let's consider a well-known AI dilemma in self-driving cars. Suppose a self-driving car encounters an emergency, where there is a potential life-threatening event. To save the driver's life, the car needs to make a sharp turn at high speed over a pedestrian crossing. Given the speed, it is certain that the person(s) on the crossing will be killed. What (programmed) decision should the self-driving car make? Should it kill the driver? Or should it kill the person crossing the street? Would the choice be different if the pedestrian crossing was an octogenarian or a teen with his or her whole life in front of them? As you can see from this example, there is no easy answer to this question. However, it is important to keep in mind that, in the end, these kinds of decisions need to be programmed into the cognitive analytics solution, whether we want to or not. As a result, the domain of AI and ethics are strongly interwoven.

Figure 41.3   The micro-capabilities of pragmatic corporate artificial intelligence

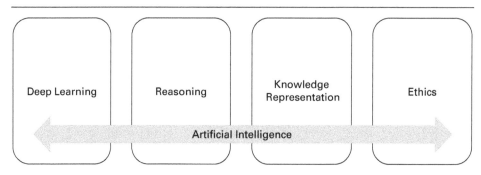

The three challenges listed above immediately give insight into the complex nature of AI and explain why most companies are only at the very initial stages of exploring how AI can support their business. To come up with a solution that makes AI actionable and pragmatic (hence the term PCAI), we will consider five micro-capabilities that organizations can establish, as depicted in Figure 41.3.

As mentioned earlier, and to avoid any doubt, this is by no means a complete overview of the scientific domain of artificial intelligence, nor is intended to be. Instead, we will focus on practical, measurable capabilities that any organization can establish and develop, in order to take the first steps to embed AI solutions into their corporate environments.

The first capability that will consider in this section is deep learning. **Deep learning** is a subset of machine learning that involves building and training artificial neural networks with multiple layers of interconnected nodes. These networks are designed to simulate the human brain's ability to recognize patterns and make decisions based on data inputs.

Deep learning algorithms are able to automatically learn and improve from experience without being explicitly programmed. They are used in a wide range of applications, including image and speech recognition, natural language processing, recommendation systems and autonomous vehicles.

The process of deep learning involves feeding large amounts of data into the neural network, which is then used to train the network to recognize patterns and make predictions. The network adjusts its weights and biases through a process called backpropagation, which helps it to improve its performance over time. The key advantage of deep learning over traditional machine learning techniques is its ability to handle large and complex datasets with high levels of accuracy. However, deep learning models are often computationally intensive and require significant amounts of training data to achieve optimal performance.

Closely related to knowledge representation is the **reasoning** capability. The reasoning capability in AI is to the ability of an AI system to make logical deductions and draw conclusions based on the information available to it. It involves using knowledge and reasoning to solve problems and make decisions in a way that mimics human thought processes.

Once a knowledge base has been built, logical reasoning needs to be used to solve business problems. Reasoning approaches and systems can be used to draw conclusions based on input data, make trade-offs between different alternatives or to make predictions about the most logical next course of action. Reasoning, because of this, is strongly intertwined with the domain of logic, the process that follows sensible steps to arrive at the most suitable conclusions. Since all computers are ultimately built from logical parts (i.e. transistors), it is only fitting that we would ultimately use computers to mimic logical decision-making. In Chapter 43, we will discuss how organizations can build reasoning capabilities, and, as a result, increase their decision-making capability.

The third major capability that is required for PCAI is the **knowledge representation capability**. Knowledge representation, very simply stated, is the way in which a computer can store (and later retrieve) knowledge. In order for computers to be deemed 'intelligent', software needs to be created with which a computer can model how beliefs, intentions and judgements of an intelligent agent can be expressed. This capability is required to transform data, which typically is only factual, to information and knowledge. There are many different ways in which organizations can structure knowledge representation (discussed further in Chapter 44), and which can help an organization to make the transition from storing data to storing real knowledge.

The last capability to be discussed in this section is the **AI ethics capability**. Whether this is a capability or an inherent moral obligation is subject to opinion, but since capabilities are inherently measurable, including it as a capability will put it under constant attention. Ethics, and the discussion about ethics, should be part of any organization that aims to leverage the power of artificial intelligence. And the reason is simple. If computers within a company make unethical choices or predications, it will reflect directly on the company itself.

In the last decade, there have been many examples of organizations that received significant negative publicity, and sometimes fines, because of unethical behaviour that was driven by AI algorithms. In 2015 Google, for example, received serious backlash when it was reported that their image recognition software classified black individual as 'gorillas'. Goldman Sachs is being investigated by regulators for using an AI algorithm that allegedly discriminated against women by granting larger credit limits to men than women on their Apple cards.[6] These examples clearly show that artificial intelligence also can bring risk to an organization, sometimes unknowingly. Besides the financial argument, it is wise to build an ethics capability right from the start in any organization. Organizations that build AI solutions according to ethical AI guidelines and principles demonstrate a sense of corporate responsibility.

Additionally, for most individuals, an organization that has a mature ethics capability will definitely be a more attractive place to work.

41.4 Artificial intelligence and Big Data

Over the last few sections, we have explained there is an inherent link between artificial intelligence and Big Data. The different AI capabilities that were introduced int the previous section all have one thing in common: they rely on suitable data architectures, suitable data storage methods and quality processing methods. To move from mere predictive analytics to cognitive analytics, AI capabilities depend on the Big Data capabilities. In the Enterprise Big Data Framework, this is the reason that AI is depicted as an external concentric ring around the other five capabilities.

A suitable visual link between the two domains can be seen in Figure 41.4, which showcases the application of an intelligent agent. An **intelligent agent** is an entity (frequently a software program) that makes the best possible decision, given a variety of different choices and input actions. The intelligent agent (also referred to as a rational agent, when the agent makes its decisions based on reason) therefore ultimately mimics human decision-making.

In a simplified representation, an intelligent agent works based on three main steps:

1 The intelligent agent **perceives** the environment around him. In essence, the environment is providing input data that provides direction or instructions for the intelligent agent to act upon.

2 The agents subsequently **reasons** the best possible course of action. To arrive at the best possible decision, the agent will need to compare the input data (from the environment) with external data (or knowledge) which is already has available in its environment and systems. This external data can be stored within the system itself or might be coming from external third parties.

3 Based on the input data (from the environment) and the data that the agent already has (from the external data), the agent calculates or determines the best possible outcome, and determines its **action** back to the environment. The action that the intelligent agent takes will (in most cases) have a direct effect on the environment, therefore changing the input again.

The three main steps and composition of an intelligent agent are shown in Figure 41.4.

In order to make the concept of an intelligent agent a bit more tangible, let's illustrate how it works with the brief example of a self-driving car. The system of a self-driving car (the intelligent agent) will constantly receive input data from the environment, like the colour of traffic lights, vicinity to other cars, etc. Based on this

Figure 41.4 Structure and steps of an intelligent agent

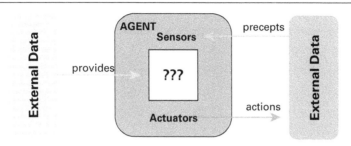

input information, the self-driving car will need to make decisions, like braking, accelerating, steering, etc. In order to make this decision, it should compare the input data with the external data. The system can for example consider the driver's driving history, or (as an external source) consider the weather conditions. Based on both the input data from the environment, and the external data, the self-driving car makes a decision to steer, accelerate, switch lane, etc. This decision will impact the environment directly.

The example above is significant for two reasons. First, understanding how rational agents work will help significantly with understanding basic AI applications. In the next few chapters, we will often refer back to intelligent agents because they are an integral component of almost every practical AI solution. Secondly, this example very clearly shows how AI is completely dependent on Big Data capabilities. A self-driving car will have hundreds of sensors, which will collect significant data, and which will subsequently need to process that data within split seconds. The agent will then need to (almost instantly) compare that input data from the environment with a database of traffic regulations, driver history or maybe even future weather forecasts. Again, each of these databases can be quite large in terms of volume, and the agent will need to conclude these calculations in milliseconds. Based on the best possible predictions, the self-driving car then needs to act to bring the driver safely to his home.

The volume, velocity and variety aspects in this self-driving car example are exemplary for modern AI solutions. As data sets grow, and sensors become better, AI systems will need to store large sets of input data efficiently, run calculations within split seconds and have the ability to query existing databases within milliseconds. All of these activities in AI systems would not be possible without the fundamental Big Data capabilities as outlined across the Enterprise Big Data Framework.

41.5 Common AI use cases and applications

Artificial intelligence has a wide range of potential applications in enterprises across industries, from improving customer service to optimizing supply chains. Table 41.1 outlines some common enterprise use cases of AI.

Table 41.1 Common enterprise use cases of AI

Industry Focus	Use Case
Customer Service	AI-powered chatbots can be used to handle routine customer inquiries and provide personalized recommendations based on customer history and preferences. These chatbots can also be integrated with natural language processing (NLP) technology to understand and respond to customer queries in a conversational manner.
Sales and Marketing	AI can be used to analyse customer data and behaviour, identify trends and patterns, and provide personalized recommendations for products and services. This can improve customer engagement, increase sales and reduce customer churn.
Supply Chain Optimization	AI can be used to optimize supply chain operations by predicting demand, identifying bottlenecks and inefficiencies, and automating inventory management. This can reduce costs, improve efficiency and enhance the customer experience.
Fraud Detection	AI can be used to detect and prevent fraudulent activity in financial transactions, such as credit card fraud and money laundering. AI models can be trained on historical data to identify patterns and anomalies that indicate fraudulent behaviour.
Predictive Maintenance	AI can be used to predict when equipment is likely to fail and schedule maintenance proactively, reducing downtime and maintenance costs. By analysing data from sensors and other sources, AI models can identify patterns and anomalies that indicate potential issues.
Human Resources	AI can be used to automate repetitive HR tasks such as résumé screening and candidate selection, reducing the time and effort required for recruitment. AI can also be used to identify high-potential employees and provide personalized career development recommendations.

AI has the potential to transform enterprises across industries by improving customer service, optimizing supply chains, reducing costs and improving the overall customer experience. By analysing data and identifying patterns and anomalies, AI models can provide insights and recommendations that enable enterprises to make better decisions and improve their operations. As AI technology continues to evolve, we can expect to see even more innovative use cases of AI in enterprises.

Notes

1 X Mou. Artificial intelligence: investment trends and selected industry uses, *International Finance Corporation*, 2019 8

2 R Hackforth, ed. (1972) *Plato's Phaedo*, vol. 120, Cambridge University Press

3 S Dick. Artificial intelligence, *Harvard Data Science Review*, 2019 1 (1)

4 A M Turing (2009) Computing machinery and intelligence. In *Parsing the Turing Test*, Springer, Dordrecht, 23–65

5 S Sicular, K Brant and G I Gartner (2018) *Hype Cycle for Artificial Intelligence*, 1–73, www.gartner.com/en/documents/3883863 (archived at https://perma.cc/C3Q3-J45W)

6 R Blackman. A practical guide to building ethical AI, *Harvard Business Review*, 2020 15

Deep Learning 42

42.1 Introduction to deep learning

Deep learning is a subset of machine learning (which we discussed in Chapter 24) that involves building and training artificial neural networks with multiple layers of interconnected nodes. These networks are designed to simulate the human brain's ability to recognize patterns and make decisions based on data inputs.[1] Deep learning algorithms are able to automatically learn and improve from experience without being explicitly programmed. They are used in a wide range of applications, including image and speech recognition, natural language processing (NLP), recommendation systems and autonomous vehicles.

The key advantage of deep learning over traditional machine learning techniques is its ability to handle large and complex datasets with high levels of accuracy. However, deep learning models are often computationally intensive and require significant amounts of training data to achieve optimal performance. For that reason, in order for deep learning to be feasible, it needs to build on an existing Big Data environment. This is the reason why artificial intelligence has been placed at the outer concentric cycle in the Enterprise Big Data Framework.

The basic building block of a deep learning network is the artificial neuron, which takes input values, applies a mathematical function to them and produces an output value. These neurons are mimicked to the neurons of the human brain. A network can contain many layers of neurons, with each layer performing a different type of computation on the input data.

The process of deep learning involves feeding large amounts of Big Data into the neural network, which is then used to train the network to recognize patterns and make predictions. The network adjusts its weights and biases through a process called back-propagation, which helps it to improve its performance over time.

One of the most widely used deep learning architectures is the convolutional neural network (CNN), which is particularly effective for image and video recognition tasks. CNNs consist of multiple layers of convolutional and pooling operations, which are designed to extract meaningful features from the input data. Another important type of deep learning architecture is the recurrent neural network (RNN), which is particularly effective for NLP tasks. RNNs have a feedback mechanism that allows them to maintain a memory of previous inputs and use this information to generate predictions based on the context of the input sequence.

In recent years, deep learning has been combined with other AI techniques, such as reinforcement learning and generative adversarial networks (GANs), to create even more powerful and sophisticated AI systems. Reinforcement learning involves training an AI agent to interact with an environment and learn from feedback, while GANs involve training two neural networks to generate realistic data samples, such as images or music.

Despite its many successes, deep learning also has some limitations and challenges. One of the main challenges is the need for large amounts of labelled data for training, which can be difficult and expensive to obtain. There is also a risk of overfitting, where the network becomes too specialized to the training data and performs poorly on new, unseen data. In addition, deep learning models can be difficult to interpret and explain, which can make it hard to identify and correct errors or biases in the model. This is particularly important in domains such as healthcare, where errors or biases in AI systems can have serious consequences.

To overcome these challenges, it is important for any AI organization to build a structure deep learning capability. Building a deep learning capability requires a combination of technical expertise, data analytics skills and domain knowledge. Organizations may need to invest in training or hiring data scientists, machine learning engineers and other experts to develop this capability. We will discuss best practices for establishing a deep learning capability in section 42.3.

42.2 Purpose and maturity levels of deep learning

Purpose

The primary purpose of the deep learning capability is to develop artificial intelligence systems that can automatically learn from data, improve over time and make accurate predictions or decisions based on that data. Deep learning algorithms are designed to recognize patterns and relationships within large and complex datasets, allowing them to identify new insights or make predictions with a high degree of accuracy.

The purpose of deep learning in an enterprise context is defined in Table 42.1.

Table 42.1   The purpose of the deep learning capability

Capability	Purpose
Deep learning	Defines the ability of an organization to use deep learning algorithms for cognitive decision-making.

For any enterprise, establishing a deep learning capability is important for organizations for several reasons:

- **Improved decision-making:** can help make more informed and accurate decisions based on data. For example, a deep learning model can be trained to predict customer preferences or forecast sales trends, which can help businesses optimize their operations and improve their bottom line.

- **Enhanced automation:** can help automate routine or repetitive tasks, such as image recognition or NLP. This can free up employees to focus on higher-value tasks and improve efficiency.

- **Increased personalization:** can help personalize their products or services to better meet the needs of individual customers. For example, a deep learning model can be used to recommend personalized products or content based on a customer's browsing history or purchase behaviour.

- **Competitive advantage:** can provide a competitive advantage by allowing them to develop innovative products or services that leverage the latest AI technologies. This can help organizations differentiate themselves from their competitors and gain market share.

- **Improved risk management:** can help identify potential risks or anomalies within their data, such as fraudulent transactions or equipment failures. This can help organizations mitigate risks and avoid costly mistakes.

Deep learning is an important capability for organizations that want to leverage the power of AI to improve their operations, enhance their products or services and gain a competitive advantage in their industry. By developing a deep learning capability, organizations can stay at the forefront of technological innovation and position themselves for success in the future.

Maturity levels

Establishing a mature deep learning capability can be a challenging process for organizations, as it requires a combination of technical expertise, data analytics skills and domain knowledge. However, as with many of the capabilities discussed throughout this book, the benefits outweigh the investments in time and money.

Many organizations have successfully established mature deep learning capabilities. To do so, they often invest in building cross-functional teams that bring together data scientists, domain experts and IT professionals to develop and maintain deep learning models. They also often focus on developing a strong data infrastructure and culture of experimentation to support ongoing learning and improvement. By taking a strategic and focused approach, organizations can overcome these challenges and establish a mature deep learning capability that delivers real business value.

Defining maturity levels for a deep learning capability can help organizations assess their current level of capability and identify areas for improvement. To assess maturity of the deep learning capability, organizations can use the five maturity levels as shown in Table 42.2.

Table 42.2 Maturity levels of the deep learning capability

Maturity Level	Description
Level 1 – Initial	The organization has established the foundational building blocks for deep learning, such as a team of data scientists and access to relevant data. However, they may lack a comprehensive deep learning strategy, infrastructure or tools, and are still in the early stages of experimentation.
Level 2 – Managed	The organization has begun to develop their deep learning capability, with a clear strategy, dedicated resources and a focus on experimentation and proof-of-concept projects. They are starting to see results and may have begun deploying deep learning models in production, but may still be refining their processes and workflows.
Level 3 – Defined	The organization has a well-established deep learning capability, with a team of experienced data scientists and machine learning engineers, a robust infrastructure and mature processes for model development and deployment. They are actively using deep learning to drive business value, and have a strong focus on continuous improvement and staying up to date with the latest research and trends in the field.
Level 4 – Controlled	The organization is a leader in deep learning, with a world-class team of experts, cutting-edge infrastructure and tools, and a culture of innovation and experimentation. They are pushing the boundaries of what is possible with deep learning, and are actively collaborating with other organizations and academia to advance the field.
Level 5 – Optimized	The organization is not just a leader in deep learning, but is actively shaping the future of the field. They are driving innovation and breakthroughs in deep learning and are recognized as thought leaders and influencers in the industry. They may be developing new approaches or technologies that have the potential to transform entire industries and are committed to advancing the field in a responsible and ethical manner.

It's important to remember that deep learning is a complex and rapidly evolving field, and building a strong capability requires a significant investment in people, infrastructure and processes. Building a mature deep learning capability can take a significant amount of time and effort.

At a minimum, it can take several years for an organization to establish a foundational deep learning capability, with a team of data scientists, access to relevant data and some basic infrastructure in place. Developing and refining the capability can take additional time, as the organization learns from experimentation, iterates on models and processes, and scales the capability across the organization. It is therefore important to always set realistic timelines and expectations about establishing this capability.

42.3 Structuring deep learning

Structuring a deep learning capability in an organization can involve several key components, including people, infrastructure and processes. Since the people component was discussed in detail in Part 7, and the processes were discussed in detail in Part 6, we will only focus on distinctive capabilities necessary for deep learning.

Convolutional neural networks

The first and most common step towards building capability in deep learning is the establishment, design, and use of convolutional neural networks (CNNs). CNNs are a class of deep learning models that are widely used for image and video recognition, object detection and other computer vision tasks. They are inspired by the structure and function of the visual cortex in the brain and are designed to process visual information in a hierarchical manner, with each layer of the network extracting more complex features from the input data.

The basic building block of a CNN is a convolutional layer, which applies a set of filters (also known as kernels or weights) to the input data, extracting local features from small regions of the input. The filters are learned through a process of backpropagation, in which the network adjusts the weights based on the error between the predicted output and the actual output. By stacking multiple convolutional layers on top of each other, the network can extract increasingly complex features from the input data, eventually learning high-level representations of the objects or patterns in the image.

In addition to convolutional layers, CNNs typically include other types of layers, such as pooling layers, which reduce the size of the output by subsampling the input data, and fully connected layers, which perform a linear transformation on the output of the previous layer and produce the final output of the network.

Figure 42.1   Example of a convolutional neural network

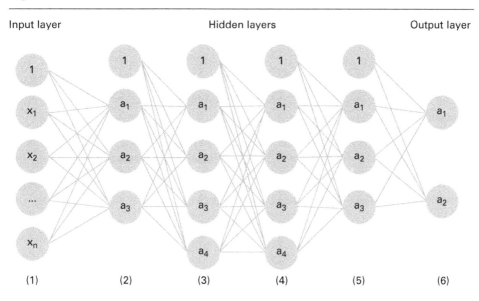

One of the key advantages of CNNs is their ability to learn features automatically from raw data, without the need for handcrafted features or domain-specific knowledge. This makes them well-suited for tasks like object recognition, where the objects may have complex shapes, textures or backgrounds. CNNs are also highly scalable and can be trained on Big Data sets, making them useful for applications like autonomous vehicles, facial recognition and medical image analysis.

CNNs have been used successfully in a wide range of applications, from identifying cats and dogs in images to diagnosing diseases from medical images. Some of the most well-known CNN architectures include AlexNet, VGGNet, ResNet and InceptionNet, each of which has its own unique structure and set of design principles.[2]

Despite their success, CNNs are not without their challenges. One of the biggest challenges is overfitting, where the network becomes too specialized to the training data and is not accurate when confronted with new data. This can be addressed through techniques like dropout, which randomly removes nodes from the network during training, and regularization, which adds a penalty term to the loss function to discourage complex models. Another challenge is interpretability, where it can be difficult to understand how the network is making its predictions. This has led to the development of techniques like saliency maps and gradient-based visualization methods, which can help to explain the features that are important for a given prediction.

To successfully apply convolutional neural networks, teams typically need knowledge about the following topics:

- **Deep learning concepts:** neural networks, backpropagation, activation functions and regularization are essential to build and train CNNs effectively.

- **Image processing:** image representation, feature extraction and image augmentation are necessary to work with image datasets and preprocess them for use in CNNs.

- **CNN architecture:** the architecture of CNNs, including the role of convolutional layers, pooling layers, and fully connected layers, is important for building and tuning effective CNN models.

- **Optimization algorithms:** stochastic gradient descent (SGD), Adam and RMSprop are essential for training CNNs efficiently and effectively.

- **Hyperparameter tuning:** how to tune hyperparameters such as learning rate, batch size and number of epochs is important for optimizing the performance of CNN models.

As you can imagine from these knowledge domains, building a convolutional neural network requires specialist knowledge.

Recurrent neural networks

A recurrent neural network (RNN) is a type of artificial neural network that is designed to handle sequential data, such as speech, text or time series data. RNNs are especially useful in applications that require processing of sequential data where the current output depends on past inputs and outputs.

At its core, an RNN is made up of a chain of interconnected nodes, or 'cells', that process sequential data one step at a time.[3] Each cell takes an input xt and produces an output ht and an internal state st that is passed on to the next cell. The output ht and the state st are both functions of the input xt and the previous state st-1.

The key feature of RNNs is their ability to 'remember' previous inputs and use this information to inform the current output. This is achieved through the use of feedback connections that allow information to be passed from one step of the sequence to the next.

The most commonly used type of RNN cell is the long short-term memory (LSTM) cell.[4] The LSTM cell includes several gating mechanisms that control the flow of information through the cell, allowing it to selectively remember or forget information from previous steps in the sequence.

One of the main advantages of RNNs is their ability to handle variable-length input sequences. Unlike traditional feedforward neural networks, which require

Figure 42.2 Recurrent neural networks

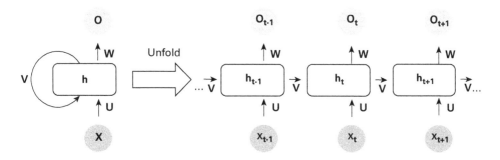

fixed-length input vectors, RNNs can process inputs of arbitrary length. This makes them well-suited to tasks such as speech recognition, where the length of the input sequence can vary depending on the length of the spoken utterance.

RNNs have been successfully applied to a wide range of tasks, including language modelling, machine translation, speech recognition and image captioning. In NLP, RNNs have been used to build language models that predict the probability of a sequence of words, which has applications in speech recognition, machine translation and text generation.

Another common application of RNNs is in time series forecasting, where the goal is to predict future values in a time series based on historical data. In this context, RNNs can be used to model the temporal dependencies in the data and generate accurate forecasts.

Building capability in RNNs is, similar to CNNs, dependent on the business problem the algorithm is trying to solve. From a capability point of view, the knowledge required to build an RNN is the same level of difficulty as the CNN.

Generative adversarial networks

Generative adversarial networks (GANs) are a type of deep learning architecture that can generate new data that resembles the training data. GANs were introduced by Ian Goodfellow in 2014, and since then they have become a popular tool for generating realistic images, videos and audio.[5]

GANs consist of two main components: a generator and a discriminator. The generator is a neural network that learns to generate new samples from random noise, while the discriminator is another neural network that learns to distinguish between real and fake samples.

The generator takes random noise as input and generates a new sample that is intended to resemble the training data. The discriminator then takes this generated sample and tries to classify it as either real or fake.[6] The two networks are trained together in a process called adversarial training, where the generator learns to generate samples that can fool the discriminator, while the discriminator learns to better distinguish between real and fake samples. As the generator learns to generate more realistic samples, the discriminator becomes better at distinguishing between real and fake samples. The goal of training is to reach a point where the generator can generate samples that are indistinguishable from the real training data.

One of the key benefits of GANs is that they can generate new samples without explicit programming. Instead of designing rules and constraints for generating new data, GANs learn to generate new samples by learning from the training data. This makes GANs very flexible and powerful tools for generating a wide range of data types.

GANs have been successfully applied to a variety of domains, including image synthesis, video synthesis, music generation and NLP. One of the most popular applications of GANs is in the generation of realistic images. GANs have been used to generate images of faces, animals and landscapes that are indistinguishable from real photographs. GANs have also been used to generate images that combine multiple styles or attributes, such as images that blend the style of one image with the content of another.

In NLP, GANs have been used to generate realistic text and dialogue. This has applications in chatbots and virtual assistants, where generating realistic dialogue is critical for creating a seamless user experience.

One of the challenges with GANs is that they can be difficult to train. The generator and discriminator must be carefully balanced to prevent one network from overpowering the other, and the training process can be unstable. Researchers have developed a number of techniques to improve the stability of GANs, including the use of different loss functions, regularization techniques and training strategies.

Figure 42.3   Generator and discriminator

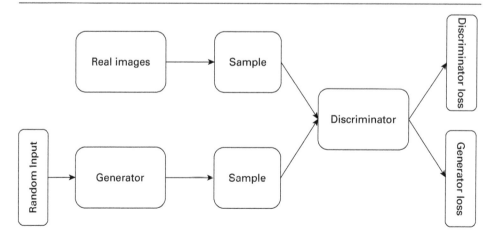

Despite their challenges, GANs are a powerful tool for generating new data that closely resembles the training data. With their ability to generate realistic images, videos and audio, GANs have the potential to revolutionize a wide range of fields, from entertainment and art to medicine and scientific research.

42.4 Deep learning summary

In this section, we looked in detail at the deep learning capability. Deep learning is a subset of machine learning that uses neural networks to learn from data and make predictions or classifications. It has become increasingly popular in recent years due to its ability to handle complex and unstructured data, such as images, audio and natural language.

To build a deep learning capability, organizations need to build upon the processes and people components that were discussed in the previous part of the Enterprise Big Data Framework. But, to build this capability, advanced knowledge about deep learning is required.

In this section, we discussed some of the most important capabilities required to build deep learning solutions: convolutional neural networks, recurrent neural networks and generative adversarial networks. Organizations that want to use the capabilities of deep learning need to specialize in these knowledge domains, and build knowledge capabilities in these areas.

Notes

1 I Goodfellow, Y Bengio and A Courville (2016) *Deep Learning*, MIT Press

2 F Tu, S Yin, P Ouyang, S Tang, L Liu and S Wei. Deep convolutional neural network architecture with reconfigurable computation patterns, *IEEE Transactions on Very Large Scale Integration (VLSI) Systems*, 2017 25 (8), 2220–33

3 L R Medsker and J C Jain. Recurrent neural networks, *Design and Applications*, 2001 5, 64–67

4 W Zaremba, I Sutskever and O Vinyals. Recurrent neural network regularization, *arXiv* preprint, 2014, arXiv:1409.2329

5 I Goodfellow, J Pouget-Abadie, M Mirza, B Xu, D Warde-Farley, S Ozair, A Courville and Y Bengio. Generative adversarial networks, *Communications of the ACM*, 2020 63 (11), 139–44

6 A Creswell, T White, V Dumoulin, K Arulkumaran, B Sengupta and A A Bharath. Generative adversarial networks: an overview, *IEEE Signal Processing Magazine*, 2018 35 (1), 53–65

Reasoning

43

43.1 Introduction to reasoning

In the context of enterprise Big Data and artificial intelligence (AI), the reasoning capability is the process of using logical rules and deductions by a computer to draw conclusions based on available information. It is an essential component of intelligent systems that enables them to make decisions and solve complex problems.

The study of reasoning is an old and fundamental field of philosophy, dating back to ancient Greek philosophers such as Aristotle.[1] Philosophers have long been interested in understanding how people reason and make decisions, and this interest has continued to the present day. Some of the most fundamental philosophical questions, such as 'what defines a human?' and 'how can we determine "intelligence"?' all question how people (and therefore machines) need to reason.

Reasoning in AI can be broadly classified into two types: deductive reasoning and inductive reasoning.[2]

Deductive reasoning is a process of logical inference that starts with a set of general rules or premises and derives specific conclusions from them. For example, if we know that all humans are mortal and that Jan is a human, we can deduce that Jan is mortal. Deductive reasoning is often used in expert systems and rule-based systems, where a set of rules are encoded and used to make decisions based on the input data.

Inductive reasoning, on the other hand, is a process of generalizing specific observations to form a more general conclusion. For example, if we observe that all the apples we have seen so far are red, we might generalize that all apples are red. Inductive reasoning is often used in machine learning and data mining, where patterns are discovered in large datasets and used to make predictions.

In AI, reasoning is often used in conjunction with other techniques such as natural language processing (NLP), computer vision and machine learning to build intelligent systems that can understand, reason and make decisions based on complex data.[3] For example, reasoning can be used to interpret natural language queries, understand complex images and make decisions in complex environments such as autonomous vehicles or robotic systems.

There are many organizations that have developed mature reasoning capabilities across a range of industries, including healthcare, finance and manufacturing. Here are a few examples:

- **IBM Watson** is a cognitive computing platform that includes a wide range of reasoning capabilities, such as NLP, machine learning and decision-making. Watson is used in a variety of industries, including healthcare, finance and retail, and has been trained on vast amounts of data to make complex decisions and provide insights into a range of business challenges.

- **GE Aviation** has developed a mature reasoning capability that uses machine learning and other AI techniques to analyse vast amounts of data from aircraft engines and other systems. The system can detect and diagnose potential issues before they become major problems, helping to minimize downtime and reduce maintenance costs.

- **Johnson & Johnson** has developed a mature reasoning capability in healthcare, using AI and machine learning to develop new drugs and treatments. The company has also used AI to analyse patient data to improve outcomes and reduce costs.

- **Amazon** has developed a mature reasoning capability in retail, using AI and machine learning to personalize the customer experience and make recommendations based on customer behaviour and preferences. The system is also used to optimize pricing and inventory management.

Establishing a sound and mature reasoning capability is an essential component of intelligent systems that enables them to make sense of complex information and make decisions based on available data.

43.2 Purpose and maturity levels of reasoning

Purpose

Reasoning is a key component of intelligent systems that allows them to process and interpret complex information, draw inferences and make decisions based on available evidence. The purpose of the reasoning capability in AI is to enable intelligent systems to make decisions and solve problems based on available data and knowledge.

The purpose of reasoning is outlined in Table 43.1.

In AI, reasoning is often used in conjunction with other techniques such as deep learning (discussed in Chapter 42) and knowledge representation (discussed in Chapter 44) to build intelligent systems that can understand and reason using massive amounts of data. For example, reasoning can be used to interpret natural

Table 43.1   The purpose of the reasoning capability

Capability	Purpose
Reasoning	Defines the ability of an organization to develop systems and solutions that can mimic human decision-making.

language queries, understand complex images and make decisions in complex environments such as autonomous vehicles or robotic systems.

There are several types of reasoning used in AI, including deductive reasoning, inductive reasoning, abductive reasoning and analogical reasoning. Each of these types of reasoning has its own strengths and weaknesses and is suited to different types of problems. We will discuss these different approaches in more detail in section 44.2.

Maturity levels

Table 43.2   Maturity levels of the reasoning capability

Maturity Level	Description
Level 1 – Initial	Reasoning is not a formalized capability within the organization. There is no standard process for how reasoning solutions should be managed or approached.
Level 2 – Managed	The organization has developed standard practices for the development of reasoning systems, but these are not yet consistently applied across the organization. The organization may have some understanding of the benefits of a more structured approach, but there may be resistance to change.
Level 3 – Defined	The reasoning process is well-defined and consistently applied across the organization. The organization has a clear understanding of the benefits of a structured approach to reasoning, and has developed a standard set of guidelines, procedures and metrics for reasoning. There may be some degree of automation in the reasoning process, which can help to improve consistency and efficiency.
Level 4 – Controlled	The organization has established a data-driven approach to reasoning, using metrics and analysis to monitor and improve the quality of reasoning outcomes. There is a focus on continuous improvement, with regular measurement and analysis of the reasoning process to identify opportunities for optimization.

(continued)

Table 43.2   (Continued)

Maturity Level	Description
Level 5 – Optimized	The organization has achieved a high level of maturity in its reasoning capabilities, with a focus on continuous optimization and innovation. The reasoning process is constantly monitored and refined, with a strong emphasis on automation and advanced reasoning techniques. The organization is able to rapidly adapt to changing circumstances and leverage new data sources to continuously improve the quality and efficiency of its reasoning outcomes.

In order to track progress and determine how well established the reasoning capability of an organization is in practice, we can use the five different maturity levels.

An organization with a mature reasoning capability would be able to leverage AI and machine learning to make better decisions, solve complex business challenges and drive innovation across the organization. Many industries such as finance, healthcare and energy, for example, require complex decision-making that cannot be easily achieved through traditional analytics. Reasoning capabilities can help organizations analyse complex data sets and identify patterns and trends that would be difficult to discern with traditional analytics.

The five levels of maturity in the reasoning capability are listed in Table 43.2.

There are many benefits to having a mature reasoning capability. In the next section, we will look at some of the core components with which organization can structure a mature reasoning capability.

43.3 Structuring reasoning

With the reasoning capability, organizations are structuring computers to follow logical rules, similar to the way that people reason. However, in computers, this is more difficult to establish, especially because most computer systems only support basic processes, like sequences and elementary logic (think about if-else statements). Reasoning in AI goes a few steps deeper in that we are training computers to make balanced trade-offs, based on a number of considerations.

In this section, we will dive into some of the most important components and activities with which organizations can structure a reasoning capability. We will discuss **reasoning techniques, knowledge bases, reasoning systems** and **training reasoning systems**.

Reasoning techniques

For any system to be able to reason, it needs to apply a way in which the computer can think. This process is known as selecting the right reasoning techniques. There are several types of reasoning techniques that can be used to build AI systems. To build suitable systems, organizations need to be able to differentiate between these different approaches and select the right one based on the business problem.

Deductive reasoning

Deductive reasoning in AI means drawing logical conclusions based on a set of given premises or assumptions. It is a process of reasoning that starts with general principles and draws specific conclusions based on those principles. In deductive reasoning, the conclusion follows necessarily from the premises. For example, if we know that 'all men are mortal' and 'Socrates is a man', we can logically conclude that 'Socrates is mortal'.

In AI, deductive reasoning is used in expert systems and rule-based systems, where a set of rules or axioms are provided and the system applies logical inference to deduce conclusions. It is also used in formal verification and theorem proving, where the goal is to prove a statement based on a set of logical rules or axioms. Deductive reasoning is a powerful tool in AI as it allows for logical deduction and can be used to validate the correctness of a system. However, it is limited by the quality of the premises and the completeness of the logical rules or axioms. If the premises are false or incomplete, or if the logical rules are not well-defined, the conclusions drawn by deductive reasoning may also be incorrect.

Inductive reasoning

Inductive reasoning is a type of reasoning in which a general rule or principle is inferred from specific examples or observations. In other words, inductive reasoning involves drawing general conclusions based on a limited set of observations or evidence.

In AI, inductive reasoning is commonly used in machine learning to train models based on a set of labelled examples or data. The algorithm learns to identify patterns and regularities in the data, and then uses these patterns to make predictions or classifications on new, unlabelled data.

For example, consider a machine learning algorithm that is being trained to recognize handwritten digits. The algorithm is fed a large dataset of labelled examples, each consisting of an image of a handwritten digit and a corresponding label indicating the correct digit (e.g. '7'). The algorithm analyses the patterns and features of the images and uses this information to learn a set of rules that can be used to identify handwritten digits in new, unlabelled images.

One of the key advantages of inductive reasoning in AI is its ability to learn from large and complex datasets, even when the underlying patterns or relationships are not well understood. However, there is always a risk of overfitting, where the algorithm learns patterns that are specific to the training data but do not generalize well to new, unseen data. To mitigate this risk, various regularization techniques and validation strategies are employed in machine learning as discussed in Chapter 24.

Abductive reasoning

Abductive reasoning is a type of reasoning in which an individual attempts to find the best explanation for a given observation or set of observations. In other words, it involves working backwards from observed effects to infer the most likely cause or explanation. Abductive reasoning is often used in AI and machine learning, particularly in tasks related to diagnosis and prediction. Abductive reasoning involves generating hypotheses or possible explanations for a given set of observations or data. The process of generating these hypotheses involves making assumptions or educated guesses about the underlying causes of the observations, based on prior knowledge and experience. These assumptions are then tested against the observed data, and refined or revised as necessary.

Abductive reasoning differs from deductive reasoning, which involves drawing logical conclusions based on given premises or assumptions, and inductive reasoning, which involves generalizing from specific observations to broader patterns or rules.

Abductive reasoning is used in many applications of AI, including medical diagnosis, fault detection in complex systems and NLP. In these applications, abductive reasoning can help to identify the most likely cause or explanation for a given problem, based on observed symptoms or behaviours. One of the key challenges in abductive reasoning is determining the most likely explanation or hypothesis from a set of possibilities. This can be addressed through various techniques, such as probabilistic reasoning and Bayesian networks, which can help to quantify the likelihood of different hypotheses based on available evidence.

Analogical reasoning

Analogical reasoning is a form of reasoning in which a conclusion is drawn by comparing the similarities between two different situations or problems. In other words, analogical reasoning involves using known information from a familiar domain to infer and make decisions about an unfamiliar domain.

In AI, analogical reasoning is often used in the field of knowledge representation and reasoning. By drawing analogies between different situations or problems, AI systems can generalize their understanding of concepts and transfer knowledge from one domain to another. This can lead to more efficient problem-solving and decision-making processes.

For example, an AI system designed to diagnose medical conditions may use analogical reasoning to compare the symptoms of a patient to those of previously diagnosed cases. By finding similarities between different cases, the AI system can make a more accurate diagnosis for the current patient. Analogical reasoning is also used in NLP, where AI systems use analogies to understand the meaning of words and phrases in context. This allows them to understand and generate more natural and human-like language.

Knowledge base

A **knowledge base** is a critical component of an AI system's reasoning capabilities. It provides the necessary information and rules for the AI system to make informed decisions and draw logical conclusions. A knowledge base is a repository of information and rules that an AI system can use to reason and make decisions.[4] The knowledge base contains a set of facts and rules about a specific domain that the AI system can use to draw conclusions or make predictions based on new data.

A knowledge base can be created manually by experts in a domain, or it can be generated automatically by the AI system through machine learning techniques such as supervised learning, unsupervised learning or reinforcement learning. The knowledge base is used for reasoning by applying inference rules to the facts and rules stored in the knowledge base. Inference is the process of using logical rules to draw conclusions based on the available evidence. The AI system uses the knowledge base to answer questions, make predictions and solve problems in the domain.

There are various examples of knowledge bases that can be used for reasoning in AI, depending on the specific domain and purpose. Here are a few examples:

- **Medical diagnosis:** A knowledge base for medical diagnosis could include information about symptoms, medical history, lab results and possible diseases or conditions that match the patient's symptoms. A reasoning system using this knowledge base could then determine the most likely diagnosis based on the available data.

- **Fraud detection:** A knowledge base for fraud detection could include information about common fraud patterns, known fraudulent activities and typical behaviours associated with fraud. A reasoning system using this knowledge base could then analyse transaction data to identify potential fraudulent activity.

- **Customer support:** A knowledge base for customer support could include information about common customer issues, troubleshooting steps and solutions to common problems. A reasoning system using this knowledge base could then guide customer support agents through the process of diagnosing and solving customer problems.

The amount of data in a knowledge base depends on the specific application and the complexity of the problem being addressed. In some cases, a relatively small knowledge base may be sufficient to achieve a desired level of reasoning. In other cases, a large and complex knowledge base may be necessary to support more sophisticated reasoning capabilities. Additionally, as we discussed in Chapter 35, the quality of the data in the knowledge base is just as important as the quantity, as inaccurate or incomplete data can lead to flawed reasoning and incorrect conclusions.

Reasoning system

Once the knowledge base is developed, the reasoning system can be implemented. This involves building the algorithms and software that will process the data, perform the reasoning and make decisions.

A reasoning system is an AI system that is designed to perform logical and inferential reasoning based on a knowledge base. The knowledge base contains a set of rules, axioms and facts that the reasoning system uses to draw conclusions, make inferences and generate new knowledge.[5]

A reasoning system can be designed to use different types of reasoning techniques, such as deductive reasoning, inductive reasoning, abductive reasoning or analogical reasoning, depending on the specific problem and the domain of knowledge. The system can also be designed to use different types of inference mechanisms, such as forward or backward chaining, to process the information in the knowledge base.

A reasoning system typically consists of four main components:

- **Knowledge base:** A structured set of data that represents the domain knowledge and rules used for reasoning.
- **Inference engine:** The component that processes the rules and knowledge in the knowledge base to make inferences or draw conclusions.
- **User interface:** The component that allows the user to interact with the reasoning system, input data and retrieve the results of the reasoning process.
- **Explanation system:** The component that provides explanations for the reasoning process and results to the user.

Reasoning systems are useful in situations where there is a need to make decisions based on complex knowledge, uncertain or incomplete data, or multiple criteria.

Train and test the reasoning system

In reasoning systems, training is the process of creating or improving the system's knowledge base and rules based on available data and domain expertise. The training process can involve various techniques, such as machine learning algorithms, to learn patterns from the data and generate rules that can be used for reasoning. The goal of training is to create a robust and accurate knowledge base that can be used for reasoning in a given domain.

Once the reasoning system is trained, it can be tested to evaluate its accuracy and effectiveness. Testing involves applying the reasoning system to a set of test data or scenarios and comparing the output with expected results. The testing process can reveal weaknesses or limitations in the system, which can then be addressed through additional training or refinement of the system's rules and knowledge base.

43.4 Reasoning summary

Reasoning plays a crucial role in enabling AI systems to make intelligent decisions and provide valuable insights in various fields. It helps in solving complex problems, making predictions and providing explanations for the decisions made. Developing mature reasoning capabilities can help organizations in many ways, most notably in supporting automated decision making.

To build a mature reasoning capability, organizations should think about the way they establish reasoning techniques, and on which data the reasoning will be applied. Different reasoning techniques, such as deductive, inductive, abductive and analogical reasoning, can be used. A knowledge base can be used to store and retrieve information for reasoning, and it can be built through various methods, such as expert systems and machine learning algorithms.

This data, known as the knowledge base, will allow an organization to establish a reasoning system and to finally test this system for accuracy of results. Ultimately, reasoning is a critical capability in any AI system and building a mature reasoning capability can provide significant benefits to organizations.

Notes

1   J M Cooper (1986) *Reason and Human Good in Aristotle*, Hackett Publishing
2   P A Flach and A C Kakas. Abductive and inductive reasoning: background and issues, *Abduction and Induction: Essays on their relation and integration*, 2000, 1–27
3   D C Parkes and M P Wellman. Economic reasoning and artificial intelligence, *Science*, 2015 349 (6245), 267–72

4 R Socher, D Chen, C D Manning and A Ng. Reasoning with neural tensor networks for knowledge base completion, *Advances in Neural Information Processing Systems*, 2013 26

5 M P Georgeff and F Ingrand (1989) Decision-making in an embedded reasoning system, In International Joint Conference on Artificial Intelligence

Knowledge Representation   44

44.1 Introduction to knowledge representation

Knowledge representation is a crucial component of artificial intelligence (AI), as it provides a means of storing, manipulating and reasoning with knowledge. In essence, it involves the process of encoding information in a way that a computer can understand and use to make intelligent decisions.

The main goal of knowledge representation is to enable computers to perform intelligent tasks that normally require human-like reasoning, such as understanding natural language, recognizing objects in images and solving complex problems. The key challenge of knowledge representation is to develop methods for representing knowledge in a way that is both meaningful and computationally tractable.

The reason that knowledge representation is a separate capability (and not part of reasoning) is that building systems that can represent knowledge requires significant technical knowledge and skills. In effect, this capability allows organizations to store and retrieve information effectively.

Because it is so specialist, knowledge representation is typically conducted by **knowledge engineers**. Knowledge engineers are responsible for designing and implementing knowledge representation systems, which involves selecting an appropriate representation language or technique and designing the schema or ontology to represent the relevant knowledge. They may work with subject matter experts to elicit and formalize domain-specific knowledge, and they may also be responsible for integrating the knowledge representation system with other components of an AI system.

Knowledge representation is an essential component of AI because it allows us to formalize and organize knowledge in a way that can be processed by computer systems. Without effective methods for representing knowledge, it would be difficult, if not impossible, for computers to reason, learn or communicate with humans. Here are some key reasons why knowledge representation is important in AI:

- **Facilitating reasoning and decision-making:** Knowledge representation provides a means of organizing and structuring knowledge in a way that supports reasoning and decision-making. By representing knowledge in a structured format, AI systems can use inference mechanisms to derive new knowledge or make decisions based on existing knowledge.

- **Enabling machine learning:** Machine learning algorithms rely on data to learn patterns and make predictions. Effective knowledge representation is necessary to structure the data and ensure that it can be processed by machine learning algorithms.

- **Supporting natural language processing:** Natural language processing (NLP) is a subfield of AI that focuses on enabling computers to understand and generate human language. Effective knowledge representation is essential for NLP, as it provides a means of representing the meaning of words and sentences in a way that can be processed by computers.

- **Facilitating knowledge sharing and reuse:** Knowledge representation provides a means of capturing and organizing knowledge in a way that can be shared and reused across different systems or applications. This can lead to more efficient and effective AI systems, as well as greater collaboration and innovation across different domains.

- **Supporting explainability and interpretability:** As AI systems become more complex and sophisticated, there is a growing need for them to be explainable and interpretable. Effective knowledge representation can facilitate explainability by making it easier to understand how an AI system arrived at a particular decision or recommendation.

Because ultimately every AI system needs to store and retrieve information, typically within very short time frames, knowledge representation has become a growing field of interest. The way in which data can be represented effectively to support AI systems and applications has become a fundamental capability to master.

44.2 Purpose and maturity levels of knowledge representation

Purpose

The purpose of knowledge representation is to provide a means of formalizing and organizing knowledge in a way that can be processed by computer systems. By representing knowledge in a structured format, AI systems can use inference mechanisms to derive new knowledge or make decisions based on existing knowledge.

The purpose of the knowledge representation capability is shown in Table 44.1.

Additionally, knowledge representation can have a significant influence on the speed and accuracy of AI systems. Effective knowledge representation can help AI

Table 44.1   The purpose of the knowledge representation capability

Capability	Purpose
Knowledge representation	Defines the ability of an organization to effectively store knowledge in the enterprise, so it can be used by information systems.

systems process information more quickly and accurately, while poor knowledge representation can lead to errors, inefficiencies and inaccuracies. For this reason, having a high level of maturity in this capability is beneficial because it will improve the performance of AI systems.

Knowledge representation can help AI systems process information more efficiently by reducing the amount of data that needs to be processed. For example, if knowledge is represented in a structured format, such as an ontology or knowledge graph, an AI system can use inference mechanisms to derive new knowledge based on existing knowledge, without having to reprocess all the original data.

Additionally, the right knowledge representation will also make AI models more accurate. Knowledge representation can help AI systems make more accurate predictions or decisions by enabling them to reason about uncertain or incomplete information. For example, if an AI system is able to represent knowledge in a probabilistic or fuzzy format, it can make more accurate predictions based on uncertain or incomplete data.

Maturity levels

The maturity of the knowledge representation capability can have a significant impact on the performance of AI systems. In general, more mature and sophisticated knowledge representation capabilities can enable AI systems to process information more efficiently and accurately, while less mature or primitive knowledge representation capabilities may lead to errors, inefficiencies and inaccuracies.

Additionally, more mature knowledge representation capabilities can facilitate interoperability between different AI systems or applications. By using standardized representations, such as ontologies or knowledge graphs (discussed in the next section), different AI systems can share and reuse knowledge more effectively, leading to more accurate and efficient processing of information.

The five different maturity levels of the knowledge representation capability are listed in Table 44.2.

As depicted in Table 44.2, the maturity of the knowledge representation capability will have a direct impact on the other AI capabilities, most notably the deep learning (see Chapter 42) and reasoning (see Chapter 43) capabilities. A low maturity in knowledge representation will hinder development or progress in other domains.

Table 44.2 Maturity levels of the knowledge representation capability

Maturity Level	Description
Level 1 – Initial	The organization uses the basic conceptualization of knowledge. It includes simple representations of knowledge, such as hierarchical taxonomies or lists of rules, which can be used to classify or reason about data. At this level, knowledge representation is typically ad hoc and may not be easily shareable or reusable.
Level 2 – Managed	The organization uses more structured representations of knowledge, such as ontologies or knowledge graphs. At this level, knowledge representation becomes more standardized and formalized, enabling better sharing and reuse of knowledge across different systems or applications.
Level 3 – Defined	The organization uses automated methods for acquiring knowledge from data, such as machine learning or natural language processing (NLP). At this level, knowledge representation becomes more adaptive and dynamic, enabling systems to learn and refine their knowledge representation based on new data.
Level 4 – Controlled	The organization uses semantic reasoning to derive new knowledge based on existing knowledge. At this level, knowledge representation becomes more inferential and sophisticated, enabling systems to make more accurate and nuanced predictions or decisions based on uncertain or incomplete data.
Level 5 – Optimized	The organization use cognitive reasoning to simulate human-level reasoning and decision-making. At this level, knowledge representation becomes more human-like, enabling systems to handle more complex and nuanced tasks that require higher-level reasoning and cognitive abilities.

44.3 Structuring knowledge representation

In order to structure knowledge representation, we will discuss different ways in which data can be represented. Some of the approaches in which to represent data are very simple (like tables), whereas others might be more complex (like knowledge graphs).

Simple list and tables

Organizations can start with simple lists or tables to represent knowledge. For example, they can create a spreadsheet that lists all the products or services they offer, along with their descriptions and prices. A simple list or table is a basic way of organizing knowledge in a structured format. It consists of a set of items that are listed in rows or columns, with each item corresponding to a specific category or attribute. For example, a company may use a simple table to organize a list of its products, with each row representing a different product and each column representing a different attribute such as the product name, price and description.

Simple lists or tables are easy to create and understand, and they can be useful for presenting information in a straightforward and concise manner. They are also easy to maintain and update, as new items can be added or removed simply by adding or deleting rows or columns.

However, simple lists or tables have limitations in terms of their expressiveness and ability to represent complex relationships between concepts. They are typically limited to representing simple one-to-one relationships between items and attributes, and they do not provide any explicit way of representing relationships between different items in the list.

Taxonomies

Taxonomies are a hierarchical way of organizing knowledge into categories and subcategories, where each category represents a different level of abstraction or granularity. Taxonomies are commonly used in areas such as e-commerce, digital asset management and content management, where they are used to classify products, assets or content into different categories for easy navigation and retrieval.

A taxonomy typically consists of a set of nodes, where each node represents a category or subcategory, and edges that connect the nodes to form a hierarchical structure. Each node can have multiple child nodes, but only one parent node. For example, a taxonomy of books may include categories such as Fiction, Non-Fiction, Biography and History, each of which can have multiple subcategories.

Taxonomies provide a more structured way of organizing knowledge than simple lists or tables, and they can help to provide a more intuitive way of navigating and exploring large knowledge domains. They can also help to ensure consistency and accuracy in the representation of knowledge, by providing a standardized and agreed-upon set of categories and subcategories.

However, taxonomies are limited in their ability to represent complex relationships between concepts, as they are typically limited to representing hierarchical relationships. They also require careful design and maintenance to ensure that they remain up to date and relevant, particularly in rapidly evolving knowledge domains.

Ontologies

Organizations can use ontologies to represent more complex and abstract knowledge domains. For example, a medical organization can create an ontology that represents the relationships between diseases, symptoms and treatments. Ontologies provide a more formalized and standardized way of representing knowledge, which enables better sharing and reuse of knowledge across different systems or applications.

Ontologies are a formal and explicit way of representing knowledge that describes a set of concepts and the relationships between them. An ontology consists of a set of classes, properties and individuals, which are organized in a structured and hierarchical manner. Each class represents a category of things, each property represents a relationship between classes and each individual represents a specific instance of a class. Ontologies are commonly used in fields such as artificial intelligence, natural language processing and semantic web technologies, where they are used to represent knowledge in a machine-readable format. They are particularly useful in areas where knowledge is complex and ambiguous, as they provide a standardized and explicit way of representing knowledge that can be shared and reused across different applications and domains.

Figure 44.1   Example of an ontology for knowledge representation

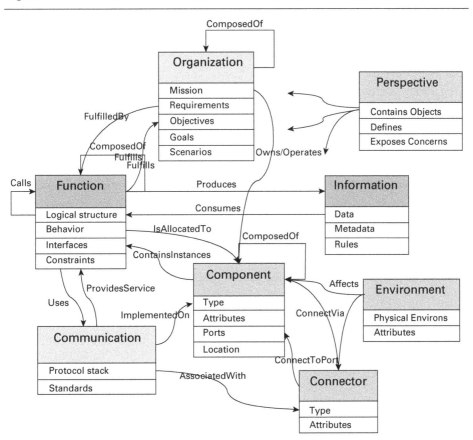

Ontologies are typically constructed using a formal ontology language, such as OWL (Web Ontology Language), RDF (Resource Description Framework) or RDFS (RDF Schema). These languages provide a rich set of constructs for defining classes, properties and individuals, as well as for expressing relationships between them.

Ontologies have several advantages over other forms of knowledge representation. They provide a more expressive and flexible way of representing complex relationships between concepts, and they can help to ensure consistency and accuracy in the representation of knowledge. They also support automated reasoning, which allows machines to draw inferences and make deductions based on the knowledge represented in the ontology.

However, ontologies can be complex to develop and maintain, and they require a significant investment of time and effort. They also require a high degree of domain expertise and may not be appropriate for all applications and domains. Ontologies are a powerful way of structuring knowledge representation, particularly in areas where knowledge is complex and ambiguous. They provide a standardized and explicit way of representing knowledge that can be shared and reused across different applications and domains, and they support automated reasoning and inference.

Knowledge graph

A knowledge graph is a type of knowledge representation that captures knowledge in the form of a graph, where nodes represent entities or concepts, and edges represent relationships between those entities or concepts. Knowledge graphs can be thought of as a network of interrelated concepts, where each concept is linked to other concepts by one or more edges.

Knowledge graphs are commonly used in areas such as NLP, machine learning and data analytics, where they are used to represent complex relationships between entities and concepts in a more intuitive and expressive way. They are particularly useful in areas where the knowledge is distributed across multiple sources and in different formats, as they provide a unified and structured way of representing that knowledge.

Knowledge graphs are typically constructed by extracting information from different sources, such as databases, web pages or documents, and linking that information together into a graph structure. The entities in the graph can be anything from people and organizations to products and events, and the relationships between them can be anything from 'is a member of' to 'is a type of' to 'is located in'.

Knowledge graphs have several advantages over other forms of knowledge representation. They provide a more expressive and flexible way of representing complex relationships between entities and concepts, and they can support automated reasoning and inference. They also enable more advanced data analytics and machine learning techniques, such as graph-based algorithms and neural networks.

Figure 44.2   Example of a knowledge graph

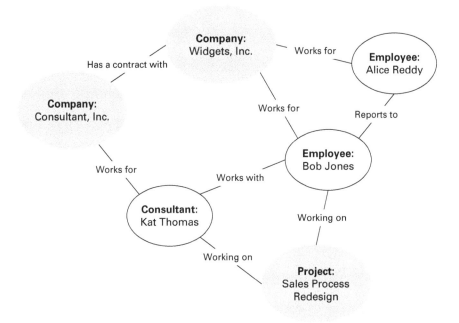

However, knowledge graphs can be complex to develop and maintain, and they require a significant investment of time and effort. They also require a high degree of domain expertise and may not be appropriate for all applications and domains.

Overall, knowledge graphs are a powerful way of structuring knowledge representation, particularly in areas where the knowledge is complex and distributed across multiple sources. They provide a unified and structured way of representing that knowledge, which can be used to support more advanced data analytics and machine learning techniques.

Machine learning models for knowledge representation

Machine learning models can be used to learn data representations directly from raw data, without the need for manual feature engineering or knowledge engineering. These learned representations can then be used as inputs to downstream machine learning models, such as classifiers or regression models.

There are several approaches to learning data representations using machine learning models. One approach is to use unsupervised learning techniques, such as autoencoders or variational autoencoders, to learn a compressed representation of the input data. These models learn to encode the input data into a lower-dimensional latent space, where the encoded representation captures the underlying structure of the input data. The learned representation can then be used as input to downstream machine learning models.

Table 44.3 Common standards for ethical AI

Standard	Description
IEEE Global Initiative on Ethics of Autonomous and Intelligent Systems:	The IEEE (Institute of Electrical and Electronics Engineers) Global Initiative has developed a set of ethical guidelines for the development and deployment of autonomous and intelligent systems. These guidelines include principles related to transparency, accountability, privacy, and human oversight.
The European Commission's Ethics Guidelines for Trustworthy AI	The European Commission has developed a set of guidelines for trustworthy AI that include principles related to human agency and oversight, technical robustness and safety, privacy and data governance, transparency, diversity, non-discrimination, and societal and environmental well-being.
AI4People Global Summit Ethical Framework for a Good AI Society	The AI4People Global Summit has developed a set of ethical guidelines for AI that include principles related to transparency, accountability, privacy and data protection, non-discrimination and fairness, environmental and societal well-being, and respect for human dignity.
The Asilomar AI Principles	The Asilomar AI Principles were developed by a group of AI researchers, scientists, and stakeholders at a conference in 2017. These principles include guidelines related to safety, transparency, privacy, open research, and ethical decision-making.
The Montreal Declaration for Responsible AI	The Montreal Declaration for Responsible AI was developed by a group of AI researchers, practitioners, and ethicists in 2018. This declaration includes principles related to respect for human rights, democratic participation, sustainable development, privacy and data governance, and transparency and explainability.

Another approach is to use supervised learning techniques, such as convolutional neural networks (CNNs) or recurrent neural networks (RNNs), to learn representations of input data for a specific task. We discussed these models in more detail in Chapter 42. For example, a CNN can be trained to learn features from images that are relevant for a particular classification task, such as identifying whether an image contains a cat or a dog. The learned features can then be used as input to a classifier to perform the classification task.

Machine learning models can also be used to learn representations of structured data, such as graphs or sequences. Graph neural networks (GNNs) can be used to learn representations of nodes and edges in a graph, where the learned representations capture the structural relationships between the nodes and edges. Similarly, RNNs can be used to learn representations of sequences, where the learned representations capture the temporal relationships between the elements in the sequence.

The advantage of using machine learning models for data representation is that they can learn representations directly from the data, without the need for manual feature engineering or knowledge engineering. This can lead to more effective and efficient representations, as the models can capture complex and subtle relationships between the input data and the output task. However, the quality of the learned representations depends on the quality and quantity of the training data, and the complexity of the model can lead to overfitting or other performance issues.

44.4 Knowledge representation summary

The knowledge representation capability is a critical aspect of artificial intelligence, which involves representing knowledge about the world in a form that can be processed by machines. The purpose of knowledge representation is to enable machines to reason about the world, make decisions and perform tasks that require understanding and knowledge.

There are several ways to represent knowledge, including simple list or table formats, taxonomies, ontologies, knowledge graphs and machine learning models for data representation. Each of these approaches has its own strengths and weaknesses, and the choice of representation depends on the specific application and the complexity of the domain.

The maturity of knowledge representation can impact the performance of AI systems, as more mature and sophisticated representations can lead to better accuracy, speed and scalability. The five levels of maturity for knowledge representation include simple lists and tables, taxonomies, ontologies, knowledge graphs and machine learning models for data representation.

AI Ethics 45

45.1 Introduction to AI ethics

Artificial intelligence (AI) has become increasingly integrated into various aspects of our daily lives, from personal assistants to healthcare, and is poised to play an even larger role in the future. As AI technology advances, there is a growing need for ethical guidelines and considerations to ensure that AI is developed and used in ways that benefit society as a whole. In this article, we will provide an introduction to AI ethics, including key principles, challenges and current initiatives.

The development and deployment of AI presents several challenges for ethical considerations. The following are some of the key challenges:

- **Bias:** AI systems can perpetuate and amplify existing biases in data and decision-making algorithms. This can lead to unfair treatment of certain groups or individuals, which can have negative social consequences.

- **Privacy:** The use of AI can raise concerns about privacy and data protection, as personal information may be collected and used in ways that individuals did not anticipate or consent to.

- **Transparency:** The complexity of many AI systems can make it difficult to understand how decisions are being made, which can lead to a lack of transparency and accountability.

- **Accountability:** As AI systems become more autonomous, it can be difficult to identify who is responsible for any negative consequences that arise from their use. This can make it difficult to hold individuals or organizations accountable for their actions.

- **Safety:** AI systems can pose a risk to individuals and society as a whole, particularly if they are not designed or deployed in a way that prioritizes safety. This can include risks related to physical harm, cybersecurity and other forms of harm.

In order to overcome these challenges, which are always present in any AI system, organizations need to build an **AI ethics** capability. An AI ethics capability helps organizations to ensure that AI can be used responsibly, with the right checks and balances in place.

To illustrate the importance of building an AI ethics capability, we only have to look at several high-profile ethical scandals related to the development and use of AI systems.[1] Some examples include:

- Bias in facial recognition: In 2018, it was discovered that facial recognition systems developed by tech giants like Amazon and Microsoft had significant bias against people with darker skin tones, leading to concerns about discrimination and racial profiling.

- Cambridge Analytica scandal: Following the US presidential election, it was revealed that political consulting firm Cambridge Analytica had used data harvested from Facebook users without their consent to target political ads during US presidential election, raising concerns about the use of AI and data analytics in political campaigning.

- Autonomous vehicle accidents: Several accidents involving self-driving cars have raised concerns about the safety of AI-powered autonomous vehicles. In 2018, an Uber self-driving car struck and killed a pedestrian in Arizona, leading to questions about the safety protocols and ethical considerations involved in testing autonomous vehicles on public roads.

- Amazon's biased hiring algorithm: In a widely published exposé, it was discovered that Amazon had developed an AI-powered hiring algorithm that was biased against women, leading to concerns about the use of AI in HR and recruitment.

These scandals highlight the potential ethical risks and challenges associated with the development and use of AI systems and demonstrate the importance of ensuring that AI is developed and used in ways that are consistent with ethical principles and values. It also emphasizes the need for organizations to build capability in AI ethics to prevent such scandals in the future.

45.2 Purpose and maturity levels of AI ethics

Purpose

The purpose of establishing an AI ethics capability in organizations is to ensure that AI is developed and used in ways that are consistent with ethical principles and values. By establishing AI ethics, organizations are ensuring that algorithms are used responsibly, without undesired bias and in line with industry best practices.

The purpose of the AI ethics capability is outlined in Table 45.1.

Building an AI ethics capability can result in several benefits for organizations: it can help to ensure that AI systems are developed and used in ways that are consistent with ethical principles and values, mitigate risks, comply with laws and regulations,

Table 45.1   The purpose of the AI ethics capability

Capability	Purpose
AI ethics	Defines the ability of an a organization to develop, create and deploy AI solutions in a responsible and socially acceptable manner.

promote innovation, gain a competitive advantage and improve decision-making. By investing in AI ethics, organizations can build public trust and confidence in AI, and help to ensure that it delivers maximum benefits to society.

Amongst the most important benefits for organizations, the AI ethics capability will help ensure the following long-term benefits:

- **Social responsibility:** Organizations have a social responsibility to develop and use AI systems in ways that benefit society as a whole. This involves ensuring that AI is developed and used in ways that are fair, transparent and accountable, and that respect privacy and human rights.

- **Legal compliance:** Many countries are introducing laws and regulations that require organizations to ensure that AI systems are developed and used in ways that are consistent with ethical principles and values. Failure to comply with these laws and regulations can result in legal and financial penalties, as well as damage to an organization's reputation.

- **Risk management:** Developing and deploying AI systems can involve significant risks, including the risk of bias, discrimination and other ethical issues. By establishing an AI ethics capability, organizations can identify and mitigate these risks, and ensure that AI is developed and used in ways that minimize harm and maximize benefits.

- **Innovation:** Ensuring that AI is developed and used in ways that are consistent with ethical principles and values can help to promote innovation by building public trust and confidence in AI. This can encourage greater investment in AI research and development, as well as greater adoption of AI in various industries and sectors.

- **Competitive advantage:** Organizations that establish an AI ethics capability can gain a competitive advantage by demonstrating their commitment to ethical values and principles. This can help to build customer loyalty and attract and retain top talent.

Establishing an AI ethics capability is an integral part of an organization's governance system, and should be deeply interwoven with an organization's Big Data strategy (as discussed in Part 3). Effective governance is essential for ensuring that AI is developed and used in ways that are consistent with ethical principles and values. This involves establishing clear policies and procedures for the development and use of AI, and ensuring that these policies and procedures are regularly reviewed and updated to reflect evolving ethical and legal standards. We will discuss the establishment of an ethical AI framework in further detail in section 45.3.

Maturity levels

Not only is it important that an AI ethics capability is established, it needs to operate a significant level of maturity. Developing ethical guidelines is one thing, but the lessons from the scandals mentioned in the previous section have learned that this alone is not enough. A frequently used quote in AI ethics is[2]:

> You cannot have AI ethics without ethics.

It is not possible to have AI ethics without ethics. AI ethics is based on ethical principles and values, which guide the development and use of AI systems in a responsible and ethical manner. Without a foundation of ethics, it would not be possible to establish ethical principles and values for AI.

Ethics is a branch of philosophy that deals with moral principles and values, and it provides a framework for making decisions about what is right and wrong, good and bad, just and unjust. Ethical principles and values guide our behaviour and help us to make decisions that are consistent with our values and beliefs. Similarly, AI ethics is concerned with the development and use of AI systems in ways that are consistent with ethical principles and values. This includes ensuring that AI systems are designed and deployed in ways that are fair, transparent and accountable, and that they respect privacy and human rights.

As a result, organizations should strive to have a significant level of maturity in AI ethics. This can be evaluated by the maturity levels as outlined in Table 45.2.

As can be seen from the five different maturity levels, there are some quite practical aspects that organizations can structure to develop their AI ethics maturity. Elements like structuring an ethical AI framework and establishing a monitoring system can easily be set up. But these measures will already have a significant impact on any organization. We will discuss these and some other structuring components in the following sections.

45.3 Structuring AI ethics

Understanding AI ethics

Before an organization can start to structure AI ethics, it is first important that it understands AI ethics. Organizations should develop a comprehensive understanding of

Table 45.2 Maturity levels of the AI ethics capability

Maturity Level	Description
Level 1 – Initial	The organization has limited awareness and understanding of AI ethics. The organization does not have a well-defined AI ethics framework and does not prioritize ethical considerations in the development and use of AI systems.
Level 2 – Managed	The organization is starting to develop its AI ethics capability. The organization is working on establishing an AI ethics framework and developing processes for embedding ethical considerations into the development and use of AI systems.
Level 3 – Defined	The organization has a well-defined AI ethics framework and established processes for ensuring ethical considerations are embedded into the development and use of AI systems. The organization has a culture of ethical decision-making and regularly reviews its AI systems to ensure they are consistent with ethical principles and values.
Level 4 – Controlled	The organization has a mature AI ethics capability. The organization has a well-established AI ethics framework that is integrated into all stages of the AI development process, from design and development to deployment and monitoring. The organization has a culture of continuous improvement and regularly reviews its AI systems to ensure they are consistent with ethical principles and values.
Level 5 – Optimized	The organization has a highly mature AI ethics capability. The organization continually monitors and improves its AI ethics capability to ensure that it remains aligned with its values and objectives. The organization actively engages with stakeholders to identify emerging ethical issues related to AI and uses this information to improve its AI ethics framework and decision-making processes.

AI ethics, including the key principles, challenges and current initiatives in the field. This can involve engaging with experts in AI ethics, attending conferences and workshops, and conducting research on the topic.

Over the year, several AI ethics principles have emerged that function as a 'red thread' for most organizations, and upon which they establish the rest of their organizational measures.[3] AI ethics principles are a set of guiding values and standards that provide a framework for ethical decision-making related to the development and deployment of AI systems. While there is no single set of principles that are universally accepted, there are several commonly recognized principles that have been developed by industry groups, government agencies and academic organizations. The following are some examples of how AI systems should be designed and deployed:

1 **Fairness:** in a way that is fair and impartial, without discriminating against individuals or groups based on their race, gender, ethnicity, religion, sexual orientation or other protected characteristics.

2 **Transparency:** transparent in their design, operation and decision-making processes, so that individuals and organizations can understand how they work and how decisions are made.

3 **Accountability:** accountable for their actions and outcomes, and those responsible for their development and deployment should be held accountable for any negative consequences.

4 **Privacy and security:** in a way that protects individuals' privacy and security, and organizations should be transparent about how they collect, use and store data.

5 **Human control:** in a way that allows humans to retain control over important decisions, and that ensures AI systems do not pose a threat to human safety or wellbeing.

6 **Ethical use:** in a way that is consistent with ethical principles and values, and that promotes the public good.

These principles provide a useful starting point for organizations to develop their own AI ethics frameworks and to ensure that they are building AI systems that are ethical, trustworthy and beneficial to society.

Ethical guidelines

Organizations should develop clear and comprehensive ethical guidelines for the development and deployment of AI. These guidelines should be based on the key principles of AI ethics and should be regularly reviewed and updated as AI technology advances.

AI ethical guidelines are a set of guidelines that outline ethical considerations and best practices related to the development, deployment and use of AI systems. These guidelines are typically developed by industry groups, government agencies and academic organizations, and they provide a framework for organizations to ensure that their AI systems are designed and used in an ethical and responsible manner.[4] These best practices and standards provide guidance on how to develop ethical guidelines that are aligned with ethical principles and values, and that promote the public good. Some of the most frequently used standards are listed in Table 45.3.

By following these public standards and guidelines, organizations can ensure that their AI systems are aligned with ethical principles and values, and that they promote the public good.

Table 45.3　Common standards for ethical AI

Standard	Description
IEEE Global Initiative on Ethics of Autonomous and Intelligent Systems:	A set of ethical guidelines for the development and deployment of autonomous and intelligent systems. These guidelines include principles related to transparency, accountability, privacy and human oversight.
The European Commission's Ethics Guidelines for Trustworthy AI	A set of guidelines for trustworthy AI that include principles related to human agency and oversight, technical robustness and safety, privacy and data governance, transparency, diversity, non-discrimination, and societal and environmental wellbeing.
AI4People Global Summit Ethical Framework for a Good AI Society	A set of ethical guidelines for AI that include principles related to transparency, accountability, privacy and data protection, non-discrimination and fairness, environmental and societal wellbeing, and respect for human dignity.
The Asilomar AI Principles	Developed by a group of AI researchers, scientists and stakeholders at a conference in 2017, these principles include guidelines related to safety, transparency, privacy, open research and ethical decision-making.
The Montreal Declaration for Responsible AI	Developed by a group of AI researchers, practitioners and ethicists in 2018, this declaration includes principles related to respect for human rights, democratic participation, sustainable development, privacy and data governance, and transparency and explainability.

Ethical frameworks

Organizations should build ethical frameworks for AI decision-making that take into account potential biases and other ethical considerations. This can involve developing transparent and explainable AI algorithms that allow for greater accountability and scrutiny.

An ethical AI framework is a set of guidelines and practices that an organization uses to ensure that its AI systems are designed, developed and deployed in an ethical and responsible manner. An ethical AI framework typically includes ethical principles and values, as well as guidelines and processes for implementing those principles in practice.

The core components of an AI ethical framework are shown in Figure 45.1. The following are the key components of an ethical AI framework.

Ethical principles and values

The foundation of an ethical AI framework is a set of ethical principles and values that guide decision-making and behaviour related to AI systems. These principles and values should be grounded in the organization's core values and mission, and should reflect the ethical concerns and values of society as a whole. Common ethical principles that are relevant to AI include fairness, transparency, accountability, fairness, privacy and security, human control and ethical use.

Governance and accountability

An ethical AI framework should establish clear lines of governance and accountability for AI systems. This includes defining roles and responsibilities for key stakeholders, such as developers, managers and end-users, as well as creating oversight mechanisms

Figure 45.1   Ethical AI framework structure

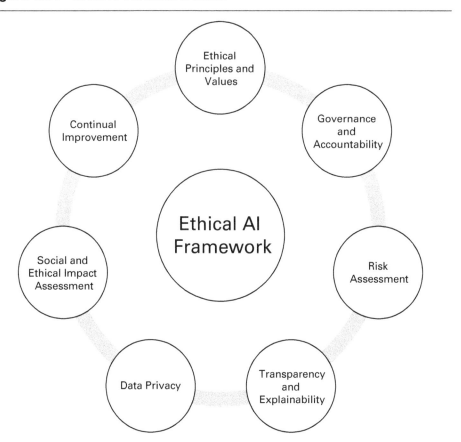

to ensure that AI systems are used in a responsible and ethical manner. Governance and accountability mechanisms may include policies and procedures, training and education programmes, internal and external audits, and reporting mechanisms.

Risk assessment

An ethical AI framework should include processes for identifying, assessing and managing risks associated with AI systems. This includes conducting thorough risk assessments of AI systems to identify potential ethical and social impacts, as well as developing strategies for mitigating those risks. Risk management strategies may include technical safeguards, such as data protection and security measures, as well as legal and regulatory compliance frameworks.

Transparency and explainability

An ethical AI framework should prioritize transparency and explainability in the design and deployment of AI systems. This includes ensuring that AI systems are designed in a way that is transparent to end-users, so that they understand how the system works and how decisions are being made. Explainability mechanisms may include providing clear and concise explanations of how AI algorithms work, as well as providing end-users with access to data and decision-making processes.

Privacy and data protection

An ethical AI framework should prioritize privacy and data protection in the design and deployment of AI systems. This includes implementing appropriate data protection and security measures to ensure that personal and sensitive data is collected, processed and stored in a secure and ethical manner. Organizations should also establish clear policies and procedures for handling data breaches and ensuring that end-users have control over their personal data.

Social and ethical impact assessment

An ethical AI framework should include processes for conducting social and ethical impact assessments of AI systems. This includes assessing the potential impact of AI systems on society, including the impact on human rights, equality and social justice. Organizations should also assess the potential impact of AI systems on the environment, and take steps to mitigate any negative impacts.

Continuous improvement and learning

An ethical AI framework should prioritize continuous improvement and learning in the design and deployment of AI systems. This includes establishing mechanisms for monitoring and evaluating the performance and impact of AI systems over time, as well as learning from ethical and social issues that arise. Organizations should also invest in ongoing education and training programmes for developers, managers and end-users to ensure that they have the knowledge and skills necessary to design, develop and deploy AI systems in an ethical and responsible manner.

Creating ethical review processes

Organizations should establish ethical review processes to ensure that AI systems are developed and deployed in ways that are consistent with ethical guidelines and frameworks. These review processes should involve experts in AI ethics and should be designed to identify and address potential ethical issues.

Once the ethical AI framework has been established, the organization should establish a set of review criteria that will be used to evaluate the AI system or application. This may include criteria related to ethical principles such as transparency, accountability, fairness, privacy and security, as well as legal and regulatory compliance requirements.

To conduct the reviews, the organization should assemble a review team consisting of individuals with relevant expertise and knowledge, such as AI developers, data scientists, legal experts and ethics specialists. The review team should also include representatives from key stakeholder groups, such as end-users, customers and communities impacted by the AI system or application. The review team should conduct a thorough review of the AI systems or applications, using the established review criteria. This may involve reviewing the code and algorithms used in the AI system, assessing the data inputs and outputs, and evaluating the system's performance against established benchmarks and standards.

Finally, based on the results of the review, the review team should identify areas for improvement in the AI system or application. This may include identifying potential ethical or social risks, as well as opportunities to improve the system's transparency, accountability, fairness and other ethical principles.

Training and education

It almost goes without saying that organizations should provide training and education on AI ethics for all employees involved in the development and deployment of AI. This can include training on ethical principles, as well as training on how to identify and address ethical issues that may arise in the development and deployment of AI.

Training in ethical AI can help developers and other stakeholders to understand the ethical principles and values that should guide the development and use of AI technology. This can promote more ethical and responsible AI development and reduce the risk of unintended consequences and negative impacts on individuals and society. By promoting ethical and responsible AI development, organizations can build trust and confidence among their customers, partners and other stakeholders. This can enhance the reputation and brand of the organization, and promote long-term success and sustainability.

Training and education for ethical AI should be integrated and coordinated with the education and skill capability that we discussed in Chapter 38.

AI ethics oversight committee

AI ethics oversight is the process of monitoring and ensuring that the development and deployment of AI technology within an organization is aligned with ethical principles and values. It involves establishing mechanisms to oversee and evaluate the ethical implications of AI systems, identifying and mitigating potential ethical risks and ensuring that the organization's AI practices are transparent and accountable.

AI ethics oversight is important because AI technology has the potential to have significant impacts on individuals, communities and society as a whole. These impacts may include issues such as bias and discrimination, invasion of privacy, lack of transparency and accountability, and negative impacts on human rights and dignity.

To ensure that AI technology is developed and deployed in a responsible and ethical manner, organizations should establish processes for ethical review and oversight. This may involve creating an AI ethics committee, conducting regular ethical audits of AI systems or implementing other mechanisms to ensure that ethical principles are being upheld throughout the organization.

The AI ethics oversight committee should also engage with stakeholders, including customers, employees and regulators, to ensure that their concerns and perspectives are taken into account. This can help to build trust and confidence in the organization's AI practices and ensure that they align with broader ethical and societal values and expectations.

45.4 AI ethics summary

The AI ethics capability is an organization's ability to develop, deploy and manage AI technology in a responsible, ethical and sustainable manner. It involves understanding the ethical principles and values that should guide AI development and use, and implementing processes and procedures to ensure that these principles are upheld.

As we have seen throughout this chapter, it is important for organizations to develop an ethical AI capability for several reasons. First, ethical AI development and use can reduce the risk of unintended consequences and negative impacts on individuals and society, and promote the long-term sustainability and success of the organization. Second, organizations that develop and use AI technology may face legal, regulatory and reputational risks and liabilities if their systems are found to be unethical or harmful. Third, ethical AI development and use can build trust and confidence among customers, partners and other stakeholders, and enhance the reputation and brand of the organization.

To structure an ethical AI capability, organizations should begin by establishing a clear ethical AI framework that outlines the ethical principles and values that should guide AI development and use and assigns roles and responsibilities for implementing these principles. This framework should also include processes for ethical decision-making and risk assessment, as well as mechanisms for monitoring and reporting on ethical AI practices.

Organizations should also invest in training and education to ensure that developers and other stakeholders understand the ethical principles and values that should guide AI development and use, and have the skills and knowledge needed to implement these principles effectively. This may include training in areas such as data privacy, bias and fairness, transparency and explainability, and human-centred design.

In addition, organizations should establish processes for ethical review and oversight of AI development and use. This may involve establishing an ethics review board or committee, conducting regular ethical audits of AI systems or implementing other mechanisms to ensure that ethical principles are being upheld throughout the organization.

Notes

1 T Hagendorff. The ethics of AI ethics: An evaluation of guidelines, *Minds and Machines*, 2020 30 (1), 99–120

2 D Lauer. You cannot have AI ethics without ethics, *AI and Ethics*, 2021 1 (1), 21–25

3 J Whittlestone, R Nyrup, A Alexandrova and S Cave (2019) The role and limits of principles in AI ethics: towards a focus on tensions. In Proceedings of the 2019 AAAI/ACM Conference on AI, Ethics, and Society, January, 195–200

4 S O'Sullivan, N Nevejans, C Allen, A Blyth, S Leonard, U Pagallo, K Holzinger, A Holzinger, M I Sajid and H Ashrafian. Legal, regulatory, and ethical frameworks for development of standards in artificial intelligence (AI) and autonomous robotic surgery, *The International Journal of Medical Robotics and Computer Assisted Surgery*, 2019 15 (1), e1968

Artificial Intelligence Maturity Assessment

Please respond to the following questions by indicating the relevant level of maturity for each activity in question and its importance to your organization.

The Capability Maturity Model levels are shown in Table 46.1.

Table 46.1 The Capability Maturity Model levels

Score	Description
0 – Non-existent	Describes a total lack of activity or lack of recognition that the activity exists.
1 – Initial	Describes evidence that the organization recognizes issues exist and need to be addressed.
2 – Managed	Describes activities designed so that similar procedures are followed by individuals. There is a high reliance on individual knowledge and skill level.
3 – Defined	Describes a standardized and documented level of activities which is being communicated through training, processes and tools.
4 – Controlled	Describes activities which are good practice and under constant improvement. Automation and tools are used to support the activities.
5 – Optimized	Describes activities that are considered leading and best practice and can be considered an example to other organizations.

Please note that responses to this survey should reflect how the organization performs the task today, not how you would like to see the organization perform the task in the future. Your choices should be based on your opinion of the organization, not just the way the task is performed in your own workgroup.

Table 46.2   Artificial Intelligence Maturity Assessment

#	Deep Learning	Score
27.1	Our organization understands the possibilities and business use cases that can be solved with deep learning algorithms.	
27.2	Our organization has the knowledge and skills to design, develop and implement deep learning algorithms.	
27.3	Our organization has the technology and tools to design, develop and implement deep learning algorithms	
27.4	Our organization has training programmes in place for the Big Data and data science teams to learn about the latest developments in deep learning.	
27.5	Our organization continuously assesses whether deep learning algorithms deliver the required results and makes improvement plans accordingly.	
27.6	Our organization actively contributes to further developments in deep learning and is considered an industry leader.	
	Reasoning	**Score**
28.1	Our organization develops reasoning products and solutions that are able to reason towards the best possible answer or solution.	
28.2	Our organization employs reasoning techniques (deductive, inductive, adductive) to develop AI products and solutions.	
28.3	Our organization actively builds and maintains a knowledge base that provides input to reasoning systems.	
28.4	Our organization utilizes documented ethical guidelines in the development and training of reasoning systems.	
28.5	Our organization has systems and processes in place to measure the accuracy and predictions of reasoning systems.	
28.6	Our organization continuously improves its reasoning systems and capabilities based on new developments and innovations.	

(continued)

Table 46.2   (Continued)

Knowledge Representation	Score
29.1 Our organization actively builds knowledge representation capabilities to store and reason with data in an effective way.	
29.2 Our organization employs knowledge engineers or similar roles that are responsible and accountable for knowledge representation.	
29.3 Our organization develops taxonomies, ontologies and knowledge graphs to ensure effective and efficient knowledge representation.	
29.4 Our organization uses cross-departmental guidelines for standardizing knowledge representation across different AI projects.	
29.5 Our organization measures and evaluates the impact of knowledge representation on the speed and accuracy of AI solutions.	
29.6 Our organization periodically reviews new developments and solutions in knowledge representation and makes improvements accordingly.	

AI Ethics	Score
30.1 Our organization has established an AI ethics policy that outlines how the organization will develop and create AI solutions in a responsible way.	
30.2 The AI ethics policy is proactively shared across the organization and training sessions are organized to familiarize employees with the policy.	
30.3 Our organization has developed an AI ethics framework that covers policies, processes, technologies and human aspects.	
30.4 Our organization utilizes AI ethics review processes so that AI products and solutions are proactively tested for compliance against ethical guidelines.	
30.5 Our organization has a procedure and process where employees or customers can report unethical use of AI solutions and every new report is thoroughly assessed and evaluated.	
30.6 Our organization has established an independent AI ethics oversight committee that oversees the AI ethics policy and advises the organization on ethical questions and dilemmas.	

INDEX

NB: page numbers in *italic* indicate figures or tables